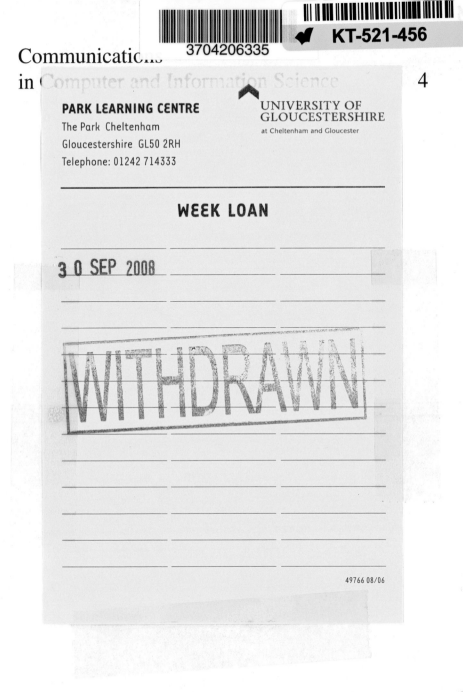

José Braz   Alpesh Ranchordas
Helder Araújo   Joaquim Jorge (Eds.)

Advances in Computer Graphics and Computer Vision

International Conferences VISAPP and GRAPP 2006
Setúbal, Portugal, February 25-28, 2006
Revised Selected Papers

 Springer

Volume Editors

José Braz
ESTSetúbal/IPS, Setúbal, Portugal
E-mail: jbraz@grapp.org

Alpesh Ranchordas
INSTICC, Setúbal, Portugal
E-mail: alpesh@visapp.org

Helder Araújo
Universidade de Coimbra, Portugal
E-mail: helder@isr.uc.pt

Joaquim Jorge
Instituto Superior Técnico/UTL, Lisboa, Portugal
E-mail: jorgej@ist.utl.pt

Library of Congress Control Number: 2007938152

CR Subject Classification (1998): I.2, I.3, I.4

ISSN   1865-0929
ISBN-10   3-540-75272-2 Springer Berlin Heidelberg New York
ISBN-13   978-3-540-75272-1 Springer Berlin Heidelberg New York

Springer is a part of Springer Science+Business Media

springer.com

© Springer-Verlag Berlin Heidelberg 2007
Printed in Germany

Typesetting: Camera-ready by author, data conversion by Scientific Publishing Services, Chennai, India
Printed on acid-free paper   SPIN: 12124459   06/3180   5 4 3 2 1 0

Preface

This book includes selected papers from the first International Conferences on Computer Vision Theory and Applications (VISAPP), and Computer Graphics Theory and Applications (GRAPP), jointly held in Setubal, Portugal, on February 25–28, 2006.

We received 314 paper submissions for both conferences, quite a high number for a first venue. We had contributions from 44 different countries covering all five continents, which confirms the success and global reach of the two conferences. After a rigorous double-blind review, a total of 116 submissions were accepted as full papers. From those, the Program Committee selected 27 for publication in this book, which were then revised by the authors. Special thanks are due to all contributors and referees, without whom this book would not have been possible.

VISAPP/GRAPP 2006 included four invited keynote lectures, presented by internationally recognized researchers. The presentations represented an important contribution to increasing the overall quality of the conference. We would like to express our appreciation to all invited keynote speakers, in alphabetical order, Marc Alexa (TU Berlin/Germany), André Gagalowicz (INRIA/France), Ken Perlin (New York University/USA), Peter Robinson (University of Cambridge/UK), whose presentations are partially included in the first section of the book. The second and third sections include selected papers from VISAPP 2006 and GRAPP 2006 respectively.

We would like to thank all organizations and people who supported and helped organize this venue. First and foremost it is a pleasure to acknowledge the generous support and collaboration of the Eurographics Association and of GPCG, its Portuguese Chapter. Moreover, we would like to thank authors of accepted contributions and the Program Committee members, whose work and expertise were instrumental in ensuring the quality of the Scientific Program. Last, but not least we would like to thank the Springer staff for their help in getting this book to print.

As we all know, every successful conference requires the dedication and concerted efforts of many people. We wish to thank all the local organizing committee members whose work and committment were invaluable to ensure a smoothly running and well organized venue. Special thanks are due to Joaquim Filipe, Marina Carvalho, Mónica Saramago, Bruno Encarnação, Hélder Coelhas and Vítor Pedrosa.

José Braz, Superior School of Technology of Setúbal, Portugal

Alpesh Ranchordas, Superior School of Technology of Setúbal, Portugal

Helder Araújo, University of Coimbra, Portugal

Joaquim Jorge, Instituto Superior Técnico, Technical University of Lisboa, Portugal

GRAPP Conference Committees

Conference Co-chairs

José Braz, EST Setúbal, Portugal

Miguel Dias, ISCTE, Portugal

Adérito Marcos, Minho University, Portugal

Program Chair

Joaquim Jorge, Instituto Superior Técnico, Technical University of Lisboa, Portugal

Program Committee

Sergey V. Ablameyko, Belarus

Marco Agus, Italy

Daniel Aliaga, USA

Ken Anjyo, Japan

Ghassan Aouad, UK

Marco Attene, Italy

António Augusto de Sousa, Portugal

Chandrajit Bajaj, USA

Prashant Banerjee, USA

Jacob Barhak, USA

Rafael Bidarra, The Netherlands

Manfred Bogen, Germany

Kadi Bouatouch, France

Dino Bouchlaghem, UK

Ronan Boulic, Switzerland

Willem F. Bronsvoort, The Netherlands

Sam Buss, USA

António Cardoso Costa, Portugal

Maria Beatriz Carmo, Portugal

Leocadio Casado, Spain

Teresa Chambel, Portugal

Chun-Fa Chang, Taiwan

Jim X. Chen, USA

Stephen Chenney, USA

Norishige Chiba, Japan

Min-Hyung Choi, USA

Jung-Hong Chuang, Taiwan

Hervé Delingette, France

Saša Divjak, Slovenia

Stéphane Donikian, France

Robin Drogemuller, Australia

Philip Dutré, Belgium

Petr Felkel, Czech Republic

Dieter W. Fellner, Germany

Jieqing Feng, China

Pablo Figueroa, Colombia

Anath Fischer, Israel

Andre Gagalowicz, France

Aphrodite Galata, UK

Stephane Garchery, Switzerland

Inmaculada García Fernández, Spain

Marina L. Gavrilova, Canada

Miguel Gea Megias, Spain

Andrew Glassner, USA

Enrico Gobbetti, Italy

Michael Goesele, USA

Abel Gomes, Portugal

Eduard Gröller, Austria

Alain Grumbach, France

Helwig Hauser, Austria

Andreas Holzinger, Austria

Toby Howard, UK

Roger Hubbold, UK

Insung Ihm, Korea

VISAPP Conference Committees

Conference Chair

Alpesh Ranchordas, EST Setúbal, Portugal

Program Chair

Helder J. Araújo, Coimbra University, Portugal

Program Committee

Henrik Aanæs, Denmark
Samer M. Abdallah, Lebanon
Rafeef Abugharbieh, Canada
Peggy Agouris, USA
Selim Aksoy, Turkey
Helder J. Araújo, Portugal
George Bebis, USA
Mohammed Bennamoun, Australia
Prabir Bhattacharya, Canada
Manuele Bicego, Italy
Stephen A. Billings, UK
Jacques Blanc-Talon, France
Isabelle Bloch, France
Pierre Boulanger, Canada
Alain Bretto, France
Thomas Breuel, Germany
Christopher Brown, USA
Rob Byrd, USA
Roberto Cesar Junior, Brazil
Kap Luk Chan, Singapore
Rama Chellappa, USA
Sheng Yong Chen, China
Loong Fah Cheong, Singapore
Hocine Cherifi, France
Chi-kit Ronald Chung, Hong Kong
James J. Clark, Canada
Isaac Cohen, USA
Eric Cohen-Solal, USA
Fabio Cuzzolin, USA

John Dingliana, Ireland
Hans du Buf, Portugal
Laurent Duval, France
Ahmed Elgammal, USA
Moumen El-Melegy, Egypt
Ali Erol, USA
Aly A. Farag, USA
Joaquim Filipe, Portugal
Robert Fisher, UK
Alejandro Frangi, Spain
Sidharta Gautama, Belgium
Bernard Gosselin, Belgium
Michael Greenspan, Canada
Jiro Gyoba, Japan
Ghassan Hamarneh, Canada
Dan Witzner Hansen, Denmark
Allen R. Hanson, USA
Xiangjian He, Australia
Christian Heipke, Germany
Thomas C. Henderson, USA
Ellen Hildreth, USA
Hsi-Chin Hsin, Taiwan
Luca Iocchi, Italy
Michael R. M. Jenkin, Canada
Tianzi Jiang, China
Xiaoyi Jiang, Germany
Ioannis Kakadiaris, USA
Geroge Kamberov, USA
Gerda Kamberova, USA

Conference Committees

Organizing Committee

Paulo Brito, INSTICC, Portugal
Marina Carvalho, INSTICC, Portugal
Helder Cide, INSTICC, Portugal
Bruno Encarnação, INSTICC, Portugal
Vitor Pedrosa, INSTICC, Portugal
Mónica Saramago,INSTICC, Portugal

Invited Speakers

Peter Robinson, University of Cambridge, UK
Ken Perlin, New York University, USA
André Gagalowicz, INRIA Rocquencourt, France
Marc Alexa, TU Berlin, Germany

Table of Contents

Invited Paper

Mesh Editing Based on Discrete Laplace and Poisson Models 3
   Marc Alexa and Andrew Nealen

Part I: Geometry and Modeling

Efficient Rendering of High-Detailed Objects Using a Reduced
Multi-resolution Hierarchy 31
   Mathias Holst and Heidrun Schumann

Mesh Retrieval by Components 44
   Ayellet Tal and Emanuel Zuckerberger

Terrain Synthesis By-Example 58
   John Brosz, Faramarz F. Samavati, and Mario Costa Sousa

Collaboration on Scene Graph Based 3D Data 78
   Lorenz Ammon and Hanspeter Bieri

Part II: Rendering

A Progressive Refinement Approach for the Visualisation of Implicit
Surfaces 93
   Manuel N. Gamito and Steve C. Maddock

Diffusion Based Photon Mapping 109
   Lars Schjøth, Ole Fogh Olsen, and Jon Sporring

An Incremental Weighted Least Squares Approach to Surface Lights
Fields 123
   Greg Coombe and Anselmo Lastra

Part III: Animation and Simulation

Motion Map Generation for Maintaining the Temporal Coherence of
Brush Strokes 139
   Youngsup Park and KyungHyun Yoon

Part IV: Interactive Environments

Distributed 3D Information Visualization – Towards Integration of the
Dynamic 3D Graphics and Web Services 155
  *Dean Vucinic, Danny Deen, Emil Oanta, Zvonimir Batarilo, and
  Chris Lacor*

Interactive Editing of Live Visuals 169
  *Pascal Müller, Stefan Müller Arisona, Simon Schubiger-Banz, and
  Matthias Specht*

Part V: Image Formation and Processing

Tolerance-Based Feature Transforms 187
  Dennie Reniers and Alexandru Telea

A Unified Theory for Steerable and Quadrature Filters 201
  Kai Krajsek and Rudolf Mester

Part VI: Image Analysis

Generalised Principal Component Analysis: Exploiting Inherent
Parameter Constraints 217
  Wojciech Chojnacki, Anton van den Hengel, and Michael J. Brooks

Ellipse Detection in Digital Image Data Using Geometric Features 229
  Lars Libuda, Ingo Grothues, and Karl-Friedrich Kraiss

A Comparison of Wavelet-Based and Ridgelet-Based Texture
Classification of Tissues in Computed Tomography 240
  Lindsay Semler and Lucia Dettori

Color Segmentation of Complex Document Images 251
  N. Nikolaou and N. Papamarkos

Improved Reconstruction of Images Distorted by Water Waves 264
  Arturo Donate and Eraldo Ribeiro

Part VII: Image Understanding

Pose Estimation Using Structured Light and Harmonic Shape
Contexts 281
  Thomas B. Moeslund and Jakob Kirkegaard

Cognitive Vision and Perceptual Grouping by Production Systems with
Blackboard Control – An Example for High-Resolution SAR-Images 293
  Eckart Michaelsen, Wolfgang Middelmann, and Uwe Sörgel

Occlusion Invariant Face Recognition Using Two-Dimensional PCA 305
  Tae Young Kim, Kyoung Mu Lee, Sang Uk Lee, and Chung-Hyuk Yim

Multidirectional Face Tracking with 3D Face Model and Learning
Half-Face Template 316
  Jun'ya Matsuyama and Kuniaki Uehara

Representing Directions for Hough Transforms 330
  Fabian Wenzel and Rolf-Rainer Grigat

Part VIII: Motion, Tracking and Stereo Vision

Dense Stereo Matching with Growing Aggregation and Neural
Learning 343
  Ignazio Gallo and Elisabetta Binaghi

Improving Appearance-Based 3D Face Tracking Using Sparse Stereo
Data 354
  Fadi Dornaika and Angel D. Sappa

3D Tracking Using 2D-3D Line Segment Correspondence and 2D Point
Motion 367
  Woobum Kang and Shigeru Eiho

Vision-Based Tracking System for Head Motion Correction in FMRI
Images 381
  Tali Lerner, Ehud Rivlin, and Moshe Gur

Learning Nonlinear Manifolds of Dynamic Textures 395
  Ishan Awasthi and Ahmed Elgammal

Author Index 407

Invited
Paper

Mesh Editing Based on Discrete Laplace and Poisson Models

Marc Alexa and Andrew Nealen

Faculty of EE & CS
TU Berlin

Abstract. Surface editing operations commonly require geometric details of the surface to be preserved as much as possible. We argue that geometric detail is an intrinsic property of a surface and that, consequently, surface editing is best performed by operating over an intrinsic surface representation. This intrinsic representation could be derived from differential properties of the mesh, i.e. its Laplacian. The modeling process poses nonzero boundary constraints so that this idea results in a Poisson model. Different ways of representing the intrinsic geometry and the boundary constraints result in alternatives for the properties of the modeling system. In particular, the Laplacian is not invariant to scaling and rotations. Either the intrinsic representation is enhanced to be invariant to (linearized) transformations, or scaling and rotation are computed in a preprocess and are modeled as boundary constraints. Based on this representation, useful editing operations can be developed: Interactive free-form deformation in a region of interest based on the transformation of a handle, transfer and mixing of geometric detail between two surfaces, and transplanting of a partial surface mesh into another surface. The main computation involved in all operations is the solution of a sparse linear system, which can be done at interactive rates. We demonstrate the effectiveness of this approach in several examples, showing that the editing operations change the shape while respecting the structural geometric detail.

Keywords: Mesh editing, detail preservation.

1 Introduction

Surfaces in computer graphics are mostly represented in global coordinate systems: explicit representations are based on points, vertices, or nodes that are typically described using absolute Euclidean coordinates. Implicit representations describe the shape as the level set of a function defined in Euclidean space. A global coordinate system is the natural choice for all operations involving other objects such as rendering, intersection testing and computation, transformations, or CSG modeling. On the other hand, for local surface modeling, it would be desirable that the representation captures the local shape (i.e. the intrinsic geometry of the surface) rather than the absolute position or orientation in Euclidean space.

Manipulating and modifying a surface while preserving the geometric details is important for various surface editing operations, including free-form deformations (Sederberg and Parry, 1986; Coquillart, 1990), cut and paste (Ranta et al., 1993;

J. Braz et al. (Eds.): VISAPP and GRAPP 2006, CCIS 4, pp. 3–28, 2007.
© Springer-Verlag Berlin Heidelberg 2007

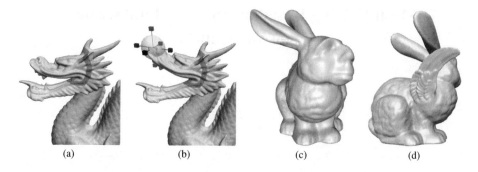

(a)   (b)   (c)   (d)

Fig. 1. Advanced mesh editing operations using Laplacian coordinates: free-form deformations (a-b), detail transfer (c) and mesh transplanting (d). Representing the geometry using the Laplacian coordinates enables preservation of detail.

Biermann et al., 2002), fusion (Kanai et al., 1999), morphing (Alexa, 2003a), and others. Note that the absolute position of the vertices in a mesh is not important for these operations, which calls for an intrinsic surface representation.

A partially intrinsic surface mesh representation are multi-resolution decompositions (Forsey and Bartels, 1988; Zorin et al., 1997; Kobbelt et al., 1998; Kobbelt et al., 1999; Guskov et al., 1999). In a multi-resolution mesh, the geometry is encoded as a base mesh and several levels of refinement. The refinement is typically described locally, so that geometric details are mostly captured in a discrete set of intrinsic coordinates. Using this representation, several modeling operations can be performed on an appropriate user-specified level-of-detail. Note, however, that the locality of multi-resolution representations is potentially limited: The support (or extent) of the representation of a single vertex increases from fine to coarse levels of the hierarchy. Thus, modeling operations are restricted to a discrete set of regions and levels-of-detail. For example, when cutting out a partial mesh for transplanting operations, the original multi-resolution representation is invalidated because parts of the base domain and (potentially) other levels of the hierarchy are missing.

This approach to encode geometric details is to use differentials as coordinates for the vertices (Alexa, 2003b; Botsch and Kobbelt, 2004; Sorkine et al., 2004; Yu et al., 2004). This provides a fully intrinsic representation of the surface mesh, where the reconstruction of global coordinates from the intrinsic representation always preserves the intrinsic geometry as much as possible given the modeling constraints. Using a differential representation for editing operations has been shown to be quite effective in image domain (Fattal et al., 2002; Pérez et al., 2003). The image domain has a natural regular parameterization and resulting inherent definition of a gradient, which allows modeling many editing tasks as a discrete Poisson equation. However, this approach cannot be directly applied or adapted to discrete (as well as continuous) surfaces.

2   The Laplacian Representation

Let the mesh $\mathscr{M}$ be described by a pair (K,V), where K is a simplicial complex representing the connectivity of vertices, edges, and faces, and $V = \{\mathbf{v}_1, \ldots, \mathbf{v}_n\}$ describes the geometric positions of the vertices in $\mathbb{R}^3$. We use the following terminology: the *neighborhood ring* of a vertex i is the set of adjacent vertices $\mathcal{N}_i = \{j|(i,j) \in K\}$ and the *degree* d_i of this vertex is the number adjacent edges (or vertices), i.e. the number of elements in $\mathcal{N}_i$. We assume that $d_i > 0$, i.e. that the mesh is connected.

Instead of using absolute coordinates V, we would like to describe the mesh geometry using a set of differentials $\Delta = \{\delta_i\}$. Specifically, coordinate i will be represented by its Laplace vector. There are different ways to define a discretized version of the Laplace operator for meshes, and each of them has certain advantages. Most of them are based on the one-ring of a vertex

$$\delta_i = \mathbf{v}_i - c_{ij} \sum_{j \in \mathcal{N}_i} \mathbf{v}_j, \quad \sum_j c_{ij} = 1, \tag{1}$$

and differ in the definition of the coefficients c_{ij}. The topological Laplacian ((Taubin, 1995)) simply uses the same weights for all neighboring vertices, i.e. $c_{ij} = 1/d_i$. In our and others' experience the the cotangent weights (e.g. (Meyer et al., 2003)) perform best in most applications.

The transformation between V and Δ can be described in matrix algebra. Let $C = \{c_{ij}\}$, then

$$\Delta = (I - C)V. \tag{2}$$

The Laplacian $L = I - C$ is invariant under translation, however, sensitive to linear transformations. Thus, L is expected to have rank $n - 1$, which means V can be recovered from Δ by fixing one vertex and solving a linear system of equations.

3 Mesh Modeling Framework

The basic idea of the modeling framework is to satisfy linear modeling constraints (exactly, or in the least squares sense), while preserving differential properties of the original geometry in the least squares sense (Alexa, 2003b; Lipman et al., 2004). Without additional linear constraints the deformed geometry V' is then defined by

$$\min_{V'} \sum_{i=1}^{n} \left\| \delta_i - \left(\mathbf{v}'_i - \frac{1}{d_i} \sum_{j \in \mathcal{N}_i} \mathbf{v}'_j \right) \right\|^2. \tag{3}$$

If the original surface was a membrane, the necessary constraints for the minimizer lead to $L^2V = 0$, which has been advocated by Botsch and Kobbelt (Botsch and Kobbelt, 2004) in the context of modeling smooth surfaces. If, in contrast, the original surface contained some detail, the right-hand side is non-zero and we arrive at a variant of the discrete Poisson modeling approach of Yu et al. (Yu et al., 2004).

The basic type of linear modeling constraints is to prescribe the absolute position of some vertices, i.e. $\mathbf{v}'_i = \hat{\mathbf{v}}_i$. These constraints are best incorporated by also satisfying them in the least squares sense, possibly weighted to trade-off between modeling constraints and the reproduction of original surface geometry.

We found that the easiest way of implementing the approach is to write the conditions to be satisfied in the least squares sense as a large rectangular system $\mathbf{A}V' = \mathbf{b}$ and then solve $\mathbf{A}^T \mathbf{A} \mathbf{V}' = \mathbf{A}^T \mathbf{b}$. Prescribing positions for some vertices then simply yields additional rows of the form

$$w_i \| \mathbf{v}_i' = \hat{\mathbf{v}}_i. \tag{4}$$

Note that in fact these are three rows for each constraint, as $\mathbf{v}$ are column vectors with three elements.

This framework can be extended towards constraints on arbitrary points on the mesh. Note that each point on the surface is the linear combination of two or three vertices. A point on an edge between vertices i and j is defined by one parameter as $(1 - \lambda)\mathbf{v}_i + \lambda \mathbf{v}_j$, $0 \le \lambda \le 1$. Similarly, a point on a triangle is defined by two parameters. We can put positional constraints $\hat{\mathbf{v}}_{ij}$ on such a point by adding rows of the form

$$(1 - \lambda)v_i' + \lambda v_j' = \hat{\mathbf{v}}_{ij} \tag{5}$$

to the system matrix A.

Furthermore, also differentials could be prescribed. Note that δ_i points roughly in normal direction at vertex i and that its length is proportional to the mean curvature. This allows us to prescribe a certain normal direction and/or curvature for a vertex, simply by adding a row of the form

$$\mathbf{v}_i' - \sum_{j \in \mathcal{N}_i} c_{ij} \mathbf{v}_j' = \hat{\delta}_i. \tag{6}$$

The modeling operation is typically localized on a part of the mesh. This part of the mesh is selected by the user as the region of interest (ROI) during the interactive modeling session. The operations are restricted to this ROI, padded by several layers of anchor vertices. The anchor vertices yield positional constraints $\mathbf{v}_i' = \hat{\mathbf{v}}_i$ in the system matrix A, which ensure a gentle transition between the altered ROI and the fixed part of the mesh.

Based on the constraints formulated so far, local surface detail is preserved if parts of the surface are translated, but changes with rotations and scales. There are several ways of dealing with linear transformations:

- They could be defined and prescribed based on the modeling operation (Yu et al., 2004).
- They could be deduced from the membrane solution (i.e. $LV' = 0$) (Lipman et al., 2004).
- They could be implicitly defined by the solution, if the rotational part is linearized (Sorkine et al., 2004).

In any case, we first need to extend the definition of the local intrinsic representation to incorporate linear transformations.

4   Incorporating Linear Transformations

The main idea to account for local linear transformations is to assign each vertex i an individual transformation T_i. These transformation are then applied to the original geometry by a transforming each local Laplacian δ_i with T_i. This results in a slightly modified functional defining the resulting geometry V':

$$\min_{V'} \sum_{i=1}^{n} \left\| T_i \delta_i - \left(\mathbf{v}'_i - \frac{1}{d_i} \sum_{j \in \mathcal{N}_i} \mathbf{v}'_j \right) \right\|^2 \tag{7}$$

Note that in the formulation of this minimization as solving a system $AV' = b$ the part $T_i \delta_i$ is contained in the right-hand side column vector b. This is important because it implies the system A can be solved independent of the transformations T_i to be applied to vertex i, allowing the T_i to be changed during interactive modeling.

The following approaches vary in how the local transformations T_i are computed.

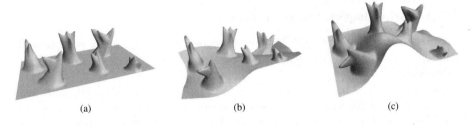

(a)   (b)   (c)

Fig. 2. Deformations of a model (a) with detail that cannot be expressed by height field. The deformation changes the global shape while respecting the structural detail as much as possible.

4.1 Prescribing the Transformations

Yu et al. (Yu et al., 2004) let the user specify a few constraint transformations and then interpolate them over the surface. In particular, the rotational and scaling parts are treated independently, i.e. the transformation is factored as $T_i = R_i S_i$, where R_i is the local rotation and S_i is a symmetric matrix containing scale and shear. Initially all vertices are assumed to be not rotated, scaled or sheared. Modeling operations might induce local linear transformations.

One could view this (slightly more general as in (Yu et al., 2004)) as a scattered data interpolation problem: In few vertices a (non-zero) rotation or non-unity scale are given. All vertices should then be assigned a scale and rotation so that the given constraints are satisfied and the field of rotations and scales is smooth. In order to apply well-known techniques only a distance measure for the vertices is necessary. Yu et al. (Yu et al., 2004) use the topological distance of vertices in the mesh.

Then, each local rotation and scale are a distance-weighted average of given transformations. The easiest way to derive the distance weights would be Shephard's approach. This defines T_i for each vertex and, thus, V'. Note that transformations can be changed interactively.

4.2 Transformations from the Membrane Solution

Lipman et al. (Lipman et al., 2004) compute the rotations from the membrane solution. They first solve $\Delta V' = 0$ and then compute each transformation T_i based on comparing the one-rings in $\mathbf{V}$ and $\mathbf{V}'$ of vertex i.

The basic idea for a definition of T_i is to derive it from the transformation of $\mathbf{v}_i$ and its neighbors to $\mathbf{v}'_i$ and its neighbors:

$$\min_{T_i} \left(\|T_i\mathbf{v}_i - \mathbf{v}_i'\|^2 + \sum_{j \in \mathcal{N}_i} \|T_i\mathbf{v}_j - \mathbf{v}_j'\|^2 \right). \tag{8}$$

This is a quadratic expression, so the minimizer is a linear function of V'.

Note that this is not significantly slower than computing the solution for the initial local identity transformations: The system matrix A has to be factored once, from the first solution all T_i are computed, b is modified accordingly, and the final positions V' are computed using back-substitution.

4.3 Linearized Implicit Transformations

The main idea of (Sorkine et al., 2004) is to compute an appropriate transformation T_i for each vertex i based on the eventual new configuration of vertices V'. Thus, $T_i(V')$ is a function of V'.

Note that in Eq. 7 both the T_i and the V' are unknown. However, if the coefficients of T_i are a linear function in V', then solving for V' implies finding T_i (though not explicitly) since Eq. 7 is still a quadratic function in V'. If we define T_i as in Eq. 8, it is a linear function in V', as required.

However, if T_i is unconstrained, the natural minimizer is a membrane solution, and all geometric detail is lost. Thus, T_i needs to be constrained in a reasonable way. We have found that T_i should include rotations, isotropic scales, and translations. In particular, we want to disallow anisotropic scales (or shears), as they would allow removing the normal component from Laplacian representation.

The transformation should be a linear function in the target configuration but constrained to isotropic scales and rotations. The class of matrices representing isotropic scales and rotation can be written as $T = s\exp(H)$, where H is a skew-symmetric matrix. In 3D, skew symmetric matrices emulate a cross product with a vector, i.e. $H\mathbf{x} = \mathbf{h} \times \mathbf{x}$. One can derive the following representation of the exponential above:

$$s \exp H = s(\alpha I + \beta H + \gamma \mathbf{h}^T\mathbf{h}) \tag{9}$$

Inspecting the terms we find that only s, I, and H are linear in the unknowns s and $\mathbf{h}$, while $\mathbf{h}^T\mathbf{h}$ is quadratic[1]. As a linear approximation of the class of constrained transformations we, therefore, use

$$T_i = \begin{pmatrix} s & h_1 & -h_2 & t_x \\ -h_1 & s & h_3 & t_y \\ h_2 & -h_3 & s & t_y \\ 0 & 0 & 0 & 1 \end{pmatrix} \tag{10}$$

This matrix is a good linear approximation for rotations with small angles.

---

[1] Figure 3 illustrates editing of a 2D mesh. Note that in 2D the matrices of class $s\exp(H)$ can be completely characterized with the linear expression

$$T_i = \begin{pmatrix} a & w & t_x \\ -w & a & t_y \\ 0 & 0 & 1 \end{pmatrix}.$$

Fig. 3. Editing 2D meshes using Laplacian-coordinates fitting. The red dots denote fixed anchor points and the yellow are the pulled handle vertices. The original meshes are colored blue.

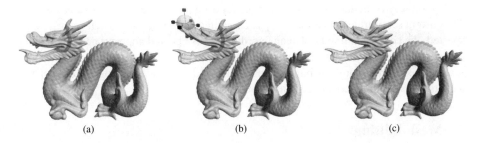

(a)   (b)   (c)

Fig. 4. The editing process. (a) The user selects the region of interest – the upper lip of the DRAGON, bounded by the belt of stationary anchors (in red). (b) The chosen handle (enclosed by the yellow sphere) is manipulated by the user: translated and rotated. (c) The editing result.

Given the matrix T_i as in Eq. 10, we can write down the linear dependency (cf. Eq. 8) of T_i on V' explicitly. Let $(s_i, \mathbf{h}_i, \mathbf{t}_i)^T$ be the vector of the unknowns in T_i, then we wish to minimize

$$\|A_i(s_i, \mathbf{h}_i, \mathbf{t}_i)^T - \mathbf{b}_i\|^2, \tag{11}$$

where A_i contains the positions of $\mathbf{v}_i$ and its neighbors and $\mathbf{b}_i$ contains the position of $\mathbf{v}_i'$ and its neighbors. The structure of $(s_i, \mathbf{h}_i, \mathbf{t}_i)^T$ yields

$$A_i = \begin{pmatrix} v_{k_x} & v_{k_y} & -v_{k_z} & 0 & 1 & 0 & 0 \\ v_{k_y} & -v_{k_x} & 0 & v_{k_z} & 0 & 1 & 0 \\ v_{k_z} & 0 & v_{k_x} & -v_{k_y} & 0 & 0 & 1 \\ \vdots & & & & & & \end{pmatrix}, k \in \{i\} \cup \mathcal{N}_i, \tag{12}$$

and

$$\mathbf{b_i} = \begin{pmatrix} v'_{k_x} \\ v'_{k_y} \\ v'_{k_z} \\ \vdots \end{pmatrix}, k \in \{i\} \cup \mathcal{N}_i. \tag{13}$$

The linear least squares problem above is solved by

$$(s_i, \mathbf{h}_i, \mathbf{t}_i)^T = \left(A_i^T A_i\right)^{-1} A_i^T \mathbf{b}_i, \tag{14}$$

which shows that the coefficients of T_i are linear functions of $\mathbf{b}_i$, since A_i is known from the initial mesh V. The entries of $\mathbf{b}_i$ are simply entries of V' so that $(s_i, \mathbf{h}_i, \mathbf{t}_i)$ and, thus, T_i is a linear function in V', as required.

4.4 Adjusting T_i

In many modeling situations solving for absolute coordinates in the way explained above is sufficient. However, there are exceptions that might require adjusting the transformations.

A good way of updating transformations for all three mentioned approaches is this: The current set of transformations $\{T_i\}$ is computed from V and V'. Then each T_i is inspected, the corresponding Laplacian coordinate δ_i is updated appropriately depending on the effect to be achieved, and the system is solved again. For example, if anisotropic scaling has been suppressed but is wanted, the $\{\delta_i\}$ are scaled by the inverse of the anisotropic scale implied by the constraints.

5 Mesh Editing

There are many different tools to manipulate an existing mesh. Perhaps the simplest form consists of manipulating a *handle*, which is a set of vertices that can be moved, rotated and scaled by the user. The manipulation of the handle is propagated to the shape such that the modification is intuitive and resembles the outcome of manipulating an object made of some physical soft material. This can be generalized to a free-form deformation tool which transforms a small set of control points defining a complex of possibly weighted handles, enabling mimicking other modeling metaphors (see e.g., (Bendels and Klein, 2003) and the references therein).

The editing interaction is comprised of the following stages: First, the user defines the region of interest (ROI) for editing. Next, the handle is defined. In addition, the user can optionally define the amount of "padding" of the ROI by *stationary anchors*. These stationary anchors form a *belt* that supports the transition between the ROI and the untouched part of the mesh. Then, the user manipulates the handle, and the surface is reconstructed with respect to the relocation of the handle and displayed.

The submesh of the ROI is the only part considered during the editing process. The positions of the handle vertices and the stationary anchors constrain the reconstruction and hence the shape of the resulting surface. The handle is the means of user control,

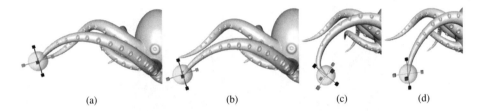

(a)   (b)   (c)   (d)

Fig. 5. Different handle manipulations. (a) The region of interest (arm), bounded by the belt of stationary anchors, and the handle. (b) Translation of the handle. (c), (d) Rotation of the handle. Note that the detail is preserved in all the manipulations.

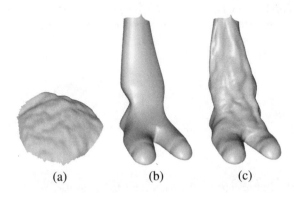

(a)   (b)   (c)

Fig. 6. Detail transfer; The details of the BUNNY (a) are transferred onto the mammal's leg (b) to yield (c)

therefore its constraints are constantly updated. The unconstrained vertices of the sub-mesh are repeatedly reconstructed to follow the user interaction. The stationary anchors are responsible for the transition from the ROI to the fixed untouched part of the mesh, resulting in a soft transition between the submesh and stationary part of the mesh. Se-lecting the amount of these padding anchor vertices depends on the user's requirements, as mentioned above. We have observed in all our experiments that setting the radius of the "padding ring" to be up to 10% of the ROI radius gives satisfying results.

The reconstruction of the submesh requires solving linear least-squares system as described in Section 2. The method of building the system matrix (Eq. 14), including the computation of a sparse factorization, is relatively slow, but constructed only once when the ROI is selected. The user interaction with the handle requires solely updating the positions of the handle vertices in the right-hand-side vector, and solve.

Figures 4 and 5 illustrate the editing process. Note that the details on the surface are preserved, as one would intuitively expect. Figure 2 demonstrates deformation of a model with large extruding features which cannot be represented by a height field.

6   Detail Transfer

Detail transfer is the process of peeling the coating of a *source* surface and transferring it onto a *target* surface. See Figure 6 for an example of such operation.

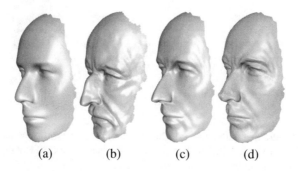

(a)   (b)   (c)   (d)

Fig. 7. The details of the MAX PLANCK are transferred onto the MANNEQUIN. Different levels of smoothing were applied to the MAX PLANCK model to peel the details, yielding the results in (c) and (d).

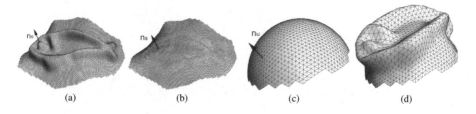

(a)   (b)   (c)   (d)

Fig. 8. Detail transfer. The orientation of details (a) are defined by the normal at the corresponding vertex in the low frequency surface in (b). The transferred detail vector needs to be rotated to match the orientation of the corresponding point in (c) to reconstruct (d).

Let S be the source surface from which we would like to extract the details, and let $\tilde{S}$ be a smooth version of S. The surface $\tilde{S}$ is a low-frequency surface associated with S, which can be generated by filtering (Desbrun et al., 1999; Fleishman et al., 2003). The amount of smoothing is a user-defined parameter, and it depends on the range of detail that the user wishes to transfer.

We encode the details of a surface based on the Laplacian representation. Let δ_i and $\tilde{\delta}_i$ be the Laplacian coordinates of the vertex i in S and $\tilde{S}$, respectively. We define ξ_i to be the encoding of the detail at vertex i defined by

$$\xi_i = \delta_i - \tilde{\delta}_i . \tag{15}$$

The values of ξ_j encode the details of S, since given the bare surface $\tilde{S}$ we can recover the original details simply by adding ξ_j to $\tilde{\delta}_i$ and reconstructing S with the inverse Laplacian transform L^{-1}. That is,

$$S = L^{-1}(\tilde{\delta} + \xi) . \tag{16}$$

In this case of a detail transfer of S onto itself, S is faithfully reconstructed. However, in general, instead of coating $\tilde{S}$ with ξ, we would like to add the details ξ onto an arbitrary surface U. If the target surface U is not smooth, it can be smoothed first, and then the detail transfer is applied. In the following we assume that the target surface

U is smooth. Before we move on, we should note that the detail transfer from S onto $\tilde{S}$ is simple, since the neighborhoods of the corresponding vertices i have the same *orientation*. We define the orientation of a vertex i in a surface S by the normal direction of i over $\tilde{S}$. Loosely speaking, the orientation of a point reflects the general orientation of its neighborhood, without respecting the high-frequencies of the surface.

When applying a detail transfer between two surfaces, the detail ξ should be first aligned, or rotated with respect to the target. This compensates for the different local surface orientations of corresponding points in the source and target surfaces.

The following is an important property of the Laplacian coordinates:

$$R \cdot L^{-1}(\delta_j) = L^{-1}(R \cdot \delta_j) \,, \tag{17}$$

where L^{-1} is the transformation from Laplacian coordinates to absolute coordinates, and R a *global* rotation applied to the entire mesh. The mapping between corresponding points in S and U defines different local orientations across the surfaces. Thus, our key idea is to use the above property of the Laplacian coordinates locally, assuming that locally the rotations are similar.

Assume that the source surface S and the target surface U share the same connectivity, but different geometry, and that the correspondence between their vertices is given. In the following we generalize this to arbitrary surfaces.

The local rotation R_i at each vertex i in S and U is taken to be the local rotation between their corresponding orientations. Let $\mathbf{n}_s$ and $\mathbf{n}_u$ be the normals associated with the orientations of i in S and U, respectively. We define the rotation operator R_i by setting the axis of rotation as $\mathbf{n}_s \times \mathbf{n}_u$ and requiring $\mathbf{n}_u = R_i(n_s)$. Denote the rotated detail encoding of vertex i by $\xi_i' = R_i(\xi_i)$. Having all the R_i associated with the ξ_i, the detail transfer from S onto U is expressed as follows:

$$U' = L^{-1}(\Delta + \xi') \tag{18}$$

where Δ denotes the Laplacian coordinates of the vertices of U. Now the new surface U' has the details of U.

6.1 Mapping and Resampling

So far we assumed that the source and target meshes (S and U) share the same connectivity, and hence the correspondence is readily given. However, detail transfer between arbitrary surfaces is more involved. To sample the Laplacian coordinates, we need to define a mapping between the two surfaces.

This mapping is established by parameterizing the meshes over a common domain. Both patches are assumed to be homeomorphic to a disk, so we may chose either the unit circle or the unit square as common domain. We apply the mean-value coordinates parameterization (Floater, 2003), as it efficiently produces a quasi-conformal mapping, which is guaranteed to be valid for convex domains. We fix the boundary conditions for the parameterization such that a correspondence between the source and target surfaces is achieved, i.e. we identify corresponding boundary vertices and fix them at the same domain points. In practice, this is a single vertex in S and in U that constrains rotation for the unit circle domain, or four boundary vertices for the unit square domain.

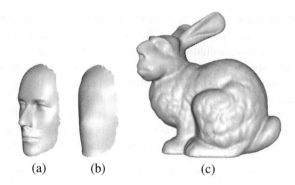

(a)   (b)   (c)

Fig. 9. Transferring the details of the MANNEQUIN onto the face of the BUNNY. (a) The source surface S. It is significantly smoothed to peel the details. (b) The smoothed surface $\tilde{S}$. (c) The result of detail transfer onto the BUNNY.

Some applications require a more careful correspondence than what can be achieved from choosing boundary conditions. For example, the mapping between two faces (see Figure 7) should link relevant details like facial features such as the brow wrinkles of the MAX PLANCK. In this case the user provides a few additional (inner) point-to-point constraints which define a warp of the mean-value parameterization. In our implementation we use a radial basis function elastic warp, but any reasonable warping function can do.

In general, a vertex $i \in U$ is mapped to some arbitrary point inside a triangle $\tau \in S$. We experimented with several methods for sampling the Laplacian for a vertex. The best results are obtained by first mapping the 1-ring of i onto S using the parameterization, and then computing the Laplacian from this mapped 1-ring. Note that this approach assumes a locally similar distortion in the mapping. This is usually the case for the detail transfer; we used the 1-ring sampling in all the respective examples. We obtain similar results by linear interpolation of the three Laplacian coordinates sampled at the vertices of the triangle τ. While this approach leads to some more "blurring" compared to the first one, it is even simpler and does not suffer from extremely different parametric distortion. In addition, no special treatment is required at the boundary of the domain in case the patch was initially cut to be homeomorphic to a disk.

After the mapping between U and S has been established and the Laplacians have been sampled, the detail transfer proceeds as explained before. Note that now the corresponding ξ_i is the difference between the *sampled* Laplacian coordinates in S and $\tilde{S}$. See the examples in Figures 6, 7 and 9.

6.2 Mixing Details

Given two meshes with the same connectivity and different details, the above transfer mechanism can be applied on a third target mesh from the two sources. Figure 10 illustrates the effect of blending the details. This example emphasizes the mixing of details, as the details of the two source meshes differ in the smoothness, form and orientation. Note that the details are gradually mixed and the global shape of the target

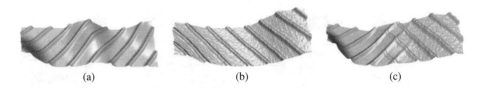

Fig. 10. Mixing details using Laplacian coordinates. The Laplacian coordinates of surfaces in (a) and (b) are linearly blended in the middle to yield the shape in (c).

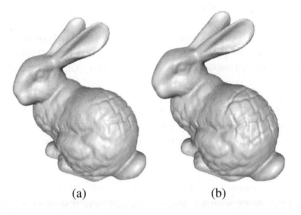

Fig. 11. Transplanting of ARMADILLO's details onto the BUNNY back with a soft transition (a) and a sharp transition (b) between the two types of details. The size of the transition area in which the Laplacians are blended is large in (a) and small in (b).

mesh is deformed respectively. By adding anchor points over the target, its shape can be further deformed. Figure 11 shows the application of this mechanism to transplant ARMADILLO's details onto the BUNNY's back with a soft transition. In the next section we further discuss this transplanting operation.

7   Transplanting Surface Patches

In the previous sections we showed how the Laplacian coordinates allow to transfer the details of surface onto another and how to gradually mix details of two surfaces. These techniques are refined to allow a seamless transplanting of one shape onto another. The transplanting operation consists of two apparently independent classes of operations: topological and geometrical. The topological operation creates one consistent triangulation from the connectivities of the two submeshes. The geometrical operation creates a gradual change of the geometrical structure of one shape into the other. The latter operation is based on the Laplacian coordinates and the reconstruction mechanism.

Let S denote the mesh that is transplanted onto a surface U. See Figure 12, where the right wing (S) of the FELINE is transplanted onto the BUNNY (U). The transplanting requires the user to first register the two parts in world coordinates. This defines the desired location and orientation of the transplanted shape, as well as its scale.

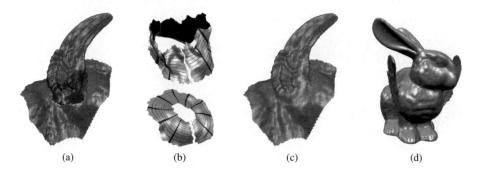

(a)   (b)   (c)   (d)

Fig. 12. Transplanting of FELINE's wings onto the BUNNY. (a) After cutting the parts and fixing the desired pose, the zipping (in green) defines the target connectivity D. The transitional region D' is marked red. Additional cut in D' (in yellow) enables mapping onto a square. (b) D' is sampled over the respective regions $U' \subset U_o$ (U_o is the cut part of the BUNNY's back) and S' (the bottom of the wing). The texture with uv-isolines visualizes the mapping over the unit square. The cut (in yellow) aligns the two maps. (c) The result of reconstruction. The ROI is padded by a belt of anchors (in red). Note the change of the zipping seam triangles (green) and the details within the transition region. (d) The flying BUNNY (see also Figure 1(d)).

The user selects a region $U_o \subset U$ onto which S will be transplanted. In the rest of the process we only work with U_o and do not alter the rest of U. U_o is cut such that the remaining boundary is homeomorphic to the boundary of S. We simply project the boundary of S onto U_o. The two boundary loops are zipped, thus creating the connectivity of the resulting mesh D (Figure 12(a)).

The remaining transplanting algorithm is similar to detail transfer and mixing. The user specifies a region of interest on D, vertices outside the ROI remain fixed.

Next, the respective *transitional regions* $S' \subset S$ and $U' \subset U_o$ are selected starting from the cut boundaries on S and U_o. Since $S' \subset D$, this implicitly defines the transitional region $D' \subset D$ along with a trivial mapping between vertices of S' and D'.

For sampling, we require an additional correspondence between S' and U', hence we parameterize both meshes over the unit square. The user guides this construction by cutting S' and U' such that both meshes are homeomorphic to a disk. The cuts enable the mapping to the common domain, and in addition they serve as intuitive means to align the mappings such that there is a correspondence between the patches. In our experiments no further warping was necessary to improve the correspondence (cf. Section 6.1).

Once the transitional regions and the mappings are defined, the transplanting procedure is ready to sample the Laplacian coordinates of S' and U' over D'. The corresponding Laplacian coordinates are linearly blended with weights defined by their relative position in the unit square parameter domain. More precisely, if $v \in [0, 1]$ defines the coordinate along the "height" axis (the blue and red lines in Figure 12(b), then the weights are v and $(1 - v)$, respectively. Since the length distortion of the maps may significantly differ, we linearly interpolate the Laplacian coordinates for sampling (cf. Section 6.1). The remainder of the ROI is sampled over D, and the reconstruction respects the belt of anchors which is placed to pad the boundaries of the ROI. Figures 12(c),(d) show the result.

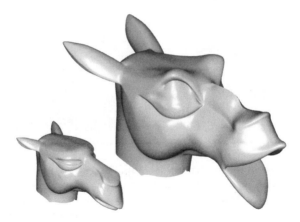

Fig. 13. With a few strokes we have greatly increased the expressiveness of the CAMEL model (bottom left). See Fig. 14 for details.

8   Sketch-Based Mesh Editing

A few strokes suffice to sketch the main features of a shape. This is why designers still prefer using pen and paper to invent and communicate, and explains the great success of sketch-based shape modeling approaches, such as SKETCH (Zeleznik et al., 1996) and Teddy (Igarashi et al., 1999). Our contribution in this Section is a tool for sketching significant shape details on already existing coarse or detailed shapes. Ideally, a sketch-based modeling system for 3D shapes should use the very same sketches that designers would draw on a piece of paper to convey the shape. As pointed out by Hoffman and Singh (Hoffman and Singh, 1997), the human visual system uses silhouettes as the first index into its memory of shapes, making everyday objects recognizable without color, shading or texture, but solely by their contours.

We believe that **sketching** a shape is **inverse NPR** (Gooch and Gooch, 2001). Consequently, we have designed a sketch-based modeling interface using silhouettes and sketches as input, and producing contours, or suggestive contours (DeCarlo et al., 2003), and ridges/ravines. The user can sketch a curve, and the system adapts the shape so that the sketch becomes a feature line on the model, while preserving global and local geometry as much as possible. As the requested properties of the sketch cannot or should not always be accommodated exactly, users only *suggest* feature lines.

Within our sketch-based modeling environment, it is easy to displace a set of edges (e.g., sketch a new position of an identified contour) while preserving the geometric details of the surface as much as possible. In the following sections, we explain how to use these basic ideas for satisfying user-defined feature lines on a mesh.

8.1   Silhouette Sketching

Our goal is to identify areas of the model which are easily recognized, and for which our memories hold vast databases of possible variations, and then apply these variations

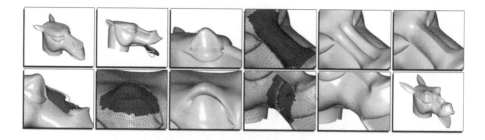

Fig. 14. Sketch-based mesh editing. Top row [(1)-(6)]: First, we open the mouth of the CAMEL model (1) by detecting an object silhouette, and sketching an approximation of the lip shape we want (2) (See Section 8.1). Note that in (2) the yellow curve is the original object silhouette, the green curve is the user sketch, and the dark blue region is the result of a previously placed sketch. By sketching directly onto the model (3) we produce a handle (yellow) by which we can lift the eyebrow with the green sketch. For the creation of sharp features we sketch the feature line (4) and then scale the affected Laplacians to produce either a ravine (5) or a ridge (6) (See Section 8.2.2). Bottom row [(7)-(12)]: If we are not yet satisfied with the ridge in (6), we can edit the newly created object contour using our silhouette tool (7). Sketching a ravine under the eye by geometry adjustment (See Section 8.2.1) is shown in (8) and (9). Finally, we sketch a subtle suggestive contour near the corner of the mouth in (10) and (11) (See Section 8.2.3), resulting in the SCREAMING CAMEL model (12), shown in Fig. 13.

by sketching them. The idea is simple yet effective: after defining a region of interest on the surface and a camera viewpoint, we select (and trim) one of the resulting silhouettes, and then sketch a new shape for this silhouette (see Fig. 15).

For the computation of silhouettes on polygonal meshes, various methods are available, see (Hertzmann, 1999). We have chosen to use object space silhouettes, and include the ability to switch between edge silhouettes (mesh edges, for which one adjacent face is front-facing and one is back-facing) and smooth surface silhouettes (Hertzmann and Zorin, 2000). Hertzmann and Zorin (Hertzmann and Zorin, 2000) determine the silhouette on mesh edges $e = (\mathbf{v}_i, \mathbf{v}_j)$ by linearly interpolating corresponding vertex normals $\mathbf{n}_i, \mathbf{n}_j$: a silhouette point $\mathbf{p} = (1 - \lambda)\mathbf{v}_i + \lambda\mathbf{v}_j$ on e has to satisfy $((1 - \lambda)\mathbf{n}_i + \lambda\mathbf{n}_j) \cdot (\mathbf{p} - \mathbf{c}) = 0$, where $\mathbf{c}$ is the viewpoint. Silhouette points on edges are connected by segments over faces.

During editing, the user first picks one of the connected components, and then interactively adjusts the start and end point by dragging them with the mouse. Note that degenerate silhouette edge paths might lead to multiply connected curves, resulting in non-intuitive user interaction. Smooth silhouettes (Hertzmann, 1999) remedy this problem on smoothly varying surfaces, and only for models with distinct sharp features (such as CAD models), mesh edges are used as silhouettes. In any case, the selected silhouette segment is represented as a set of points $\mathbf{q}_i$ on the mesh.

After selecting a silhouette segment, the user sketches a curve on the screen, representing the suggested new silhouette segment. The sketch is represented as a polyline in screen space. The vertex locations $\mathbf{s}_i$ on this polyline result in constraints on mesh vertices as follows: First, silhouette vertices $\mathbf{q}_i$ are transformed to screen space, i.e. the first two components contain screen space coordinates, while the third contains the

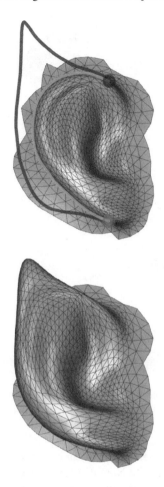

Fig. 15. Sketching a very recognizable ear silhouette: we detect, select, crop and parameterize an object silhouette (yellow, the green and red balls represent begin and end vertices respectively), and then sketch a new desired silhouette (green)

z-value. Then, both curves are parameterized over $[0, 1]$ based on edge lengths of the screen space polylines. This induces a mapping from $\mathbf{q}_i$ to $\{\mathbf{s}_j\}$, defining a new screen space position $\mathbf{q}_i'$ (note that $\mathbf{q}_i'$ retains the z-value of $\mathbf{q}_i$).

The new position $\mathbf{q}_i'$ in screen space is transformed back to model space and serves as a positional constraint. Note that when using smooth surface silhouettes, on-edge constraints have to be used (see Eq. 5). Additionally, varying the weighting of positional constraints along the silhouette against Laplacian constraints leads to a trade off between the accurate positioning of silhouette vertices under the sketch curve, and the preservation of surface details in the ROI. To achieve this, we simply multiply the affected rows in **A** and **b** with the selected weighting factor. For example, the result in Fig. 15 follows the sketch closely, whereas the sketch in Fig. 16 only hints at the desired lip position.

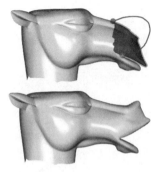

Fig. 16. Sketching an *approximate* CAMEL lip by reducing the weights on the positional constraints for silhouette vertices

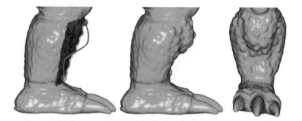

Fig. 17. Editing the bumpy ARMADILLO leg: although the silhouette (yellow) in the ROI (blue) has substantial depth variation and the desired silhouette (green) is smooth, properly weighting the positional constraints retains the surface characteristics after the edit

This method works well even for moderately noisy and bumpy surfaces and preserves details nicely (see Fig. 17). Note that for very noisy surfaces, object space silhouette paths and loops may become arbitrarily segmented, in which case our silhouette sketching method is no longer applicable. In such cases, sketch editing can be performed relative to any user-defined curve sketched manually onto the surface, as was done for lifting the eyebrows of the CAMEL, see Fig. 14(3).

The matrix $\mathbf{A}^T\mathbf{A}$ is computed and factored once for each ROI and silhouette curve selection, and we simply solve for each sketch by back substitution (Toledo, 2003). Some editing results in Fig. 13 were obtained by using the silhouette editing capabilities of our system: sketching larger ears, opening the mouth and modifying the nose contour.

8.2   Feature and Contour Sketching

8.2.1   Geometry Adjustment

Suppose we intend to create a potentially sharp feature where we have drawn our sketch *onto* the mesh. To create a meaningful feature (i.e. a ridge, ravine or crease) on a mesh, we must first adjust the mesh geometry to accommodate such a feature directly under the sketch, since in our setting the sketch need not run along an edge path of the mesh. To illustrate this, see Fig. 18(a), where the sketch path $\{\mathbf{s}_i\}$ (green) follows the edges on the

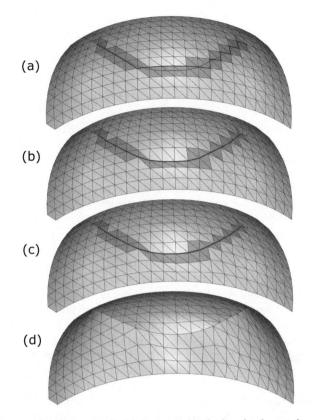

Fig. 18. Creating a ravine-like crease: in (a) the green sketch given by the user is approximated by the red edge path on the original geometry. We adjust the geometry to lie directly under the sketch by orthogonal projection along the tangent plane (b), and then relax the area around the sketch (c). Now we can create the crease by scaling the Laplacians along the edge path (d), resulting in a sharp feature, even for this coarsely sampled surface.

left, but runs perpendicular to them on the right. By applying repeated subdivision we could have locally adjusted the mesh resolution, but for situations similar to the one in Fig. 18(a), many levels of subdivision would be necessary to properly approximate the sketch with an edge path. Another option would be to cut the mesh along the sketch; however, we have found a simpler method that avoids increasing the mesh complexity, yields nice feature lines and well-shaped triangles while retaining the original mesh topology.

We incorporate a tangential mesh regularization, which moves edges onto sharp features while ensuring well-shaped triangles. To access the tangential location of vertices, we relate the topological to the cotangent weighted Laplace operator (see Section 2 for an explanation of these operators). We exploit this for regularizing the mesh in tangential direction, by asking that

$$\mathbf{v}_i' - d_i^{-1} \sum_{j \in \mathcal{N}_i} \mathbf{v}_j' = \mathbf{v}_i - \sum_{j \in \mathcal{N}_i} c_{ij} \mathbf{v}_j, \tag{19}$$

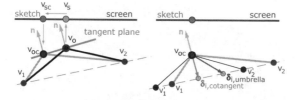

Fig. 19. Adjusting edge path vertices to lie under the sketch curve (left): an object-space edge path vertex $\mathbf{v}_o$ is projected to $\mathbf{v}_s$ in screen space, from there orthogonally projected onto $\mathbf{v}_{sc}$ on the sketch curve, and then projected back onto the tangent plane defined by the normal at $\mathbf{v}_o$, yielding the new vertex position $\mathbf{v}_{oc}$. Relaxing the sketch region (right): to ensure a good triangulation after adjusting the geometry, we perform a relaxation of the edge-path vertices (allow them to move along the sketch path) and nearby vertices by constraining $\delta_{i,umbrella}$ to $\delta_{i,cotangent}$ in the least squares sense. Qualitatively, this moves $\mathbf{v}_1$ and $\mathbf{v}_2$ to $\mathbf{v}_1'$ and $\mathbf{v}_2'$, while keeping $\mathbf{v}_{oc}$ under the sketch.

where d_i is the degree of vertex i. The rationale behind this operation is this: the uniformly weighted operator generates a tangential component, while the cotangent weighting does not. Asking that they are equivalent is essentially solving the Laplace equation but only for the tangential components. The result is a mesh with well shaped triangles, preserving the original mean curvatures as long as the tangential offset is not too large. Note that we typically restrict this operation to small regions, so that large tangential drift cannot occur.

In detail, the geometry adjustment procedure breaks down as follows:

– The triangles in the ROI are transformed to screen space; triangles intersecting $\{\mathbf{s}_i\}$ are gathered (Fig. 18(a), dark triangles) and the begin and end mesh vertices are identified.
– An edge path $\mathbf{V}_p = (\mathbf{v}_{p_1}, \mathbf{v}_{p_2}, \ldots, \mathbf{v}_{p_n})$ that is close to $\{\mathbf{s}_i\}$ is computed by solving a weighted shortest path problem in the edge graph of the ROI. The weight for each edge is the sum of its vertices' screen space distance to $\{\mathbf{s}_i\}$. The resulting edge path vertices are generally not on, but close to $\{\mathbf{s}_i\}$ (shown in red in Fig. 18(a)).
– The path vertices $\mathbf{V}_p$ are mapped onto closest edges of the sketch path $\{\mathbf{s}_i\}$ in screen space; corresponding z-values are computed from restricting each vertex to move on its tangent plane, as defined by the original vertex normal (Fig. 19, left). The resulting edge path closely follows the sketch curve (Fig. 18(b)), yet may introduce badly shaped triangles.
– Triangle shapes are improved by relaxing vertices close to the sketch so that their umbrella Laplacian equals the cotangent Laplacian (Eq. 19) in the least squares sense (See Fig. 19, right). For the vertex relaxation we must solve a linear system, much like the actual editing solver (Section 3), but with additional constraints given by Eq. 19. Obviously, the edge path vertices must remain under the sketch path during this procedure. To ensure this, while also giving the edge path vertices a valid degree of freedom, we add them as positional constraints (Section 3), and additionally add averaging constraints of the form

$$\mathbf{v}_{p_i}' - \frac{1}{2}\mathbf{v}_{p_{i-1}}' - \frac{1}{2}\mathbf{v}_{p_{i+1}}' = 0, \tag{20}$$

for all vertices in $\mathbf{V}_p$ excluding the begin and end vertices. The averaging constraint *loosens* the positional constraint, allowing edge path vertices to move between their adjacent vertices in the path. Adjusting the ratio of weights between positional and averaging constraints leads to a trade-off between accurately approximating the sketch, and some possibly desired path smoothing.

We have experienced no detrimental effects when applying this procedure on meshes which approximate the underlying smooth surface well, even in areas of high curvature. Also, small changes might be tolerable, as this region will be subsequently edited.

After the geometry adjustment step, the surface is prepared for editing operations in the vicinity of the sketch.

8.2.2 Sharp Features

To create a sharp feature along the edge path, we adjust the Laplacians of path vertices when constructing the **A** matrix by prescribing the Laplacian transform for sketch vertices without flexibility to rotate or scale (i.e., as in Eq. 6). Since we discretize the Laplacian using the cotangent weights, we can simply scale the Laplacians of edge path vertices, resulting in a ridge or ravine, depending on the sign. If the Laplacian evaluates to zero, as is the case for flat surfaces, we instead scale the surface normal and prescribe it as the new Laplacian. As described in Section 8.1, we factor the matrix $\mathbf{A}^T\mathbf{A}$ once we have selected a sketch, and can then quickly evaluate the results of varying scales by dragging the mouse up and down. The creation of a sharp ridge is shown in Fig. 18(d). Alternatively, we can add some amount to the Laplacians, making the change absolute rather than relative. This works well in regions with high curvature variation along the sketch.

We have found it to be very convenient to create a ridge using our modeling framework, and thereafter treat it as a silhouette from a different camera position and edit it as outlined in Section 8.1. This technique was applied in the creation of the wavy ridge along the nose of the CAMEL model in Figures 13 and 14(7).

8.2.3 Smooth Features and Suggestive Contours

Applying the editing metaphor described in the previous section can only create sharp features. To enable smooth features or suggestive contours, we need to influence the Laplacians of more vertices than only those lying on the edge path. Additionally, for suggestive contours, we intend to manipulate curvature in the viewing direction. Thus, we need to rotate the Laplacians w.r.t. an axis which is orthogonal to both viewing and normal vectors. After performing the geometry adjustment of Section 8.2.1, given the viewing position $\mathbf{c}$, we gather and segment vertices within a user-defined sketch region around the edge path as follows (Fig. 20, top):

- For each path vertex $\mathbf{v}_{p_i}$ with normal $\mathbf{n}_{p_i}$ (the yellow vectors in Fig. 20) we compute the radial plane $\mathbf{r}_i$, which passes through $\mathbf{v}_{p_i}$ with plane normal $\mathbf{n}_{r_i} = (\mathbf{v}_{p_i} - \mathbf{c}) \times \mathbf{n}_{p_i}$ (the blue vectors in Fig. 20). Now we can segment the vertices in the sketch region $\mathbf{V}_s = (\mathbf{v}_{s_1}, \mathbf{v}_{s_2}, \dots, \mathbf{v}_{s_n})$ such that each sketch region vertex is associated with one such plane (ergo, each vertex in $\mathbf{V}_s$ *belongs* to one edge path vertex).
- Each vertex in $\mathbf{V}_s$ is assigned to the radial plane it is closest to, where the distance of $\mathbf{v}_{s_j}$ to plane $\mathbf{r}_i$ is measured as $d_j = orthodist(\mathbf{r}_i, \mathbf{v}_{s_j}) + dist(\mathbf{v}_{p_i}, \mathbf{v}_{s_j})$. Here,

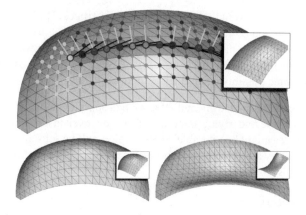

Fig. 20. Top: view dependent vertex segmentation and rotation axis assignment. Bottom left: scaling all Laplacians in the sketch region by the same factor produces smooth ridges and ravines. Bottom right: rotating all Laplacians by an angle of $-\pi/2$ w.r.t. the blue rotation axes results in a suggestive contour.

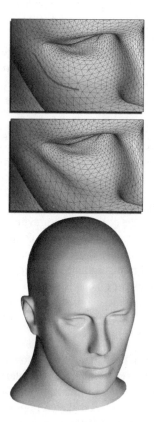

Fig. 21. Adding a strong cheekbone to the MANNEQUIN model by sketching a suggestive contour

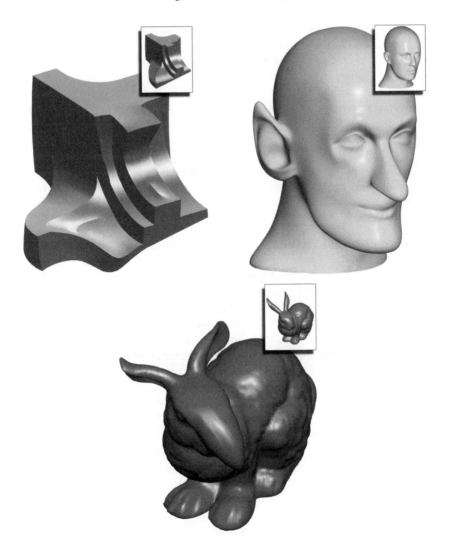

Fig. 22. Some sketch-based mesh editing results: a deformed FANDISK with a few more sharp features, a rather surprised MANNEQUIN with more than just an extra contour around the eye, and droopy-eared, big-nose BUNNY with large feet.

orthodist measures orthogonal distance to the plane, and *dist* is the Euclidean distance between $\mathbf{v}_{p_i}$ and $\mathbf{v}_{s_j}$. We take Euclidean distance into account to avoid problems which occur when two different path vertices have similar radial planes, and furthermore to limit the support of the sketch region.

In Fig. 20 (top image), we show one such segmentation, where the edge path vertices are highlighted with red circles and the segmentation is color coded (i.e. all vertices of the same color are associated with the path vertex of that color).

Once we have this segmentation, one possible operation is to uniformly scale (or add to) the Laplacians of all sketch region vertices. Complementing the sharp features of Section 8.2.2, this operation gives us smooth bumps and valleys (Fig. 20, bottom left). By setting the Laplacians to zero we can flatten specific regions of the mesh.

An alternative editing behavior results from rotating all Laplacians w.r.t. their respective rotation axes (given by above segmentation) by a user-defined angle, determined by dragging the mouse left or right. Note that rotation by π is identical to scaling by minus one. For angles in the ranges $[0, \pi)$ and $(\pi, 2\pi]$ we create varying radial curvature inflection points (Fig. 20, bottom right), resulting in suggestive contours (DeCarlo et al., 2003) such as the cheekbone shown in Fig. 21. Note that these inflection points are not necessarily directly under the sketch, since they result from the Laplacian surface reconstruction and the boundary constraints around the ROI.

9   Implementation Details

All the techniques presented in this paper are implemented and tested on a Pentium 4 2.0 GHz computer. The main computational core of the surface reconstruction algorithm is solving a sparse linear least-squares problem. We use a direct solver which first computes a sparse triangular factorization of the normal equations and then finds the minimizer by back-substitution. As mentioned in Section 5, constructing the matrix of the least-squares system and factorizing it takes the bulk of the computation time. This might seem as a heavy operation for such an application as interactive mesh editing; however, it is done only once per ROI selection. The solve by back-substitution is quite fast and enables to reconstruct the surface interactively, following the user's manipulations of the handle. It should be noted that the system is comprised only of the vertices that fall into the ROI; thus the complexity is not directly dependent on the size of the entire mesh, but rather on the size of the ROI. We experimented with various ROIs of sizes in the order of tens of thousands of vertices. The "intermediate preprocess" times observed were a few seconds, while the actual editing process runs at interactive framerates. Some short editing sessions are demonstrated in the accompanying video.

10   Conclusions

Intrinsic geometry representation for meshes fosters several local surface editing operations. Geometry is essentially encoded using differential properties of the surface, so that the local shape (or, surface detail) is preserved as much as possible given the constraints posed by the user. We show how to use this representation for interactive free-form deformations, detail transfer or mixing, transplanting partial surface meshes, and sketch-based mesh editing.

It is interesting to compare the Laplacian-based approach to multi-resolution approaches: Because each vertex is represented individually as a Laplacian coordinate, the user can freely choose the editing region and model arbitrary boundary constraints, however, computing absolute coordinates requires the solution of a linear system. On the other hand, the non-local bases in multi-resolution representations limit the choice of the editing region and boundary constraints, but absolute coordinates are computed much simpler and faster by summing displacements through the hierarchy. Additionally, we would like to mention that we have found the Laplacian approach to be easier to implement and less brittle in practice.

In general, modeling geometry should be coupled to modeling other surface properties, such as textures. The machinery of discrete Poisson equations has already shown to be effective for image editing, so that editing textured surface should probably be performed on a combined differential geometry/texture representation.

Acknowledgements

Models are courtesy of Stanford University and Max-Planck-Institut für Informatik.

References

Alexa, M.: Differential coordinates for local mesh morphing and deformation. The Visual Computer 19(2), 105–114 (2003a)

Alexa, M.: Differential coordinates for local mesh morphing and deformation. The Visual Computer 19(2), 105–114 (2003b)

Bendels, G.H., Klein, R.: Mesh forging: editing of 3d-meshes using implicitly defined occluders. In: Proceedings of the Eurographics/ACM SIGGRAPH Symposium on Geometry Processing, pp. 207–217. ACM Press, New York (2003)

Biermann, H., Martin, I., Bernardini, F., Zorin, D.: Cut-and-paste editing of multiresolution surfaces. In: Proceedings of the 29th annual conference on Computer graphics and interactive techniques, pp. 312–321 (2002)

Botsch, M., Kobbelt, L.: An intuitive framework for real-time freeform modeling. ACM Trans. Graph 23(3), 630–634 (2004)

Coquillart, S.: Extended free-form deformation: A sculpturing tool for 3D geometric modeling. In: Proceedings of SIGGRAPH 90, pp. 187–196 (1990)

DeCarlo, D., Finkelstein, A., Rusinkiewicz, S., Santella, A.: Suggestive contours for conveying shape. ACM Trans. Graph 22(3), 848–855 (2003)

Desbrun, M., Meyer, M., Schröder, P., Barr, A.H.: Implicit fairing of irregular meshes using diffusion and curvature flow. In: Proceedings of ACM SIGGRAPH 99, pp. 317–324. ACM Press, New York (1999)

Fattal, R., Lischinski, D., Werman, M.: Gradient domain high dynamic range compression. In: Proceedings of ACM SIGGRAPH 2002, pp. 249–256. ACM Press, New York (2002)

Fleishman, S., Drori, I., Cohen-Or, D.: Bilateral mesh denoising. In: Proceedings of ACM SIGGRAPH 2003, pp. 950–953. ACM Press, New York (2003)

Floater, M.S.: Mean-value coordinates. Computer Aided Geometric Design 20, 19–27 (2003)

Forsey, D., Bartels, R.: Hierarchical b-spline refinement. In: Proceedings of ACM SIGGRAPH 88, pp. 205–212. ACM Press, New York (1988)

Gooch, B., Gooch, A.: Non-Photorealistic Rendering. A.K. Peters (2001)

Guskov, I., Sweldens, W., Schröder, P.: Multiresolution signal processing for meshes. In: Proceedings of ACM SIGGRAPH 99, pp. 325–334. ACM Press, New York (1999)

Hertzmann, A.: Introduction to 3D non-photorealistic rendering: Silhouettes and outlines. In: Green, S. (ed.) Non-Photorealistic Rendering. SIGGRAPH 99 Course Notes (1999)

Hertzmann, A., Zorin, D.: Illustrating smooth surfaces. In: Proceedings of the 27th annual conference on Computer graphics and interactive techniques, pp. 517–526 (2000)

Hoffman, D.D., Singh, M.: Salience of visual parts. Cognition 63(1), 29–78 (1997)

Igarashi, T., Matsuoka, S., Tanaka, H.: Teddy: A sketching interface for 3D freeform design. In: Proceedings of SIGGRAPH 99, Computer Graphics Proceedings, Annual Conference Series, pp. 409–416 (1999)

Kanai, T., Suzuki, H., Mitani, J., Kimura, F.: Interactive mesh fusion based on local 3D metamorphosis. In: Graphics Interface '99, pp. 148–156 (1999)

Kobbelt, L., Campagna, S., Vorsatz, J., Seidel, H.-P.: Interactive multi-resolution modeling on arbitrary meshes. In: Proceedings of ACM SIGGRAPH 98, pp. 105–114. ACM Press, New York (1998)

Kobbelt, L., Vorsatz, J., Seidel, H.-P.: Multiresolution hierarchies on unstructured triangle meshes. Computational Geometry: Theory and Applications 14, 5–24 (1999)

Lipman, Y., Sorkine, O., Cohen-Or, D., Levin, D.: Differential coordinates for interactive mesh editing. In: International Conference on Shape Modeling and Applications 2004 (SMI'04), pp. 181–190 (2004)

Meyer, M., Desbrun, M., Schröder, P., Barr, A.H.: Discrete differential-geometry operators for triangulated 2-manifolds. In: Visualization and Mathematics III, pp. 35–57 (2003)

Pérez, P., Gangnet, M., Blake, A.: Poisson image editing. In: Proceedings of ACM SIGGRAPH 2003, pp. 313–318. ACM Press, New York (2003)

Ranta, M., Inui, M., Kimura, F., Mäntylä, M.: Cut and paste based modeling with boundary features. In: SMA '93: Proceedings of the Second Symposium on Solid Modeling and Applications, pp. 303–312 (1993)

Sederberg, T.W., Parry, S.R.: Free-form deformation of solid geometric models. In: Proceedings of SIGGRAPH 86, pp. 151–160 (1986)

Sorkine, O., Lipman, Y., Cohen-Or, D., Alexa, M., Rössl, C., Seidel, H.-P.: Laplacian surface editing. In: Proceedings of the Eurographics/ACM SIGGRAPH Symposium on Geometry processing. Eurographics Association, pp. 179–188. ACM Press, New York (2004)

Taubin, G.: A signal processing approach to fair surface design. In: Proceedings of ACM SIGGRAPH 95, pp. 351–358. ACM Press, New York (1995)

Toledo, S.: Taucs: A Library of Sparse Linear Solvers. Tel. Aviv. University (2003)

Yu, Y., Zhou, K., Xu, D., Shi, X., Bao, H., Guo, B., Shum, H.-Y.: Mesh editing with poisson-based gradient field manipulation. ACM Trans. Graph. 23(3), 644–651 (2004)

Zeleznik, R.C., Herndon, K.P., Hughes, J.F.: Sketch: An interface for sketching 3D scenes. In: Proceedings of SIGGRAPH 96. Computer Graphics Proceedings. Annual Conference Series, pp. 163–170 (1996)

Zorin, D., Schröder, P., Sweldens, W.: Interactive multiresolution mesh editing. In: Proceedings of ACM SIGGRAPH 97, pp. 259–268. ACM Press, New York (1997)

Part I

Geometry
and Modeling

Efficient Rendering of High-Detailed Objects Using a Reduced Multi-resolution Hierarchy

Mathias Holst and Heidrun Schumann

University of Rostock
Albert-Einstein-Str. 21, 18059 Rostock, Germany
mholst@informatik.uni-rostock.de
University of Rostock
Albert-Einstein-Str. 21, 18059 Rostock, Germany
schumann@informatik.uni-rostock.de

Abstract. In the field of view-dependant continuous level of detail of triangle-meshes it is often necessary to extract the current LOD triangle by triangle. Thus, triangle strips are only of very limited use, or only usable with a high effort. In this work a method is proposed that allows a stepwise reduction of a great, fine stepped LOD hierarchy by merging nodes. The result of this process is a reduced hierarchy, which allows the extraction of many neighboring static triangles in one step, so that triangle strips are applicable more efficiently. We show that this results in a significant decimation of processed vertices without loosing a smooth LOD transition.

Keywords: Multi-Resolution Modeling, Real-Time Rendering.

1 Introduction

It is not possible to render high-detailed triangle meshes with interactive framerates even with current hardware. In many cases the triangle size in image space is very low (< 1 pixel) and it is often more necessary to achieve interactive framerates than showing fine details. Thus, level of detail techniques are an important part of many rendering techniques for large scenes and high-detailed objects. For this purpose, the original triangle mesh is simplified using global or local operations (see (Luebke et al., 2002) for an overwiew). Every operation creates a level of detail (short LOD) of the original mesh. During rendering a certain LOD is selected with respect to a high image quality versus low costs.

For doing so, there are two techniques: Discrete techniques save a certain number of offline generated LOD. Then, in every frame, an appropriate LOD is selected, e.g. depending on the viewer distance. On the other hand, continuous techniques use a data structure to extract an appropriate LOD, which contains the whole detail spectra of the original mesh. The advantage of continuous techniques is a very smooth LOD transition in contrast to discrete approaches, and they adapt the LOD better to the viewing situation, so that in most cases less triangles have to be rendered compared to using a discrete LOD.

On the other side graphics cards are specialized to accelerate the rendering of large triangles sets, e.g. using *triangle strips*. A triangle strip is a sequence of triangles in

J. Braz et al. (Eds.): VISAPP and GRAPP 2006, CCIS 4, pp. 31–43, 2007.

which adjacent triangles share a common edge. A strip of k triangles is described as a sequence of $k + 2$ vertices: three vertices for the first triangle and one for each additional triangle. A set of triangle strips that contains all triangles of a mesh is called a *striptification* of that mesh.

Triangle strips are very useful when using discrete LOD techniques, because the whole LOD is rendered at once. In contrast, triangle strips are less useful when using continuous techniques. This is because triangles, that belong to LOD are extracted in small sets only. Thus, the triangle strip length is limited to this set size. To overcome this limitation more sophisticated and time consuming striptification techniques have to be used. Thus, sometimes discrete LOD techniques are more efficient than continuous LOD, although discrete LOD contain more triangles (but less vertices because of longer triangle strips).

To decrease the number of processed vertices in continuous LOD by using triangle strips, a trade-off has to be found: On the one hand the calculation effort should be small (time-consuming calculations should be done offline), and triangle strips should be as long as possible on the other hand.

In this paper a continuous technique is proposed that uses triangle strips more efficiently. Thus, the rendering process is accelerated significantly. A LOD is created by small patches in our approach. Every patch contains a small amount of adjacent triangles. Such a patch is described by a few triangle strips. We have developed a technique to enlarge these patches offline before rendering, so that longer triangle strips are useable. In contrast to other approaches these triangle strips are static, so that the striptification is computed offline, too. This results in a fast LOD extraction during rendering time.

The remainder of this paper is structured as follows. First, in section 2, we will give a short overview on related works. Section 3 describes the basic LOD structure we use. In section 4 we demonstrate, how the patch size is increased by reducing this structure. After this, we will discuss the achieved results in section 5. We conclude with a short summary and an outlook to future work in section 6.

2   Related Work

The rendering acceleration of continuous LOD meshes by using triangle strips was the issue of some previous works. The *Skip Strip* algorithm (El-Sana et al., 1999) uses a merge tree that is represented by a skip strip. For the original mesh a striptification is created, which is updated and repaired during traversal the strip. In addition, the generated triangle strips are scanned for redundant vertices before rendering.

In (Stewart, 2001) an elegant and efficient algorithm for creating a striptifaction of a static mesh is proposed using a so called *tunneling-operator*. This operator connects previously given triangle strips iteratively to reduce their number. They show how this operator can be used to update a striptification that was broken by a local vertex-split (resp. edge-collapse) operation. Thus, it can be used for continuous LOD, too.

In (Velho et al., 1999) an initial striptification is generated for a low detailed mesh. After this, the mesh is refined by inserting new vertices and edges, so that the resulting new triangles can be inserted in the initial striptification, without requiring more triangle strips. The position of an inserted vertex is estimated from an implicit or parametric surface description.

All these techniques do not limit the length of triangle strips. On the other side triangle strips are not static and have to be updated from LOD to LOD, so potentially in every frame. This is time consuming, especially the LOD changes a lot. In our approach the triangle strip length is limited, but they are static, and can be generated offline. Since the benefit of triangle strips decreases with their length, the overhead for processed vertices is small (as shown in section 5). In addition the whole striptification can be stored in a vertex buffer on the graphics card to further reduce the rendering time. This is not possible using dynamic triangle strips, as are used in the described approaches.

Beside these works, there are algorithms that focus on special object types, unlike our approach, which can be used for nearly all kind of objects: In (Lindstrom et al., 1996) an efficient algorithm for height fields is proposed. The single LOD of these landscapes are represented by *Quad-Trees*. The ROAM-Renderer (Duchaineau et al., 1997) was developed for landscapes, as well. It includes an iterative algorithm to get and update triangle strips with a length of four or five triangles. Both approaches also create triangle strips during or after LOD selection, unlike our approach, which uses static triangle strips.

3   Basic LOD Hierarchy

To render an original mesh regarding the viewing distance and other parameters, a data structure is needed that allows the access to all surface areas in different resolutions. These structures are in general hierarchies or trees, like the *merge tree* (Xia et al., 1997). We use the elegant *MT-hierarchy* developed in (Floriani et al., 1997). Using this, it is already possible to extract a small patch of two or more fixed triangles that belong to a certain LOD at once. This is an important property as shown in section 4.

The MT-hierarchy is a directed acyclic graph (abbreviated *DAG*) $G = (\mathcal{N}, \mathcal{A})$. Its nodes $\mathcal{N}$ represent local simplification operation and are labeled by a simplification error. Hierarchy arcs[1] are labeled by triangle sets. We denote a triangle set of an arc a as a patch p_a. The outgoing arcs of a node contain all triangles that are changed (or deleted) by this simplification operation, and its ingoing arcs contain these changed triangles (figure 1). There are two special nodes: The *drain node* n_D at the bottom of the hierarchy (with simplification error 0), whose ingoing arcs represents the original mesh, and the *source node* n_S on top of the hierarchy (with simplification error ∞), whose outgoing arcs contains the most simplified mesh.

3.1   Hierarchy Creation

The hierarchy is generated bottom up, as described in (Floriani et al., 1997). We use edge-collapse operations (Hoppe et al., 1993) to simplify the original mesh iteratively: All possible edge-collapse operations are ordered in a priority queue, in respect to their

---

[1] Since we operate on meshes, the term "edge" already has a meaning. For clarity the term "arc" is used for a hierarchy edge.

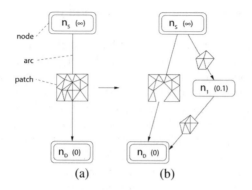

Fig. 1. Hierarchy creation steps: basic mesh, the dashed edge is collapsed (a), patch hierarchy after this edge-collapse operation with simplification error 0.1 (b)

simplification error. This queue is processed until it is empty. We calculate the simplification error using the widely used *quadric error metric* (short: QEM) (Garland and Heckbert, 1997). By this iterative creation and by the QEM it is ensured that the simplification error of the father node n_i of every arc (n_i, n_j) is greater than (or equal to) the simplification error of its child node n_j.

3.2 LOD Selection

To extract a LOD out of the hierarchy it is necessary to create a *cut*. A cut is an arc subset $C \subseteq A$ with the following two properties:

1. $\forall a = (n_i, n_j), a' = (n_k, n_l) \in C : \not\exists n_j \rightarrow^* n_k$
   ($\rightarrow^*$ denotes a path of any length)
2. C is *maximal* (no arc can be added to C without breaking property 1).

The first property ensures that there are no overlapping arc patches. The second property ensures on the other hand, that the whole original mesh is covered by the arc patches of the cut.

Since the simplification error e_i, that is stored in every node n_i, decreases monotonically from top to bottom of the hierarchy, a cut is uniquely defined by:

$$C = \{(n_i, n_j) \in A : e_i \geq \varepsilon > e_j\} \tag{1}$$

as shown in figure 2. The parameter ε describes the desired LOD accuracy. A simple algorithm scans A linearly for cut determination. Since the hierarchy has a logarithmic height, it is of course more efficient to traverse the hierarchy bottom up or top down to avoid unnecessary arc tests. Usually a cut does not change very much from frame to frame. Thus, it is even better to update the cut of the last frame up or down to get the cut for the current frame as described in (Floriani et al., 1998).

Since the QEM measures a *quadratic* distance in object space, ε has to be interpreted as a quadratic distance, too. However, using an image error in pixels is more intuitive. Thus, we propose to define ε by a pixel value γ in image space: Using a perspective

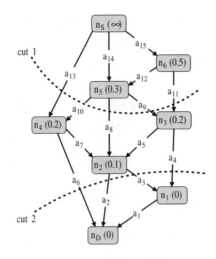

Fig. 2. Demonstration of two cuts specifying different LOD. The first cut $\mathcal{C}_1 = \{a_8, a_9, a_{10}, a_{11}, a_{13}\}$ for $\varepsilon = 0.25$ and the second cut $\mathcal{C}_2 = \{a_2, a_3, a_4, a_6\}$ for $\varepsilon = 0.05$.

projection the length l of a line defined in object space with a distance d to the viewer has the maximum pixel length s in image space of

$$s(l, d) = \frac{l}{d} \cdot \frac{h}{2 \tan \left(\frac{\alpha}{2} \right)}, \tag{2}$$

where h is the output image height (in pixels) and α is the field of view angle.

If the user defines an image error γ in pixels, then its *quadratic* length in object space is given by

$$\varepsilon = (s(l, d_O)^{-1})^2 = \left(\frac{d_O}{\gamma} \cdot \frac{2 \tan \left(\frac{\alpha}{2} \right)}{h} \right)^2, \tag{3}$$

where d_O is the object distance to the viewer. Using the bounding sphere of the object with center M_O and radius r_O, the value of d_O is bounded below by

$$d_O = \max(|M_O - V| - r_O, 0), \tag{4}$$

where V is the viewer position in object space. If γ, d_O, the image dimension h or the field of view angle α change, ε is recalculated and a new cut is determined.

In figure 3 examples for different choices of γ and their effect on image quality are shown.

This cut estimation only considers the object distance to the viewer. But it is of course extensible by using a more sophisticated cost and benefit heuristic as proposed in (Funkhouser and Sequin, 1993).

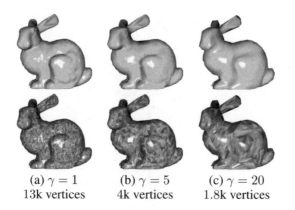

(a) $\gamma = 1$ (b) $\gamma = 5$ (c) $\gamma = 20$
13k vertices   4k vertices   1.8k vertices

Fig. 3. Showing LOD selection using the Stanford bunny: With increasing allowed pixel error the granularity of the mesh decreases significantly for the benefit of less vertices

4   Patch Enlargement

Our purpose is to accelerate rendering by using triangle strips, because the number of processed vertices is a frame rate limiting factor. Since we construct a certain LOD out of several patches, triangle strips can only be defined within these patches. But an arc patch of the hierarchy contains only ≈ 2 triangles in average, so triangle strips are not very efficient. Thus, it is useful to enlarge these patches.

4.1   Arc-Collapse Operator

To achieve a larger average patch size, a coarser local simplification operations than the common used edge-collapse operator could be used, e.g. the removal of more than one vertex at once, with a following retriangulation of the created mesh hole. But it is hard to archive a specified average patch size using this approach. In addition other operators have to be used (and implemented), if a different patch size is desired. Thus, we propose another way: To increase the average patch size we introduce an *arc-collapse operator*, which merges two adjacent hierarchy nodes. This has the effect that the ingoing arcs (resp. outgoing arcs) of both merged nodes with the same father node (resp. child node) are merged to one arc each (figure 4). Thus, larger patches are created. This arc collapsing can be interpreted as the application of two simplification operations at once instead of one after the other.

To guarantee that the used hierarchy is still a DAG after an arc-collapse operation, it has to be ensured that there is no other path between the merged nodes than this arc, otherwise a cycle is created (figure 5). This would cause a conflict situation during cut estimation.

A collapse of randomly selected arcs is not purposeful, because several criteria should be considered: On the one hand a desired average patch size should be achieved by collapsing as few arcs as possible. On the other hand an efficient striptifaction of the resulting patches and the keeping of a smooth LOD transition are important.

For achieving an average patch size two factors are relevant.

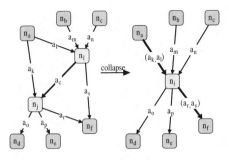

Fig. 4. Arc collapse operation: If arc $a_c = (n_i, n_j)$ is collapsed to a new node other arcs a_k, a_l and a_r, a_s are merged to new arcs, that contain larger patches

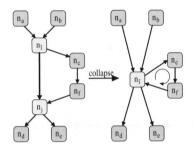

Fig. 5. Error situation: If there is another path between two nodes of an arc, this arc can not be collapsed, because a cycle would be created

1. The number of triangles in the patch p_a of the collapsed arc a, denoted as $|p_a|$: If $|p_a|$ is small the average patch size is bigger after collapsing this arc than if $|p_a|$ would be greater. Hence, a small $|p_a|$ should be preferred.
2. The patch sizes of merged arcs: $\mathcal{M}_a$ denotes the set of the merged arc pairs (in figure 4: $\mathcal{M}_a = \{(a_k, a_l), (a_r, a_s)\}$). Using this, the sum ps of the patch sizes is estimated by:

$$ps(a) = \sum_{(a', a'') \in \mathcal{M}_a} |p_{a'}| + |p_{a''}| \tag{5}$$

If ps is big, few large, or many small patches are created, which yields a bigger average patch number as wanted. On the other side, it is better to merge as many small patches as possible in order to get a nearly constant patch size over the whole hierarchy, because patches can only be enlarged. Thus, it is useful to use ps in relation to the number of merged arcs:

$$ps_{rel}(a) = \frac{ps(a)}{|\mathcal{M}_a|}. \tag{6}$$

It sometimes happens that merging two arcs in $\mathcal{M}_a$ does not form a contiguous patch. Thus, for these patches at least 2 triangle strips have to be used, so that there would be

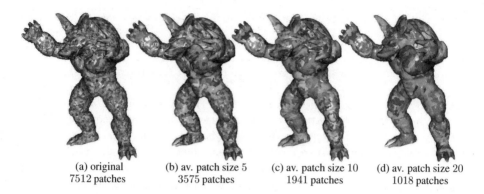

| (a) original | (b) av. patch size 5 | (c) av. patch size 10 | (d) av. patch size 20 |
| 7512 patches | 3575 patches | 1941 patches | 1018 patches |

Fig. 6. Rendering of the same LOD of the Armadillo model with different average patch sizes (each patch is differently colored)

no benefit in the number of processed vertices. Denotes $\mathcal{U}_a \subseteq \mathcal{M}_a$ the set of arc-pairs with neighboring patches:

$$\mathcal{U}_a = \{(a', a'') \in \mathcal{M}_a : p_{a'}, p_{a''} \text{ neighboring}\}, \tag{7}$$

then a relation adj that considers this is given by:

$$adj(a) = \frac{|\mathcal{U}_a|}{|\mathcal{M}_a|} \tag{8}$$

and should be considered for selecting an arc to collapse, whereas adj should be as large as possible.

To preserve a smooth LOD transition inside the hierarchy as far as possible, the relation e_{diff} of the simplification errors of a collapsed arc's father node and child node is considered. If it is *small*, a smooth LOD transition is preserved after collapsing this arc. The value e_{diff} for every $a = (n_i, n_j)$ is given by:

$$e_{diff}(a) = \frac{\max(e_i, \mu)}{\max(e_j, \mu)}, \tag{9}$$

where μ is a very small constant. This constant is necessary because e_j can be 0 (e.g. if n_j is the drain node n_D). Thus, $e_{diff} = \infty$, which would have the effect that such edges would not be collapsed, although a smooth LOD transition could be given. Our choice for μ is the smallest simplification error $\neq 0$ of all nodes in $\mathcal{N}$ divided by 10, which seems to be a practicable value.

To use all these factors for creating an order of arc collapse operations, it is useful to combine them to a single weight $w(a)$ for every arc a. We found that it is very effective to multiply these factors (or their reciprocal) equally weighted, so that a small weight means to collapse an arc before higher weighted arcs.

$$w(a) = |p_a| \cdot e_{diff}(a) \cdot ps_{rel}(a) \cdot \frac{1}{adj(a)}. \tag{10}$$

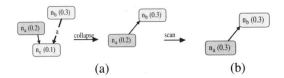

Fig. 7. After collapsing arc a the monotonic bottom-up increase of simplification errors is broken

To achieve a specific average patch size our procedure is as follows: All arcs are ordered in a priority queue, starting with the smallest weight. Then, iteratively, the arc at the head of this queue is collapsed (if it does not produce a cycle, of course). During this, weights of the in- and outgoing arcs of the merged nodes are updated. We stop collapsing arcs if the desired average patch size is reached (or if there is only one arc left in the hierarchy).

Results of such a hierarchy reduction by using arc-collapse operations are shown in figure 6: The number of patches gets significantly smaller with bigger patch sizes.

4.2 Node Error Adjustment

As illustrated in figure 7(a) the simplification error of an arc's father node can get smaller than its child node after an arc-collapse operation. Thus, the LOD selection algorithm (3.2) is non-deterministic. To solve this problem the hierarchy is repaired by an additional breadth-first traversal after reduction. This traversal detects these problematic arcs. If such an arc is found the simplification error of its father node is set to its child's simplification error (figure 7(b)). This slightly decreases the LOD selection precision. Thus, a higher LOD is selected than necessary, which reduces exiguously the efficiency of the reduced hierarchy.

5   Discussion and Results

After introducing a possible way to achieve a certain average patch size easily, in this section we will discuss, what patch size is appropriate for what purpose. In addition the efficiency of our approach is shown, especially in comparison to discrete LOD.

5.1   Appropriate Patch Sizes

To answer the question what average patch size provides most benefits, we first look at the saving factor that triangle strips provide. This is the number of vertices of a strip in relation to the number of triangle vertices:

$$s_{ts}(t) = \frac{2+t}{3t}, \tag{11}$$

where t is the number of triangles. As you can see in figure 8, the benefit of triangle strips converges to $1/3$ very fast with increasing triangle number. Using the original hierarchy with an average patch size of 2 you can save $\approx 33\%$ vertices by using triangle strips (assuming that every patch is represented by only one strip). If the patch size is

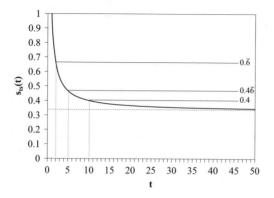

Fig. 8. Efficiency of triangle strips in comparison to render each triangle of the strip separately

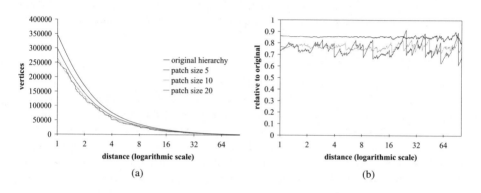

Fig. 9. Number of triangle strip vertices of different LOD at different distances using different patch sizes (a) and these numbers of vertices in relation to to the original hierarchy (b)

increased to 10, an additional 27% is saved, which is only $6.\bar{6}\%$ above the theoretical minimum. That this benefit is nearly reached can be seen in figure 9(a), which shows the number of processed vertices for our Armadillo model at different LOD for some different average patch sizes, and in figure 9(b), which shows the vertex number in relation to the original hierarchy. In some cases the results are not exactly as good as expected. This is because for some large patches more than one triangle strip is needed.

It can also be seen in figure 9(b) that the results for using bigger patch sizes are always better than using the original hierarchy, which shows that the patch size is very uniform over the whole reduced hierarchy. It is also easy to see in figure 9(b) that the relation varies significantly on low LOD using bigger patch sizes. This is because the LOD transitions get coarser with higher distances too, and the LOD do not adapt to user distance as well as when using the original hierarchy.

Another positive effect of reducing the hierarchy is that by collapsing arcs, the patches of these arcs are deleted, too. Thus, the number of vertices that are held in memory is reduced additionally. As shown in table 1 the number of arcs in a hierarchy with an average patch size of 20 is 13 times less than the number in the original

Table 1. Number of arcs and needed vertex-buffer memory using hierarchies for the Armadillo model with different patch sizes

patch size	#arcs	vb size	saving
original (≈ 2)	722076	147.8MB	–
5	258504	99.1MB	32.9%
10	118403	84.5MB	42.8%
20	55612	76.5MB	48.2%

hierarchy. If the triangle strip vertices of all patches are stored in one vertex buffer, using three attributes each (position, normal and color), for the Armadillo model you need 147.8MB using the original hierarchy. If the hierarchy of patch size 20 is used, this is reduced by over 48%. In addition, the cut estimation (as shown in section 3.2) is even faster, because less arcs have to be checked, whether they belong to cut or not.

We can conclude that if a fine LOD transition is important, an average patch size of $5 - 10$ is a good choice. If the memory requirements of the vertex buffer is more important, e.g. it should fit in the very limited graphics card memory, a value over 10 should be used instead. Hence, an average patch size of 10 is a good compromise between a fine LOD transition, vertex number and memory requirements.

5.2   Patch Striptification

The used triangle strip algorithm has a big influence on our approach. We use the tunneling-algorithm (Stewart, 2001), because it always reaches better results than the classical *SGI* algorithm (Akeley et al., 1990) or the *STRIPE* algorithm (Evans et al., 1996). Using this we reach an average triangle strip number per patch of less than 2 even when using a patch size of 50.

5.3   Comparison to Discrete LOD

A discrete LOD transition has several benefits compared to a continuous LOD, because the whole LOD mesh is given explicitly. Thus, no LOD extraction is necessary. In addition the whole LOD mesh can be striptified. Thus, the triangle strip length is not limited, which generally results in less triangle strips, unlike in our approach. Hence, also fewer vertices are used to render the LOD. As shown in section 5.1 and figure 8, the theoretical maximum of this vertex decimation is over 33% compared to the original hierarchy with a patch size of 2. But if an average patch size of 10 is used, this decimation is only about 7%. In addition a discrete LOD algorithm does not produce a smooth LOD transition.

We compared our approach with a discrete LOD mechanism. To do so, we created a cut using the original hierarchy for every distance with a positive integer power of 2, and used these cuts to create discrete LOD. Every discrete LOD got a validity up to the next lower LOD. In figure 10(a) the number of vertices used for rendering is shown for these discrete LOD in comparison to the original hierarchy and a hierarchy with patch size 10. As you can see, the discrete LOD is better at the beginning of each distance

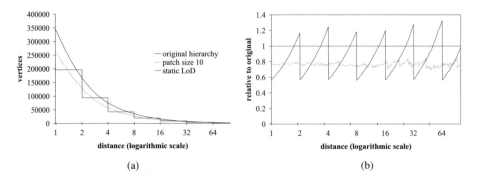

Fig. 10. Processed vertices using the original hierarchy and a hierarchy of patch size 10 in comparison to discrete LOD (a) and in relation to the original hierarchy resp. (b)

interval. But the reduced hierarchy adapts the number of vertices better to distance, so that it is more efficient towards the end of each interval. In figure 10(b) the number of vertices in relation to the original hierarchy is shown. Especially here you can see the range of distance where our approach delivers better results (compared to discrete LOD) exceeds the number of distance intervals where the results are poorer, while it also provides smooth LOD transitions, that discrete LOD does not.

6   Conclusion and Future Work

In this paper we described a technique that allows to use the benefits of continuous LOD (smooth LOD transition) and discrete LOD (good striptification, fast LOD selection). Using a fine-granular LOD-hierarchy as a base, we reduce this by iteratively using an introduced $arc - collapse$ operator. This reduced hierarchy allows the access to larger surface areas (patches) of a specific resolution than before. Thus, using triangle strips for these patches, a certain LOD is described by less vertices, which yields a significant reduction in vertices that have to be processed by the graphics card. Since the number of vertices adapts well to the viewing situation, our approach mostly uses even less vertices than a discrete LOD. This is shown by results.

Our technique works well for all kind of objects that can be described by previous multi-resolution techniques, too. For objects of a high complexity, like plants, this is not the case because these objects can not be simplified by local triangle based simplification operations very efficiently. Thus, even the lowest LOD contains many triangles. For such objects, point based approaches or combined approaches using hybrid hierarchies in the sense of (Cohen et al., 2001) should be preferred, because points are not defined by edges as triangles are, but by isolated vertices. One could imagine to use our approach for point hierarchies as well. Since point hierarchies mostly store points in nodes and not in arcs, a *node-collapse operator* is imaginable to reduce such point hierarchies. Thus, larger amounts of points could be rendered at once. This may accelerate point based LOD rendering using such reduced point hierarchies.

References

Akeley, K., Haeberli, P., Burns, D.: The tomesh.c program. In: Technical report. Silicon Graphics. Available on SGI Developers Toolbox CD (1990)

Cohen, J.D., Aliaga, D.G., Zhang, W.: Hybrid simplification: combining multi-resolution polygon and point rendering. In: Proceedings of the conference on Visualization '01, pp. 37–44. IEEE Computer Society Press, Los Alamitos (2001)

Duchaineau, M., Wolinsky, M., Sigeti, D.E., Aldrich, M.C.M.C., Mineev-Weinstein, M.B.: Roaming terrain: Real-time optimally adapting meshes. In: IEEE Visualization '97, pp. 81–88. IEEE Computer Society Press, Los Alamitos (1997)

El-Sana, J., Azanli, E., Varshney, A.: Skip strips: maintaining triangle strips for view-dependent rendering. In: VIS '99: Proceedings of the conference on Visualization '99, pp. 131–138. IEEE Computer Society Press, Los Alamitos, CA, USA (1999)

Evans, F., Skiena, S., Varshney, A.: Optimizing triangle strips for fast rendering. In: VIS '96: Proceedings of the 7th conference on Visualization '96, pp. 319–326. IEEE Computer Society Press, Los Alamitos, CA, USA (1996)

Floriani, L.D., Magillo, P., Puppo, E.: Building and traversing a surface at variable resolution. In: Proceedings of the 8th conference on Visualization '97, p. 103. IEEE Computer Society Press, Los Alamitos (1997)

Floriani, L.D., Magillo, P., Puppo, E.: Efficient implementation of multi-triangulations. In: Proceedings of the conference on Visualization '98, pp. 43–50. IEEE Computer Society Press, Los Alamitos (1998)

Funkhouser, T.A., Sequin, C.H.: Adaptive display algorithm for interactive frame rates during visualization of complex virtual environments. In: Proceedings of the 20th annual conference on Computer graphics and interactive techniques, pp. 247–254. ACM Press, New York (1993)

Garland, M., Heckbert, P.S.: Surface simplification using quadric error metrics. In: Proceedings of the 24th annual conference on Computer graphics and interactive techniques, pp. 209–216. ACM Press/Addison-Wesley Publishing Co, New York (1997)

Hoppe, H., DeRose, T., Duchamp, T., McDonald, J., Stuetzle, W.: Mesh optimization. In: SIGGRAPH '93: Proceedings of the 20th annual conference on Computer graphics and interactive techniques, pp. 19–26. ACM Press, New York (1993)

Lindstrom, P., Koller, D., Ribarsky, W., Hodges, L.F., Faust, N., Turner, G.A.: Real-time, continuous level of detail rendering of height fields. In: SIGGRAPH '96: Proceedings of the 23rd annual conference on Computer graphics and interactive techniques, pp. 109–118. ACM Press, New York (1996)

Luebke, D., Reddy, M., Cohen, J., Varshney, A., Watson, B., Huebner, R.: Level of Detail for 3D Graphics. Computer Graphics and Geometric Modeling. Morgan Kaufmann, San Francisco (2002)

Stewart, A.J.: Tunneling for triangle strips in continuous level-of-detail meshes. In: GRIN'01: No description on Graphics interface 2001, pp. 91–100. Canadian Information Processing Society, Toronto, Ont. Canada, Canada (2001)

Velho, L., de Figueiredo, L.H., Gomes, J.: Hierarchical generalized triangle strips. The Visual Computer 15, 21–35 (1999)

Xia, J.C., El-Sana, J., Varshney, A.: Adaptive real-time level-of-detail-based rendering for polygonal models. IEEE Transactions on Visualization and Computer Graphics 3(2), 171–183 (1997)

Mesh Retrieval by Components

Ayellet Tal* and Emanuel Zuckerberger

Department of Electrical Engineering
Technion
ayellet@ee.technion.ac.il
Department of Electrical Engineering
Technion

Abstract. This paper examines the application of the human vision theories of
Marr and Biederman to the retrieval of three-dimensional objects. The key idea
is to represent an object by an attributed graph that consists of the object's meaningful components as nodes, where each node is fit to a basic shape. A system
that realizes this approach was built and tested on a database of about 400 objects
and achieves promising results. It is shown that this representation of 3D objects
is very compact. Moreover, it gives rise to a retrieval algorithm that is invariant
to non-rigid transformations and does not require normalization.

Keywords: 3D shape retrieval, 3D shape matching.

1 Introduction

In his seminal work (Marr, 1982), Marr claims that the human brain constructs a 3D
viewpoint-independent model of the image seen. This model consists of objects and
spatial inter-relations between them. Every 3D object is segmented into primitives,
which can be well approximated by a few simple shapes. Biederman's Recognition-By-
Components (RBC) theory (Biederman, 1987; Biederman, 1988) claims that the human
visual system tends to segment complex objects at regions of deep concavities into simple basic shapes, *geons*. The simple attributed shapes along with the relations between
them form a stable 3D mental representation of an object.

The current paper proposes a retrieval approach that attempts to succeed these theories. The key idea is to decompose each object into its "meaningful" components at the
object's deep concavities, and to match each component to a basic shape. After determining the relations between these components, an attributed graph that represents the
decomposition is constructed and considered the object's *signature*. Given a database
of signatures and one specific signature, the latter is compared to other signatures in the
database, and the most similar objects are retrieved.

Retrieving 3D objects has become a lively topic of research in recent years
(Veltkamp, 2001). A common practice is to represent each object by a few properties – a *signature* – and base the retrieval on the similarity of the signatures. Some

---

* This work was partially supported by European FP6 NoE grant 506766 (AIM@SHAPE) and
by the Smoler Research Funds.

Fig. 1. Retrieval of the top 20 objects similar to to the top left-most human figure

signatures consist of local properties of the shapes such as histograms of colors and normals (Paquet et al., 2000), probability shape distributions (Osada et al., 2001), reflective symmetry (Kazhdan et al., 2003a), spherical harmonics (Vranic and Saupe, 2002; Kazhdan et al., 2003b) and more. Other papers consider global properties, such as shape moments (Elad et al., 2001) or *sphere projection* (Leifman et al., 2005). In these cases, the objects need to be normalized ahead of time.

Our global approach is mostly related to graph-based algorithms. The Reeb graph is a skeleton determined using a scalar function, which is chosen in this case to be the geodesic distance (Hilaga et al., 2001). In (Sundar et al., 2003; Cornea et al., 2005), it is proposed to represent an object by its skeleton and an algorithm for comparing shock graphs is presented. Our approach succeeds these methods, yet differs in several ways. First, the graphs are constructed differently, focusing on segmentation at deep concavities, following (Marr, 1982; Biederman, 1995). Second, each node and edge in the graph is associated with properties, resulting in an attributed graph. Third, a different graph matching procedure is utilized.

Our proposed signature has a few important properties. First, it is invariant to non-rigid-transformations. For instance, given a human object, we expect its signature to be similar to signatures of other humans, whether they bend, fold their legs or point forward, as illustrated in Figure 1. In this figure, all the 19 humans in a database consisting of 388 objects, were ranked among the top 21 objects, and 17 among the top 17. Invariance to non-rigid-transformations is hard to achieve when only geometry is considered.

Second, normalization is not required, since the signature is a graph that is invariant to rigid transformations.

Third, the signature tolerates degenerated meshes and noise. This is so because the object is represented by its general structure, ignoring small features.

Finally, the proposed signature is very compact. Thus, signatures can be easily stored and transfered.

The remaining of the paper is structured as follows. Section 2 outlines our approach. Sections 3–4 address the main issues involved in the construction of a signatures. In particular, Section 3 discusses mesh decomposition into meaningful components while

Section 4 describes the determination of basic shapes. Section 5 presents our experimental results. Section 6 concludes the paper.

2   System Overview

Given a database of meshes in a standard representation consisting of vertices and faces (e.g., VRML) and one specific object O, the goal is to retrieve from the database objects similar to O.

This section starts by outlining the signature computation technique. This is the main contribution of the paper and thus the next sections elaborate on the steps involved. Then, the section briefly describes the graph matching algorithm used during retrieval.

SIGNATURE COMPUTATION: Let S be an orientable mesh.

Definition 2.1. Decomposition: $S_1, S_2, \ldots S_k$ *is a decomposition of S iff (i)* $\forall i, 1 \leq i \leq k$, $S_i \subseteq S$, *(ii)* $\forall i$, S_i *is connected, (iii)* $\forall i \neq j, 1 \leq i, j \leq k$, S_i *and S_j are face-wise disjoint and (iv)* $\cup_{i=1}^{k} S_i = S$.

Definition 2.2. Decomposition graph: *Given a decomposition* $S_1, S_2, \cdots S_k$ *of a mesh S, a graph $G(V,E)$ is its corresponding decomposition graph iff each component S_i is represented by a node $v_i \in V$ and there is an arc between two nodes in the graph iff the two corresponding components share an edge in S.*

Definition 2.3. Attributed decomposition graph: *Given a decomposition graph $G(V, E)$, $G = (V, E, \mu, \nu)$ is an attributed decomposition graph if μ is a function which assigns attributes to nodes and ν is a function which assigns attributes to arcs.*

For each object in the database, its attributed decomposition graph, the object's *signature*, is computed and stored. Signature computation is done in three steps. First, the object is decomposed into a small number of meaningful components. Second, a decomposition graph is constructed. Third, each node and arc of the decomposition graph is given attributes, following (Biederman, 1987; Biederman, 1988). Specifically, each component is classified as a basic shape: a spherical surface, a cylindrical surface, a cone surface or a planar surface. The corresponding graph node is given the appropriate shape attribute. Each graph arc is attributed by the relative surface area of its endpoint components (i.e., greater, smaller, equal). We elaborate on signature construction in the next couple of sections.

RETRIEVAL: Given a specific object by the user, the goal of the system is to retrieve from the database the most similar objects to this object.

This step requires the comparison of graphs. Graph matching and subgraph isomorphism has been applied to many problems in computer vision and pattern recognition e.g., (Rocha and Pavlidis, 1994; Wang et al., 1997; Lee et al., 1990; Pearce et al., 1994; Wong, 1992). In the current paper, we follow (Messmer, 1995), which uses error-correcting subgraph isomorphism.

The key idea of error correction algorithm is as follows. A graph edit operation is defined for each possible error type. Possible operations are deletion, insertion and substitution (i.e., changing attributes) of nodes and arcs. A cost function is associated with each type of edit operation. Given a couple graphs, the algorithm aims at finding a sequence of edit operations with a minimal cost, such that applying the sequence to one graph results in a subgraph isomorphism with the other.

Formally, the algorithm is given two graphs, $G = (V, E, \mu, \nu)$ and $G' = (V', E', \mu', \nu')$, where V (V') is the set of nodes of G (G'), E (E') is its set of arcs, μ (μ') is a function which assigns attributes to nodes and ν (ν') is a function which assigns attributes to arcs. It is also given a set of graph edit operations and their corresponding cost functions. The goal is to find the optimal error-correcting subgraph isomorphism (Δ, g), where Δ is a sequence of edit operations and g is an isomorphism, such that there is a subgraph isomorphism g from $\Delta(G)$ to G' and the cost $C(\Delta)$ of Δ is minimal.

The algorithm maintains a search tree. The root of the search tree contains an empty mapping and is associated with cost 0. At the next level of the search tree, the first node of G is mapped onto nodes in G'. Each such mapping, along with its corresponding cost of the relevant edit operation, is a node in the search tree. The generation of the next nodes is guided by the cost of the edit operations. The node representing the mapping with the lowest cost in the current search tree is explored by mapping a new node of G onto every node of G' that has not yet been used in the path and the corresponding costs are calculated.

When the first mapping γ' describing a complete subgraph isomorphism from G to G' is found, a threshold parameter is set to the cost $C(\gamma')$ of γ'. A node having a cost greater than the threshold is never explored. Other nodes are explored until a mapping with the minimal cost is found.

This procedure is applied to the graph representing the query object against each graph in the database. It returns a corresponding error value for each pair. The lower the error, the less edit operations are required (or the "cheaper" these operations are), and thus the more similar the objects are. The objects are therefore retrieved in an ascending order of their error values.

3   Mesh Decomposition

The first step in signature construction is mesh decomposition into its meaningful components. In recent years, there have been several papers addressing this problem, e.g. (Katz and Tal, 2003; Li et al., 2001; Lee et al., 2005; Shamir, 2004; Katz et al., 2005). These techniques produce very nice decompositions. However, we will show below that simpler, linear algorithms are sufficient for retrieval.

Our approach follows Biederman's observation that "*the human visual system tends to segment complex objects at regions of deep concavities into simple basic shapes*". Thus, algorithms that generate rough decompositions at deep concavities are used.

In (Chazelle et al., 1997), a sub-mesh is called *convex* if it lies entirely on the boundary of its convex hull. It is proved that the optimization problem is NP-complete. Nevertheless, linear greedy flooding heuristics are used for generating convex decompositions. These heuristics work on the dual graph H of mesh S, where nodes represents facets and arcs join nodes associated with adjacent facets. The algorithm starts from some node in H and traverses H, collecting nodes along the way as long as the associated facets form a convex sub-mesh. When no adjacent nodes can be added to the current component, a new component is started and the traversal resumes.

Another simple linear decomposition algorithm is *Watershed decomposition* (Mangan and Whitaker, 1999) which decomposes a mesh into *catchment basins*, or *watersheds*. Let $h : E \rightarrow R$ be a discrete height function defined over E, the set of elements (vertices, edges or faces) of the mesh. A *watershed* is a subset of E, consisting of elements whose path of steepest descent terminates in the same local minimum of h. In our implementation, the height function is defined over the edges and is a function of the dihedral angle.

The key idea of the Watershed decomposition algorithm is to let the elements descend until a labeled region is encountered, where all the minima are labeled as a first step.

The major problem with watershed as well as with convex decomposition is over-segmentation (i.e., obtaining a large number of components), due to many small concavities. The goal of our application, however, is to obtain only a handful of components.

To solve over-segmentation, it is proposed in (Mangan and Whitaker, 1999) to merge regions whose watershed depth is below a certain threshold. A couple of other possible solutions are studied in (Zuckerberger et al., 2002) and described below.

First, since small components are less vital to recognition (Biederman, 1987), the components are merged based on their surface areas. Thus, a small component is merged with a neighboring component having the largest surface area. This process is done in ascending order of surface areas and continues until all the components become sufficiently large.

The drawback of merging is that it might result with complex shapes, which might not fit any basic shape.

Another solution is to ignore the small components altogether. Only the original large components are taken into account both in the construction of the decomposition graph and in determining the components' basic shapes. The small components are used only to determine the adjacency relations between the large components.

Figure 2 presents an example of the results, obtained by four variants of the general scheme: Convex vs. Watershed decomposition and merging vs. ignoring small components. As can be seen, even when the small components are ignored, there is still sufficient information to visually recognize the rook. Figures 2(c) demonstrates the drawback of merging – the red component does not resemble any basic shape.

In summary, the first step in constructing a signature of an object is to decompose it into a handful of meaningful components. This can be done by augmenting linear

| Convex | Convex | Watershed | Watershed |
| merging | ignoring | merging | ignoring |

Fig. 2. Decompositions of a rook

algorithms – the *watershed decomposition* and a *greedy convex decomposition* – with a post-processing step which either eliminates small components or merges them with their neighbors.

4   Basic Shape Determination

The second issue in the construction of a signature is basic shape determination. Given a sub-mesh, which basic shape better fits this component? In this paper four basic shapes are considered – a spherical surface, a cylindrical surface, a cone surface and a planar surface.

Our problem is related to the problem of fitting implicit polynomials to data and using polynomial invariants to recognize three-dimensional objects. In (Taubin, 1991), a method based on minimizing the mean square distance of the data points to the surface is described. A first-order approximation of the real distance is used. In (Keren et al., 1994), a fourth-degree polynomial $f(x,y,z)$ is sought, such that the zero set of $f(x,y,z)$ is stably bounded and approximates the object's boundary. A probabilistic framework with an asymptotic Bayesian approximation is used in (Subrahmonia et al., 1996).

In order to fit a basic shape to a component, the given component is first sampled. A non-linear least-squares optimization problem, which fits each basic shape to the set of sample points, is then solved. The approximate mean square distance from the sample points to each of the basic surfaces is minimized with respect to a few parameters specific for each basic shape. The basic shape with the minimal fitting error represents the shape attribute of the component. The algorithm for fitting the points to a surface is based on (Taubin, 1991). We formalize it below.

Let $f : R^n \to R^k$ be a smooth map, having continuous first and second derivatives at every point. The set of zeros of f, $Z(f) = \{Y | f(Y) = 0\}$, $Y \in R^n$ is defined by the implicit equations $f_1(Y) = 0, \cdots, f_k(Y) = 0$ where $f_i(Y)$ is the i-th element of f, $1 \le i \le k$.

The goal is to find the approximate distance from a point $X \in R^n$ to the set of zeros $Z(f)$ of f. In the linear case, the Jacobian matrix $Jf(X)$ of f with respect to X is a constant $Jf(X) = \mathbf{C}$, and $f(Y) = f(X) + \mathbf{C}(Y - X)$. The unique point $\hat{Y}$ that minimizes the distance $\|Y - X\|$, constrained by $f(Y) = 0$, is given by $\hat{Y} = X - \mathbf{C}^\dagger f(X)$, where $\mathbf{C}^\dagger = \mathbf{C}^\mathbf{T}(\mathbf{C}\mathbf{C}^\mathbf{T})^{-1}$ is the pseudo-inverse (Duda et al., 2000). If C is invertible then $\mathbf{C}^\dagger = \mathbf{C}^{-1}$. Finally, the square of the distance from X to $Z(f)$ is given by

$$dist(X, Z(f))^2 = \|\hat{Y} - X\|^2 = f(X)^T (\mathbf{C}\mathbf{C}^T)^{-1} f(X).$$

For the nonlinear case, Taubin (Taubin, 1991) proposes to approximate the distance from X to $Z(f)$ with the distance from X to the set of zeros of a linear model of f at X, $\tilde{f} : R^n \to R^k$, where $\tilde{f}$ is defined by the truncated Taylor series expansion of f, $\tilde{f}(Y) = f(X) + Jf(X)(Y - X)$. But, $\tilde{f}(X) = f(X)$, $J\tilde{f}(X) = Jf(X)$, and the square of the approximated distance from a point $X \in R^n$ to the set of zeros $Z(f)$ of f is given by

$$dist(X, Z(f))^2 \approx f(X)^T (Jf(X)Jf(X)^T)^{-1} f(X).$$

Specifically, for the basic shapes we are considering, $n = 3$, $k = 1$, and the set of zeros $Z(f)$ of f is a surface in three-dimensions. The Jacobian $Jf(X)$ has only one row and $Jf(X) = (\nabla f(X))^T$, where $\nabla f(X)$ is the gradient of $f(X)$.

In this case, the approximated distance becomes

$$dist(X, Z(f))^2 \approx f(X)^2 / \|\nabla f(X)\|^2.$$

Moreover, we are interested in maps described by a finite number of parameters $(\alpha_1, \cdots, \alpha_r)$. Let $\phi : R^{n+r} \to R^k$ be a smooth function, and consider maps $f : R^n \to R^k$, which can be written as $f(X) \equiv \phi(\alpha, X)$, where $\alpha = (\alpha_1, \cdots, \alpha_r)^T$, $X = (X_1, \cdots, X_n)$ and $\alpha_1, \cdots, \alpha_r$ are the parameters.

The approximated distance from X to $Z(\phi(\alpha, X))$ is then

$$dist(X, Z(\phi(\alpha, X)))^2 = \delta_\phi(\alpha, X)^2$$
$$\approx \phi(\alpha, X)^T (J\phi(\alpha, X)J\phi(\alpha, X)^T)^{-1} \phi(\alpha, X).$$

In particular, in three-dimensional space

$$\delta_\phi(\alpha, X)^2 \approx \phi(\alpha, X)^2 / \|\nabla \phi(\alpha, X)\|^2.$$

We can now formalize the fitting problem. Let $P = \{p_1, \cdots, p_m\}$ be a set of n-dimensional data points and $Z(\phi(\alpha, X))$ the set of zeros of the smooth function $\phi(\alpha, X)$. In order to fit P to $Z(\phi(\alpha, X))$ we need to minimize the approximated mean square distance $\Delta_P^2(\alpha)$ from P to $Z(\phi(\alpha, X))$:

$$\Delta_P^2(\alpha) = \frac{1}{m} \sum_{i=1}^{m} \delta_\phi(\alpha, p_i)^2$$

with respect to the unknown parameters $\alpha = (\alpha_1, \cdots, \alpha_r)^T$.

This is equivalent to minimizing the length of the residual vector $Q = (Q_1, \cdots, Q_m)^T$

$$\|Q(\alpha)\|^2 = \sum_{i=1}^{m} Q_i(\alpha)^2 = m\Delta_P^2(\alpha)$$

where $Q_i(\alpha) = \delta_\phi(\alpha, p_i)$, $i = 1, \cdots, m$.

The Levenberg-Marquardt algorithm can be used to solve this nonlinear least squares problem (Bates and Watts, 1988). This algorithm iterates the following step

$$\alpha^{n+1} = \alpha^n - (JQ(\alpha^n)JQ(\alpha^n)^T + \mu_n I_m)^{-1} JQ(\alpha^n)^T Q(\alpha^n),$$

where $JQ(\alpha)$ is the Jacobian of Q with respect to α: $J_{ij}Q(\alpha) = \frac{\partial Q_i}{\partial \alpha_j}(\alpha)$, for $i = 1, \cdots, m$, and $j = 1, \cdots, r$, and μ_n is a small nonnegative constant which makes the matrix $JQ(\alpha^n)$ $JQ(\alpha^n)^T + \mu_n I_m$ positive defined.

At each iteration, the algorithm reduces the length of the residual vector, converging to a local minimum.

4.1 Distance 3D Point – Basic Shape

We can now explicitly define the square of the distance $\delta_\phi(\alpha, X)$ from a three-dimensional point X to the set of zeros $Z(\phi(\alpha, X))$ of $\phi(\alpha, X)$ for our basic shapes, three of which are quadrics (i.e., sphere, cylinder, cone) and the fourth is linear (i.e., plane).

A quadric, in homogeneous coordinates, is given by $X^T M X = 0$ in the global coordinate system, where M is a 4×4 matrix and X is a vector in R^4. In its local coordinate system, it is given by $X'^T M' X' = 0$, where $X = T_r R_x R_y R_z S_c X'$, T_r is a translation matrix, R_x, R_y, R_z are rotation matrices and S_c is a scale matrix.

If M' is known, M can be calculated and the equation of the quadric in the global coordinate system can be obtained.

$$\phi(t_x, t_y, t_z, \theta_x, \theta_y, \theta_z, s_x, s_y, s_z, X) = X^T M X = 0,$$

where the parameters are the translation, rotation and scale.

Then, for each basic quadric, the square of the approximated distance $\delta_\phi(t_x, t_y, t_z, \theta_x, \theta_y, \theta_z, s_x, s_y, s_z, X_p)$ from a three-dimensional point X_p to the quadric can be determined by

$$\delta_\phi(t_x, t_y, t_z, \theta_x, \theta_y, \theta_z, s_x, s_y, s_z, X_p)^2 \approx \tag{1}$$

$$\approx \frac{\phi(t_x, t_y, t_z, \theta_x, \theta_y, \theta_z, s_x, s_y, s_z, X_p)^2}{\|\nabla\phi(t_x, t_y, t_z, \theta_x, \theta_y, \theta_z, s_x, s_y, s_z, X_p)\|^2} =$$

$$= \frac{\phi(t_x, t_y, t_z, \theta_x, \theta_y, \theta_z, s_x, s_y, s_z, X_p)^2}{(\frac{\partial\phi}{\partial x})^2 + (\frac{\partial\phi}{\partial y})^2 + (\frac{\partial\phi}{\partial z})^2}$$

Hereafter we use the above equation to calculate δ_ϕ for each quadric basic shape, which are all special cases of the above.

For a spherical surface with radius $r_0 = 1$, defined in its local coordinate system centered at the center of the sphere, we have

$$M' = \begin{pmatrix} 1 & 0 & 0 & 0 \\ 0 & 1 & 0 & 0 \\ 0 & 0 & 1 & 0 \\ 0 & 0 & 0 & -1 \end{pmatrix}.$$

$$\phi(t_x, t_y, t_z, r, x, y, z) = (x - t_x)^2 + (y - t_y)^2 + (z - t_z)^2 - r^2 = 0.$$

For a cylindrical surface with radius $r_0 = 1$, defined in its local coordinate system, where the z axis is the axis of the cylinder,

$$M' = \begin{pmatrix} 1 & 0 & 0 & 0 \\ 0 & 1 & 0 & 0 \\ 0 & 0 & 0 & 0 \\ 0 & 0 & 0 & -1 \end{pmatrix}.$$

The implicit equation in the global coordinate system is

$$\phi(t_x, t_y, t_z, \theta_x, \theta_y, r, x, y, z) = \tag{2}$$

$$= D_1(x - t_x)^2 + D_2(y - t_y)^2 + D_3(z - t_z)^2 +$$

$$+ 2C_1(x - t_x)(y - t_y) + 2C_2(x - t_x)(z - t_z) +$$

$$+ 2C_3(y - t_y)(z - t_z) - r^2 = 0$$

where

$$
\begin{aligned}
D_1 &= \cos^2 \theta_y, \\
D_2 &= \cos^2 \theta_x + \sin^2 \theta_x \sin^2 \theta_y, \\
D_3 &= \sin^2 \theta_x + \cos^2 \theta_x \sin^2 \theta_y, \\
C_1 &= \sin \theta_x \sin \theta_y \cos \theta_y, \\
C_2 &= -\cos \theta_x \sin \theta_y \cos \theta_y, \\
C_3 &= \sin \theta_x \cos \theta_x \cos^2 \theta_y, \\
B_1 &= -t_x D_1 - t_y C_1 - t_z C_2, \\
B_2 &= -t_x C_1 - t_y D_2 - t_z C_3, \\
B_3 &= -t_x C_2 - t_y C_3 - t_z D_3.
\end{aligned}
$$

Note that (t_x, t_y, t_z) can be any point on the cylinder axis, thus the cylinder is over parameterized. This can be solved by setting one of these three parameters to zero.

For a cone surface with $g_0 = r_0/h_0 = 1$, where r_0 is the radius and h_0 is the height, defined in its local coordinate system, where the z axis is the axis of the cone and the origin of the coordinate system is the apex of the cone,

$$
M' = \begin{pmatrix}
1 & 0 & 0 & 0 \\
0 & 1 & 0 & 0 \\
0 & 0 & -1 & 0 \\
0 & 0 & 0 & 0
\end{pmatrix}.
$$

The implicit equation in the global coordinate system is

$$
\begin{aligned}
\phi(t_x, t_y, t_z, \theta_x, \theta_y, g, x, y, z) &= \\
&= D_1(x - t_x)^2 + D_2(y - t_y)^2 + D_3(z - t_z)^2 + \\
&\quad + 2C_1(x - t_x)(y - t_y) + 2C_2(x - t_x)(z - t_z) + \\
&\quad + 2C_3(y - t_y)(z - t_z) = 0
\end{aligned} \tag{3}
$$

where

$$
\begin{aligned}
D_1 &= \cos^2 \theta_y - g^2 \sin^2 \theta_y, \\
D_2 &= \cos^2 \theta_x + \sin^2 \theta_x \sin^2 \theta_y - g^2 \sin^2 \theta_x \cos^2 \theta_y, \\
D_3 &= \sin^2 \theta_x + \cos^2 \theta_x \sin^2 \theta_y - g^2 \cos^2 \theta_x \cos^2 \theta_y, \\
C_1 &= (1 + g^2) \sin \theta_x \sin \theta_y \cos \theta_y, \\
C_2 &= -(1 + g^2) \cos \theta_x \sin \theta_y \cos \theta_y, \\
C_3 &= (1 + g^2) \sin \theta_x \cos \theta_x \cos^2 \theta_y, \\
B_1 &= -t_x D_1 - t_y C_1 - t_z C_2, \\
B_2 &= -t_x C_1 - t_y D_2 - t_z C_3, \\
B_3 &= -t_x C_2 - t_y C_3 - t_z D_3.
\end{aligned}
$$

Finally, a plane is defined by the equation $ax + by + cz + d = 0$. The square of the distance from a point $p = (x_p, y_p, z_p)$ to the plane is simply

$$\delta_\phi(a,b,c,d,x_p,y_p,z_p)^2 = \frac{(ax_p + by_p + cz_p + d)^2}{a^2 + b^2 + c^2}.$$

5   Experimental Results

Our goal is to examine whether Biederman's observation, claiming that recognition can be accurate even if only a few geons of a complex object are visible (Biederman, 1995), is indeed feasible.

We tested our retrieval algorithm on a database consisting of 388 objects. Among the 388 objects we identified six classes: 19 models of human figures, 18 models of four-legged animals, 9 models of knives, 8 models of airplanes, 7 models of missiles and 7 models of bottles. The other models are unclassified.

Four different decomposition techniques were used in our experiments: (1) Greedy convex decomposition, where small patches are ignored; (2) Greedy convex decomposition, where small patches are merged with their neighbors; (3) Watershed decomposition, where small patches are ignored; (4) Watershed decomposition, where small patches are merged with their neighbors.

Based on these four decomposition techniques, four signature databases were built. Identical retrieval experiments were applied to each database. In each experiment, a test object was chosen and the system was queried to retrieve the most similar objects to this test object in ascending order. At least one member from each of the six classes was used as a test object.

Figures 3– 6 demonstrate some of our results. In each figure, the test object is the left-most, top object, and the objects retrieved are ranked from left to right. In particular, Figure 3 presents the most similar objects to *Detpl* (at the top-left), as retrieved by our algorithm. All the eight airplanes of the class were retrieved among the top eleven. Figure 4 presents the results of retrieving objects similar to *Cat2*. Sixteen out the eighteen members of the 4-legged animal class were retrieved among the top twenty. Figure 5 presents the retrieved most similar objects to *Knifech*. Eight out of the nine knifes of the class were retrieved among the top ten. Figure 6 demonstrates the most similar objects to the missile at the top left, as retrieved by our algorithm. Six out of the the seven

Fig. 3. The most similar objects to *Detpl* (top left)

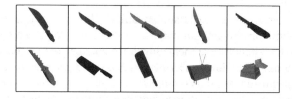

Fig. 4. The most similar objects to *Cat2*

Fig. 5. The most similar objects to *Knifech*

Fig. 6. The most similar objects to *Aram*

class members were retrieved among the top nine. Note that in all the above cases the members of each class differ geometrically. Yet, their decomposition graphs are similar and therefore they were found to be similar.

On the class of bottles, the algorithm does not perform as well. This class contains seven members (see Figure 7). Though the objects seem similar geometrically, their connectivity differs. The *Beer, Ketchup* and *Tabasco* bottles consist each of 4-8 disconnected components while *Bottle3, Champagne, Whiskey* and *Plastbtl* consist each of only one or two components. Since connectivity determines the graph structure and the graphs differ, the results of the retrieval experiments are inferior to the other classes.

All four sub-methods performed well. The Watershed decomposition performed slightly better than convex decomposition. This fact might be surprising since convexity is the main factor in human segmentation. This can be explained by the fact

Fig. 7. The bottle class

Table 1. Summary of the experimental results for the Watershed / ignore sub-method

Class(N)/ Object	Retrieved / Top results		
Airplanes(8)			
Detplane	5/6	7/9	8/16
Worldw	6/6	6/9	8/16
747	5/6	5/9	7/16
Animals(18)			
Cat2	6/8	11/14	14/20
Tiger3	7/8	11/14	13/20
Deer	8/8	11/14	15/20
Humans(19)			
Woman2	10/10	17/17	19/24
Child3y	10/10	15/17	19/24
Knives(9)			
Knifech	6/6	8/8	8/15
Knifest	6/6	6/8	8/15
Missiles(7)			
Aram		3/6	5/10
Bottles(7)			
Beer		1/3	1/6

that optimal convex decomposition cannot be achieved. Moreover, the height function used in the Watershed algorithm considers convexity as well.

Considering only the original large components and ignoring the small ones performs better than merging small components with their neighbors, both for watershed decomposition and for convex decomposition. This can be explained by the fact that merging results in complex shapes which might cause a failure of the basic shape determination procedure.

Table 1 shows some of our results for one sub-method – Watershed, ignoring small components. The first column shows the classes and the test objects. For each class, the number of members of the class N is shown. The next column of the table summarizes the results obtained for each test object. Each result (n/m) represents the number of the members of the same class n retrieved among the top m objects.

6   Conclusion

This paper examines the adaptation of the human vision theories of Marr and Biederman to three dimensions. According to these theories, an object is represented by an attributed graph, where each node represents a meaningful component of the object, and there are arcs between nodes whose corresponding components are adjacent in the model. Every node is attributed with the basic shape found to best match the component, while each arc is attributed with the relative surface area of its adjacent nodes.

It was demonstrated that simple and efficient decomposition algorithms suffice to construct such a signature. We examined a couple of post-processing steps on top of well-known segmentation algorithms, in order to get only a handful of components. Moreover, a technique was presented for finding the best match between a given sub-mesh and pre-defined basic shapes. An error-correcting subgraph isomorphism algorithm was used for matching.

The experimental results presented in the paper are generally good. The major benefits of the signature is being invariant to non-rigid transformations and avoiding normalization as a pre-processing step. In addition, the algorithm for generating signatures is simple and efficient and produces very compact signatures.

The technique has a couple of drawbacks. First, the signature depends on the connectivity of the given objects, which might cause geometrically-similar objects to be considered different. Second, the graph matching algorithm we use is relatively slow. While the first drawback can be solved by fixing the models, the second problem is inherent to graph-based representations. More efficient graph matching algorithms should be sought.

References

Bates, D., Watts, D.: Nonlinear Regression and Its Applications. John Wiley & Sons, New York (1988)

Biederman, I.: Recognition-by-components: A theory of human image understanding. Psychological Review 94, 115–147 (1987)

Biederman, I.: Aspects and extensions of a theory of human image understanding. In: Pylyshyn, Z. (ed.) Computational Processes in Human Vision: An Interdisciplinary Perspective, pp. 370–428 (1988)

Biederman, I.: Visual object recognition. In: Kosslyn, S., Osherson, D. (eds.) An Invitation to Cognitive Science, vol. 2, pp. 121–165 (1995)

Chazelle, B., Dobkin, D., Shourhura, N., Tal, A.: Strategies for polyhedral surface decomposition: An experimental study. Computational Geometry: Theory and Applications 7(4-5), 327–342 (1997)

Cornea, N., Demirci, M., Silver, D., Shokoufandeh, A., Dickinson, S., Kantor, P.: 3D object retrieval using many-to-many matching of curve skeletons. In: IEEE International Conference on Shape Modeling and Applications, pp. 368–373. IEEE Computer Society Press, Los Alamitos (2005)

Duda, R., Hart, P., Stork, D.: Pattern Classification. John Wiley & Sons, New York (2000)

Elad, M., Tal, A., Ar, S.: Content based retrieval of vrml objects - an iterative and interactive approach. EG Multimedia 39, 97–108 (2001)

Hilaga, M., Shinagawa, Y., Kohmura, T., Kunii, T.: Topology matching for fully automatic similarity estimation of 3D shapes. In: SIGGRAPH, pp. 203–212 (2001)

Katz, S., Leifman, G., Tal, A.: Mesh segmentation using feature point and core extraction. The Visual Computer 21(8-10), 865–875 (2005)

Katz, S., Tal, A.: Hierarchical mesh decomposition using fuzzy clustering and cuts. ACM Trans. Graph (SIGGRAPH) 22(3), 954–961 (2003)

Kazhdan, M., Chazelle, B., Dobkin, D., Funkhouser, T.: A reflective symmetry descriptor for 3D models. Algorithmica (to appear 2003a)

Kazhdan, M., Funkhouser, T., Rusinkiewicz, S.: Rotation invariant spherical harmonic representation of 3D shape descriptors. In: Symposium on Geometry Processing (2003b)

Keren, D., Cooper, D., Subrahmonia, J.: Describing complicated objects by implicit polynomials. IEEE Transactions on Pattern Analysis and Machine Intelligence 16(1), 38–53 (1994)

Lee, S., Kim, J., Groen, F.: Translation-, rotation-, and scale-invariant recognition of hand-drawn symbols in schematic diagrams. Int. J. Pattern Recognition and Artificial Intelligence 4(1), 1–15 (1990)

Lee, Y., Lee, S., Shamir, A., Cohen-Or, D., Seidel, H.-P.: Mesh scissoring with minima rule and part salience. Computer Aided Geometric Design (2005)

Leifman, G., Meir, R., Tal, A.: Semantic-oriented 3D shape retrieval using relevance feedback. The Visual Computer 21(8-10), 649–658 (2005)

Li, X., Toon, T., Tan, T., Huang, Z.: Decomposing polygon meshes for interactive applications. In: Proceedings of the 2001 symposium on Interactive 3D graphics, pp. 35–42 (2001)

Mangan, A., Whitaker, R.: Partitioning 3D surface meshes using watershed segmentation. IEEE Transactions on Visualization and Computer Graphics 5(4), 308–321 (1999)

Marr, D.: Vision - A computational investigation into the human representation and processing of visual information. W.H. Freeman, San Francisco (1982)

Messmer, B.: GMT - Graph Matching Toolkit. PhD thesis, University of Bern (1995)

Osada, R., Funkhouser, T., Chazelle, B., Dobkin, D.: Matching 3D models with shape distributions. In: Proceedings of the International Conference on Shape Modeling and Applications, pp. 154–166 (2001)

Paquet, E., Murching, A., Naveen, T., Tabatabai, A., Rioux, M.: Description of shape information for 2-D and 3-D objects. Signal Processing: Image Communication, pp. 103–122 (2000)

Pearce, A., Caelli, T., Bischof, W.: Rulegraphs for graph matching in pattern recognition. Pattern Recognition 27(9), 1231–1246 (1994)

Rocha, J., Pavlidis, T.: A shape analysis model with applications to a character recognition system. IEEE Trans. Pattern Analysis and Machine Intelligence 16, 393–404 (1994)

Shamir, A.: A formalization of boundary mesh segmentation. In: Proceedings of the second International Symposium on 3DPVT (2004)

Subrahmonia, J., Cooper, D., Keren, D.: Practical reliable bayesian recognition of 2d and 3D objects using implicit polynomials and algebraic invariants. IEEE Transactions on Pattern Analysis and Machine Intelligence 18(5), 7505–7519 (1996)

Sundar, H., Silver, D., Gagvani, N., Dickinson, S.: Skeleton based shape matching and retrieval. In: Shape Modelling and Applications (2003)

Taubin, G.: Estimation of planar curves, surfaces, and nonplanar space curves defined by implicit equations with applications to edge and range image segmentation. IEEE Transactions on Pattern Analysis and Machine Intelligence 13(11), 1115–1138 (1991)

Veltkamp, R.: Shape matching: Similarity measures and algorithms. In: Shape Modelling International, pp. 188–197 (2001)

Vranic, D., Saupe, D.: Description of 3D-shape using a complex function on the sphere. In: Proceedings IEEE International Conference on Multimedia and Expo, pp. 177–180. IEEE Computer Society Press, Los Alamitos (2002)

Wang, Y.-K., Fan, K.-C., Horng, J.-T.: Genetic-based search for error-correcting graph isomorphism. IEEE Trans. Systems, Man, and Cybernetics 27, 588–597 (1997)

Wong, E.: Model matching in robot vision by subgraph isomorphism. Pattern Recognition 25(3), 287–304 (1992)

Zuckerberger, E., Tal, A., Shlafman, S.: Polyhedral surface decomposition with applications. Computers & Graphics 26(5), 733–743 (2002)

Terrain Synthesis By-Example

John Brosz, Faramarz F. Samavati, and Mario Costa Sousa

University of Calgary
2500 University Drive NW, Calgary, Canada
{brosz,samavati,mario}@cpsc.ucalgary.ca

Abstract. Synthesizing terrain or adding detail to terrains manually is a long and tedious process. With procedural synthesis methods this process is faster but more difficult to control. This paper presents a new technique of terrain synthesis that uses an existing terrain to synthesize new terrain. To do this we use multi-resolution analysis to extract the high-resolution details from existing models and apply them to increase the resolution of terrain. Our synthesized terrains are more heterogeneous than procedural results, are superior to terrains created by texture transfer, and retain the large-scale characteristics of the original terrain.

Keywords: Terrain synthesis, modeling, multi-resolution analysis, multi-fractals.

1 Introduction

Terrain synthesis is the process of creating the artificial terrains used in games, movies, and simulations. Artificial terrains are necessary whenever terrain information is not available, lacks resolution and detail, or must meet specific feature criteria. Creating artificial terrain is not easy as large, high-resolution terrains often involve millions of data points.

There are two major applications of terrain synthesis. The first is in creating a synthetic terrain guided by a user who provides a rough outline of the desired characteristics. In this case the goal is to retain the attributes of the given outline, while adding realistic features to fill out the terrain. The second application is in increasing the resolution of an existing terrain for close-up viewing. Although any type of surface interpolation can increase resolution, it will also make the terrain look overly smooth. Extra information in the form of deviation from the smooth surface is necessary to make the terrain interesting and realistic. Terrains synthesized for both applications should appear visually realistic, meet desired topology requirements, and be inexpensive in terms of modeling time (Roettger and Frick, 2002).

Presently in commercial systems like Bryce (Bryce, 2005) and Terragen (McLusky, 2005), artificial terrains are created through a mixture of procedural methods and user painting of height fields (Roettger and Frick, 2002). The procedural methods, usually based on fractal subdivision, are controlled by user specified parameters. These methods have major shortcomings in that they lack erosion features and create homogeneous terrains. To compensate for this, erosion processes can be simulated on these surfaces, adding missing erosion features. Unfortunately erosion simulation is slow and introduces many more parameters for the user to control.

J. Braz et al. (Eds.): VISAPP and GRAPP 2006, CCIS 4, pp. 58–77, 2007.

Fig. 1. Terrain synthesis by-example. The left image is a user-created 20×20 base terrain. The middle image is the chosen target terrain, a 30m NED model. The right image is the result of our synthesis, a 146×146 synthesized terrain.

In general, creating any new model, especially a detailed and complex model is difficult. However, if an example with similar attributes to what is being created can be used for inspiration, the task becomes easier. It is more natural for a user to specify that they want their terrain to look like a particular example, but with their specified features, rather than by providing a large number of parameters. Moreover, high resolution terrains are available to the public through the internet (U.S.G.S., 2005). The major goal of this work is to replace procedural and erosion synthesis parameters with use of an example terrain to make it easier to synthesize realistic, heterogeneous terrain.

1.1   System Overview

There are two different terrains that are used to create a terrain by example. The first we call the *base* terrain. This is the terrain that is either a rough estimate of the desired terrain's large-scale characteristics, or it is a real terrain where we would like to increase the resolution. The other is the *target* terrain. This is the terrain that displays the high frequency, small-scale characteristics that the user desires to have in their synthetic terrain. The target terrain must have a resolution greater than or equal to the desired resolution of the synthetic terrain in order to provide small-scale information of the correct resolution. Our goal is to extract the small-scale characteristics from the target terrain and apply them to the large-scale characteristics of the base terrain as is shown in Figure 1.

Our system has three major steps. The first step is to extract the details from the base terrain. The next step is to find the areas in the base and target terrains that best match one another and produce a map of these relationships. The last step is to re-organize the details to match the mapping and then add these details through subdivision, refining the base terrain.

To extract these details and copy them from one terrain to another, we use the subdivision and reverse subdivision filters created by Samavati and Bartels (Samavati and Bartels, 1999). We also explore another method of extraction where we estimate the local fractal scale and use this estimate to create multi-fractal terrains by-example.

When copying the details from target terrain to the base terrain it is important that information coming from one type of feature, gets applied to that same type of feature. For example the peak of a mountain should get applied to another mountain peak. To achieve this mapping we have developed two methods. The first is interactive, relying upon the user to select matching areas. The other method is automatic, based on a texture synthesis technique.

1.2 Contributions and Organization

This work makes the following contributions: (1) use of multi-resolution analysis to extract and apply high-resolution terrain information, (2) two techniques for matching similar areas of the example terrain and the terrain being synthesized are presented, (3) adaptation and use of Image Quilting (Efros and Freeman, 2001) to automatic matching of terrain features, and (4) adaptation of Losasso and Hoppe's residuals measurement (Losasso and Hoppe, 2004) to estimate fractal scale when creating multi-fractals.

The remainder of this paper is organized as follows. Section 2 reviews work related to terrain synthesis. The data we use is described in Section 3. Section 4 discusses multi-resolution modeling and our reasons for using multi-resolution analysis. Section 5 presents the terrain by-example system. Section 6 discusses terrain rendering. Lastly, Section 7 shows results and Section 8 presents conclusions and future work.

2 Background

Fournier et. al (Fournier et al., 1982) and Lewis (Lewis, 1987) developed fractal and general stochastic subdivision methods for creating synthetic terrains. These two techniques succeed in creating a variety of terrain-like objects. Although the terrains produced by these systems look interesting and impressive, there are problems with the created terrains. The first is that they lack the characteristics of erosion. The second is that it is difficult to control the fractal or stochastic functions to create a specific terrain. The last is that these terrains tend to be homogeneous (i.e., they are similarly rough, or smooth, over the entire terrain).

Miller (Miller, 1986) improved Fournier et. al's midpoint insertion technique by replacing linear interpolation with third order B-spline based subdivision. This removes artifacts associated with the original midpoint technique.

There exist several works where the resolution of existing terrain models is increased through estimating the fractal dimension of the terrain (Pumar, 1996) (Brivio and Marini, 1996) (Losasso and Hoppe, 2004). This estimate is used to provide fractal values to fill in the new data points. Our multi-fractal by-example technique differs from these works in that we estimate the size of the fractal displacement on the target terrain at high resolution, rather than by the displacements present in the base terrain.

Musgrave et. al (Musgrave et al., 1989), Kelley (Kelley et al., 1988), Benes and Forsbach (Benes and Forsbach, 2001), and Nagashima (Nagashima, 1997) are among the researchers that have developed erosion simulations to increase the realism of procedurally created terrains. Such systems reproduce the effects of water, thermal, and other types of erosion.

However, there are problems with these processes. The first is that these methods usually take a large amount of time to simulate the erosion. The second problem is that these processes introduce a large number of new parameters (e.g., number of time steps, rainfall patterns, soil conditions, wind patterns, etc.) that must be accurate to achieve realistic and predictable results. These parameters are difficult to select accurately (Nagashima, 1997). Another problem is the evaluation of accuracy. All the proposed systems admit to being mostly empirical models that aim to capture the essential behavior of a few of the most noticeable erosion processes. Lastly, it has not been determined how erosion effects can be simulated in scenarios where the user wishes to increase the resolution of real terrain data. In this situation we do not want the erosion to eliminate existing features.

Musgrave in Ebert's book (Ebert, 1994) discusses a variation on fractal synthesis known as multi-fractals. This technique improves upon fractal terrains by varying the fractal scale over the terrain, resulting in heterogeneous features. Unfortunately, automatic application of multifractals is difficult and can easily produce undesired effects as is shown in (Ebert, 1994).

Chiang et. al (Chiang et al., 2005) present an interactive approach to terrain synthesis. In their system the underlying shape of the terrain is created from simple geometric objects (e.g., prisms, cones, etc). These primitives are matched to terrain units by cross-section, mountain ridge, or contour similarity. Terrain units are extracted from a database of terrain data that has been manually segmented to contain one mountain, ridge, or other feature (Chiang et al., 2005).

3 Terrain Data

The terrain data we use is Digital Elevation Model (DEM) data. These terrain models are composed of a regularly spaced, two dimensional array of floating point elevation values. The DEMs used in this work come from the United States Geological Survey (U.S.G.S., 2005).

There are several different sets of elevation data available, we have used the two that were available for the most areas within North America. The first set is Shuttle Radar Topology Mission (SRTM) data. This data is canopy based and is available in 90m and 30m resolutions (U.S.G.S., 2005). The other set is the National Elevation Dataset (NED). This is composed of bare ground readings from a variety of sources including aerial photographs and physical measurements (U.S.G.S., 2005). NED data comes in several resolutions including 30m, 10m, and 3m resolutions.

4 Multi-resolution

Multi-resolution modeling is important for our synthesis technique since these techniques describe the differences between high and low-resolution versions of models. We interpret these differences as being characteristic of a terrain's small-scale features that can be used to add the target terrain's small-scale features to the base terrain's large-scale features. In particular, we have chosen to use multi-resolution analysis (MRA) to extract and copy these small-scale features. MRA is available for curves and arbitrary topology models, however since DEMs can be treated as tensor product surfaces we limit our discussion to only the curve application.

MRA operations fulfill four necessary conditions for our system: (1) the ability to coarsen terrain models, (2) separates and retains the high-frequency information lost in coarsening, (3) has capacity to refine terrain with high frequency information from other terrains, and (4) has the ability to perform these operations efficiently in both time and memory space.

We describe each row or column of terrain as a set of sequenced points: c_1^k, c_2^k, ..., c_n^k, and present these points in the column $C^k = [c_1^k, c_2^k, ..., c_n^k]^T$. Subdivision produces a refined, higher resolution set of n' points, C^{k+1}, through multiplication by a matrix:

$$C^{k+1} = P^k C^k \tag{1}$$

where P^k is a $n' \times n$ subdivision matrix that doubles the resolution of the curve. To reverse this process we start with a fine set of n points, C^k. A coarse set of n' points, C^{k-1}, is produced by application of a decomposition matrix:

$$C^{k-1} = A^k C^k \tag{2}$$

where A^k is the $n' \times n$ matrix that halves the resolution. Since C^{k-1} has fewer points, some high frequency information (details) about the curve C^k have been lost. These $n - n'$ details, D^{k-1}, are captured by applying another matrix on the original points:

$$D^{k-1} = B^k C^k \tag{3}$$

where B^k is a $(n - n') \times n$ detail extraction matrix that is dependent on A. These details, D^{k-1}, are vectors that describe the differences between C^k and PC^{k-1}. The last component of MRA, Q, is a $n \times (n' - n)$ matrix that adds the contributions of the details, D, when refining the coarse points into our original data set. So, if we decompose a curve using equations 2 and 3, we can reconstruct the initial curve exactly using:

$$C^k = P^k C^{k-1} + Q^k D^{k-1}. \tag{4}$$

The matrices A^k and B^k should produce details that are as small as possible. If the details are small, then C^k and PC^{k-1} are almost the same, loosely indicating that C^{k-1} is a good approximation of C^k. We also desire small details since this ensures that most of the contribution to the final terrain is from the base terrain, rather than the target terrain. This preserves the large-scale features of the base terrain.

We chose to use the local Chaikin matrices derived by Samavati and Bartels (Samavati and Bartels, 2004). These matrices are derived from a local least squares analysis of Chaikin subdivision, based on third order B-splines. We chose Chaikin over higher order methods due to its simplicity and compactness and over lower order methods, such as Haar or Faber, because it yields surfaces with greater continuity and is better suited for smooth surfaces (Samavati and Bartels, 1999). Chaikin also underlies the fractal synthesis results obtained by Miller (Miller, 1986). Readers interested in the values of the matrices should refer to Samavati and Bartels (Samavati and Bartels, 2004).

To justify our choice of MRA rather than other multi-resolution techniques we now briefly examine alternatives. Although many multi-resolution methods exist, we are only concerned with surface simplification methods that create coarse approximations of models. The goal of these techniques is to create coarse models that retain the shape of the original model. We can also limit our discussion to methods that can exactly reconstruct the original representation from the coarsened version. For exact reconstruction some form of details are necessary and the construction of the details is very important to our technique.

One such method is Image Pyramids. This techniques use a hierarchy of images formed with the original image as the bottom level, and at each higher level the image has half the resolution of the preceding image. The reduction in resolution is obtained with a low-pass filter and sub-sampling. There are a variety of filters and MRA filters are obvious candidates. We chose not to use filters unique to Image Pyramids because they oversample the image or only approximately reconstruct the original image (Simoncelli et al., 1992).

Triangle decimation (Schroeder et al., 1992) removes triangles that make little contribution to the model. Surface Simplification using Quadrics (Garland and Heckbert, 1997), Progressive Meshes (Hoppe, 1996), and other techniques use edge contraction to remove edges, coarsening the model. These techniques are inappropriate for our purposes as they do not describe a uniform change in resolution over the entire object and because they produce triangulated irregular networks (TINs) rather than DEMs. Furthermore, the behavior and effects of the details generated by these methods have not been researched to the same extent that MRA details have.

5   Terrain By-Example

To reduce the resolution and extract the details of the target terrain, we apply the reverse subdivision matrices A and B (Equations 2 and 3) to each column of height values. This gives us an array of coarse points with almost half the height of the original as well as a set of details. We refer to this first set of details as the *column details*. Then we use the filters on each row, leaving us with a coarsened terrain of half the resolution and another set of details, the *row details*.

To refine our base terrain to double its resolution we use the subdivision matrices P and Q (Equation 4) on each row of the array with the target's row details generating an array with double the width. Then P and Q are used on each column in conjunction with captured column details, resulting in a terrain with double the resolution.

First consider the case where the target terrain is exactly double the resolution of the base terrain. Our first step is to extract the high-frequency noise from the target with reverse subdivision. The resulting row and column details are our high-frequency noise. The simplest method of using these extracted details with our base is to simply apply them via subdivision to the base terrain. Unfortunately, simply applying these details in the order they were extracted leads to problems. As shown in Figure 2, the details extracted from a terrain correspond to features of that terrain. If we apply these details in the same order that we extracted them, we could apply the wrong details to the features in the base terrain. E.g., we might apply the details from a mountain in the target to a plateau in the base terrain. Section 5.2 describes two methods of matching features in the base to features in the target terrain.

Once a mapping has been specified we rearrange the target's row and column details into the order determined by the mapping. Subdivision is used to apply the details to the rows and then the columns of the base, doubling its resolution, producing our

Fig. 2. Top is a valley in Nevada, USA. Bottom is the result of extracting one level of details and applying them to a flat surface. The features in the terrain clearly correspond to features in the details. Colored by slope steepness.

synthesized result. This process is referred to as applying one level of details or as performing one iteration of subdivision.

Now consider the case where the target terrain has a much higher resolution than the base terrain. In this case we perform reverse subdivision to the target several several times, until the target has approximately the same resolution as the base. As before our next step is to perform matching between the base and target terrains, and then subdivide the base terrain using the last set of details extracted from the target. We use the last set since these are the details that will describe the difference between the base's current resolution and double this resolution. We can then repeat this matching and subdividing until we have used up all the details in reverse order and our synthesized terrain has the same resolution as the original target.

5.1 Multi-fractals By-Example

Another way of creating terrain by-example is with multi-fractals. This technique has drawbacks but provides another method of creating terrains by-example.

The difference between fractal terrains and multi-fractal terrains is that the fractal scale changes over the terrain producing terrains that are less homogeneous. To produce multi-fractals by example we need to capture the fractal scale from the target terrain. To do this we must determine an estimate of the fractal scale and use this parameter on the feature-mapped areas of the base terrain. Losasso and Hoppe

(Losasso and Hoppe, 2004) have obtained fractal scale estimates for entire terrains by using the variance of *residuals*. The residuals used are essentially the details resulting from linear interpolation.

In our work, we estimate the fractal scale in a similar manner. We use Miller's Chaikin based terrain fractals (Miller, 1986), consequently the fractal scale becomes the variance of the displacements created by the Chaikin details. To implement our by-example multi-fractals we use this estimate of fractal scale over small areas of the target and then use these to decide the fractal scale on mapped areas of the base terrain.

With multi-fractals by-example we estimate residuals over selected areas of the target terrain and store these fractal scales to be used on the base terrain. The mapping procedure (see Section 5.2) is still performed, making this algorithm execute at approximately the same speed as MRA by-example.

Multi-fractals by-example have a major drawbacks in applying small-characteristic features. To understand why we must examine the generation of the fractal displacement. When using our multi-fractals we take the variance of the details and use this to scale Gaussian noise. By doing this we are discarding an accurate and real distribution of details from the target, and replacing this with a Gaussian distribution. In essence, we are discarding most of the noise we have gone to the trouble of extracting from the target. This is one of the reasons why multi-fractal by-example results tend to resemble the target less than MRA by-example results as will be shown in Section 7.3.

5.2   Mapping Terrain Features

The goal of this section is to find a mapping between similar areas and features on the target and base terrains. We have made use of two existing techniques for handling this problem. The first is interactive, relying on human interpretation to solve the matching problem. The other technique is automatic and based on Texture Quilting (Efros and Freeman, 2001). We chose this technique because of its speed and quality.

5.2.1   Interactive Mapping

The simplest technique of solving the mapping problem is to leave it up to the user. We replace the guessing at assorted parameters required for fractal synthesis or erosion simulation with a more intuitive mechanism. This mechanism is having the user perceive similar areas in the base and target terrains.

In this system the user selects a section of the target terrain and then a section of the same size of the base terrain. These sections may have any shape; we have chosen to use rectangles in our system for speed of calculation and ease of implementation. If mapped-to areas on the base terrain already posses details we replace the existing details. The user can also specify the number of levels of details to copy. The number of levels to copy is dependent on the desired resolution but in our tests we have found that copying three levels of detail provides good results. An example of this process can be seen in Figures 3 and 4.

Performing the MRA is very fast (Samavati and Bartels, 1999), allowing users to easily and quickly see the results of their specified mapping. This interactive method can also be used to edit the details of an existing terrain. By specifying a new mapping of an area, the base terrain's details are replaced, changing the small-scale characteristics

Fig. 3. The interactive system copied the bumpy details from the highlighted area of the target (left) changing a smooth area of the base terrain (middle) into a more rough area (right)

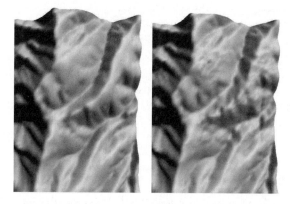

Fig. 4. Close-up of the terrain in Figure 3, before (left) and after (right) synthesis. The red lines have been removed to allow examination of the borders.

of the selected area. This method also easily allows more than one target terrain to be used to refine a single base terrain.

5.2.2   Automatic Mapping: Terrain Quilting

In order to reduce the amount of user interaction we have also created an automatic mapping system. This automatic system is based on the Image Quilting algorithm (Efros and Freeman, 2001) used for texture synthesis and texture transfer.

The first step of the automatic mapping is to break the base terrain into blocks. We do this by dividing the base terrain into a grid of overlapping square blocks. By choosing a smaller block sizes, smaller features are matched and better mappings can be produced; however, this also increases the time required for the algorithm to run. Our default setting uses blocks that are approximately one-fifteenth of the average of the base terrain's width and length, however, the block size is adjustable by the user. For the best possible results the block size should be determined by the resolution of the small-scale characteristics the user desires to capture.

For each block in the base terrain we attempt to find a similar block in the target terrain. This is done by testing the similarity of some number of randomly selected blocks in the target. The number of candidate blocks we test is the smaller of forty or the number of blocks that fit equally into the target. This gives a good trade off between speed and quality, however if poor matches occur this setting is user adjustable.

In the Image Quilting algorithm (Efros and Freeman, 2001), the difference (or conversely the similarity) between two blocks is described by the sum of squares between the pixel brightness values. For terrains, the values we are comparing are elevations rather than pixel brightness so we more concerned with features (e.g., a mountain peak in the base terrain should be mapped to a mountain peak in the target terrain). Consequently, we need to examine the shape portrayed by the block, rather than the absolute height values of the block.

The metric we created to calculate the difference in shape between two blocks, i from the base, and j from the target, where we have indexed the height values in the blocks with a single index, is:

$$e_{i,j} = \sum_{k=1}^{n} ((i_k - m_i) - (j_k - m_j))^2$$

where n is the number of height values per block, i_k is the kth height value of block i, and m_i is the mean height value of block i. Unlike Image Quilting, when calculating the difference between blocks we ignore the blending between blocks (since we are copying details, not pieces of terrain) so this does not contribute to the difference calculation.

5.2.3   Constructing the Detail Quilts

Once we have found the best match for each base terrain block, we construct a quilt of the target's details. This is done for both the row and the column details. We quilt the details, rather than the actual height values, because we want a new synthesized terrain, not a terrain that was created through mixing and matching pieces of the target. A mix and match terrain would suffer block blending issues and could alter large-scale characteristics of the base terrain. Instead, the system quilts the details so that the resulting terrain contains merely the addition of the details from the target. In Image Quilting a minimum error boundary cut is used to blend overlapping areas. In our work we use a linear blend of the details between the blocks. We do this because details are small in respect to the curve presented by the low-resolution data for the reason described in Section 4.

6   Terrain Rendering

Rendering in our system is not just a matter of simply displaying terrains. Rather it is a tool that can allow us to more easily evaluate, compare, and contrast synthetic terrains. This is especially important when presenting synthesis results in one or two images. We use four rendering techniques that provide easier discrimination between and evaluation of terrains.

Our standard rendering method uses Gouraud shading on grey colored triangles to maximize contrast and make terrain evaluation possible when the images are printed in black and white.

The second rendering style uses Gouraud shading but with triangles colored based on elevation. From lowest elevation to highest, triangles are colored brown, green, red, orange, yellow, and white. This coloring makes the terrain easier to understand, especially when the terrain is viewed from the top. This is shown in Figure 7.

We also desired to make it easier to determine how smooth (or rough) a terrain is. To do this we color based on slope steepness. This is the rate of change in elevation making it a good measure to indicate the smoothness of a terrain (Shary et al., 2002). In our slope steepness figures, from most steep to least steep, the triangles are colored yellow, red, green, or grey. We have found this gives good insight into the amount of heterogeneity of rendered terrains and can emphasize features such as the riverbed in Figure 2.

Our last technique uses a non-photorealistic rendering technique to place small ink strokes. This rendering technique uses silhouette stability edges with the direction of the edge changed to point in the tangent direction as described in Brosz's work (Brosz, 2005). For evaluating terrains, this rendering technique emphasizes the differences between rough and smooth areas of synthesized terrains. We have used this rendering technique in Figure 9.

7 Results and Discussion

There are several criteria for the success of our system. The most important is that the synthesized terrain should appear more detailed than if the base was subdivided without details. Our next expectation is that the terrain gains detail in a manner that is more predictable and realistic than current procedural methods. A related point is that we expect the synthesized terrain to show small-scale characteristics similar to those of the target. Another important goal for the success of the system is in the simplicity of the user interaction.

7.1 Providing a Control Synthesis

To compare the results of the terrain by-example system to the results of a fractal-based synthesis, we implemented fBm subdivision as described by Miller (Miller, 1986) with Voss' successive random additions (Peitgen and Saupe, 1988) to further reduce fractal artifacts. We estimate the initial fractal scale based on our residual calculation. H, the parameter controlling the change in fractal scale (Fournier et al., 1982), has been set 0.85 as we found this value produces good results.

We have not considered erosion techniques due to two problems. The first is that they involve many parameters that must be provided. These parameters depend on the type of terrain as well as many environmental conditions. The other is that these erosion simulations are likely to remove or significantly alter previously existing features of the base terrain that are real features and desired in the resulting model.

7.2 Experimentation

In this subsection we present two trials using Chaikin MRA. In the first trial we synthesized a terrain from a small, low resolution, hand-made terrain. The second trial compares a real, high-resolution terrain with a synthesized terrain that uses low resolution data from the same area as its base terrain. In both trials we used the default

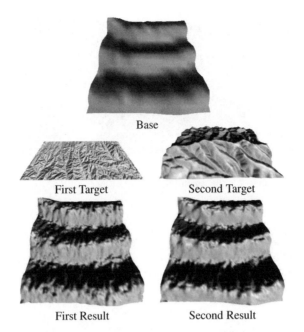

Base

First Target   Second Target

First Result   Second Result

Fig. 5. The first trial. The base is a user created 20×20 terrain. The results are 146×146, produced by copying three levels of details from their respective target terrains.

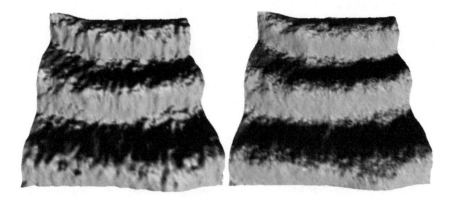

Fig. 6. Trial 1 comparison between by-example (top) and fBm synthesis (bottom). Notice the homogeneous nature fBm result when compared to the by-example result.

block size. Timings were performed on an AMD 2600XP+ with 1.5GB RAM and an ATI 9800 128MB video card.

The base and target terrains used in our first trial, as well as the terrains resulting from our synthesis, are shown in Figure 5. The first target is a 30m NED from Kansas, USA, the second is a 30m NED from Utah, USA. The base terrain's resolution was increased from approximately 240m to 30m resolution. Figure 6 compares the result of fBm synthesis to a result achieved with terrain by-example synthesis. The terrain

Fig. 7. The target terrain used in the second trial, colored by elevation. This is a 10m NED from the Utah Salt Flats.

Fig. 8. The second trial. The top image is the base terrain (30m NED data from the Utah Salt Flats), the middle is the Chaikin, terrain by-example result, and the bottom is the result of fBm synthesis.

by-example synthesis in this trial took approximately 3 seconds while the fBm synthesis required less than 1 second.

In comparing our two synthesized results, we can see that changing the target significantly changes the synthesis result. The first result has more jagged features, similar to the jagged hills in the Kansas target whereas the second result is smoother, more like the Utah target. Looking at our results, especially the sides of the hills, we can see that they have interesting bumps added while also appearing smooth, much like the target terrains. In contrast, the fBm result is very rough all over. The fBm synthesis, because it changes the height at random is uniformly noisy, whereas the by-example results are more coherent.

Our second trial uses a 30m NED of an area within the Utah salt flats as its base terrain. We chose a 10m NED from another portion of the Utah salt flats as our target (shown

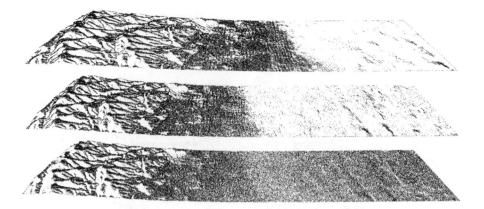

Fig. 9. Non-photorealistically rendered comparison between the real, 10m resolution NED (top), our second trial's 7.5m by-example result (middle), and the 7.5m result of fBm synthesis (bottom). Notice the roughness of the salt flat fBm result.

in Figure 7). The base and the results of by-example and fBm synthesis are shown in Figure 8. Figure 9 provides comparison between 10m NED data of the same area and the two synthesized 7.5m results. The by-example result (2794×394), obtained from two levels of copied details, was created in 8 seconds; the fBm result required 2.5 seconds.

In Figure 8 our synthesized terrain shows very little introduced roughness. This is due to the smoothed nature of the NED as well as the smooth nature of the salt flats. Close inspection reveals small irregularities added to several of the mountain ridges and a few small bumps in the flat area. In the fBm terrain we see that the introduced noise obscures some of the stream beds in the middle of the terrain. The most noticeable difference is that the fBm synthesis adds a large number of undesirable bumps to the flat area.

This trial, with the mountainous terrain at one end and the very flat terrain at the other, emphasizes the drawback of fBm synthesis. The estimated fractal scale is the average residual from the entire terrain, resulting in terrain that is too rough at the flat end and too smooth at the other. Use of multi-fractals could fix this, but even then the scale is still estimated over some area and, if that area has heterogeneous features, the scale can again be wrong. MRA however, is based on wavelets that are able to effectively capture and represent these different scales.

It is important to note that the flats cannot easily be synthesized in a better fashion by simply adding erosion to the fBm synthesis. Thermal weathering erosion (Musgrave et al., 1989) may somewhat reduce the size of the fractal bumps, but not completely because the bumps are small and have very little slope. Hydraulic erosion techniques can smooth these bumps out but are designed to, and will, introduce new rivers and valleys, destroying the features of the base terrain.

7.3   Chaikin vs. Multi-fractals

In Section 5 we have discussed two different techniques of extracting and applying details. Chaikin MRA, is useful because it is based on third order B-Splines that

Fig. 10. Repeat of Trial 1 (Figure 5) with Chaikin MRA (top) and multi-fractals by-example (bottom). In the left column are the results that used Kansas target, the right column presents the results of the Utah target.

effectively capture the smooth underlying nature of terrains. Multi-fractals by-example provide a close link to existing procedural methods. To compare these techniques we have repeated the first trial using multi-fractals. Figure 10 shows the results.

In Figure 10 it is clear that the multi-fractals are not as successful in capturing the character of the target terrain. It is not clear that the left multi-fractal result came from the ridge-filled Kansas target while the right came from Utah target. The Chaikin MRA results show these differences.

7.4   Texture Transfer Compared

An important topic is why current texture transfer techniques are not suitable for synthesizing terrain. In some senses they are suitable. Can a target terrain be broken into pieces and then sewn together to form a realistic terrain or, as in Image Analogies, two different resolutions of the target terrain could provide a filter to increase the resolution of the base terrain?

The key difference between our method and texture transfer approaches is that we do not copy pieces of terrain; instead we copy details. This ensures that our result is composed mostly of the features of the base terrain. Texture transfer rearranges pieces of the target to fit the base, making these methods unsuitable for increasing the resolution of existing terrain. By using details, since they are such small contributions to the result, we also avoid the blending artifacts that appear in texture transfer methods.

To test this we compare a terrain synthesized by-example with results of two texture transfer systems: Image Quilting (Efros and Freeman, 2001) implemented by Robert Burke (Burke, 2005) and the Image Analogies system (Hertzmann et al., 2001). Figure 11 shows the base, target, and our synthesis.

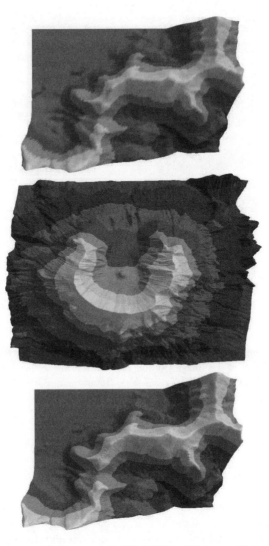

Fig. 11. The left image is of the base terrain (30m NED of Harmony Flats, Washington, USA), the middle is the target (10m NED of Mount St. Helens, Washington, USA) and the right is the by-example synthesis result

To perform the Image Quilting texture transfer, we convert the DEM to a height encoded image (i.e., an image where the highest areas are white and the lowest are black). Next, we resample the 30m base to a 10m resolution. This is akin to subdividing without adding details, producing a smooth, high-resolution terrain. We then apply texture transfer between the target and the resampled base producing the result shown in Figure 12. It is clear that directly using the original terrain has introduced blending problems, failing to produce a realistic terrain.

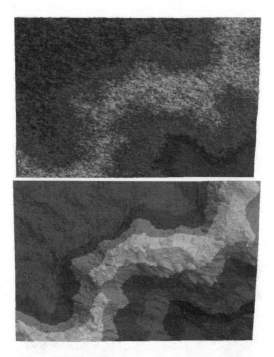

Fig. 12. Top is the result of the Image Quilting algorithm using settings of 3 iterations, initial block size of 16, 17% overlap, and 50 candidates. Bottom is a result of the Image Analogies algorithm using steered filters and the default settings. Both are rendered with elevation coloring.

For the Image Analogies texture transfer we used height encoded images of the 30m and 10m NED target terrain as the learning pair. As both of these images had to be the same size, we resampled the 30m image to achieve 10m resolution. Similarly the 30m base image was also resampled. The chosen matching method was Hertzmann et. al's recommended approximate nearest neighbor search. Figure 12 presents our best result with this system. More results of our testing can be seen in Brosz's work (Brosz, 2005). The result of the Image Analogies system does not reproduce the flat area of the upper left base terrain and generally produces terrains with a speckled appearance. The hillsides have new ridges and lines, giving an interesting but unwelcome terraced look. It does not appear to be a bad result unless one considers that neither the base nor the target has these features. Both terrains have ridges but these ridges are mostly smooth, not noisy like synthesis result. Since neither the base nor the target terrains have speckles, these must be artifacts created by blending problems when placing pixels.

The results of two texture transfer systems show that they have problems in maintaining flat terrain due to the problems of blending images (as opposed to blending details). It is also due to the fact that they are designed to preserve the source image (the target terrain) rather than to keep the features of the target image (the base terrain). The Image Analogies system performed better than the Image Quilting system but overall we feel it is clear that terrain by-example is superior for synthesizing terrain.

8   Conclusions

In this work a technique to synthesize terrains based on an example terrain has been presented. This system simplifies user interaction, replacing procedural and erosion parameters with selection of a target terrain. The resulting terrains show influence from the target terrain and have heterogeneous features. Lastly the synthesis is completed quickly, achieving synthesis in seconds. Freely available high resolution terrain data for use as targets makes this system feasible and inexpensive.

In examining our criteria for success, we can see that our synthesized terrains are more detailed than the base terrain. Moreover, the terrains gain details that seem realistic. This is shown in all of our results, but particularly the second trial where the by-example synthesis maintained the flatness of the salt flats. The interactive system copies details from the target to the base in a predictable manner. The automatic system also results in terrains that show characteristics of the target terrain (Figure 5). The by-example results appear similar to the real high resolution data of the same area, even if they do not exactly match. Our system simplifies user interaction, producing user-specified terrain without input of a plethora of parameters. By-example synthesis can create completely synthetic terrains as well as add levels of detail to existing terrain.

Multi-resolution analysis provides an efficient and effective method for capturing and copying the character of a terrain. Multi-fractals present another method of extracting details from the target terrain, however this technique is unable to capture a target's character as well as Chaikin MRA.

Both the interactive and the automatic methods provide good starting points for feature matching in this pipeline. These techniques work well for most terrains, however, both methods have drawbacks. The interactive method requires more input from the user. For large terrains this could become time consuming and tedious. However, this system offers the potential for editing of existing details in terrains that proves an interesting and potentially useful feature.

The automatic feature mapping system has several limitations. Our random block matching technique, adapted from Image Quilting, is not ideal because it does not guarantee that the best matching block in the target terrain is found. An exhaustive search or variation of simulated annealing could ensure better matching. From our examination of the matches made by our system it seems that the current system works well without modification. Other techniques for comparing shapes could increase the effectiveness or speed of automatic matching.

There is also the issue of how the block size should be chosen. Small block sizes can achieve more accurate matches, but when the block size is too small, neighboring information is lost, causing bad matches. The values we have used produce qualitatively good results, however, a more quantitative examination would be useful. Adding a contribution from the neighboring area to the error metric might also alleviate the small block problem.

8.1   Future Work

Introducing a painting interface to specify specific mappings could increase the functionality of the by-example system. This could be similar to the paint by numbers used with Image Analogies (Hertzmann et al., 2001). This could make it easier for users to indicate mappings and to specify different target terrains. E.g., half a base terrain could be painted yellow, with yellow mapped to a desert target, and the rest could be mapped to a mountainous target.

There exist methods (Pumar, 1996), (Brivio and Marini, 1996) that use estimates of fractal dimension (opposed to our estimate of fractal scale) to increase the resolution of terrains. It is possible that these alternative estimates may improve the quality of the terrain synthesized with multi-fractals by-example. It is our intuition however, that the poor performance of multi-fractals is more greatly due to the randomness of displacements as opposed to the size of those displacements. Consequently, we are not optimistic of improving the multi-fractal by-example technique.

Triangulated Irregular Networks (TINs) abandon the regular grid format of DEMs, reducing the number of data points necessary to represent terrains. TINs are able to better represent sharp features, such as ridges, by aligning triangle edges with feature edges (DEM's edges seldom coincide with features). A more sophisticated shape analysis technique in conjunction with the details extracted with progressive meshes (Hoppe, 1996), arbitrary topology MRA, or another multi-resolution technique could create a TIN by-example system.

References

Benes, B., Forsbach, R.: Layered data representation for visual simulation of terrain erosion. In: Proceedings of SCCG '01, pp. 80–86 (2001)

Brivio, P.A., Marini, D.: A fractal method for digital elevation model construction and its application to a mountain region. Computer Graphics Forum 12(5), 297–309 (1996)

Brosz, J.: Terrain modeling by example. University of Calgary, Department of Computer Science (2005)

Bryce, Bryce 5.0 User Manual. Daz Software (2005)
    http://bryce.daz3d.com/Bryce_Manual_DAZ.pdf

Burke, R.: Image quilting, texture transfer, and wang tiling implementation (2005)

Chiang, M., Huang, J., Tai, W., Liu, C., Chang, C.: Terrain synthesis: An interactive approach. In: International Workshop on Advanced Image Tech (2005)

Ebert, D.S. (ed.): Texturing and Modeling: A Procedural Approach. AP Professional (1994)

Efros, A.A., Freeman, W.T.: Image quilting for texture synthesis and transfer. In: Proceedings of SIGGRAPH '01, pp. 341–346 (2001)

Fournier, A., Fussell, D., Carpenter, L.: Computer rendering of stochastic models. Commun. ACM 25(6), 371–384 (1982)

Garland, M., Heckbert, P.S.: Surface simplification using quadric error metrics. In: Proceedings of SIGGRAPH '97, pp. 209–216 (1997)

Hertzmann, A., Jacobs, C.E., Oliver, N., Curless, B., Salesin, D.H.: Image analogies. In: Proceedings of SIGGRAPH '01, pp. 327–340 (2001)

Hoppe, H.: Progressive meshes. In: Proceedings of SIGGRAPH '96, pp. 99–108 (1996)

Kelley, A., Malin, M., Nielson, G.: Terrain simulation using a model of stream erosion. In: Proceedings of SIGGRAPH '88, pp. 263–268 (1988)

Lewis, J.P.: Generalized stochastic subdivision. ACM Transactions on Graphics 6(3), 167–190 (1987)

Losasso, F., Hoppe, H.: Geometry clipmaps: terrain rendering using nested regular grids. ACM Transactions on Graphics 23, 769–776 (2004)

McLusky, J.: Terrain dialog description (2005),
   http://www.planetside.co.uk/terragen/guidde/dlg_terrain.html

Miller, G.S.P.: The definition and rendering of terrain maps. In: Proceedings of SIGGRAPH '86, pp. 39–48 (1986)

Musgrave, F., Kolb, C., Mace, R.: The synthesis and rendering of eroded fractal terrains. In: Proceedings of SIGGRAPH '89, pp. 41–50 (1989)

Nagashima, K.: Computer generation of eroded valley and mountain terrain. The Visual Computer, pp. 456–464 (1997)

Peitgen, H.-O., Saupe, D. (eds.): The Science of Fractal Images. Springer, Heidelberg (1988)

Pumar, M.A.: Zooming of terrain imagery using fractal-based interpolation. Computers and Graphics 20(1), 171–176 (1996)

Roettger, S., Frick, I.: The terrain rendering pipeline. In: Proc. of East-West Vision '02, pp. 195–199 (2002)

Samavati, F.F., Bartels, R.H.: Multiresolution curve and surface representation by reversing subdivision rules. Computer Graphics Forum 18(2), 97–120 (1999)

Samavati, F.F., Bartels, R.H.: Local bspline wavelets. In: Proceedings of the International Workshop on Biometric Technologies (2004)

Schroeder, W.J., Zarge, J.A., Lorensen, W.E.: Decimation of triangle meshes. In: Proceedings of SIGGRAPH '92, pp. 65–70 (1992)

Shary, P.A., Sharaya, L.S., Mitusov, A.V.: Fundamental quantitative methods of land surface analysis. Geoderma 107(1-2), 1–32 (2002)

Simoncelli, E.P., Freeman, W.T., Adelson, E.H., Heeger, D.J.: Shiftable multi-scale transforms. IEEE Trans. on Informations Theory 38(2), 587–607 (1992)

U.S.G.S, Seamless data distribution system (2005), http://seamless.usgs.gov

Collaboration on Scene Graph Based 3D Data

Lorenz Ammon and Hanspeter Bieri

Institute of Computer Science and Applied Mathematics, University of Bern
Neubrückstrasse 10, 3012 Bern, Switzerland
ammon@iam.unibe.ch, bieri@iam.unibe.ch

Abstract. Professional 3D digital content creation tools, like Alias Maya or discreet 3ds max, offer only limited support for a team of artists to work on a 3D model collaboratively. We present a scene graph repository system that enables fine-grained collaboration on scenes built using standard 3D DCC tools by applying the concept of collaborative versions to a general attributed scene graph. Artists can work on the same scene in parallel without locking out each other. The artists' changes to a scene are regularly merged to ensure that all artists can see each others progress and collaborate on current data. We introduce the concept of indirect changes and indirect conflicts to systematically inspect the effects that collaborative changes have on a scene. Inspecting indirect conflicts helps maintaining scene consistency by systematically looking for inconsistencies at the right places.

Keywords: Collaboration, DCC (digital content creation), attributed scene graph, automatic merging, conflict resolution.

1 Introduction

3D modeling can be a challenging task, and usually several specialized artists have to work collaboratively on different aspects of the same 3D scene. Especially if content creation is an evolutionary team process, as it is often the case in highly creative environments, a rather immediate collaboration on a scene is essential. Also, sometimes a scene gets too large for one single artist to finish it in time and several people have to work on it in parallel (e.g. large *seamless worlds* are one of the challenges in content creation for next generation console games). Quite often a scene does not evolve just linearly, i.e. alternative designs are considered, refined, rejected and finally taken over.

Unfortunately, today's professional 3D *digital content creation tools* (DCC tools), like Alias Maya or discreet 3ds max, offer only limited support for a team of artists to work on a 3D model collaboratively. Usually they store 3D scenes in a simple file, and the file system's locking mechanism is applied, so only one artist can work on a scene file at a time. A work around for this locking problem are *reference files*. Reference files allow the decomposition of a scene into several parts. A main scene file then references all part scene files. Artists can work in parallel on separate reference files, but the decomposition of the scene into parts also puts barriers to the artists' collaborative work. In order to see what the others are doing, an artist has to open the main scene file or explicitly reference the corresponding part files. Changes to a scene are coordinated

J. Braz et al. (Eds.): VISAPP and GRAPP 2006, CCIS 4, pp. 78–90, 2007.

using the main scene file, but to make the necessary adjustments the artist always has to find and open the corresponding part file. Therefore reference files only make possible a coarse-grained collaboration on rather statically defined parts of a scene. In addition, managing the separately evolving parts can get quite cumbersome, as more parts and especially lots of revisions of them are created.

Exactly this problem is attacked by Alienbrain Studio (Alienbrain, 2005) which is today's leading digital asset management solution in content creation for video games. It stores scenes in a central repository, manages their revisions and is aware of the reference file mechanism. But it does not provide support for two artists to work in parallel on the same scene file and for merging their changes. This support is only provided for text documents (e.g. program code). Text files are merged using a standard line-based *diff and merge* approach. Such line-based merging does not work for scene files because it would invalidate their usually complex internal structure. There exist approaches in software development (Magnusson et al., 1993) to make use of the structure of programs within text files to implement versioning at the finer-grained level of functions, i.e. not just at the file level. Yet such approaches do not translate directly to 3D scenes because program code is inherently text- and line-based while scenes of standard DCC tools usually are coded in a proprietary binary format.

The graphics database system GSCOPE (Collison and Bieri, 2000) implements versioning at the scene graph object level. But it focusses on reuse of 3D models rather than on collaboration on them. There is no support for the merging of changes that different artists have made to a scene in parallel. Another approach to add versioning support to CAD/CASE databases (Wieczerzycki and Rykowski, 1994) extends the *database version approach* by a merge transaction that merges database versions by object comparison. But it focusses rather on extending the versioning model and does neither really detail scene graph and change representations nor conflict resolution and scene consistency.

There exist systems, like Scene-Graph-As-Bus (Zeleznik et al., 2000), blue-c (Naef et al., 2003), Mu3D (Galli and Luo, 2000) and Distributed Open Inventor (Hesina et al., 1999), that directly operate on the internal structure of a scene to implement a fine-grained and immediate kind of collaboration. These systems provide a single distributed scene graph that usually is replicated on each collaborator's system. Changes made to the scene graph by one collaborator are immediately propagated to the replicated scene graphs of the other collaborators. Objects worked on by one collaborator are locked for all other collaborators to ensure scene consistency. Because collaborators always share the same instance of the distributed scene graph, such systems do not have to implement the merging of scene graphs.

Distributed scene graph systems usually form the basis for collaboration in virtual reality environments. But they are not well suited for enabling collaboration between users of standard DCC tools, because such tools use their own proprietary scene graphs that were not designed to get distributed. Also their scene graph APIs tend to hide internal structures and were not meant to support efficient scene graph replication and synchronization. In addition, distributed scene graph systems need all collaborators to be connected by a common high speed network.

Because there exists always only one instance of the distributed scene graph, collaboration is immediate. Artists are not able to privately evaluate different experimental designs before making an initial version of their design known to the other artists. Therefore some collaborators possibly base their work on a design that might still change heavily.

In the following sections we shall present a system that supports fine-grained collaboration on scenes of standard 3D DCC tools. It enables collaboration on the scene graph at the object level, as opposed to the coarse reference file level. Several artists can work on the same scene in parallel without locking out each other. Because of that, dynamic work assignments become possible. The artists' changes to a scene are regularly merged to make sure that all artists can see each other's progress and collaborate on current data. Artists may work privately on a scene and make their results public only when they are really ready. Merging is carried out automatically if there arise no conflicts between the artists' different changes to the scene. In addition, we present a number of strategies for automatic conflict resolution. The effects that local changes may have on a scene as a whole are tracked, and possible consistency problems caused by side effects of these changes are registered as indirect conflicts and are brought to the artists' attention. We give a practical example for the collaboration made possible among artists by our system by discussing its application to the development of a 3D model of the old part of the city of Bern. Finally, we list some conclusions.

2   Collaborative Versions

To enable several artists to work collaboratively on a single 3D scene, we adopt the concept of *collaborative versions* which is widely and successfully used in software development. We only give a short overview here and then concentrate on the critical points when applying this concept to enable collaboration on scene graph based data created by common 3D DCC tools. Key elements of our concept are a *repository* for storing scenes, the versioning of scenes, and the automatic merging of scenes.

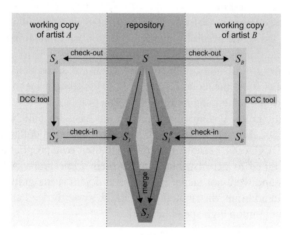

Fig. 1. Collaborative versions

Figure 1 illustrates how two artists A and B work in parallel on a scene S. Artist A starts working on S by checking-out the scene from the repository to a private local working copy S_A on his[1] system. This check-out operation does not put a lock on the scene S. Therefore artist B is also allowed to check-out the scene S from the repository to a local working copy S_B on his system, and the same holds for any other artist. Both artists now make changes to their local working copies of the scene using a standard DCC tool. When artist A finishes his work or a consistent piece of it, he wants to make his changes to S available to the other artists. To do so he simply checks his local working copy back into the repository. The repository registers the changes artist A made to S and stores his scene as the new current version S_1 of S. In the meantime, artist B is also satisfied with the changes he made to S and wants to make them public by checking his private working copy back into the repository. Of course, the current version of S is no longer the version artist B checked-out, but equal to the version S_1 which artist A recently checked-in. In order not to get lost, the changes artist A made to S must be merged with the changes artist B wants to check-in. The result is the now current version S_2 of the scene. If both artists made changes to different parts of the scene, these changes can usually be merged automatically. If there arise conflicts, they must be resolved either automatically by the repository or manually by the artists involved. Even if some changes by artist B were dropped during conflict resolution, they would not be lost, because before the merging takes place, artist B's working copy S'_B is checked-in to the repository as an alternative version S_1^B to what artist A checked-in earlier. So the whole work of artist B can be reviewed again at any time if necessary.

Obviously the merging of different scene versions is the critical point of the concept of collaborative versions. Standard revision control systems, like CVS, ClearCase, Perforce, etc., are not able to automatically merge 3D scene files because they are specialized in line-based diff and merge of text files and cannot handle the usually proprietary binary formats of 3D scene files. Such tools can detect bitwise changes but do not know how to interpret them and thus are not able to merge such changes to form a valid 3D scene again. Therefore, to implement the concept of collaborative versions, a repository must know the internal structure of scenes and be able to interpret the changes that are applied to them. Fortunately, 3D DCC tools share an important common concept for managing scene data, i.e. the *scene graph*. That allows us to develop a repository system enabling collaboration on scenes originating not only from one special 3D DCC tool, but also on scenes coming from the other tools. What is needed is a general scene graph model being able to hold the scene graphs coming from the different 3D DCC tools.

3 Attributed Scene Graphs

Text books usually define scene graphs to be directed acyclic graphs (DAG) that model the composition and transformation hierarchy of a scene. However, 3D DCC tools normally use a more sophisticated kind of scene graph, as a careful analysis of Alias Maya, discreet 3ds max, Softimage XSI, OpenGL Performer, VRML, X3D, Java 3D, OpenSG

---

[1] Here and in the following "he" stands also for "she".

and Open Scene Graph shows. Usually there is a DAG part that models hierarchical relationships between scene graph nodes, but in addition there exist also many other relationships between nodes which usually express some kinds of constraints that do not explicitly form an acyclic graph. Such additional relationships occur in different forms (e.g. as routes in VRML, as dependencies in Maya, as references in 3ds max) and are implemented in different ways (e.g. by explicitly connecting attributes of scene graph nodes or by using general message passing between nodes). A general scene graph model must, of course, be able to model such additional relationships between nodes. To do so, we opted for an *attributed scene graph model* as it is shown in a simplified UML diagram in Figure 2.

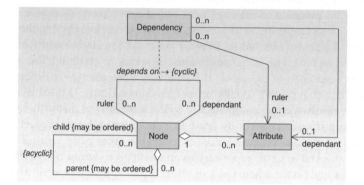

Fig. 2. The attributed scene graph model

This model centers around nodes that may have an arbitrary number of attributes of different types to store data. Every node has a unique identifier and a type. Node attributes are identified by names. A node can be connected to an arbitrary number of child and/or parent nodes. The latter enables nodes to be shared in a scene graph's composition hierarchy, a feature that not all 3D DCC tools provide. A node's children and parents may be ordered. To order child nodes is e.g. needed for the so-called *switch nodes*. There are no cycles allowed in the parent-child hierarchy, i.e. this part of the attributed scene graph model corresponds to the classic DAG structure.

The cyclic part of our model provides dependency relationships to express that one node depends on another one (e.g. because it needs to access the other node's data or adapt itself to certain changes of the other node). Dependencies bear a description and may reference attributes of nodes. This feature allows us to easily map scene graph models that have been designed or influenced by Silicon Graphics — and therefore use some kind of routes — to our attributed scene graph model.

We have formally defined our attributed scene graph model in an XML schema which allows us to code and exchange such scene graphs as XML files. We did not use an existing XML based digital asset exchange solution, like COLLADA (Barnes, 2005), because these tend to concentrate on aspects that are less important to our application purpose, like e.g. finding common ways to represent graphical and animation primitives. Our main focus is not on the scene content's detailed representation but on its structure and dependencies. We also need a scene's mapping to our general scene graph model to

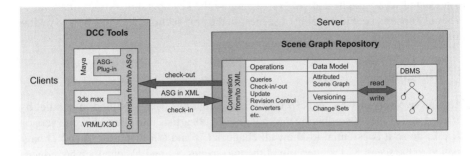

Fig. 3. Architecture of the scene graph repository system

be absolutely lossless, which exchange formats usually do not provide: Creating a scene with a 3D DCC tool, exporting it into an exchange format file and then reimporting the file into the DCC tool, usually does not yield exactly the same scene graph, but only a scene that looks the same. The next section will explain how the attributed scene graph model fits into the overall architecture of our system.

4 System Architecture

The central part in our system is the *scene graph repository server* which provides operations for managing and versioning scenes in the attributed scene graph model. The actual scene data is stored in a database using an OODBMS, but a graph-oriented database systems, like GRAS (Kiesel et al., 1995), would also be a suitable choice. Artists access the scene graph repository through plug-ins for their DCC tools. The following example demonstrates how scene graph data "flows" through the repository system's architecture which is shown in Figure 3.

Let us assume that a Maya artist has created a new 3D scene and wants to store it in the scene graph repository. He does so by invoking the check-in operation of the attributed scene graph (ASG) plug-in for Maya. This plug-in traverses the Maya scene graph and maps it losslessly to an attributed scene graph which is encoded in XML and sent to the scene graph repository. The repository server parses the XML data into its own attributed scene graph implementation, registers a new version for the scene and stores it in the database. If the artist later wants to make changes to his scene, he uses the Maya plug-in to query the scene graph repository for the scene and then invokes the check-out operation. The repository server reads the scene from its database and encodes its attributed scene graph data in XML and sends the XML data to the Maya plug-in. The plug-in parses the XML data and recreates exactly the same Maya scene graph that was checked-in by the artist before.

The same processes hold for any other supported DCC tool, because application specific tasks (e.g. encoding losslessly the complete application scene graph into ASG XML data) are encapsulated into the corresponding ASG plug-ins. With scene description languages, like VRML, no plug-in is needed, as the scene graph data can be directly parsed from a scene file. Checking-out or -in scenes that have not been worked on in parallel by different artists mainly involves the mapping of application scene graphs to attributed scene graphs and vice versa, but not the key operation of the collaborative versions concept, i.e. the merging of scenes. In the next sections we show how to realize this key operation.

5 Merging

Merging two versions S_A and S_B of a scene S that has been modified in parallel by artists A and B means combining the changes of both artists into one new scene version S_M. To do so it is essential to know all changes C_A and C_B that artist A and B have applied to the scene S. The merging of the two scenes S_A and S_B can then be reduced to the merging of the so-called *change sets* C_A and C_B into a single change set C_M. The merged scene S_M results from applying all changes in C_M to S. We show now how change sets can be determined.

5.1 Change Sets

There are two different approaches to track scene changes, i.e. *state-based* and *operation-based*. To determine operation-based changes, a plug-in for every DCC tool would have to record all the tool's operations on a scene as an artist is modifying it. Unfortunately, detailed monitoring of operations is not supported by all DCC tools. In addition, working with operation-based changes requires the necessary recording plug-ins to be installed. If an external artist, who does not have such a plug-in installed, is handed over a scene from the repository to work on, it is difficult to later incorporate his modifications to the scene into the scene graph repository because of the missing set of changes. Therefore we use a state-based approach.

To determine changes between two scene versions, their attributed scene graphs are compared node by node and changes in state are collected into a change set. As mentioned before, every node has a unique ID, and node attributes are identified by names. This allows us to reliably and efficiently find the corresponding nodes and attributes that have to be compared between two attributed scene graphs. Without node IDs, corresponding nodes would have to be deduced from the scene graph structure alone, which is a costly and error prone task as related work (Cobéna et al., 2002) shows that deals with the comparison of hierarchical XML data. The following list shows the types of changes we determine when comparing two attributed scene graphs:

- AddNode, DeleteNode
- AddAttribute, RemoveAttribute
- SetAttribute
- AddDependency, RemoveDependency
- AddHierarchy, RemoveHierarchy, ReoderChildren, ReorderParents

Each change affects a specific node and possibly a specific attribute (e.g. an *AddNode* change only affects a node whereas a *SetAttribute* change also affects an attribute). After having determined the change sets C_A and C_B, merging can be easily done by building their union $C_M = C_A \cup C_B$, but only if there occur no changes in C_A and C_B that conflict with each other. How to detect conflicting changes will be explained in the next section.

5.2 Conflict Detection

For the detection of conflicts we set up a *conflict detection matrix* with the change types listed above as labels for both the rows and the columns. Each matrix position holds a Boolean expression whose arguments are expressed using the change types of the corresponding row and column. If such an expression evaluates to "true" for two changes, these changes conflict with each other. Evaluating such a conflict detection expression for each possible change pair would be rather inefficient. Fortunately it is sufficient to only evaluate changes that affect the same node, because changes that affect different nodes obviously cannot directly conflict with each other.

Conflict detection may be implemented at the node level or finer at the attribute level. In the first case, changes from two different change sets conflict with each other if they affect the same node and are not identical. This leads to a simple conflict detection matrix containing simple expressions. For every change pair it is sufficient to only check the IDs of the nodes affected by its changes. But such a conservative scheme may report two changes as conflicting that actually are compatible. E.g. modifying a node's position attributes and adding an additional child to that node hardly conflict with each other.

The second form of conflict detection works at the attribute level and demands more complicated conflict detection matrices. Of course, if two changes try to set the same node attribute using different values they always conflict with each other. Yet in some other cases, actual conflicts may depend on special properties of the DCC tool's scene graph. For a DCC tool that allows node attributes to have a fan-in of dependencies, two changes adding dependencies which affect the same node attribute do not conflict with each other, but for a DCC tool that forbids such fan-ins they do. If such properties are global to a DCC tool's scene graph they can be directly encoded in the corresponding conflict detection matrix' expressions. But if these properties are local to nodes and their attributes, they have to be encoded in the node types, and this information has then to be taken into account by the corresponding expressions in the conflict detection matrix.

By adding more information to the node type descriptions and more complexity to the conflict detection matrix expressions, conflicts can be detected more precisely, but to do so the DCC tool's scene graph model has to be analyzed first. Therefore when making a new DCC tool's scene graph known to the repository it is reasonable to start with a node based conflict detection matrix and then refine it for cases where conflicts have been detected too pessimistically.

5.3 Conflict Resolution

Merging two change sets C_A and C_B by building their union $C_M = C_A \cup C_B$ is not possible if there are changes $c_A \in C_A$ and $c_B \in C_B$ that conflict with each other. Essentially there is only one way to resolve such a conflict, i.e. either c_A or c_B has to be dropped. Therefore, resolving conflicts means choosing from conflicting changes those to be kept and those to be dropped.

When an artist checks-in his local working copy to the repository and his changes must be merged with another artist's changes, his complete working copy is first registered as a new alternative scene version before the merging takes place. This makes sure that the artist's changes cannot get lost and that changes that were dropped during the merging can later be selected and ported to another scene version, if required. This feature allows us to establish aggressive automatic merging policies.

If there is a strict hierarchy defined among the artists, a reasonable automatic merging policy consists in always dropping changes by a junior artist that conflict with changes by a senior artist. If required, the senior artist may still port some of the junior artist's changes later to the current version of the scene. If the artists are collaborating peers, the artist checking-in his local working copy of a scene to the repository may be given the opportunity to decide himself if his conflicting changes should override other artists' changes or should be overridden themselves. Of course, artists may also analyze their conflicting changes together and choose the changes to keep or drop on a per conflict basis.

More advanced conflict resolution does not only involve discarding changes which conflict with other changes, but also changes that relate to conflicting changes. If conflicts have been found in a certain part of a scene, an artist sometimes does not only want to make sure that his changes override other conflicting changes in that part but also that the part as a whole remains exactly the same as in his version. Therefore, while checking-in a scene, an artist may specify a subgraph of the scene where only his changes are taken into account and where changes from other artists to this subgraph are dropped.

At the end of the conflict resolution process results the merged change set C_M containing changes from C_A that do not conflict with changes from C_B and vice versa. Changes in C_A and in C_B but not in C_M are not lost and can still be applied later to a selected scene version if required.

5.4 Indirect Conflicts

Even if artists A and B make only changes to a scene that do not conflict, their changes might still not be consistent. We illustrate this by giving a simple example for such inconsistent collaborative scene changes in Figure 4. It shows a scene graph (a) that groups two rectangles to model the character T in the scene S (b). Obviously there occurs a problem, i.e. a small gap arises between the two rectangles. Let us assume that artists A and B both close this gap within collaborative versions. To do so, artist A extends the vertical rectangle as shown in (c), and artist B extends the horizontal rectangle as shown in (d). Because both artists only modify different nodes, merging their collaborative versions S_A and S_B into S_M does not yield any conflicts, yet S_M does not look right as it is shown in (e): The gap between the rectangles in S has disappeared, but they now overlap in S_M.

The problem just shown is an illustration of what we call *indirect changes*. The group node in (a) aggregates the two rectangle nodes and therefore depends on them. Changing one of the group node's children indirectly also changes the group node itself. More generally, a change to a scene graph node indirectly changes all nodes that depend on it, i.e. by propagation of indirect changes along hierarchy and dependency relationships.

An indirect change affects a node and possibly also a node attribute. Indirect changes introduced by hierarchy relationships only affect nodes whereas indirect changes introduced by dependency relationships may also affect node attributes for attribute

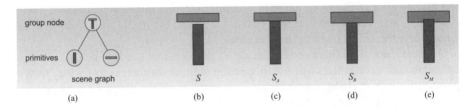

Fig. 4. An indirect conflict resulting in overlapping rectangles

dependencies. Indirect changes can be computed recursively: A change or indirect change that affects a node introduces an additional indirect change for every node that depends on that node by hierarchy or dependency. Because of possible cycles in dependency relationships, care must be taken when computing indirect changes. Every indirect change includes a root change where it originates from and knows its preceding indirect change if there is one.

Computing all indirect changes for all direct changes $c \in C_A$ that artist A applied to S yields the set I_A of all changes artist A made indirectly. When merging the two change sets C_A and C_B, not only direct conflicts but also *indirect conflicts* can now be detected. If an indirect change $i_A \in I_A$ affects the same node as an indirect change $i_B \in I_B$, and i_A and i_B originate from different root changes, the two indirect changes conflict. That is exactly what happens at the group node in Figure 4 and leads to the overlapping rectangles in (e). Indirect conflicts identify nodes where the effects of different changes from artists A and B meet. For the group node in (e) these changes are the extensions of the vertical and horizontal rectangles caused by A and B.

If an indirect conflict has been detected in a node it propagates along dependency and especially hierarchy relationships. Such propagated indirect conflicts are only of limited interest because they are just a manifestation of an indirect conflict that has already occurred deeper within the scene graph. Therefore we only consider indirect conflicts in nodes where the changes from artists A and B meet for the first time. For indirect changes $i_A \in I_A$ and $i_B \in I_B$ affecting the same node n, no indirect conflict is registered if both their preceding indirect changes have already affected the same node m.

Detecting indirect conflicts allows us to systematically check the effects that collaborative changes have on each other and to track down unexpected side effects of changes that may not have been taken into account by the artists. Therefore, inspecting nodes with indirect conflicts helps ensuring a scene's consistency. If the indirect conflict in the group node of the scene S_M in Figure 4 had been reviewed by an artist, the overlapping problem would have been identified and could have been fixed.

To bring possible problems caused by indirect changes to an an artist's attention, nodes with indirect conflicts must be isolated in the scene and, if possible, be visually presented to the reviewing artist. If an artist detects a problem, the root changes of the conflicting indirect changes can be consulted in order to figure out what went wrong. Indirect conflicts result from the effects that changes by two different artists have on a scene graph. Therefore resolving indirect conflicts is similar to resolving direct conflicts: If the indirect changes $i_A \in I_A$ and $i_B \in I_B$ conflict with each other, either the root change of i_A or that of i_B has to be dropped to resolve this indirect conflict. Yet an artist may also prefer not to deal with changes at all and to directly fix a problem in the scene where the indirect conflict has occurred.

Of course, not all indirect conflicts lead to a problem that needs to be addressed; in fact, most indirect conflicts will not. Inspecting indirect conflicts is just a way to systematically and purposefully look for possible problems at the right places, as opposed to randomly scanning the whole scene.

For every indirect conflict we register the distances from the originating root change nodes to the node where the indirect changes meet in a conflict. The reason is that we assume that local indirect conflicts, whose causing root changes are not far away, are more likely to identify problems than rather global indirect conflicts, whose causing root changes are spread far away in different parts of the scene graph. This makes it possible to first review indirect conflicts that are more likely to be critical.

Computing indirect changes and detecting indirect conflicts are only possible because of the underlying general attributed scene graph model which makes the exact structure of a scene known to the scene graph repository. In addition to the hierarchy and dependency relationships between nodes, also internal attribute dependencies of nodes have to be taken into consideration. Such internal dependencies are defined within the node types.

6   A Practical Example

The authors' research group is currently developing a 3D model of the old part of the city of Bern. A prototype version of the scene graph repository system has been applied to this model, and its capability to enable collaboration could be successfully tested.

To be able to model all the buildings needed in reasonable time a special plug-in for Maya has been developed (Zaugg, 2005). It allows us to automatically construct a building typical for the city of Bern from a building's ground plan and from some additional parameters that are directly attached as attributes to its ground plan polygons in Maya. Historically important or complex buildings, like towers, churches, fountains, etc., have to be manually modeled in Maya from scratch.

There are several people involved in building this city model. One modeler acquires ground plan polygons and defines the rough parameters for the houses to be built upon them. Another modeler erects houses from the ground plan polygons using the special building plug-in and fine-tunes their parameters to achieve a consistent overall appearance of the city. Some of the ground plan polygons correspond to those important buildings that need to be manually modeled in detail by additional modelers. Yet another modeler decorates buildings with advertisement signs, flowers, etc. to add further "realism" to the city model.

All these modelers can work in parallel on the same model without locking out each other. Each time they check-in or update their scene they can see what their collaborating modelers added or changed and can adapt their own work accordingly. This helps to ensure an overall consistent appearance of the model and to sort out different opinions on aspects of the model as early as possible.

A modeler of a historical building can create his model directly within the city model, which allows him to adjust his model to the surrounding buildings at the time he creates it. If he needs to change some of the surrounding buildings to fit in his model correctly, he can do so immediately in his own scene and does not have to search for and to open the reference file which contains the buildings he wants to change. Therefore he will also not run into the problem that a specific reference file might already be in use by someone else and is not available for him to work on.

Detection and resolution of conflicting changes by the repository system during the check-in of scenes keeps the city model in a clean state. In addition, the detection and inspection of indirect conflicts helps to keep the city model consistent. If two modelers have accidentally decorated the same building this would result in an indirect conflict in the affected building. During a check-in or an update this indirect conflict would be brought to the modelers' attention and the problem could be fixed.

7   Conclusions

Today's professional 3D digital content creation tools only offer limited support for several artists to work collaboratively on a 3D scene, and also standard group authoring tools are only of limited assistance, because they are not able to merge collaborative changes made to 3D scenes. To make the merging of 3D scenes possible we have presented an attributed scene graph model that is general enough to handle scene graphs of different DCC tools.

We have also presented a scene graph repository system that enables fine-grained collaboration on scenes of standard 3D DCC tools by implementing the concept of collaborative versions. Artists can now work on the same scene in parallel without locking out each other. The artists' changes to a scene are regularly merged to make sure that all artists can see each other's progress and can collaborate on current data. We have reduced the merging of scenes to the merging of state-based change sets and have shown how to detect and resolve conflicts between such change sets using different conflict resolution policies.

We have also introduced the concept of indirect changes and indirect conflicts which help maintaining scene consistency by systematically looking for inconsistencies at the right places. Computing indirect conflicts is based on our attributed scene graph model's capability to depict detailed dependencies between nodes.

Our approach has been implemented in a prototype scene graph repository server in Java and a Maya ASG plug-in in C++. We have successfully tested our prototype implementation by applying it to our model of the old part of the city of Bern. Merging different versions of a city model Maya scene, which is about 50 MB in size, by applying an automatic conflict resolution policy takes less than 15 seconds on a today's standard PC.

References

Alienbrain, Alienbrain studio 7. (2005), http://www.alienbrain.com
Barnes, M.: Collada, digital asset schema release 1.3.0, specification (2005),
    http://www.collada.org

Cobéna, G., Abiteboul, S., Marian, A.: Detecting changes in XML documents. In: Proceedings of the 18th International Conference on Data Engineering (ICDE'02), pp. 41–52. IEEE, Los Alamitos (2002)

Collison, A., Bieri, H.: A component-based system for storing and manipulating graphics objects of different representations. The Visual Computer 16(6), 322–338 (2000)

Galli, R., Luo, Y.: Mu3d: a causal consistency protocol for a collaborative vrml editor. In: VRML '00: Proceedings of the fifth symposium on virtual reality modeling language (Web3D-VRML), pp. 53–62. ACM Press, New York (2000)

Hesina, G., Schmalstieg, D., Fuhrmann, A.L., Purgathofer, W.: Distributed open inventor: a practical approach to distributed 3d graphics. In: VRST, pp. 74–81 (1999)

Kiesel, N., Schürr, A., Westfechtel, B.: Gras, a graph-oriented (software) engineering database system. Information Systems 20(1), 21–51 (1995)

Magnusson, B., Asklund, U., Minör, S.: Fine-grained revision control for collaborative software development. In: Proceedings of the first ACM symposium on Foundations of software engineering, pp. 33–41. ACM Press, New York (1993)

Naef, M., Lamboray, E., Staadt, O., Gross, M.: The blue-c distributed scene graph. In: Proceedings of the IPT/EGVE Workshop 2003, pp. 125–133 (2003)

Wieczerzycki, W., Rykowski, J.: Version support for cad/case databases. In: Proceedings East/West Database Workshop, Workshops in Computing, pp. 249–260 (1994)

Zaugg, M.: Generische Gebäudemodellierung in Maya. Master Thesis, Institute of Computer Science and Applied Mathematics, University of Bern (2005)

Zeleznik, B., Holden, L., Capps, M., Abrams, H., Miller, T.: Scene-graph-as-bus: Collaboration between heterogeneous stand-alone 3-D graphical applications. Computer Graphics Forum (Eurographics 2000) 19(3) (2000)

Part II

Rendering

A Progressive Refinement Approach for the Visualisation of Implicit Surfaces

Manuel N. Gamito[*] and Steve C. Maddock

Department of Computer Science, The University of Sheffield
M.Gamito@dcs.shef.ac.uk, S.Maddock@dcs.shef.ac.uk

Abstract. Visualising implicit surfaces with the ray casting method is a slow procedure. The design cycle of a new implicit surface is, therefore, fraught with long latency times as a user must wait for the surface to be rendered before being able to decide what changes should be introduced in the next iteration. In this paper, we present an attempt at reducing the design cycle of an implicit surface modeler by introducing a progressive refinement rendering approach to the visualisation of implicit surfaces. This progressive refinement renderer provides a quick previewing facility. It first displays a low quality estimate of what the final rendering is going to be and, as the computation progresses, increases the quality of this estimate at a steady rate. The progressive refinement algorithm is based on the adaptive subdivision of the viewing frustrum into smaller cells. An estimate for the variation of the implicit function inside each cell is obtained with an affine arithmetic range estimation technique. Overall, we show that our progressive refinement approach not only provides the user with visual feedback as the rendering advances but is also capable of completing the image faster than a conventional implicit surface rendering algorithm based on ray casting.

Keywords: Affine arithmetic, implicit surface, progressive refinement, ray casting.

1 Introduction

Implicit surfaces play an important role in Computer Graphics. Surfaces exhibiting complex topologies, i.e. with many holes or disconnected pieces, can be easily modelled in implicit form. An implicit surface is defined as the set of all points $\mathbf{x}$ that verify the condition $f(\mathbf{x}) = 0$ for some function $f : \mathbb{R}^3 \mapsto \mathbb{R}$. Modelling with implicit surfaces amounts to the construction of an appropriate function f that will generate the desired surface.

Rendering algorithms for implicit surfaces can be broadly divided into meshing algorithms and ray casting algorithms. Meshing algorithms convert an implicit surface to a polygonal mesh format, which can be subsequently rendered in real time with modern graphics processor boards (Lorensen and Cline, 1987; Bloomenthal, 1988; Velho, 1996). Ray casting algorithms compute the projection of an implicit surface on

---

[*] Supported by grant SFRH/BD/16249/2004 from Fundação para a Ciência e a Tecnologia, Portugal.

J. Braz et al. (Eds.): VISAPP and GRAPP 2006, CCIS 4, pp. 93–108, 2007.

the screen by casting rays from each pixel into three-dimensional space and finding their intersection with the surface (Roth, 1982).

Our ultimate goal is to use implicit surfaces as a tool to model and visualise realistic procedural planets over a very wide range of scales. The function f that generates the surface terrain for such a planet must have fractal scaling properties and exhibit a large amount of small scale detail. Examples of this type of terrain generating function can be found in the Computer Graphics literature (Ebert et al., 2003). In our planet modelling scenario, meshing algorithms are too cumbersome as they generate meshes with a very high polygon count in order to preserve all the visible surface detail. Furthermore, as the viewing distance changes, the amount of surface detail varies accordingly and the whole polygon mesh needs to be regenerated. For these reasons, we have preferred a ray casting approach because of its ability to render the surface directly without the need for an intermediate polygonal representation.

The visualisation of an implicit surface with ray casting is not without its problems, however. When the surface is complex, many iterations have to be performed along each ray in order to locate the intersection point with an acceptable accuracy (Mitchell, 1990). Imaging an implicit surface with ray casting can then become a slow procedure. This is further compounded by the fact that an anti-aliased image requires that many rays be shot for each pixel (Cook, 1989).

We propose to alleviate the long rendering times associated with the modelling and subsequent ray casting of complex fractal surfaces by providing a quick previewer based on a progressive refinement rendering principle. The idea of progressive refinement for image rendering was first formalised in 1986 (Bergman et al., 1986). Progressive refinement rendering has received much attention in the fields of radiosity and global illumination (Cohen et al., 1988; Guo, 1998; Farrugia and Peroche, 2004). Progressive refinement approaches to volume rendering have also been developed (Laur and Hanrahan, 1991; Lippert and Gross, 1995). Our previewer uses progressive rendering to visualise an increasingly better approximation to the final implicit surface. It allows the user to make quick editing decisions without having to wait for a full ray casting solution to be computed. Because the rendering is progressive, the previewer can be terminated as soon as the user is satisfied or not with the look of the surface.

Our progressive refinement previewing method relies on affine arithmetic to compute an estimate of the variation of the implicit function f inside some region (Comba and Stolfi, 1993). Affine arithmetic is a framework for evaluating algebraic functions with arguments that are bounded but otherwise unknown. It is a generalisation of the older interval arithmetic framework (Moore, 1966). Affine arithmetic, when compared against interval arithmetic, is capable of returning much tighter estimates for the variation of a function, given input arguments that vary over the same given range. Affine arithmetic has been used with success in an increasing number of Computer Graphics problems, including the ray casting of implicit surfaces (de Cusatis Jr. et al., 1999). We use a modified form of affine arithmetic that we term *reduced affine arithmetic* (Gamito and Maddock, 2005). Reduced affine arithmetic, in the context of ray casting implicit surfaces made from procedural fractal functions, returns the same results as standard affine arithmetic while being faster to compute and requiring smaller data structures.

2 Previous Work

One of the best known techniques for previewing implicit surfaces at interactive frame rates is based on the dynamic placement of discs that are tangent to the surface (Witkin and Heckbert, 1994; Hart et al., 2002). The discs are kept apart by the application of repulsive forces and are constrained to remain on the implicit surface. Each disc is also made tangent to the surface by sharing the surface normal at the point where it is located. This previewing system relies on a characteristic of our visual system whereby we are able to infer the existence of an object based solely on the distribution of a small number of features on the surface of that object. This visual trait only works, however, when the surface of the object is simple and fairly smooth. If the surface is irregular, an apparently random distribution of discs is visible and no object is perceived.

An approximate representation of an implicit surface can be generated by subdividing the space in which the surface is embedded into progressively smaller voxels and using a surface classification technique to identify which voxels are potentially intersecting with the surface. One such spatial subdivision method employs interval arithmetic to perform the surface classification step (Duff, 1992). The subdivision strategy of this method is adapted from an earlier work and is not suitable for interactive previewing (Woodwark and Quinlan, 1982). One must wait for the subdivision to finish before any surface approximation can be visualised unless some additional data processing is added, which will tend to slow down the algorithm. Another spatial subdivision method employs affine arithmetic to perform surface classification and subdivides space with an octree data structure (de Figueiredo and Stolfi, 1996). The octree voxels are rendered from back to front, relative to the viewpoint, with a painter's algorithm. This subdivision strategy is wasteful as it tracks the entire surface through subdivision, including parts that are occluded and that could be safely discarded for a given viewing configuration.

Rather than performing object space subdivision, one can also perform image space subdivision in order to obtain a progressive rendering mechanism. Sample subdivision in image space was originally proposed as an anti-aliasing method for ray tracing (Whitted, 1980). Four rays are shot at the corners of each rectangular sample. If the computed colours for these rays differ by more than some specified amount, the sample is subdivided into four smaller samples and more rays are shot through the corners of the new samples. This type of image space subdivision can also be used for progressive refinement previewing (Painter and Sloan, 1989; Maillot et al., 1992). The problem with image space subdivision algorithms is that they rely entirely on probabilistic methods to determine when to subdivide the image samples. The decision to subdivide a sample is based on a probabilistic analysis of the set of rays traced so far in the neighbourhood of that sample. Because this discrete set of rays is only an approximation of a continuous image intensity distribution, wrong subdivision decisions can sometimes occur.

3 Rendering with Progressive Refinement

The main stage of our method consists in the binary subdivision of the space, visible from the camera, into progressively smaller cells that are known to straddle the boundary of the surface. The subdivision mechanism stops as soon as the projected size of a cell on the screen becomes smaller than the size of a pixel. Information about the behaviour of the implicit function f inside a cell is returned by evaluating the function with reduced affine arithmetic. The procedure for rendering implicit surfaces with progressive refinement can be broken down into the following steps:

1. Build an initial cell coincident with the camera's viewing frustrum. The near and far clipping planes are determined so as to bound the implicit surface.
2. Recursively subdivide this cell into smaller cells. Discard cells that do not intersect with the implicit surface. Stop subdivision if the size of the cell's projection on the image plane falls below the size of a pixel.
3. Assign the shading value of a cell to all pixels that are contained inside its projection on the image plane. The shading value for a cell is taken from the evaluation of the shading model at the centre point of the cell.

The following sections will explain how each of the steps in our rendering method work, starting with a presentation of the reduced affine arithmetic framework in Section 3.1. We then explain the geometry of a cell inside the camera's viewing frustrum (Section 3.2) and how a cell is subdivided and rendered (Sections 3.3 and 3.4). We also explain in Section 3.5 how a region of interest can be optionally defined so as to provide the user with interactive control during the rendering process.

3.1 Reduced Affine Arithmetic

A variable is represented with reduced affine arithmetic (rAA) as a central value plus a series of noise symbols. In contrast to the standard affine arithmetic model, the number of noise symbols is constant, being given by the fundamental degrees of freedom of the problem under consideration (Gamito and Maddock, 2005). In the rendering method that is being described in this paper, the degrees of freedom are the three parameters necessary to locate any point inside the viewing frustrum of the camera. These parameters are the horizontal distance u along the image plane, the vertical distance v along the same image plane and the distance t along the ray that passes through the point at (u, v). A rAA variable $\hat{a}$ has, therefore, the following representation:

$$\hat{a} = a_0 + a_u e_u + a_v e_v + a_t e_t + a_k e_k. \tag{1}$$

The noise symbols e_u, e_v and e_t are shared between all rAA variables in the system, which allows for the representation of correlation information between rAA variables relative to the u, v and t degrees of freedom. The extra noise symbol e_k is included to account for uncertainties in the $\hat{a}$ variable that are not shared with any other variable.

Non-affine operations on rAA variables are performed by updating the a_u, a_v and a_t noise coefficients with their new uncertainties and clumping all other uncertainties into the a_k coefficient. We give an example of how non-affine rAA operations work by considering the case of the multiplication between two variables $\hat{a}$ and $\hat{b}$ of the form (1). In the original standard affine arithmetic framework, the result $\hat{c} = \hat{a}\hat{b}$ would be written as:

$$\hat{c} = c_0 + c_u e_u + c_v e_v + c_t e_t + c_k e_k + c_n e_n. \tag{2}$$

The new noise symbol e_n is introduced to account for the non-linearity of the multiplication operator. The coefficients for the variable $\hat{c}$ are:

$$
\begin{aligned}
c_0 &= a_0 b_0, \\
c_u &= a_0 b_u + b_0 a_u, \\
c_v &= a_0 b_v + b_0 a_v, \\
c_t &= a_0 b_t + b_0 a_t, \\
c_k &= a_0 b_k + b_0 a_k, \\
c_n &= (|a_u| + |a_v| + |a_t| + |a_k|) \times \\
&\quad (|b_u| + |b_v| + |b_t| + |b_k|).
\end{aligned}
\tag{3}
$$

As a sequence of standard affine arithmetic computations progresses, new noise symbols keep being introduced into the system. For a sufficiently complex expression, the number of noise symbols that have to be considered makes the system increasingly difficult to manage, both in terms of memory requirements and of computational expense. One technique to keep the number of error symbols down to a manageable level is to periodically invoke a procedure called *condensation* (Stolfi and de Figueiredo, 1997). Condensation reduces the number of error symbols of a standard affine arithmetic variable at the cost of destroying correlation information. If the variable $\hat{c}$ in (2) is condensed into a new variable $\hat{d}$ with one less error symbol, we will have for the coefficients of $\hat{d}$:

$$
\begin{aligned}
d_0 &= c_0, \\
d_u &= c_u, \\
d_v &= c_v, \\
d_t &= c_t, \\
d_k &= |c_k| + |c_n|.
\end{aligned}
\tag{4}
$$

The condensed variable $\hat{d}$ is now in the rAA form, according to (1). With the reduced affine arithmetic framework, all non-affine operations are always followed by a condensation step to keep a constant number of error symbols for every variable throughout the computation. In practice, all non-affine operations in reduced affine arithmetic are modified so that the condensation step (4) is automatically built into them. The multiplication $\hat{c} = \hat{a}\hat{b}$, that in standard affine arithmetic was given by (3), now becomes:

$$
\begin{aligned}
c_0 &= a_0 b_0, \\
c_u &= a_0 b_u + b_0 a_u, \\
c_v &= a_0 b_v + b_0 a_v, \\
c_t &= a_0 b_t + b_0 a_t, \\
c_k &= |a_0 b_k + b_0 a_k| + \\
&\quad (|a_u| + |a_v| + |a_t| + |a_k|) \times \\
&\quad (|b_u| + |b_v| + |b_t| + |b_k|).
\end{aligned}
\tag{5}
$$

Reduced affine arithmetic is more efficient than standard affine arithmetic because it keeps only the required minimum amount of correlation information between all rAA quantities. In our progressive refinement renderer, much faster convergence rates can be obtained towards the final image by using affine arithmetic in reduced form.

For an implicit surface, the value $f(\mathbf{x})$ at some point $\mathbf{x}$ in space can be computed with reduced affine arithmetic. The rAA representation $\hat{\mathbf{x}}$ of the vector $\mathbf{x}$ is a tuple of three rAA coordinates, similar to (1), where each coordinate has its own independent noise symbol e_{k_i}, with $i = 1, 2, 3$. The rAA vector $\hat{\mathbf{x}}$ describes not a point but a region of space spanned by the uncertainties associated with its three coordinates. Evaluation of the expression $\hat{y} = f(\hat{\mathbf{x}})$ leads to a range estimate $\hat{y}$ for the variation of $f(\hat{\mathbf{x}})$ inside the region spanned by $\hat{\mathbf{x}}$. Knowing $\hat{y}$, the average value $\bar{y}$ and the variance $\langle y \rangle$ for that range estimate can be computed as follows:

$$\bar{y} \triangleq y_0, \tag{6a}$$

$$\langle y \rangle \triangleq |y_u| + |y_v| + |y_t| + |y_k|. \tag{6b}$$

The range estimate $\hat{y}$ is then known to lie inside the interval $[\bar{y} - \langle y \rangle, \bar{y} + \langle y \rangle]$. If this interval contains zero, the region spanned by $\hat{\mathbf{x}}$ may or may not intersect with the implicit function. This is because affine arithmetic (both in its standard and reduced forms) always computes conservative range estimates and it is possible that the exact range resulting from $f(\hat{\mathbf{x}})$ may be smaller than $\hat{y}$. What is certain is that if $[\bar{y} - \langle y \rangle, \bar{y} + \langle y \rangle]$ does not contain zero the region spanned by $\hat{\mathbf{x}}$ is either completely inside or completely outside the implicit surface and therefore does not intersect it.

3.2   The Anatomy of a Cell

A cell is a portion of the camera's viewing frustrum that results from a recursive subdivision along the u, v and t parameters. Figure 1 depicts the geometry of a cell. It has the shape of a truncated pyramid of quadrangular cross-section, similar to the shape of the viewing frustrum itself. Four vectors, taken from the camera's viewing system, are used to define the spatial extent of a cell. These vectors are:

The vector o This is the location of the camera in the world coordinate system.

The vectors $\mathbf{p}_u$ and $\mathbf{p}_v$ They represent the horizontal and vertical direction along the image plane. The length of these vectors gives the width and height, respectively, of a pixel in the image plane.

The vector $\mathbf{p}_t$ It is the vector from the camera's viewpoint and orthogonal to the image plane. The length of this vector gives the distance from the viewpoint to the image plane.

The vectors $\mathbf{p}_u$, $\mathbf{p}_v$ and $\mathbf{p}_t$ define a left-handed perspective viewing system. The position of any point $\mathbf{x}$ inside the cell is given by the following inverse perspective transformation:

$$\begin{aligned}
\mathbf{x} &= \mathbf{o} + (u\mathbf{p}_u + v\mathbf{p}_v + \mathbf{p}_t)t \\
&= \mathbf{o} + ut\mathbf{p}_u + vt\mathbf{p}_v + t\mathbf{p}_t.
\end{aligned} \tag{7}$$

The spatial extent of a cell is obtained from the above by having the u, v and t parameters vary over appropriate intervals $[u_a, u_b]$, $[v_a, v_b]$ and $[t_a, t_b]$. We must consider

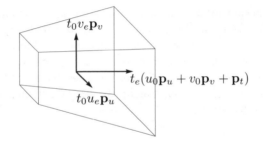

Fig. 1. The geometry of a cell. The vectors show the three medial axes of the cell.

how to compute the rAA representation $\hat{\mathbf{x}}$ of this spatial extent. To do so a change of variables must first be performed. The rAA variable $\hat{u} = u_0 + u_e e_u$ will span the same interval $[u_a, u_b]$ as u does if we have:

$$u_0 = (u_b + u_a)/2, \tag{8a}$$
$$u_e = (u_b - u_a)/2. \tag{8b}$$

Similar results apply for the v and t parameters. Substituting $\hat{u}$, $\hat{v}$ and $\hat{t}$ in (7) for u, v and t, we get:

$$\begin{aligned}
\mathbf{x} = {}& \mathbf{o} + t_0 u_0 \mathbf{p}_u + t_0 v_0 \mathbf{p}_v + t_0 \mathbf{p}_t \\
& + t_0 u_e e_u \mathbf{p}_u + t_0 v_e e_v \mathbf{p}_v \\
& + u_0 t_e e_t \mathbf{p}_u + v_0 t_e e_t \mathbf{p}_v + t_e e_t \mathbf{p}_t \\
& + t_e u_e e_u e_t \mathbf{p}_u + t_e v_e e_v e_t \mathbf{p}_v.
\end{aligned} \tag{9}$$

The first line of (9) contains only constant terms. The second and third lines contain linear terms of the noise symbols e_u, e_v and e_t. The fourth line contains two non-linear terms $e_u e_t$ and $e_v e_t$, which are a consequence of the non-linearity of the perspective transformation. Since a rAA representation cannot accommodate such non-linear terms they are replaced by the independent noise terms e_{k_1}, e_{k_2} and e_{k_3} for each of the three cartesian coordinates of $\hat{\mathbf{x}}$. The rAA vector $\hat{\mathbf{x}}$ is finally given by:

$$\begin{aligned}
\hat{\mathbf{x}} = {}& \mathbf{o} + t_0 (u_0 \mathbf{p}_u + v_0 \mathbf{p}_v + \mathbf{p}_t) \\
& + t_0 u_e \mathbf{p}_u e_u + t_0 v_e \mathbf{p}_v e_v \\
& + t_e (u_0 \mathbf{p}_u + v_0 \mathbf{p}_v + \mathbf{p}_t) e_t \\
& + \left[x_{k_1} e_{k_1} \; x_{k_2} e_{k_2} \; x_{k_3} e_{k_3} \right]^T,
\end{aligned} \tag{10}$$

with

$$x_{k_i} = |t_e u_e p_{u_i}| + |t_e v_e p_{v_i}|, \quad i = 1, 2, 3. \tag{11}$$

A consequence of the non-linearity of the perspective projection and its subsequent approximation with rAA is that the region spanned by $\hat{\mathbf{x}}$ is going to be larger than the spatial extent of the cell. Figure 2 shows the geometry of a cell and the region spanned by its rAA representation in profile. Because the rAA representation has been linearised, its spatial extent is a prism rather than a truncated pyramid. This has further consequences in that the evaluation of $f(\hat{x})$ is going to include information from the regions of the prism outside the cell and will, therefore, lead to range estimates that are larger than necessary. The linearisation error is more pronounced for cells that exist early in the subdivision process. As subdivision continues and the cells become progressively smaller, their geometry becomes more like that of a prism and the discrepancy with the geometry of $\hat{x}$ decreases[1].

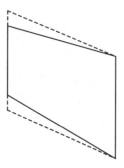

Fig. 2. The outline of a cell (solid line) and the outline of its rAA representation (dashed line) shown in profile. The rAA representation is a prism that forms a tight enclosure of the cell.

The subdivision of a cell proceeds by first choosing one of the three perspective projection parameters u, v or t and splitting the cell in half along that parameter. This scheme leads to a k-d tree of cells where the sequence of dimensional splits is only determined at run time. The choice of which parameter to split along is based on the average width, height and depth of the cell:

$$\bar{w}_u = 2\,t_0 u_e \|\mathbf{p}_u\|, \tag{12a}$$

$$\bar{w}_v = 2\,t_0 v_e \|\mathbf{p}_v\|, \tag{12b}$$

$$\bar{w}_t = 2\,t_e \|u_0 \mathbf{p_u} + v_0 \mathbf{p_v} + \mathbf{p}_t\|. \tag{12c}$$

If, say, $\bar{w}_u$ is the largest of these three measures, the cell is split along the u parameter. The two child cells will have their u parameters ranging inside the intervals $[u_a, u_0]$ and $[u_0, u_b]$, where $[u_a, u_b]$ was the interval spanned by u in the mother cell. In practice, the factors of 2 in (12) can be ignored without changing the outcome of the subdivision. This subdivision strategy ensures that, after a few iterations, all the cells will have an evenly distributed shape, even when the initial cell is very long and thin.

3.3   The Process of Cell Subdivision

Cell subdivision is implemented in an iterative manner rather than using a recursive procedure. The cells are kept sorted in a priority queue based on their level of subdivision. A cell has priority over another if it has undergone less subdivision. For cells at

---

[1] This can be demonstrated by the fact that the terms $t_e u_e$ and $t_e v_e$ in (9) decrease more rapidly than any of the linear terms u_e, v_e and t_e of the same equation as the latter converge to zero.

the same subdivision level, the one that is closer to the camera will have priority. The algorithm starts by placing the initial cell, which corresponds to the complete viewing frustrum, on the priority queue. At the start of every new iteration, a cell is removed from the head of the queue. If the extent of the cell's projection on the image plane is larger than the extent of a pixel, the cell is subdivided and its two children are examined. In the opposite case, the cell is considered a leaf cell and is discarded after being rendered. The two conditions that indicate whether a cell should be subdivided are:

$$u_b - u_a > 1, \tag{13a}$$

$$v_b - v_a > 1. \tag{13b}$$

The values on the right hand sides of (13) are a consequence of the definition of $\mathbf{p}_u$ and $\mathbf{p}_v$ in Section 3.2, which cause all pixels to have a unit width and height.

The sequence of events after a cell has been subdivided depends on which of the parameters u, v or t was used to perform the subdivision. If the subdivision occurred along t, there will be two child cells with one in front of the other and totally occluding it. The front cell is first checked for the condition $0 \in f(\hat{\mathbf{x}})$. If the condition holds, the cell is pushed into the priority queue and the back cell is ignored. If the condition does not hold, the back cell is also checked for the same condition. The difference now is that, if $0 \notin f(\hat{\mathbf{x}})$ for the back cell, a new cell must be searched by marching along the t direction. The first cell scanned, at the same subdivision level of the front and back cells, for which $0 \in f(\hat{\mathbf{x}})$ holds is the one that is pushed into the priority queue. On the other hand, if the subdivision occurred along the u or v directions, there will be two child cells that sit side by side relative to the camera without occluding each other. Both cells are processed in the same way. If, for any of the two cells, $0 \in f(\hat{\mathbf{x}})$ holds, that cell is placed on the priority queue, otherwise a farther cell must be searched by marching forward in depth.

The process of marching forward from a cell along the depth direction t tries to find a new cell that has a possibility of intersecting the implicit surface by verifying the condition $0 \in f(\hat{\mathbf{x}})$. The process is invoked when the starting cell has been determined not to verify the same condition. The reason for having this scanning in depth is because cells that do not intersect with the surface must be discarded. Only cells that verify $0 \in f(\hat{\mathbf{x}})$ are allowed into the priority queue for further processing. Figure 3 shows an example of this marching process. The scanning is performed by following a depth-first ordering relative to the tree that results from subdividing in t. The scanning sequence skips over the children of cells for which $0 \notin f(\hat{\mathbf{x}})$. The possibility of scanning in breadth-first order, by marching along all the cells at the same level of subdivision, is not recommended because in deeply subdivided trees a very high number of cells would have to be tested.

As mentioned before, when subdivision is performed along t, the back cell is ignored whenever the front cell verifies $0 \in f(\hat{\mathbf{x}})$. This does not mean, however, that the volume occupied by this back cell will be totally discarded from further consideration. The front cell may happen to be subdivided during subsequent iterations of the algorithm and portions of the volume occupied by the back cell may then be revisited by the depth marching procedure.

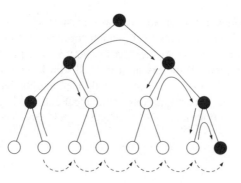

Fig. 3. Scanning along the depth subdivision tree. Cells represented by black nodes may intersect with the surface. Cells represented by white nodes do not. The solid arrows show progression by depth-first order. The dotted arrows show progression by breadth-first order.

3.4   Rendering a Cell

The shading value of a cell is obtained by evaluating the shading function at the centre of the cell. The central point $\mathbf{x}_0$ for the cell is determined from (10) to be:

$$\mathbf{x}_0 = \mathbf{o} + t_0(u_0\mathbf{p}_u + v_0\mathbf{p}_v + \mathbf{p}_t). \tag{14}$$

During rendering, the shading value of a cell is assigned to all the pixels that are contained within its image plane projection. The centre of a pixel (i, j) occupies the coordinates $\mathbf{c}_{ij} = (i + 1/2, j + 1/2)$ on the image plane. All the pixels that verify $\mathbf{c}_{ij} \in [u_a, u_b] \times [v_a, v_b]$ for the cell being rendered will be assigned its shading value. Any previous shading values stored in these pixels will be overwritten. This process happens after cell subdivision and before the newly subdivided cells are placed on the priority queue. The subdivided cells will overwrite the shading value of their mother cell on the image buffer. The same process also takes place for leaf cells before they are discarded. In this way, the image buffer always contains the best possible representation of the image at the start of every new iteration.

3.5   Specifying a Region of Interest

A user can interactively influence the rendering algorithm by drawing a rectangular region of interest (ROI) over the image. The algorithm will then refine the image only inside the specified region. This is accomplished by creating a secondary priority queue that stores the cells that are relevant to the ROI. When the user finishes drawing the region, the primary queue is scanned and all cells whose image projection intersects with the rectangle corresponding to that ROI are transferred to the secondary queue. The algorithm then proceeds as explained in Section 3.3 with the difference that the secondary queue is now being used. Once this queue becomes empty, the portion of the image inside the ROI is fully rendered and the algorithm returns to subdividing the cells that were left in the primary queue. It is also possible to cancel the ROI at any time by flushing any cells still in the secondary queue back to the primary queue.

3.6   Some Implementation Remarks

The best implementation strategy for our rendering method is to have an application that runs two threads concurrently: a subdivision thread and a rendering thread. An internal image buffer is used to store the rendering of the surface as it is being refined. The subdivision thread requires read-write access to this buffer while the rendering thread requires read-only access to the same buffer. The rendering thread is responsible for periodically updating the graphical output of the application with the latest results from the subdivision thread. Its task is to invoke a single graphics library call that transfers the content of the internal image buffer to the frame buffer of the GPU card. A timer is used to keep a constant frame refresh rate. Except for the periodical invocation of the timer handler routine, the rendering thread remains in a sleep state so that the subdivision thread can use all the CPU resources.

It is possible that, on machines with a small amount of main memory, excessive paging may occur due to the need to store a large number of samples in the priority queue. We have implemented our application on a Pentium 4 1.8GHz with 1Gb of memory. All the results shown in the next section were tested on this computer and it was found that the use of swap memory was never necessary. In any case, it is advisable that the data structure used to hold a sample be as light as possible.

4   Results

Figure 5 on the next page shows four snapshots taken during the progressive refinement rendering of an implicit sphere modulated with a Perlin procedural noise function (Perlin, 2002). The last snapshot shows the final rendering of the surface. The large scale features of the surface become settled quite early and the latter stages of the refinement are mostly concerned with resolving small scale details.

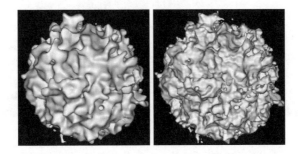

Fig. 4. An implicit surface with two layers (left) and three layers (right) of a Perlin noise function

Figure 4 shows an implicit sphere modulated with two and three layers of the Perlin noise function. Table 1 shows the total number of iterations and the computation time for the surfaces that were rendered in Figures 4 and 5. The table also shows the computation time for ray casting the same surfaces by shooting a single ray through the centre of each pixel. The number of iterations required to complete the progressive rendering algorithm

Table 1. Rendering statistics for an implicit sphere with several layers of Perlin noise

Layers	Iterations	Time	Raycasting
1	350759	27.8s	1m10.4s
2	349465	1m16.8s	4m16.7s
3	359659	3m01.5s	8m51.7s

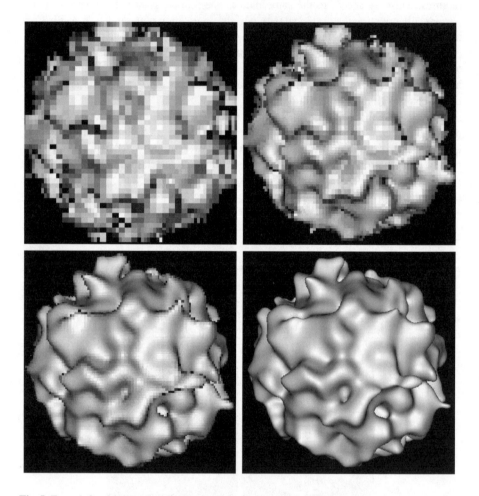

Fig. 5. From left to right, top to bottom, snapshots taken during the progressive refinement rendering of a procedural noise function. The snapshots were taken after 5000, 10000, 28000 and 350759 iterations, respectively. The wall clock times at each snapshot are 1.02s, 1.98s, 4.18s and 27.80s, respectively.

is largely independent of the complexity of each surface. It depends only on the image resolution and on the percentage of the image that is covered by the projected surface.

As estimated by the results in Table 1, previewing by progressive refinement is approximately three times faster than previewing by ray casting without anti-aliasing. It

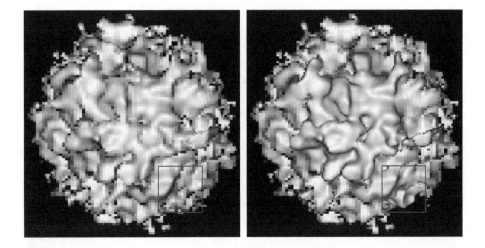

Fig. 6. Progressive refinement rendering with an active region of interest shown as a red frame. Once rendering is complete inside the region, refinement continues on the rest of the image.

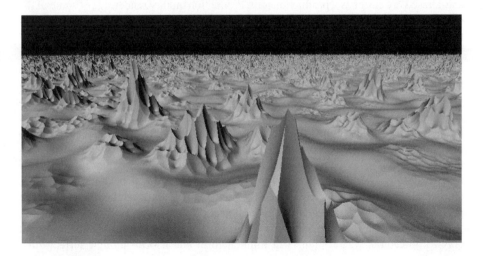

Fig. 7. The visualisation of a procedural landscape that corresponds to a small section of an entire fractal planet. The image shows the final rendering result obtained with progressive refinement.

should be added that these numbers do not entirely reflect the reality of the situation because, as demonstrated in the example of Figure 5, progressive refinement previewing already gives an accurate rendering of the surface at early stages of refinement. From a perceptual point of view, therefore, the difference between the two previewing techniques is greater than what is shown in Table 1.

Figure 6 shows two snapshots of a progressive refinement rendering where a region of interest is active. The surface being rendered is the same two layer Perlin noise surface that was shown in Figure 4. The rectangular ROI is defined on the lower right corner of the image. The portion of the surface that projects inside the ROI is given priority during progressive refinement.

Figure 7 shows the final rendering result obtained with our progressive refinement renderer for a procedural planet modelled as an implicit surface and built from a combination of different types of procedural noise functions that include Perlin noise, sparse convolution noise and cellular texture noise (Perlin, 2002; Lewis, 1989; Worley, 1996). The landscape is obtained by modulating the surface of a sphere at a very small scale.

5   Conclusions

The rendering method, here presented, offers the possibility of visualising implicit surfaces with progressive refinement. The main features of a surface become visible early in the rendering process, which makes this method ideal as a previewing tool during the editing stages of an implicit surface modeler. In comparison, a meshing method would generate expensive high resolution preview meshes for the more complex surfaces while a ray caster would be slower and without the progressive refinement feature. Our rendering method, however, does not implement anti-aliasing and cannot compete with an anti-aliased ray caster as a production tool. Production quality renderings of some of the surfaces shown in this paper are typically done overnight, a fact which further justifies the need for a previewing tool.

It would have been straightforward to incorporate anti-aliasing into our rendering method by allowing cells to be subdivided down to sub-pixel size and then applying a low-pass filter to reconstruct the pixel samples. There is, however, one issue that prevents the use of our method for high quality renderings and which makes such implementation effort not worthwhile. As explained in Section 3.1, the computation of range estimates with affine arithmetic is always conservative. This conservativeness implies that some cells a small distance away from the surface may be incorrectly flagged as intersecting with it. As a consequence, some portions of the surface may appear dilated after rendering. The offset error at some point on the surface is in the same order as the size of a pixel times the distance to the point. This artifact can be tolerated during previewing but is not acceptable for production quality renderings.

We intend in the future to apply our progressive refinement previewing strategy not only to procedural fractal planets in implicit form but also to implicit surfaces that interpolate scattered data points.

References

Bergman, L., Fuchs, H., Grant, E., Spach, S.: Image rendering by adaptive refinement. In: Evans, D.C., Athay, R.J. (eds.) Computer Graphics (SIGGRAPH '86 Proceedings), vol. 20, pp. 29–37. ACM Press, New York (1986)

Bloomenthal, J.: Polygonisation of implicit surfaces. Computer Aided Geometric Design 5(4), 341–355 (1988)

Cohen, M.F., Chen, S.E., Wallace, J.R., Greenberg, D.P.: A progressive refinement approach to fast radiosity image generation. In: Dill, J. (ed.) Computer Graphics (SIGGRAPH '88 Proceedings), vol. 22, pp. 75–84. ACM Press, New York (1988)

Comba, J.L.D., Stolfi, J.: Affine arithmetic and its applications to computer graphics. In: Proc. VI Brazilian Symposium on Computer Graphics and Image Processing (SIBGRAPI '93), pp. 9–18 (1993)

Cook, R.L.: Stochastic sampling and distributed ray tracing. In: Glassner, A.S. (ed.) An Introduction to Ray Tracing, ch. 5, pp. 161–199. Academic Press, London (1989)

de Cusatis, Jr. A., de Figueiredo, L.H., Gattas, M.: Interval methods for raycasting implicit surfaces with affine arithmetic. In: Proc. XII Brazilian Symposium on Computer Graphics and Image Processing (SIBGRAPI '99), pp. 65–71 (1999)

de Figueiredo, L.H., Stolfi, J.: Adaptive enumeration of implicit surfaces with affine arithmetic. Computer Graphics Forum 15(5), 287–296 (1996)

Duff, T.: Interval arithmetic and recursive subdivision for implicit functions and constructive solid geometry. In: Catmull, E.E. (ed.) Computer Graphics (SIGGRAPH '92 Proceedings, vol. 26, pp. 131–138. ACM Press, New York (1992)

Ebert, D.S., Musgrave, F.K., Peachey, D.R., Perlin, K., Worley, S.P.: Texturing & Modeling: A Procedural Approach, 3rd edn. Morgan Kaufmann, San Francisco (2003)

Farrugia, J.P., Peroche, B.: A progressive rendering algorithm using an adaptive perceptually based image metric. Computer Graphics Forum 23(3), 605–614 (2004)

Gamito, M.N., Maddock, S.C.: Ray casting implicit procedural noises with reduced affine arithmetic. Memorandum CS – 05 – 04, Dept. of Comp. Science, The University of Sheffield (2005)

Guo, B.: Progressive radiance evaluation using directional coherence maps. In: Beach, R.J. (ed.) Computer Graphics (SIGGRAPH '98 Proceedings), vol. 22, pp. 255–266. ACM Press, New York (1998)

Hart, J.C., Jarosz, W., Fleury, T.: Using particles to sample and control more complex implicit surfaces. In: Proceedings Shape Modeling International, pp. 129–136 (2002)

Laur, D., Hanrahan, P.: Hierarchical splatting: A progressive refinement algorithm for volume rendering. In: Sederberg, T.W (ed.) Computer Graphics (SIGGRAPH '91 Proceedings), vol. 25, pp. 285–288. ACM Press, New York (1991)

Lewis, J.-P.: Algorithms for solid noise synthesis. In: Lane, J. (ed.) Computer Graphics (SIGGRAPH '89 Proceedings), vol. 23, pp. 263–270. ACM Press, New York (1989)

Lippert, L., Gross, M.H.: Fast wavelet based volume rendering by accumulation of transparent texture maps. Computer Graphics Forum 14(3), 431–444 (1995)

Lorensen, W.E., Cline, H.E.: Marching cubes: A high resolution 3D surface construction algorithm. In: Stone, M.C. (ed.) Computer Graphics (SIGGRAPH '87 Proceedings), vol. 21, pp. 163–169. ACM Press, New York (1987)

Maillot, J.-L., Carraro, L., Peroche, B.: Progressive ray tracing. In: Chalmers, A., Paddon, D., Sillion, F. (eds.) Third Eurographics Workshop on Rendering, pp. 9–19. Eurographics, Consolidation Express Publishing, Bristol (1992)

Mitchell, D. P.: Robust ray intersection with interval arithmetic. In: Proceedings of Graphics Interface '90, pp. 68–74. Canadian Information Processing Society (1990)

Moore, R.: Interval Arithmetic. Prentice-Hall, Englewood Cliffs (1966)

Painter, J., Sloan, K.: Antialiased ray tracing by adaptive progressive refinement. In: Lane, J. (ed.) Computer Graphics (SIGGRAPH '89 Proceedings), vol. 23, pp. 281–288. ACM Press, New York (1989)

Perlin, K.: Improving noise. In: ACM Transactions on Graphics (SIGGRAPH '02 Proceedings), vol. 21(3), pp. 681–682. ACM, New York (2002)

Roth, S.D.: Ray casting for modeling solids. Computer Graphics and Image Processing 18(2), 109–144 (1982)

Stolfi, J., de Figueiredo, L.H.: Self-validated numerical methods and applications. Course notes for the 21st Brazilian Mathematics Colloquium (1997)

Velho, L.: Simple and efficient polygonization of implicit surfaces. Journal of Graphics Tools 1(2), 5–24 (1996)

Whitted, T.: An improved illumination model for shaded display. Communications of the ACM 23(6), 343–349 (1980)

Witkin, A.P., Heckbert, P.S.: Using particles to sample and control implicit surfaces. In: Glassner, A. (ed.) Computer Graphics (SIGGRAPH '94 Proceedings), vol. 28, pp. 269–278. ACM Press, New York (1994)

Woodwark, J.R., Quinlan, K.M.: Reducing the effect of complexity on volume model evaluation. Computer Aided Design 14(2), 89–95 (1982)

Worley, S.P.: A cellular texture basis function. In: Rushmeier, H. (ed.) Computer Graphics (SIGGRAPH '96 Proceedings), vol. 30, pp. 291–294. ACM Press, New York (1996)

Diffusion Based Photon Mapping

Lars Schjøth[1], Ole Fogh Olsen[1], and Jon Sporring[2]

[1] IT University of Copenhagen
Rued Langgaards Vej 7, 2300 Copenhagen S
lsc@itu.dk and fogh@itu.dk
[2] University of Copenhagen
Universitetsparken 1, 2100 Copenhagen Ø
sporring@diku.dk

Abstract. Density estimation employed in multi-pass global illumination algorithms give cause to a trade-off problem between bias and noise. The problem is seen most evident as blurring of strong illumination features. In particular this blurring erodes fine structures and sharp lines prominent in caustics. To address this problem we introduce a novel photon mapping algorithm based on nonlinear anisotropic diffusion. Our algorithm adapts according to the structure of the photon map such that smoothing occurs along edges and structures and not across. In this way we preserve the important illumination features, while eliminating noise. We call our method *diffusion based photon mapping*.

Keywords: Ray-tracing, global illumination, photon mapping, caustics, density estimation, diffusion filtering.

1 Introduction

Particle tracing is an important concept in global illumination. Particle tracing algorithms usually employ two passes. A first pass in which particles representing light are emitted from light sources and reflected around a scene, and a second pass which generates an image of the scene using the light transport information from the first pass. Common to all algorithms using particle tracing is that they trace light from the light sources. This generates information about lights propagation through the scene. In turn this information is used to reconstruct the illumination seen in the generated image. The advantage of particle tracing algorithms is that they effectively simulate all possible light paths. In particular they can simulate lighting phenomena such as color bleeding and caustics.

However, particle tracing algorithms are faced with a severe problem. In the particle tracing pass, particles are stochastically emitted from the light sources and furthermore often stochastically traced through possible light paths. This procedure induces noise, which has to be coped with in the reconstruction of the scene illumination. Unfortunately, the technique used to reduce noise also introduce a systematic error (bias) seen as a blurring of the reconstructed illumination. This is not necessarily a bad effect when concerned with slowly changing illumination, but it becomes an important problem when the illumination intensity changes quickly such as when concerned with caustics and shadows. This is a density estimation problem well-known in classical statistics.

J. Braz et al. (Eds.): VISAPP and GRAPP 2006, CCIS 4, pp. 109–122, 2007.
© Springer-Verlag Berlin Heidelberg 2007

In this paper we develop an algorithm which reduces noise and in addition preserve strong illumination features such as those seen in caustics. We have chosen to implement it in photon mapping. Photon mapping is a popular particle tracing algorithm developed by Henrik Wann Jensen (Jensen, 1996).

Our algorithm is inspired by a filtering method called *nonlinear anisotropic diffusion*. Nonlinear anisotropic diffusion is a popular method commonly used in image processing. It has the property of smoothing along edges in an image instead of across edges. Thus it preserves structures in an images while smoothing out noise. We call this novel algorithm *diffusion based photon mapping*.

Figure 1 illustrates two renderings; one using regular photon mapping and the other using diffusion based photon mapping. The images shows how diffusion based photon mapping reproduces caustics in higher detail than regular photon mapping.

Despite the fact that diffusion filtering is almost exclusively employed to process images, our method is not a post-processing step applied to photon mapping generated images. In diffusion based photon mapping we have adapted diffusion filtering in order to employ it on densities of photons during the illumination reconstruction.

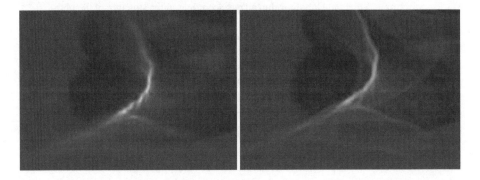

Fig. 1. [a b] Rendering of caustics created by a glass torus knot. Region zoom from Figure 3. a) Using regular photon mapping with cone filtering, b) using diffusion based photon mapping.

2   Density Estimation in Photon Mapping

In photon mapping indirect illumination is reconstruction through a series of queries to the photon maps. A photon map is a collection of photons created during a particle tracing phase in which photons are reflected around a scene using Monte Carlo ray tracing. Each query is used to estimate the reflected radiance at a surface point as the result of a local photon density estimate. This estimate is called *the radiance estimate*.

2.1   The Radiance Estimate

In his book (Jensen, 2001) Jensen derives an equation which approximates the reflected radiance using the photon map. This is done by letting the incoming radiance, L_i, at a point be represented by the incoming flux and letting the incoming flux at that point be approximated using the point's k nearest photons. In this way the equation for the reflected radiance becomes

$$L_r(\mathbf{x}, \boldsymbol{\omega}) \approx$$

$$\widehat{L}_r(\mathbf{x}, \boldsymbol{\omega}) = \frac{1}{\pi r(\mathbf{x})^2} \sum_{i=1}^{k} f_r(\mathbf{x}, \boldsymbol{\omega}_i, \boldsymbol{\omega}) \Phi_i. \tag{1}$$

The equation sums over the k photons nearest the point $\mathbf{x}$. Φ_i is the flux represented by the i'th photon, f_r is the *bidirectional reflectance distribution function* (abbreviated BRDF), and $r(\mathbf{x})$ is the radius of a sphere encompassing the k nearest photons, where $\pi r(\mathbf{x})^2$ is the sphere's cross-sectional area through its center. The radius dependens on $\mathbf{x}$, as the its value is determined by the photon density in the proximity of $\mathbf{x}$. In density estimation $r(\mathbf{x})$ is the called the bandwidth, smoothing parameter or the windows width, we will use the terms bandwidth and support radius in this article.

The support radius is important because its size controls the trade-off between variance and bias. A small radius gives a limited support of photons in the estimate; it reduces the bias but increases the variance of the estimate. Inversely, estimating the radiance using a large radius results in an increase in bias and a decrease in variance.

Using a k'th nearest neighbor search to decide the support radius, Jensen helps limit bias and variance in the estimate by smoothing more where the photon density is sparse and less where the photon density is dense.

The radiance estimate in Equation 1 is simple insofar it weights each photon in the estimate equally. Jensen refined the radiance estimate in (Jensen, 1996) such that filtering was used to weight each photon according to its distance to the point of estimation.

It is possible to reformulate the radiance estimate to a general form such that it can be used with different filtering techniques. We formulate this general radiance estimate as

$$\widehat{L}_r(\mathbf{x}, \boldsymbol{\omega}) = \frac{1}{r(\mathbf{x})^2} \cdot$$

$$\cdot \sum_{i=1}^{k} K\left(\frac{(\mathbf{x} - \mathbf{x}_i)^T (\mathbf{x} - \mathbf{x}_i)}{r(\mathbf{x})^2} \right) \cdot \tag{2}$$

$$\cdot f_r(\mathbf{x}, \boldsymbol{\omega}_i, \boldsymbol{\omega}) \Phi_i,$$

where $\mathbf{x}_i$ is the position of the i'th photon and $K(\mathbf{y})$ is a function that weights the photons according to their distance from $\mathbf{x}$. This function should be symmetric around $\mathbf{x}$ and it should be normalized such that it integrates to unity within the distance $r(\mathbf{x})$ to $\mathbf{x}$. In density estimation $K(\mathbf{y})$ is known as the kernel function. Usually, the kernel function decreases monotonically, weighting photons near $\mathbf{x}$ higher than those farther away. In this way the kernel function reduce bias where the change in density is significant.

In his PhD thesis (Jensen, 1996) Jensen presents the *cone filter*. This filter is used to reduce bias, such that edges and structure in the illumination are less blurred. As a kernel in the general radiance estimate the cone filter has the following form

$$K(\mathbf{y}) = \begin{cases} K(\mathbf{y}) = \frac{1 - \frac{\sqrt{|\mathbf{y}|}}{k}}{(1 - \frac{2}{3k})\pi} & \text{if } \sqrt{|\mathbf{y}|} < 1, \\ 0 & \text{otherwise,} \end{cases} \tag{3}$$

where $k \geq 1$ is a constant which controls the steepness of the filter slope.

Another useful kernel is the Epanechnikov kernel. The Epanechnikov kernel is known from statistics for its bias reducing properties and it is furthermore popular because it is computationally inexpensive. In computer graphics, Walter has employed it with good results in (Walter, 1998). In 2D the Epanechnikov kernel is given by

$$K(\mathbf{y}) = \begin{cases} \frac{2}{\pi}(1 - \mathbf{y}) \text{ if } \mathbf{y} < 1, \\ 0 \qquad \text{otherwise.} \end{cases} \tag{4}$$

In this paper we use the Epanechnikov kernel to examine our proposed method.

2.2 Bias Reduction

Bias reduction is a well examined subject, when concerned with density estimation both within the field of statistics and the field of computer graphics. Besides filtering, numerous methods addressing the issue has been presented.

The first method for reducing bias in photon mapping was suggested by Jensen (Jensen and Christensen, 1995). The method is called *differential checking* and it reduces bias by making sure that the support radius of the radiance estimate does not cross boundaries of distinct lighting features. This is done by expanding the support radius ensuring that the estimate does not increase or decrease, when more photons are included in the estimate.

Myszkowsky *et al.* (Myszkowski, 1997) suggested to solve the problem in much the same way as Jensen did with differential checking, however, they made the method easier to control and more robust with respect to noise. Myszkowsky *et al.* increase the support radius iteratively estimating the radiance in each step. If new estimates differ more from previous than what can be contributed variance, the iteration stops as the difference is then assumed to be caused by bias. More recently Schregle (Schregle, 2003) followed-up their work using the same strategy but optimizing speed and usability. Speed is optimized by using a binary search for the optimal support radius. This search starts in a range between a maximum and a minimum user-defined support radius. The range is split up, and the candidate, whose error is most likely to be caused by variance and not bias, is searched.

Shirley *et al.* (Shirley et al., 1995) introduced an algorithm for estimating global illumination. Like photon mapping this algorithm uses density estimation to approximate the illumination from particles generated during a Monte Carlo-based particle tracing step. However, unlike photon mapping the algorithm is gemoetry-dependent - the illumination is tied to the geometry. They called the algorithm *the density estimation framework* and they refined it in a series of papers.

The first edition of their framework did not try to control bias. In (Walter et al., 1997) they extended the framework to handle bias near polygonal boundaries. This was done by converting the density estimation problem into one of regression. In this way they could use common regression techniques[1] to eliminate boundary bias.

Later Walter in his PhD thesis (Walter, 1998), reduced bias by controlling the support radius of the estimate using statistics to recognize noise from bias. Benefiting from the

---

[1] Specifically they used locally-weighted polynomial least-squares regression to eliminate boundary bias.

field of human perception he used a measure for controlling the support radius such that noise in the estimate was imperceptible to the human eye.

Walter recognized that if bias was to be significantly reduced, using his method, perceptual noise had to be accepted in the vicinity of prominent edges and other strong lighting features. This is a common problem which also affects differential checking and both Schregle's and Myszkowsky's method. Hence, in the proximity of strong features such as the edges of a caustic the support radius stops expanding and the foundation on which the estimate is made is supported by few photons. This means that when estimates are made close to edges the support is limited and noise may occur.

In *diffusion based photon mapping* we employ the concept of nonlinear anisotropic diffusion in the radiance estimate of photon mapping. Nonlinear anisotropic diffusion is a well examined and popular technique within the field of image analysis. It is a filtering technique that adapts its smoothing according to the image structure. This means that it smoothes along edges and not across. It is known to be robust and effective (Weickert, 1998). To our knowledge the technique has not been employed in connection with photon mapping.

In contrast to Myszkowsky, Schregle and Walter's approach our method will smooth along edges and structures, it follows that its support will not be limited in the proximity of these.

3   Anisotropic Filtering in Photon Mapping

To be able to use anisotropic filtering in photon mapping, we in some way have to be able describe the structure of the photon map, to get some guidance as how to adapt the filtering. It follows that it is necessary to modify the radiance estimate such that the kernel adapts according to the structure description and that we, furthermore, need to normalize this modified radiance estimate in order to preserve energy when the kernel changes shape.

3.1   Structure Description

The gradient of the illumination function denotes the orientation in which the illumination intensity changes and therefore describes the first order structure of the illumination. This information will be used to steer the filtering.

As the illumination function is estimated in the radiance estimate, the differentiated radiance estimate approximates the gradient of the photon map.

To differentiate the radiance estimate we combine the generalized radiance estimate from Equation 2, with a suitable kernel function. Furthermore, it is convenient to simplify the radiance estimate by assuming that all surfaces hit by photons are ideal diffuse reflectors. This means that the BRDF, f_r, is constant regardless of the incoming and outgoing direction of light. In this way the BRDF does not need to be differentiated as it does not depend on the position, x, which is the variable in respect to which we differentiate.

This of course is a radical assumption as photons can be affected much by the type of surfaces they encounter. However, photons are only stored on diffuse surfaces, so the surfaces involved in the radiance estimate are most likely diffuse and need therefore not differ much from an ideal diffuse surface. Furthermore if we were to differentiate the BRDF then our algorithm would not be able to handle arbitrary BRDFs as we would have to know the BRDF in order to do so. In effect we would not retain the beneficial qualities of photon mapping. Another solution would of course be to do reverse engineering, to numerically estimate the BRDF in question, however, this approach is both cumbersome and computationally expensive.

Additionally, we have to make a constraint on the generalized radiance estimate. The estimate should use a fixed support radius for $r(\mathbf{x})$ such that the radius is independent of $\mathbf{x}$. Though this effectively reduces the radiance estimate to a common multivariate kernel estimator - rather than a k'th nearest neighbor estimator - this is not a severe constraint. The advantage of the k'th nearest neighbor search is its ability to reduce bias. This ability is important in the radiance estimate, however, when estimating the gradient, smoothing is an advantage as the gradient is perceptible to noise.

Combining a simplified version of the generalized radiance estimate with the two-dimensional Epanechnikov kernel we get

$$\widehat{L}_r(\mathbf{x}, \boldsymbol{\omega}) =$$
$$\frac{2f_r}{\pi r^2} \sum_{i=1}^{k} \left(1 - \frac{(\mathbf{x} - \mathbf{x}_i)^T (\mathbf{x} - \mathbf{x}_i)}{r^2} \right) \Phi_i, \tag{5}$$

This equation can be differentiated giving us the gradient function of the estimated illumination function. Differentiating Equation 5 with respect to the j'th component of $\mathbf{x}$ gives the partial derivative

$$\frac{\partial \widehat{L}_r(\mathbf{x}, \boldsymbol{\omega})}{\partial x_j} = \frac{4f_r}{\pi r^2} \sum_{i=1}^{k} -\frac{x_j - x_{ij}}{r^2} \Phi_i. \tag{6}$$

As seen from Figure 2, the gradient of the photon map is a plausible structure descriptor. Figure 2a is a distribution of photons and Figure 2b is a gradient field of the distribution. The gradient vectors are calculated using the photons nearest the center of each quadrant

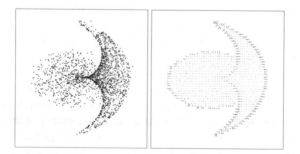

Fig. 2. [a b] a) Cardioid shaped photon distribution created by light reflection within a metal ring, b) gradient field of the photon distribution in a)

in the grid of the field. The gradient vectors along the edges of the distribution are those with greatest magnitude and the vectors are as expected perpendicular to edges and structures.

We denote the gradient of the photon map $\nabla\mathbf{M}$, where $\mathbf{M}$ is the photon map.

A more advanced way is to describe the first order structure is with the *structure tensor*. The structure tensor was introduced to diffusion filtering by Weickert (Weickert, 1995). The advantage of the structure tensor is that even though it does not contain more information than the gradient descriptor, it is, unlike the gradient, possible to smooth it without losing important structure information. Being able to smooth the structure descriptor makes the orientation information less perceptible to noise.

The structure tensor is the tensor product of the gradient. In three dimensions it is given by

$$\nabla\mathbf{M} \otimes \nabla\mathbf{M} =$$
$$\begin{pmatrix} M_x^2 & M_x M_y & M_x M_z \\ M_x M_y & M_y^2 & M_y M_z \\ M_x M_z & M_y M_z & M_z^2 \end{pmatrix}. \tag{7}$$

In diffusion based photon mapping we use the structure tensor to describe the structure of the photon map.

3.2 Diffusion Tensor

In diffusion filtering the filtering is controlled by a symmetric positive semidefinite matrix called the diffusion tensor (Weickert, 1998). This matrix can be constructed using information derived from a structure descriptor. One possible construction is for edge enhancing which will be apply in this paper to preserve the finer structures of the illumination.

For edge enhancing, smoothing should occur parallel to the edges not across them. The orientation of the local edge structure is derived from the structure tensor. The primary eigenvector of the structure tensor is simply the gradient which is perpendicular to the local edge orientation. The direction parallel to edges can be calculated as the cross-product of the surface normal and the vector representing the direction parallel to the structure. This will be the main direction of diffusion.

The eigenvectors and eigenvalues of the diffusion tensor describe respectively the main directions of diffusion and the amount of diffusion in the corresponding direction. Hence by constructing the diffusion tensor from the primary eigenvector of the structure tensor diffusion can be steered to enhance the edges.

The gradient of the illumination function (derived from the structure tensor) is only in the tangent plane to the surface if the surface is locally flat. Since the photon energy should stay on the surface we must insure that the main diffusion direction is the tangent plane.

Consequently, the diffusion directions are constructed in the following way.

The primary eigenvector of the structure tensor is projected to the plane perpendicular to the surface normal. This is our second diffusion direction X_2. The third diffusion direction is the surface normal X_3 and the primary diffusion direction is the cross product of the second and third diffusion direction X_1. All vectors should be normalized.

The diffusion tensor is constructed as

$$\mathbf{D} = \mathbf{X} \ \mathrm{diag}(\lambda_1, \lambda_2, \lambda_3) \ \mathbf{X}^T, \tag{8}$$

where $\mathbf{X}$ is $[\mathbf{X_1}\mathbf{X_2}\mathbf{X_3}]$ and $\mathrm{diag}(\cdot)$ is the diagonal matrix containing the eigenvalues of $\mathbf{D}$ along the diagonal.

It remains to determine the amount of diffusion. That is the eigenvalues, λ:

$$\lambda_1 = 1,$$
$$\lambda_2 = \frac{1}{1+\left(\frac{\mu_1}{K}\right)^{1+\alpha}}, \quad \alpha > 0, \tag{9}$$
$$\lambda_3 = 0.1,$$

where the secondary eigenvalue, λ_2, is estimated using a function called the *diffusivity function*, introduced to diffusion filtering by Perona and Mallik (Perona and Malik, 1990). The diffusivity coefficient, K, decides when the function starts to monotonically decrease and α the steepness of the decline. In practice what it means is, that K is the threshold deciding what value of the primary eigenvalue of the structure tensor, μ_1, is considered an edge and what is considered noise, and α controls the smoothness of transition.

We suggest that the tertiary eigenvalue, λ_3 should be set to 0.1. The reason why the tertiary vector should have such a low eigenvalue is that it limits certain forms of bias. It is comparable to using a disc instead of a sphere to collect photons; a techniques to reduce bias in corners (Jensen, 2001).

We have now constructed a diffusion tensor which favors diffusion parallel to structures while limiting diffusion perpendicular to structures. We will utilize this tensor such that it controls the filtering of the photon map.

3.3 The Diffusion Based Radiance Estimate

The next step is to use the diffusion tensor to shape the kernel of the radiance estimate such that it smoothes along structures and edges and not across. To do this we have to shape our kernel in some way.

If we take a look at the multivariate kernel density estimator on which the radiance estimate is based,

$$\widehat{f}(\mathbf{x}) =$$
$$\frac{1}{nh^d} \sum_{i=1}^{n} K\left(\frac{(\mathbf{x} - \mathbf{x}_i)^T (\mathbf{x} - \mathbf{x}_i)}{h^2}\right), \tag{10}$$

it is important to note that the kernel is uniform insofar that only a single parameter, h is used. Data points, $\mathbf{x}_i$, are scaled equally according to the bandwidth, h, and their distance to the center, $\mathbf{x}$. Smoothing occurs equally in all directions.

Now considering a simple two dimensional normal distribution:

$$f(\mathbf{x}) =$$
$$\frac{1}{2\pi\sigma_1\sigma_2} \exp\left(-\frac{(x_1 - \mu_1)^2}{\sqrt{2}\sigma_1} - \frac{(x_2 - \mu_2)^2}{\sqrt{2}\sigma_2}\right), \tag{11}$$

where σ_1 and σ_2 are the standard deviations with respect to the axes and μ is the center of the distribution. Here we have a Gaussian kernel whose shape is specified by the two parameters for the standard deviation. Unfortunately, this equation only gives control in two directions.

However, generalizing the equation to d dimensions, we can use an inversed $d \times d$ covariance matrix, Σ^{-1}, to shape the normal distribution:

$$
f(\mathbf{x}) = \frac{1}{(2\pi)^{d/2}\sqrt{\det \Sigma}} \cdot
\cdot \exp\left(-\frac{(\mathbf{x}-\mu)^T \Sigma^{-1}(\mathbf{x}-\mu)}{2} \right).
\tag{12}
$$

In two dimensions using a diagonal covariance matrix with the variance values in the diagonal this equation is exactly the same as Equation 11. However, using a matrix we are not limited to control the shape of the Gaussian in only two direction. If we for example had shaped our Gaussian kernel to form an ellipse, we could rotate this kernel by rotating the covariance matrix. The equation will remain normalized as the determinant of a matrix is rotational invariant. So the shape of normal distribution in Equation 12 is controlled by the covariance matrix.

We can use Equation 12 to extend the generalized radiance estimate from Equation 2. To generalize the shape adapting properties we use the Mahalanobis distance from Equation 12 to shape the kernel. The Mahalanobis distance is a statistical distance. It is given by:

$$
d(\mathbf{x}, \mathbf{y}) = (\mathbf{x}-\mathbf{y})^T \Sigma^{-1}(\mathbf{x}-\mathbf{y}).
\tag{13}
$$

As the shape of the kernel should be controlled by the diffusion tensor we use the tensor in place of the covariance matrix. We can reformulate the generalized radiance estimate as:

$$
\widehat{L}_r(\mathbf{x}, \boldsymbol{\omega}) = \frac{1}{r^2\sqrt{\det \mathbf{D}}} \cdot
\cdot \sum_{i=1}^{k} K\left(\frac{(\mathbf{x}-\mathbf{x}_i)^T \mathbf{D}^{-1}(\mathbf{x}-\mathbf{x}_i)}{r^2} \right).
\cdot f_r(\mathbf{x}, \boldsymbol{\omega}_i, \boldsymbol{\omega})\Phi_i.
\tag{14}
$$

We now have a general diffusion based radiance estimate, which filters the photon map adapting the shape of the kernel according to the diffusion tensor. Or to be even more general we have a radiance estimator which estimates the illumination function taking into consideration the structure of the photon map, such that edges and structures are preserved.

3.4   Implementation

Diffusion based photon mapping can be implemented in different ways depending on which structure descriptor is used, however, we propose to use the structure tensor and for this reason we need to estimate it or have it available during the radiance estimate in order to construct the diffusion tensor.

We do this using a preprocessing step that approximates the gradient of the photon map. The preprocessing step occurs between the photon tracing pass and the rendering pass. To approximate the gradient we sample it at all photon positions. The advantage of this procedure is that we can store the local gradient along with the photon and in this way does not need a separate gradient map. Additionally, we know the sampling positions to be located on a surface, as photons are only stored in connection with a surface. This is useful as the gradient is only relevant at surface positions.

During the radiance estimate we calculate the structure tensors at the photon positions near x. In this way we can estimate the local structure tensor as the weighted average of the surrounding structure tensors. Smoothing the structure tensor reduces noise and furthermore gives a broader foundation from which to steer the filtering after.

Having calculated the local structure tensor we construct the diffusion tensor as described in the former section. This then is used in the general diffusion based radiance estimate together with a suitable kernel.

For a more thorough examination of diffusion based photon mapping refer to (Schjøth, 2005).

4   Results

Figure 3 is a rendering of a scene consists of a simple glass torus knot positioned over a plane in space. A spherical light source above the torus knot creates the caustic on the plane.

Figure 3a illustrates the scene visualized employing the k'th nearest neighbor estimate in conjunction with the cone kernel whereas Figure 3b is visualized using diffusion based photon mapping.

The difference in the two images is seen in the caustics. The structure of the caustic in Figure 3b is much more detailed than the caustic in Figure 3a. Fine patterns are visible in the caustic in the image estimate using the diffusion based radiance estimate that are not visible in the image estimated using the cone kernel.

To further test diffusion based photon mapping we have constructed a photon distribution. The constructed distribution is rather simple yet it contains both edges and ridges and circular and rectangular shapes.

4.1   The Cone Kernel

We first test Jensen's cone kernel on the constructed distribution. This is done by first combining the cone kernel from Equation 3, with the general radiance estimate from Equation 2. We then estimate the radiance of the constructed photon distribution a number of times, iteratively expanding the support radius, allowing an increasing amount of photons in each estimation. This is done until the result contains an acceptable low noise level. The result of this procedure is illustrated in Figure 4. It is seen from the illustration that the noise level decreases slowly with respect to the number of photons per estimate. Bias is visible as a clearly identifiable blurring of shape edges. In addition boundary bias is seen along the boundaries of the images. It should be clear that

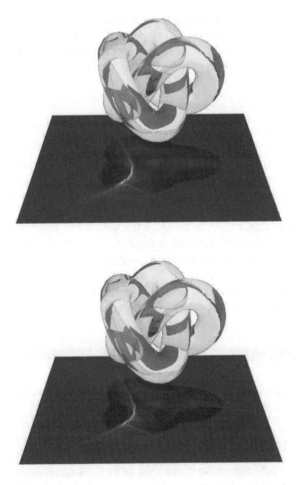

Fig. 3. [^a_b] Rendering of a glass torus positioned above a plane using a) regular photon mapping and b) diffusion based photon mapping

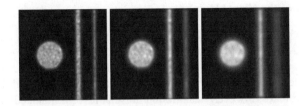

Fig. 4. [a b c] A visualization of a constructed distribution estimated using the cone kernel. a) estimated using the 200 nearest photons, b) estimated using the 400 nearest photons and, c) estimated using the 800 nearest photons.

the bias increases as the noise is reduced. This phenomenon is directly related to the bias vs. variance trade-off accounted earlier. Another thing to notice is how the thin line losses intensity as the number of photons per estimate is increased. This happens because the energy of the line is spread out over a larger area as the smoothing increase.

4.2   The Diffusion Based Radiance Estimate

To test the applicability of the structure tensor as structure descriptor, we use the diffusion based radiance estimate together with the Epanechnikov kernel. In contrast to the cone kernel radiance estimate we will not us the k nearest neighbor method to reduce bias, instead we will use a fixed support radius letting the shape adaption reduce bias.

We first set the support radius low, and then we iteratively increase the support radius until the noise level is acceptable. This is done using a large value of the diffusivity coefficient K from Equation 9. In this way the kernel will stay uniform and will not adapt according to structure. Estimating the radiance with a uniform Epanechnikov kernel using different support radii we find a support radius which reduces noise to an acceptable level.

Using this support radius we test the diffusion based radiance estimate by iteratively decreasing the value of the diffusivity coefficient such that the kernel starts to adapt its shape according to the structure described by the structure tensor. The result of this procedure is illustrated in Figure 5. From the results of the diffusion based radiance estimate we see that edges are enhanced as the diffusivity coefficient is decreasing.

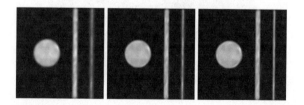

Fig. 5. [a b c] A visualization of a constructed distribution estimated using diffusion based photon mapping. a) estimated using K=0.4, b) estimated using K=0.2 and, c) estimated using K=0.1.

4.3   Summary of the Visual Results

We summarily compare the best results of the two radiance estimation methods. The results were chosen in the attempt to find the estimates with least noise and least bias. Figure 6 depicts the estimates. From the chosen results we see that the diffusion based radiance estimates reduces bias markedly better than the common k'th nearest neighbor radiance estimate. However, background noise is less pronounced in the common radiance estimate.

Another thing to notice is the thinnest line in the constructed distribution. We know that this line has photon distribution as dense as the two other shapes in the distribution. For this reason the thin line should be just as intense as the other shapes. However, as estimates are smoothed using a higher support radius and more photons per estimate, the energy is spread out. Comparing the three results it is seen that the structure based

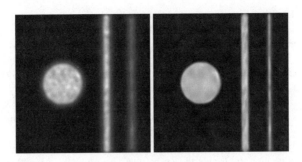

Fig. 6. [a b] A visualization of a constructed distribution estimated using different radiance estimation methods. a) estimated using a uniform cone kernel with 400 photons per estimate and b) estimated using a gradient based shape adapting Gaussian radiance estimate with a diffusivity coefficient of $K = 0.2$.

radiance estimate is most successful in preserving the energy of the thin line as it has almost the same intensity as the other shapes.

Finally, it should be mentioned that it has not been our objective to test the computationally performance diffusion based photon mapping. Despite this we will say a few things about the running time. Considering the estimates of the constructed distribution. The image in Figure 6a was estimated using the cone kernel and 400 photons per estimate. It was computed in 45 seconds. In comparison the computation time for the tensor based radiance estimate, producing Figure 6b, was 1 minute and 3 seconds from which 12 seconds was used estimating the gradient map.

5   Conclusion

In this paper we have proposed a novel method for enhancing edges and structures of caustics in particle tracing algorithms. Our method is called diffusion based photon mapping.

The method is based on nonlinear anisotropic diffusion which is a filtering algorithm known from image processing. We have implemented it in photon mapping and we have shown that our algorithm is markedly better than regular photon mapping when simulating caustics. Specifically, does diffusion based photon mapping preserve edges and other prominent features of the illumination where as regular photon mapping blur these features.

References

Jensen, H. W.: The Photon Map in Global Illumination. PhD thesis, Technical University of Denmark, Lyngby (1996)

Jensen, H.W.: Realistic image synthesis using photon mapping. A.K. Peters, Ltd, Natick, MA, USA (2001)

Jensen, H.W., Christensen, N.J.: Photon maps in bidirectional monte carlo ray tracing of complex objects. Computers & Graphics 19(2), 215–224 (1995)

Myszkowski, K.: Lighting reconstruction using fast and adaptive density estimation techniques. In: Proceedings of the Eurographics Workshop on Rendering Techniques '97, pp. 251–262. Springer, London, UK (1997)

Perona, P., Malik, J.: Scale-space and edge detection using anisotropic diffusion. IEEE Transactions on Pattern Analysis and Machine Intelligence, PAMI 12(7), 629–639 (1990)

Schjøth, L,: Diffusion based photon mapping. Technical report, IT University of Copenhagen, Copenhagen, Denmark (2005)

Schregle, R.: Bias compensation for photon maps. Computer Graphics Forum 22(4), 729–742 (2003)

Shirley, P., Wade, B., Hubbard, P.M., Zareski, D., Walter, B., Greenberg, D.P.: Global illumination via density-estimation. In: Rendering Techniques '95, pp. 219–230 (1995)

Walter, B.: Density estimation techniques for global illumination. PhD thesis, Cornell University (1998)

Walter, B., Hubbard, P.M., Shirley, P., Greenberg, D.P.: Global illumination using local linear density estimation. ACM Trans. Graph. 16(3), 217–259 (1997)

Weickert, J.: Multiscale texture enhancement. In: Hlaváč, V., Šára, R. (eds.) CAIP 1995. LNCS, vol. 970, pp. 230–237. Springer, Heidelberg (1995)

Weickert, J.: Anisotropic Diffusion in Image Processing. B.G. Teubner, Stuttgart, Germany (1998)

An Incremental Weighted Least Squares Approach to Surface Lights Fields

Greg Coombe and Anselmo Lastra

Department of Computer Science, University of North Carolina at Chapel Hill
coombe@cs.unc.edu, lastra@cs.unc.edu

Abstract. An Image-Based Rendering (IBR) approach to appearance modelling enables the capture of a wide variety of real physical surfaces with complex reflectance behaviour. The challenges with this approach are handling the large amount of data, rendering the data efficiently, and previewing the model as it is being constructed. In this paper, we introduce the Incremental Weighted Least Squares approach to the representation and rendering of spatially and directionally varying illumination. Each surface patch consists of a set of Weighted Least Squares (WLS) node centers, which are low-degree polynomial representations of the anisotropic exitant radiance. During rendering, the representations are combined in a non-linear fashion to generate a full reconstruction of the exitant radiance. The rendering algorithm is fast, efficient, and implemented entirely on the GPU. The construction algorithm is incremental, which means that images are processed as they arrive instead of in the traditional batch fashion. This human-in-the-loop process enables the user to preview the model as it is being constructed and to adapt to over-sampling and under-sampling of the surface appearance.

Keywords: Image-based rendering, surface light fields, appearance modelling, least-squares approximation.

1 Introduction

A Surface Light Field (SLF) (Wood, 2000) is a parameterized representation of the exitant radiance from the surface of a geometric model under a fixed illumination. SLFs can model arbitrarily complex surface appearance and can be rendered at real-time rates. The challenge with SLFs is to find a compact representation of surface appearance that maintains the high visual fidelity and rendering rates.

One approach to this problem is to treat it as a data approximation problem. The exitant radiance at each surface patch is represented as a function, and the input images are treated as samples from this function. Since there are no restrictions imposed on the geometry of the object or on the camera locations, the input samples are located at arbitrary positions. This is an example of a problem known as scattered data approximation (Wendland, 2005).

(Coombe, 2005) introduced the notion of *casual capture* of a SLF by moving a camera around an object, tracking the camera pose using fiducials, and incrementally updating the SLF. This enabled the operator to see the result, add views where

J. Braz et al. (Eds.): VISAPP and GRAPP 2006, CCIS 4, pp. 123–135, 2007.

Fig. 1. A model of a heart captured with our system

needed, and stop when he or she was satisfied with the result. However, one difficulty with the matrix factorization approach is that it requires fully resampled matrices, and so can be sensitive to missing data from occlusions and meshing errors.

In this paper we present Incremental Weighted Least Squares (IWLS), a fast, efficient, and incremental algorithm for the representation and rendering of surface light fields. It is a non-linear polynomial approximation for multi-variate data, based on the idea of Least Squares polynomial approximation, which fits scattered data samples to a set of polynomial basis functions. WLS is similar to piecewise polynomial approximation and splines, except that the reconstruction is non-linear.

Weighted Least Squares (Wendland, 2005) generalizes Least Squares by computing a set of approximations with associated weighting terms. These weighting terms can be either noise (in statistics) or distance (in graphics and computational geometry (Ohtake, 2003)). If we use distance, then WLS becomes a local approximation method. This local approximation is extended to a global approximation by computing the Partition of Unity (Ohtake, 2003; Shepard, 1968).

This paper offers the following contributions:

- We apply existing mathematical tools such as the Weighted Least Squares approximation technique by casting surface light fields as a scattered data approximation problem.
- We introduce Incremental Weighted Least Squares, an incremental approach to surface light field construction that enables interactive previewing of the reconstruction.
- Using the IWLS representation, we develop a real-time surface light field rendering algorithm, implemented on the GPU, which provides direct feedback about the quality of the surface light field.

The paper proceeds as follows. We first discuss previous approaches to light field capture and representation, including the difference between batch processing and incremental processing. In Section 3 we discuss Least Squares fitting and the generalization to Weighted Least Squares. We then introduce IWLS and describe how the WLS representation can be incrementally constructed and rendered. In Section 4 we discuss implementation details of the capture and rendering system, and then present results and conclusion.

2 Background

A good overview of the state of the art in material modelling by image acquisition is provided by the recent Siggraph course on Material Modelling (Ramamoorthi, 2002), and the Eurographics State of the Art Report on Acquisition, Synthesis and Rendering of Bidirectional Texture Functions (Mueller, 2004). The choice of representation of this captured data is crucial for interactive rendering. (Lensch, 2001) uses the Lafortune representation (Lafortune, 1997) and clustered samples from acquired data in order to create spatially-varying BRDFs. (Gardner, 2003) and (McAllister, 2002) describe BDRF capture devices and methods for BRDF representation.

Data-driven representation can be divided into parametric and non-parametric approaches. A parametric approach assumes a particular model for the BRDF (such as the Lafortune model (Lafortune, 1997) used by (McAllister, 2002)). These models have difficulty representing the wide variety of objects that occur in real scenes, as observed by Hawkins in (Yu, 1999).

A non-parametric approach uses the captured data to estimate the underlying function and makes few assumptions about the behavior of the reflectance. Thus non-parametric models are capable of representing a larger class of surfaces, which accounts for their recent popularity in image-based modelling (Chen, 2002; Furukawa, 2002; Matuzik, 2003; Zickler, 2005). Our approach uses a non-parametric model to represent surface light fields.

2.1 Surface Light Fields

Surface light fields (Wood, 2000) parameterize the exitant radiance directly on the surface of the model. This results in a compact representation that enables the capture and display of complex view-dependent illumination of real-world objects. This category of approaches includes view-dependent texture mapping (Debevec, 1996; Debevec, 1998; Buehler, 2001), which can be implemented with very sparse and scattered samples, as well as regular parameterizations of radiance (Levoy, 1996; Gortler, 1996). (Wood, 2000) use a generalization of Vector Quantization and Principal Component Analysis to compress surface light fields, and introduce a 2-pass rendering algorithm that displays compressed light fields at interactive rates. These functions can be constructed by using Principal Component Analysis (Nishino, 1999; Chen, 2002; Coombe, 2005) or non-linear optimization (Hillesland 2003). The function parameters can be stored in texture maps and rendered in real-time (Chen, 2002).

These approaches can suffer from difficulties stemming from the inherent irregularity of the data. If they require a complete and regularly sampled set of data, an expensive resampling step is needed. To avoid these problems, we treat surface light field reconstruction as a *scattered data approximation* problem (Wendland, 2005). Scattered data approximation can be used to construct representations of data values given samples at arbitrary locations (such as camera locations on a hemisphere or surface locations on a model).

A common scattered data approximation technique uses Radial Basis Functions (RBFs) (Moody, 1989). (Zickler, 2005) demonstrated the ability of RBFs to accurately reconstruct sparse reflectance data. Constructing this approximation requires a global technique, since every point in the reconstruction influences every other point. This is a disadvantage for an incremental algorithm, as every value must be recomputed when a new sample arrives. It is also difficult to render efficiently on graphics hardware, since many RBF algorithms rely on Fast Multipole Methods to reduce the size of the computation (Carr, 2001). We would like a method that has the scattered data representation ability of RBFs, but without the complex updating and reconstruction.

2.2 Incremental Methods

Most of the research in image-based modelling has focused on *batch-processing* systems. These systems process the set of images over multiple passes, and consequently require that the entire set of images be available. Incorporating additional images into these models requires recomputing the model from scratch.

Formulating surface light field construction as an *incremental processing* approach avoids these problems by incrementally constructing the model as the images become available. (Matusik, 2004) used this approach with a kd-tree basis system to progressively refine a radiance model from a fixed viewpoint. (Schirmacher, 1999) adaptively meshed the *uv* and *st* planes of a light field, and used an error metric along the triangle edges to determine the locations of new camera positions. (Coombe, 2005) used an incremental PCA algorithm to construct surface light fields in an online fashion, but required resampling the data for matrix computation.

3 Incremental Weighted Least Squares

IWLS is a technique to incrementally calculate an approximation to the exitant radiance at each surface patch given a set of input images. The process is divided into two parts: constructing the WLS representation from the incoming images, and rendering the result. In this section we review Least Squares fitting and the generalization to Weighted Least Squares. We then describe how these WLS representations can be incrementally constructed and rendered.

3.1 Least Squares Approximation

Least Squares methods are a set of linear approximation techniques for scattered data. Given a set of N scalar samples $f_i \in \Re$ at points $x_i \in \Re^d$, we want a globally-defined function $f(x)$ that best approximates the samples. The goal is to generate this function $f(x)$ such that the distance between the scalar data values f_i and the function evaluated at the data points $f(x_i)$ is as small as possible. This is written as

$$\min \sum_i \left| f(x_i) - f_i \right|$$

(Note: this discussion follows the notation of (Nealen, 2004)). Typically, $f(x)$ is a polynomial of degree m in d spatial dimensions. The coefficients of the polynomial are determined by minimizing this sum. Thus $f(x)$ can be written as

$$f(x) = b(x)^T c$$

where $b(x) = [b_1(x)\ b_2(x)\ ...\ b_k(x)\ ]^T$ is the polynomial basis vector and $c = [c_1\ c_2\ ...\ c_k\ ]$ is the unknown coefficient vector. A set of basis functions $b(t)$ is chosen based on the properties of the data and the dimensionality.

To determine the coefficient vector c, the minimization problem is solved by setting the partial derivatives to zero and solving the resulting system of linear equations. After rearranging the terms, the solution is:

$$c = \sum_i \left[b(x_i) b(x_i)^T \right]^{-1} \sum_i b(x_i) f_i$$

For small matrices, this can be inverted directly. For larger matrices, there are several common matrix inversion packages such as BLAS (Remington, 1996) and TGT. The size of the matrix to be inverted depends upon the dimensionality d of the data and the degree k of the polynomial basis.

3.2 Weighted Least Squares

One of the limitations of Least Squares fitting is that the solution encompasses the entire domain. This global complexity makes it difficult to handle large data sets or data sets with local high frequencies. We would prefer a method that considers samples that are nearby as more important than samples that are far away. This can be accomplished by adding a distance-weighting term $\Theta(d)$ to the Least Squares minimization. We are now trying to minimize the function

$$\min \sum_i \Theta(|x - x_i|) |f(x_i) - f_i|$$

A common choice for the distance-weighting basis function $\Theta(d)$ is the Wendland function (Wendland, 1995)

$$\Theta(d) = (1 - d/h)^4 (4d/h + 1)$$

which is 1.0 at $d = 0$, and falls off to zero at the edges of the support radius h. This function has compact support, so each sample only affects a small neighborhood. There are many other weighting functions that could be used, such as multiquadrics and thin-plate splines, but some functions have infinite support and thus must be solved globally.

Instead of evaluating a single global approximation for all of the data samples, we create a set of local approximations. These approximations are associated with a set of points $\bar{x}$, which are known as *centers*. At each of these centers, a low-degree polynomial approximation is computed using the distance-weighted samples x_i in the local neighborhood.

$$c(\bar{x}) = \sum_i \left[\Theta(|\bar{x} - x_i|) b(x_i) b(x_i)^T \right]^{-1} \sum_i \Theta(|\bar{x} - x_i|) b(x_i) f_i$$

We now have a set of local approximations at each center. During the reconstruction step, we need to combine these local approximations to form a global approximation. Since this global function is a weighted combination of the basis functions, it has the same continuity properties.

The first step is to determine the m nearby local approximations that overlap this point and combine them using a weight based on distance. However, the functions cannot just be added together, since the weights may not sum to 1.0. To get the proper weighting of the local approximations, we use a technique known as the *Partition of Unity* (Shepard, 1968), which allows us to extend the local approximations to cover the entire domain. A new set of weights $\Phi(j)$ are computed by considering all of the m local approximations that overlap this point

$$\Phi_j(x) = \frac{\Theta_j(x)}{\sum\limits_{i=1}^{m} \Theta_i(x)}$$

The global approximation of this function is computed by summing the weighted local approximations.

$$f(x) = \sum_{j=1}^{m} \Phi_j(x) b(x)^T c(\bar{x}_j)$$

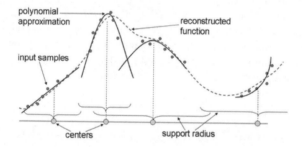

Fig. 2. A diagram of the weighted least squares approach to function representation. Each center constructs a low-degree polynomial approximation based on samples in their neighborhood. These local approximations are then combined to form a global approximation.

The WLS representation allows us to place the centers $\bar{x}$ wherever we like, but the locations are fixed. This is in contrast to the Radial Basis Function method, which optimizes the location of the centers as well as the coefficients. We discuss several strategies for center placement in Section 4.

3.3 Incremental Construction

Surface light field representation can be treated as a batch process by first collecting all of the images and then constructing and rendering the WLS representations. The advantage of batch processing is that all of the sample points are known at the time of construction, and the support radii and locations of the centers can be globally optimized.

The disadvantage to batch processing is that it provides very little feedback to the user capturing the images. There is often no way to determine if the surface appearance is adequately sampled, and undersampled regions require recomputing the WLS representation. A better approach is to update the representation as it is being constructed, which allows the user to preview the model and adjust the sampling accordingly. In this section we describe two approaches to incrementally update the WLS approximation.

3.3.1 Adaptive Construction

The adaptive construction method starts with all of the centers having the maximum support radius. As new image samples are generated, they are tested against the support radius of a center, and added to that center's neighborhood list. The WLS approximation is computed from the samples in the neighborhood list. As each center's list gets larger, the support radius is decreased, and samples are discarded if they no longer fall within the neighborhood. In our implementation, this involves several user-defined parameters; we typically decrease the radius by 25% if the number of samples is more than 4 times the rank of the approximation.

3.3.2 Hierarchical Construction

The adaptive approach has the disadvantage that a single sample can cause the recomputation of numerous WLS coefficients, particularly in the initial phases when the support radii are large. The hierarchical approach avoids this computation by subdividing the domain as a quadtree. Initially, the representation consists of a single WLS center with a large support radius. When a new image sample arrives, the hierarchy is traversed until a leaf node is reached. The sample is deposited at the leaf node and the WLS is recalculated. If the number of samples in a leaf node is larger than a pre-determined threshold, the leaf node is split into four children. Each child decreases its support radius and recomputes its WLS coefficients. Note that a sample can be a member of more than one leaf node, since the support radii of the nodes can overlap. There are several user-defined parameters; we have had good results splitting the nodes if the number of samples exceeds 4 times the rank of the approximation, and decreasing the area of the neighborhood by half (decreasing the radius by $1/\sqrt{2}$).

3.4 Rendering

Weighted Least Squares conforms well to the stream-processing model of modern graphics hardware. Each surface patch is independent and is calculated using a series of simple mathematical operations (polynomial reconstruction and Partition of Unity). More importantly, the local support of the WLS centers means that reconstruction only requires a few texture lookups in a small neighborhood.

After the centers and the WLS coefficients have been computed (using either the adaptive or the hierarchical technique), they are stored in a texture map for each surface patch. The coefficients are laid out in a grid pattern for fast access by the texture hardware. The adaptive centers are typically arranged in a grid pattern, but the hierarchical pattern must be fully expanded before it is saved to texture. This is done by copying down any leaf nodes that are not fully expanded.

During rendering, the viewpoint is projected onto the UV basis of the surface patch and used to index into the coefficient texture. The samples from the neighborhood around this element comprise the set of overlapping WLS approximations. Texture lookups are used to collect the neighboring centers and their coefficients. These polynomial coefficients are evaluated and weighted by their distance. The weights are computed using the Partition of Unity, which generates the final color for this surface patch.

Once the color at each patch has been determined, we need a method to interpolate the colors across the model to smoothly blend between surface patches. One approach is to simply interpolate the colors directly. However this approach is incorrect, as it interpolates the values after the Partition of Unity normalization step. This generates artifacts similar to those encountered when linearly interpolating normal vectors across a triangle. The correct approach is to perform the normalization after the interpolation. For our system, we can accomplish this by interpolating the weights and colors independently, and using a fragment program to normalize the weights at every pixel.

4 Implementation

The data structure and camera capture are managed on the CPU and function reconstruction and rendering is handled by the GPU. In this section we discuss how input images are converted into surface patch samples, which involves camera capture, pose estimation, and visibility computation. A diagram of the system is shown in Figure 3.

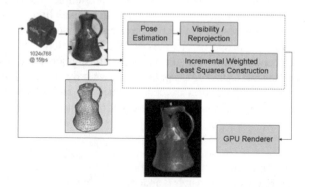

Fig. 3. A diagram of the surface lightfield capture and rendering system. Images are captured using a handheld video camera, and passed to the system. Using the mesh information, visibility is computed and the surface locations are back-projected into the image. Each of these samples are incorporated into the Incremental Weighted Least Squares approximation, and sent to the card for rendering. The user can use this direct feedback to decide where to move the video camera to capture more images.

In order to project the image samples onto the geometry, the camera's position and orientation must be known. Our system uses a tracked video camera to capture images of the object. The camera was calibrated with Bouguet's Camera Calibration Toolbox, and images are rectified using Intel's Open Source Computer Vision Library. To determine the pose of the camera with respect to the object, a stage was created with fiducials along the border. The 3D positions of the fiducials are located in the camera's coordinate system in real-time using the ARToolkit Library. This library uses image segmentation, corner extraction, and matching techniques for tracking the fiducials. This system is similar to the system presented in our earlier paper (Coombe, 2005).

Table 1. A description of the models and construction methods used for timing data

Model	# Vertices	Construction	# Centers
Bust A	31K	Hierarchical	16
Heart A	4K	Hierarchical	16
Pitcher A	29K	Hierarchical	16
Bust B	14K	Hierarchical	16
Bust C	14K	Hierarchical	64
Heart B	4K	Adaptive	16

Once the camera pose has been estimated, the visibility is computed by rendering the mesh from the point of view of the camera. The depth buffer is read back to the CPU, where it is compared against the projected depth of each vertex. If the vertex passes the depth test, it samples a color from the projected position on the input image.

For rendering efficiency, the coefficient textures are packed into a larger texture map. Each texture stores the coefficients for one term of the polynomial basis. For all of the examples in this paper we use a 3-term polynomial basis. We found that higher-order polynomial bases were susceptible to *over-fitting* (Geman, 1992), which occurs when the number of input samples is small enough that the polynomial bases try to fit minor errors in the data, rather than the overall shape. The consequence is that reconstruction is very accurate at sample positions, but oscillates wildly around the edges. Using a lower-degree polynomial avoids this problem.

The positions of the surface patches, which are determined *a priori*, are represented as either vertices or texels. For most of the models we use vertices, and the renderer uses a vertex texture fetch to associate surface patches with vertices.

4.1 Results

We have implemented this system on a 3.2 GHz Intel Pentium processor with an Nvidia GeForce 7800. A graph of timing results from several different models is shown in Figure 4, and the parameters used for these timings are shown in Table 1. The rendering algorithm is compact, fast, and efficient and can render all of the models in this paper at over 200 frames per second. An image generated with our system is shown in Figure 1, and a side-by-side comparison is shown in Figure 5.

The hierarchical construction method is much faster than the adaptive construction method due to the fact that the adaptive construction method can potentially cause the recomputation of a number of coefficients. For the 4K-vertex heart model, the

Fig. 4. Timing results (in seconds per image) for the IWLS construction. We measured three quantities; the time to compute the visibility and reproject the vertices into the image, the Least Squares fitting times, and the time to transfer the computed results to the graphics card for rendering.

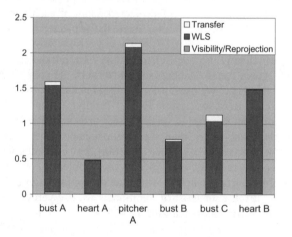

Fig. 5. A side-by-side comparison of the WLS reconstruction with an input image that was not included in the training set

adaptive construction generated about 5.1 Least Squares fitting computations per image, while the hierarchical construction only generated about 1.7. As this is the most time-consuming aspect of the process, reducing the number of Least Squares fits is important to achieve good performance. This performance gain enables higher resolution reconstruction; note that the bust model with 64 centers is only 1.4 times slower than the 16 center version, even though it has 4 times as many coefficients. However, the increased number of coefficients is reflected in the data transfer time, which is close to 4 times longer.

A potential issue with the hierarchical construction is that it could introduce error. We conducted an experiment to compare the quality of the reconstruction with a reference batch process which has global knowledge. The results are shown in Figure 6.

We have tried several center placement strategies; a uniform grid over projected hemisphere directions, a uniform disk using Shirley's concentric mapping (Shirley, 1997), and jittered versions of each. A comparison is shown in Table 2. For most of the models in this paper we use the grid method due to its ease of implementation.

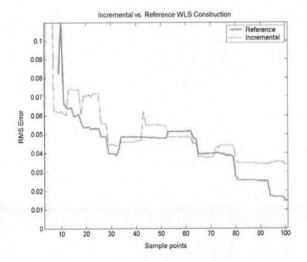

Fig. 6. The reconstruction error of the hierarchical construction versus a batch construction for a single surface patch of the bust model. Each method used only the input samples available, and the error was measured against the full set of samples. The hierarchical algorithm is initially superior to the batch algorithm, and continues to be similar in error behavior while also being much faster to compute.

Table 2. RMS Error values from reconstructing a WLS approximation while varying the center layout. The error was computed with a training set of 64 images and an evaluation set of 74 images. The disk is a slight improvement in terms of error compared to the grid, and it has a large benefit in terms of reducing the variability of the error.

Layout	Mean RMS Error	StD RMS Error
Uniform Grid	0.0519	0.0086
Jittered Grid	0.0608	0.0148
Uniform Disk	0.0497	0.0045
Jittered Disk	0.0498	0.0036

5 Conclusion

We have introduced Incremental Weighted Least Squares (IWLS), a fast, efficient, and incremental algorithm for the representation and rendering of surface light fields.

IWLS can be used to render high quality images of surfaces with complex reflectance properties. The incremental construction is useful for visualizing the representation as it is being captured, which can guide the user to collect more images in undersampled regions of the model and minimize redundant capture of sufficiently sampled regions. The rendering algorithm, which is implemented on the GPU for real-time performance, provides immediate feedback to the user.

5.1 Future Work

There are several improvements to our system that we are interested in pursuing. Currently, the surface patches are computed independently and do not share information. This choice was made in order to allow the algorithm to reconstruct as broad a class of surfaces as possible. However, many surfaces have slowly-varying reflectance properties which could be exploited for computational gain. Each surface patch could collect WLS coefficients from itself as well as its neighbors. This would involve adjusting the distance weighting to reflect the distance along the surface of the model. We could also use an approach similar to Zickler (Zickler, 2005) to share reflectance values across a surface.

This system was designed to construct and render surface light fields, which allow arbitrary viewpoints but a fixed lighting. We are interested in applying IWLS to the problem of reconstructing arbitrary lighting, but from a static viewpoint. This is similar to Polynomial Texture Mapping (Malzbender, 2001), which used Least Squares fitting and custom hardware to render images with varying lighting.

Mathematically, the Weighted Least Squares approach generalizes easily to multiple dimensions by simply modifying the polynomial basis. However, the substantial increase in data would require re-thinking the construction and rendering components of our system.

References

Buehler, C., et al.: Unstructured Lumigraph Rendering. In: SIGGRAPH 2001 (2001)

Carr, J.C., et al.: Reconstruction and Representation of 3D Objects with Radial Basis Functions. In: SIGGRAPH (2001)

Chen, W.-C., et al.: Light Field Mapping: Efficient Representation and Hardware Rendering of Surface Light Fields. In: SIGGRAPH (2002)

Coombe, G., et al.: Online Construction of Surface Light Fields. In: Eurographics Symposium on Rendering (2005)

Debevec, P.E., Taylor, C.J., Malik, J.: Modeling and Rendering Architecture from Photographs: A Hybrid Geometry- and Image-Based Approach. In: SIGGRAPH 1996 (1996)

Debevec, P.E., Yu, Y., Borshukov, G.D.: Efficient View-Dependent Image-Based Rendering with Projective Texture-Mapping. In: Eurographics Rendering Workshop, Vienna, Austria (1998)

Furukawa, R., et al.: Appearance based object modeling using texture database: acquisition, compression and rendering. In: Proceedings of the 13th Eurographics workshop on Rendering, pp. 257–266 (2002)

Gardner, A., et al.: Linear Light Source Reflectometry. In: SIGGRAPH 2003 (2003)

Geman, S., Bienenstock, E., Doursat, R.: Neural Networks and the Bias/Variance Dilemma. Neural Computation 4, 1–58 (1992)

Gortler, S.J., et al.: The Lumigraph. In: SIGGRAPH 96 Conference Proceedings, pp. 43–54 (1996)

Hillesland, K., Molinov, S., Grzeszczuk, R.: Nonlinear Optimization Framework for Image-Based Modeling on Programmable Graphics Hardware. In: SIGGRAPH 2003 (2003)

Lafortune, E.P.F., et al.: Non-Linear Approximation of Reflectance Functions. In: SIGGRAPH 97 (1997)

Lensch, H.P.A., et al.: Image-Based Reconstruction of Spatially Varying Materials. In: Eurographics Workshop on Rendering (2001)

Levoy, M., Hanrahan, P.: Light Field Rendering. In: SIGGRAPH 1996 (1996)

Malzbender, T., Gelb, D., Wolters, H.: Polynomial Texture Maps. In: SIGGRAPH 2001 (2001)

Matusik, W., et al.: A Data-Driven Reflectance Model. In: SIGGRAPH (2003)

Matusik, W., Loper, M., Pfister, H.: Progressively-Refined Reflectance Functions from Natural Illumination. In: Eurographics Symposium on Rendering (2004)

McAllister, D.K., Lastra, A.A., Heidrich, W.: Efficient Rendering of Spatial Bi-directional Reflectance Distribution Functions. In: Graphics Hardware 2002, Saarbruecken, Germany (2002)

Moody, J.E., Darken, C.: Fast learning in networks of locally-tuned processing units. Neural Computation 1, 281–294 (1989)

Mueller, G., et al.: Acquisition, Synthesis and Rendering of Bidirectional Texture Functions. In: Eurographics State of the Art Reports (2004)

Nealen, A.: An As-Short-As-Possible Introduction to Least Squares, Weighted Least Squares and Moving Least Squares Methods for Scattered Data Approximation and Interpolation (2004)

Nishino, K., Sato, Y., Ikeuchi, K.: Eigen-Texture Method: Appearance Compression Based on 3D Model. In: Proceedings of CVPR-99 (1999)

Ohtake, Y., et al.: Multi-level Partition of Unity Implicits. In: SIGGRAPH 2003 (2003)

Ramamoorthi, R., Marschner, S.: Acquiring Material Models by Inverse Rendering. In: SIGGRAPH 2002 Course Materials (2002)

Remington, K.A., Pozo, R.: NIST Sparse BLAS User's Guide. National Institute of Standards and Technology (1996)

Schirmacher, H., Heidrich, W., Seidel, H.-P.: Adaptive Acquisition of Lumigraphs from Synthetic Scenes in Computer Graphics Forum (1999)

Shepard, D.: A two-dimensional interpolation function for irregularly-spaced data. In: Proceedings of the 1968 23rd ACM national conference, ACM Press, New York (1968)

Shirley, P., Chiu, K.: A Low Distortion Map Between Disk And Square. Journal of Graphics Tools 2(3), 45–52 (1997)

Wendland, H.: Piecewise polynomial,positive definite and compactly supported radial basis functions of minimal degree. Advances in Computational Mathematics 4, 389–396 (1995)

Wendland, H.: Scattered Data Approximation. Cambridge Monographs on Applied and Computational Mathematics. In: Ciarlet, P.G. (ed.) Scattered Data Approximation, Cambridge University Press, Cambridge (2005)

Wood, D., et al.: Surface Light Fields for 3D Photography. In: SIGGRAPH (2000)

Yu, Y., et al.: Inverse Global Illumination: Recovering Reflectance Models of Real Scenes from Photographs. In: Siggraph 99, Los Angeles (1999)

Zickler, T., et al.: Reflectance Sharing: Image-based Rendering from a Sparse Set of Images. In: Eurographics Symposium on Rendering (2005)

Part III

Animation
and Simulation

Motion Map Generation for Maintaining the Temporal Coherence of Brush Strokes

Youngsup Park and KyungHyun Yoon

Chung-Ang University 221 HukSeok-Dong, DongJak-Gu, Seoul, Korea
aupres98@hanmail.net, khyoon@cau.ac.kr

Abstract. Painterly animation is a method that expresses images with a hand-painted appearance from a video, and the most crucial element for it is the coherence between frames. A motion map generation is proposed in this paper as a resolution to the issue of maintaining the coherence in the brush strokes between the frames. A motion map refers to the range of motion calculated by their magnitudes and directions between the frames with the edge of the previous frame as a point of reference. The different methods of motion estimation used in this paper include the optical flow method and the block-based method, and the method that yielded the biggest PSNR using the motion information (the directions and magnitudes) acquired by various methods of motion estimation has been chosen as the final motion information to form a motion map. The created motion map determined the part of the frame that should be re-painted. In order to maintain the temporal coherence, the motion information was applied to only the strong edges that determine the directions of the brush strokes. Also, this paper sought to reduce the flickering phenomenon between the frames by using the multiple exposure method and the difference map created by the difference between images of the source and the canvas. Maintenance of the coherence in the direction of the brush strokes was also attempted by a local gradient interpolation in an attempt to maintain the structural coherence.

Keywords: Non-photorealistic Animation, Painterly Animation, Motion Map, Temporal Coherence, Strong Edge, Local Gradient Interpolation.

1 Introduction

The most crucial element in a painterly animation with an input of a video is to maintain the coherence in the brush strokes between frames. This paper proposes a motion map in order to resolve the issue of maintaining the coherence of brush strokes between frames in a painterly animation.

One of the basic information needed for the perception of the objects moving between frames (the foreground and the background) is the information of edges. The information of edges is a standard that distinguishes between the objects in a video and an essential element that visualize the motion. The motion map suggested in this paper is created using the information of edges as well as the motion information. In other words, a motion map refers to the range of a motion calculated by the magnitudes and directions of the motions of each object between frames with the edge of a previous

J. Braz et al. (Eds.): VISAPP and GRAPP 2006, CCIS 4, pp. 139–152, 2007.

frame as a point of reference, and the area where brush strokes should be newly created when passing on to the next frame. Our painting algorithm, applying the similar
methods applied to the paint-on-glass animations, has sought to maintain the coherence
of brush strokes between frames by applying new brush strokes by determining at the
area of the motion map the area of the previous canvas where it should be re-painted to
produce the images of the next frame.

Motion information can be acquired by the methods of motion estimation, such as
the optical flow method(Horn and Schunck, 1981)(Lucas and Kanade, 1981) and the
block-based method(Koga et al., 1981) (Tekalp, 1995). The motion information created by using the optical flow method accurately shows the direction of the motion,
but it does not accurately depict the exact magnitude of the motion as a result of the
noise and/or occlusion problem of the images(Tekalp, 1995). Although Litwinowicz
(Litwinowicz, 1997) and Hertzmann(Hertzmann and Perlin, 2000) have produced motion information using the optical flow method, this paper sought to improve the accuracy of the motion information by choosing among the three methods of motion
estimation(Horn and Schunck, 1981)(Lucas and Kanade, 1981)(Koga et al., 1981) the
method that yields the greatest PSNR. This paper also sought to maintain the coherence
between frames by applying the motion information to strong edges that determine the
direction of brush strokes among other elements.

The character of brush strokes is determined by such elements as the color, the direction, the size, and the shape. Most of the painterly rendering algorithms
(Litwinowicz, 1997)(Hertzmann, 1998)(Hays and Essa, 2004) use a very simple form
of brush strokes that have the same shapes and sizes among the characteristics of
brush strokes. For such reasons, the resulting images convey a static, machine-like
atmosphere, unlike the active and intense effects of the actual paintings. This paper,
however, created brush strokes of diverse directions, sizes, and lengths using the linear
and curvy shapes and local gradient interpolation, and applied them to the motion map
in order to produce a painterly animation.

2   Related Work

Litwinowicz and Hertzmann used the optical flow method for motion estimation in order to move the brush strokes from the previous frame to the current one
(Litwinowicz, 1997)(Hertzmann and Perlin, 2000). This method, however, calculates
the motion using only the intensity information between neighboring pixels, and thus,
the occlusion problem between a foreground and a background and between a foreground and another foreground is neglected. This paper used both the optical flow
method(Horn and Schunck, 1981)(Lucas and Kanade, 1981) and the block-based
method (Koga et al., 1981) in order to resolve the problems associated with using twodi-
mensional image, among the various methods of motion estimation chose the method
with the biggest PSNR.

Hertzmann(Hertzmann and Perlin, 2000), in order to maintain the coherence of the
brush strokes between frames, applied new brush strokes on the re-painting part of
the next frame by using the paintover method, similar to the paint-on-glass method,
difference masking, and the motion data. His method, however, has two problems.

First, because a video has noises and/or the occlusion problem, the motion information calculated between frames is not accurate. Hertzmann failed to resolve the problem of flickering by applying his motion data to every element such as the directions, locations, and shapes of the brush strokes(Hertzmann and Perlin, 2000). This paper sought to decrease the flickering phenomenon by applying the motion data only to the strong edges that determine the directions of the strokes and using the motion map elsewhere. Second, in a real paint-on-glass animation, the coherence between frames is maintained by using the canvas of the previous frame as the initial canvas for the next frame and by applying brush strokes only to where it should be re-painted. Hertzmann(Hertzmann and Perlin, 2000), however, warped the canvas of the previous frame using the inaccurate motion data, and used that warped canvas as the initial canvas for the next frame. Also, he calculated the difference masking not by using the images of the current source and the initial canvas, but by comparing the images of the previous sources with the images of the current sources. When using the difference masking calculated in such a way to paint the brush on the previously warped canvas, it may show much difference from the images of the current source and continue the flickering phenomenon onto the next frame. It is because the image with the most maintained coherence is an image of a source. This paper sought to maintain the coherence between frames by calculating the difference map between the image of the current source and the canvas onto which the motion map had been applied.

Hays redefined the characteristics of the brush strokes and produced brush strokes for each frame because a hole had appeared on the canvas due to the imperfect motion information and/or a phenomenon of partially erased characteristics of the brush strokes had appeared on the canvas(Hays and Essa, 2004). Hays method, however, also has disadvantages as it applies a process of decreasing the opacity by 10% for each frame in an attempt to avoid the flickering that emerge in the process of the redefinition of brush strokes. It is too dependent on opacity, in other words. The method also conveys a feeling of mere movement of brush strokes between frames by using only line brush strokes for the texture.

3   Creation of the Motion Map

Motion estimation refers to the estimation of the vectors of the motion between the previous frame and the current frame. The method proposed by in this paper employed for motion estimation include: the method of finding the pixel with the minimum pixel-to-pixel variation among the flow vectors(Horn and Schunck, 1981); the method of motion estimation based on an assumption that the motion vector remains unchanged over a particular block of pixels(Lucas and Kanade, 1981); and the block-based method that, using the block mask, finds the pixels with the best-matching block of the same size(Koga et al., 1981). Based on the motion information(the directions and the magnitudes) gathered by using these methods, this paper chooses the method with the biggest PSNR.

A motion map is created by applying the method of perceiving an object in the channel that handle the forms and movements among other channels of handling the visual information, and this method of perception is reflected upon the edges of the moving object in focus. This paper creates a motion map by finding the range of the motion with the edge of the previous frame as a point of reference using the motion vectors found by the motion estimation. The newly created motion map determines where should be re-painted in the next frame and maintains the coherence in brush strokes between the frames.

3.1   Motion Estimation

The HS(Horn and Schunck, 1981) and LK(Lucas and Kanade, 1981) optical flow method can apply motion estimation to the whole range of an image and the direction of the motion in its information is accurate, while the magnitude of the motion is not. On the contrary, the BM(Koga et al., 1981) method that looks for the pixels with the most correspondence to the previous frame as much as the size of a block mask per pixel provides the direction and the magnitude of the motion more accurate than those of the optical flow method, despite its disadvantage that the area 2 of Figure 1(C) cannot calculate the motion information. This paper chose the method with the biggest PSNR after calculating each motion vector by dividing the whole area into area 1 and area 2 just as in Figure 1. Table 1 is the result of the calculation of the peak signal to noise applying the optical flow method and the block-based method to each area. In case of calculating the motion vectors regarding the image in Figure 1(A–B), similar to the results shown in Table 1, after applying the motion information calculated by the BM method to Area 1 and the motion information calculated by the LK method to Area 2, the PSNR is calculated again based on the whole area(Area 1 + Area 2). Table 2 is the result of the calculation of the PSNRs from the optical flow method(Horn and Schunck, 1981)(Lucas and Kanade, 1981) and other method suggested in this paper. Equation 1–2 is the formula used to calculate the PSNR, and Element A is the warped image of the image of the previous source using the estimated

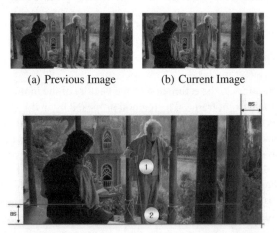

(a) Previous Image   (b) Current Image

(c) Dividing the whole area into area 1 and area 2 for Motion Estimation (BS : Block Size)

Fig. 1. Images applied Motion Estimation and Area Segmentation for Motion Estimation Method

Table 1. 3 PSNR Values for each Area of Figure 1(C)

	PSNR(dB)(Area 1)	PSNR(dB)(Area 2)
HS	18.86403	19.70797
LK	20.90547	19.75762
BM	26.14414	

Table 2. 3 PSNR Values for the whole area of Figure 1(C)

	PSNR(dB) (Area 1 + Area 2)
HS	18.91518
LK	20.81920
OURS (Area 1:BM + Area 2:LK)	24.83612

motion information, and Element B is the image of the current source. This paper does not always choose the LK and BM methods as in Tables 1-2, but chooses the method with the biggest PSNR for each image. This paper also shortened the rendering time by calculating the motion information for all the images as a preprocessing step.

$$T = \sum_{i=1}^{SZ}(A_i - B_i)^2 \tag{1}$$

$$PSNR(dB) = 10 * \log(\frac{65025.0}{T/SZ}) \tag{2}$$

3.2 Motion Map

The edge information is one of the important elements for the visual perception of movements. This paper created a motion map based on the motion vectors and the edge information.

Figure 2 shows how a motion map is developed when a circle moves downward to the right. When a circle composed of Areas A and B of the previous frame moves to a circle composed of Areas B and C in the current frame, Area A transforms from a foreground into a background, Area B maintains its foreground status despite the movements, and Area C transforms from a background to a foreground. This paper creates a motion map that includes Areas A and C by assuming the area of re-painting for the next frame as Areas A and C just as it is in the method of making the paint-on-glass animation. This method makes a motion map that includes the Areas A and C by drawing a line from Point P on the edge to Point Q when the Point P of the previous frame has moved to Point Q in the current frame. The motion map proposed in this paper has an advantage of easy creating using the edge and motion information without separating the foreground and the background. Figure 3 is a motion map using the method suggested by this paper.

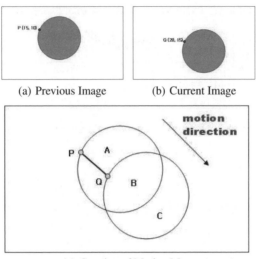

(a) Previous Image   (b) Current Image

(c) Creation of Motion Map

Fig. 2. Motion map is developed when a circle moves downward to the right (The point P and Q are a meeting point between frames, F(x,y,t)=(5 pixels, 5 pixels))

Because the motion map is an area where the visual changes between frames are apparent, brush strokes of various sizes were applied in layers to the initial canvas of the current frame. The method to decide what size to use for the brush strokes when applying to a motion map in layers is similar to Hertzmanns method(Hertzmann, 1998) that forms one brush stroke in one grid. However, the brush strokes that go beyond the motion map can be removed by applying the brush strokes only when the proportion of the grid area and the area of the motion map exceeds a certain threshold. Figure 3(d) and Figure 3(e) show the brush strokes created using the motion map of Figure 3(C). As shown in Figure 3(D), applying brush strokes of various kinds to the next frame without regarding the size of the motion map area can cause much difference from the previous frame, bringing up much more flickering.

4 Motion Map Based Painterly Animation

4.1 Direction

Painters usually draw a picture of an object following the edgy line of that object. Litwinowicz(Litwinowicz, 1997) proposed a local gradient interpolation. This method determines the directions of the brush strokes by interpolating the gradients of the surrounding pixels in case of a pixel with a gradient located in a certain area with a magnitude near 0. Because this method applies the interpolation to the area where the direction of the strokes is not certain, the direction of the brush strokes does not comply with the direction of the edges. In order to resolve this problem, this paper set strong edges that determine the direction, and made the direction of the surrounding pixels correspond to the direction set by the edges. This is similar to the Hays method(Hays and Essa, 2004),

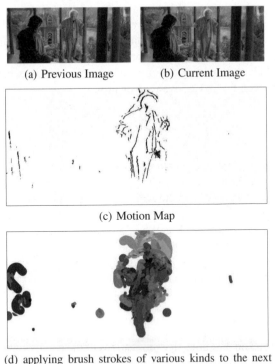

(a) Previous Image   (b) Current Image

(c) Motion Map

(d) applying brush strokes of various kinds to the next frame without regarding the size of the motion map area

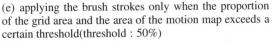

(e) applying the brush strokes only when the proportion of the grid area and the area of the motion map exceeds a certain threshold(threshold : 50%)

Fig. 3. Motion map and the canvas created using the motion map

but while Hays(Hays and Essa, 2004) used the gradient interpolation of the whole area, this paper used the local gradient interpolation.

There are three steps to finding strong edges: first, calculating the magnitudes of the gradients of pixels on the edges using thinned images; second, organize the calculated sizes of the gradients in a descending order; third, choose the biggest gradient as a strong edge and remove the surrounding edges only when their difference from the strong edge in direction is smaller than a fixed threshold. Many strong edges can be found by repeating this process.

The local gradient interpolation method using the strong edges calculated the weight of the distances between the edges that are within R radius, which is N times the shortest distance with the location of P as a point of reference(Park and Yoon, 2004). The gradients in pixels were calculated by adding the gradients and weights of the strong edges on the radius R and dividing the number. Variable N is an experimental number, and the values between 1.5 and 2.5 were given to it.

$$Weight(i) = \left(\frac{MinDistance}{Distance(i)} \right)^{b}, i = 1, \ldots, M \tag{3}$$

Equation 3 is a gradient interpolation function in order to calculate the weighted gradient value at each pixel (x, y). The MinDistance of a element is the shortest distance from Point P to the strong edges on the radius R and is expressed as MD. The distance is the length between Point P and the strong edges on the radius R. M is the number of the strong edges on the radius R and b is a constant. Figure 4(c) explains Point P, MD and Radius R. This method is a variation of the method of interpolation used in morphing (Beier and Neely, 1992). Figure 4 shows the strong edges created and the interpolated gradient images using the method suggested in this paper.

4.2   Color

Colors largely depend on the subjective motivations of the painters, and each painter has his own palette of distinctive colors. The Impressionists in particular were influenced by the flat form of the Japanese color prints. Considering this, this paper has attempted the method of flatizing the range of luminosity from 256 levels to 12 levels and the method of quantizing the colors (Deng et al., 1999b) (Deng et al., 1999a) (Park and Yoon, 2004). The painterly rendering in particular is handled by the units of random areas where the brush strokes are made, not by the pixel units, and thus, it is unnecessary to apply every color that forms an image of a source.

4.3   Shape and Size

Brush strokes have sizes of 4 to 32 pixels depending on the area of their application. The divided areas are painted using big brushes first, and then smaller brushes. The brush strokes are expressed in spline curves as well as the linear lines as a result of the application of the edge clipping. The control points of the spline curves are chosen in reference to the gradient interpolation of each pixel, and expanded upward and downward or left and right with the spline curve as a line of reference that follows the minimum of 2 and the maximum of 10 control points along the gradient from the starting point.

4.4   Maintenance of the Coherence Between Frames

Accurate motion information is necessary for the maintenance of coherence between frames. The existing methods of calculating motion information (Horn and Schunck, 1981) (Lucas and Kanade, 1981) (Koga et al., 1981) do

(a) Source Image

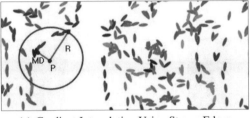

(b) Strong Edges Image

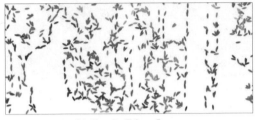

(c) Gradient Intepolation Using Strong Edges

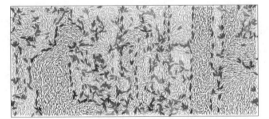

(d) Gradient Interpolated Image

Fig. 4. Strong Edge Image and Gradient Interpolated Image

not provide accurate motion information due to the noise or occlusion problem in the video(Tekalp, 1995). Those who studied the painterly animation
earlier(Litwinowicz, 1997)(Hertzmann and Perlin, 2000)(Hays and Essa, 2004) cause
the flickering phenomenon by applying the inaccurate motion information to every
element of the brush strokes. The Hays method especially has a high dependency on
opacity, conveying a feeling of mere movements of the brush strokes rather than a
feeling of re-painting. This paper has applied motion information only to the strong
edges that determined the element of direction of the brush strokes in an attempt to
maintain coherence between frames. It is because the edge images found using random

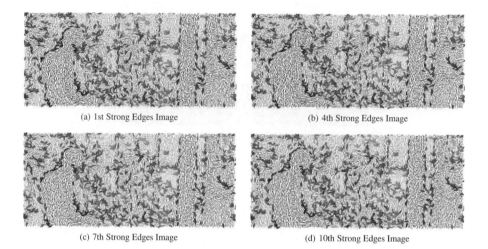

(a) 1st Strong Edges Image   (b) 4th Strong Edges Image

(c) 7th Strong Edges Image   (d) 10th Strong Edges Image

Fig. 5. An image resulting from determining the directions of the brush strokes by applying motion information only to the strong edges between frames

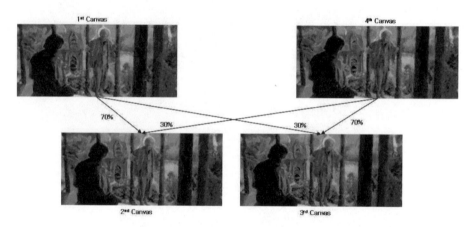

Fig. 6. An image resulting from applying the multi-exposure method

thresholds produce different results per frame, which may dislocate the strong edges. When the strong edges change their locations per frame, so does the direction of brush strokes. Figure 5 is an image resulting from moving the strong edges by applying the motion information in an attempt to maintain coherence of the directions of brush strokes.

Another method to maintain coherence between frames is to express the natural movements of the object by applying the multi-exposure method(Laybourne, 1998) as shown in Figure 6. This method expressed natural movements of the object by creating an in-between frame, blending Canvas 2 in a proportion of 7 (Canvas 1): 3(Canvas 4), and Canvas 3 in a proportion of 3 (Canvas 1):7(Canvas 2) after rendering only Canvases 1 and 4. This method is effective for the usage in a video with many movements, and has an

(a) 1st Source Image

(b) 1st Final Canvas and 4th Initial Canvas

(c) 4th Source Image

(d) Motion Map

(e) applying brush strokes of various kinds to the next frame with regarding the size of the motion map area

(f) (b)Image + (e)Image

(g) an Image applyied the smallest brush strokes by difference map between (f)canvas and (c)Image

(h) 4th Final Canvas ((f) Image + (g) Image)

Fig. 7. An image resulting from each step taken to maintain coherence between frames

advantage to alleviate the flickering phenomenon that can be caused by many differences in the colors of the brush strokes that are applied to the same location between frames.

The last method to maintain coherence between frames is to make a difference map between the canvas onto which a motion map has been applied and the image of the source and the re-paint it using a small brush. The area of effect of this method is Area B of Figure 2(c). This Area B had not appeared in the motion map, despite its motion, because its difference in intensity was not apparent from the surrounding pixels. Changes of each frame were probable in this area, so a difference map was made using the difference between the canvas of the applied brush strokes in the motion map and the image of the source, and Area B was re-painted with that map as a reference. Unlike Hertzmanns method(Hertzmann and Perlin, 2000) that makes a difference map between

Fig. 8. The images resulting from many scenes

the warped image of the previous source and the image of the current source, the method applied in this paper made a difference map between the canvas where the area of the motion map had been re-painted and the image of the current source in an attempt to lessen the flickering phenomenon between frames. It is due to the fact that the image with the most coherence between frames is an image of a source, and the difference between a warped image of the previous source and the image of the current source is different from the difference between the previously warped canvas and the present canvas. Figure 7(G) is an image resulting from the area without the motion map, and the smallest brush was used to produce it.

5   Results

Figure 5 is an image resulting from determining the directions of the brush strokes by applying motion information only to the strong edges between frames. This was an attempt to maintain coherence between frames by applying the motion information, which could be inaccurate due to the noise and the occlusion problem of the image, not to every element of the brush strokes (the direction, the location, the color, the form), but by applying it to only the direction between frames. Figure 6 is an image resulting from applying the multi-exposure method. Movements are naturally expressed by extracting the images of the source that have 8 frames per second from the video, rendering them, and blending the images between them. Figure 7 shows an image resulting from each step taken to maintain coherence between frames. Coherence is maintained by making a difference map between the image whose brush strokes are created and repainted by the motion map and the image of the source. Figure 8 is the images resulting from many scenes. You can find more images and videos created by the methods outlined in this paper on the website at : http://cglab.cse.cau.ac.kr/npr/index.html.

6   Conclusion and Future Work

This paper has suggested the method of using a motion map in creating a painterly animation. The areas of repainting between frames are distinguished by the motion map made by the edge and motion information acquired from motion estimation. In an attempt to maintain coherence between frames, motion information was applied to only the strong edges that determined the directions of the brush strokes, and the multi-exposure method was used in order to express the natural movements of the object(Laybourne, 1998). Also, by making a difference map between the previous canvas and the current image of the source and applying the smallest brush strokes, the flickering phenomenon was also lessened.

Among the characteristics of brush strokes, the effects of color contrast, the brush texture expressed using rough brushes or knives, and the glazing effects need to be analyzed and simulated.

Acknowledgements

This work was supported in part by MIC & IITA through IT Leading R&D Support Project.

References

Beier, T., Neely, S.: Feature based image metamorphosis. In: SIGGRAPH'92, pp. 35–42 (1992)

Deng, Y., Kenney, C., Moore, M., Manjunath, B.: Peer group filtering and perceptual color image quantization. In: ISCAS'99, pp. 21–24 (1999a)

Deng, Y., Manjunath, B., Shin, H.: Color image segmentation. In: CVPR'99, pp. 2446–2451 (1999b)

Hays, J., Essa, I.: Image and video based painterly animation. In: NPAR'2004, pp. 113–120 (2004)

Hertzmann, A.: Painterly rendering with curved brush strokes of multiple sizes. In: SIG-GRAPH'98, pp. 453–460 (1998)

Hertzmann, A., Perlin, K.: Painterly rendering for video and interaction. In: NPAR'2000, pp. 7–12 (2000)

Horn, B., Schunck, B.: Determining optical flow. In: Artifitial Intelligence, pp. 185–203 (1981)

Koga, T., Iinuma, K., Hirano, A., Iijima, Y., Ishiguro, T.: Motion-compensated interframe coding for video. In: NTC'81, pp. 531–534 (1981)

Laybourne, K.: Animation Book, 2nd edn. Three Reviers Press (1998)

Litwinowicz, P.: Processing images and video for an impressionist. In: SIGGRAPH'97, pp. 407–414 (1997)

Lucas, B., Kanade, T.: An iterative image registration technique with an application to stereo vision. In: DARPA Image Understanding Workshop, pp. 121–130 (1981)

Park, Y., Yoon, K.: Adaptive brush stroke generation for painterly rendering. In: EG'04 - Short Presentations, pp. 65–68 (2004)

Tekalp, A.M.: Digital Video Processing, 2nd edn. Prentice Hall, Englewood Cliffs (1995)

Part IV

Interactive Environments

Distributed 3D Information Visualization – Towards Integration of the Dynamic 3D Graphics and Web Services

Dean Vucinic, Danny Deen, Emil Oanta, Zvonimir Batarilo, and Chris Lacor

Faculty of Engineering, Department of Mechanical Engineering, Fluid Mechanics and
Thermodynamics Research Group
Vrije Universiteit Brussel, Pleinlaan 2, B- 1050 Brussels, Belgium
dean@stro.vub.ac.be, danny@stro.vub.ac.be

Abstract. This paper focuses on visualization and manipulation of graphical
content in distributed network environments. The developed graphical
middleware and 3D desktop prototypes were specialized for situational
awareness. This research was done in the LArge Scale COllaborative decision
support Technology (LASCOT) project, which explored and combined software
technologies to support human-centred decision support system for crisis
management (earthquake, tsunami, flooding, airplane or oil-tanker incidents,
chemical, radio-active or other pollutants spreading, etc.). The performed state-
of-the-art review did not identify any publicly available large scale distributed
application of this kind. Existing proprietary solutions rely on the conventional
technologies and 2D representations. Our challenge was to apply the "latest"
available technologies, such Java3D, X3D and SOAP, compatible with average
computer graphics hardware. The selected technologies are integrated and we
demonstrate: the flow of data, which originates from heterogeneous data
sources; interoperability across different operating systems and 3D visual
representations to enhance the end-users interactions.

Keywords: X3D graphics, distributed 3D content.

1 Introduction

Two decades of research in developing fluid flow simulation software has build up
our expertise in scientific visualization; see Figure 1 (Vucinic, 1992). Our continuous
objective is to applied visualization techniques to enhance the analysis of fluid flow
simulations and experiments (Vucinic, 2001). In this paper we present the
visualization framework developed within the European ITEA program (LASCOT
2005). LASCOT has underpinned our research in finding new ways to apply graphics
to visualize and present diversified and dynamically changing information.

The Computer Graphics technology has reached the point where non-technical
people can comprehend complex information looking to their visual counterparts.
Thus, we applied Model-View-Controller (MVC) paradigm (Vuorenmaa, 2000) to
enhance interactivity of our 3D software components for: visualization, monitoring

J. Braz et al. (Eds.): VISAPP and GRAPP 2006, CCIS 4, pp. 155–168, 2007.
© Springer-Verlag Berlin Heidelberg 2007

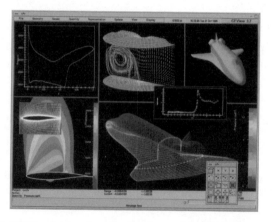

Fig. 1. CFView interactive visualization tool for fluid flow analysis

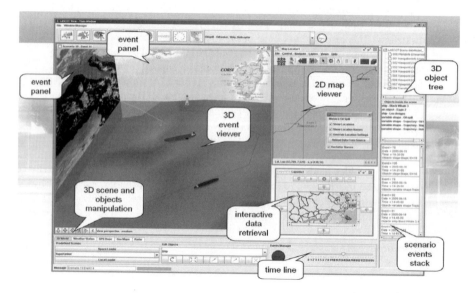

Fig. 2. The LASCOT application

and exchange of dynamic information, including spatial and time-dependent data, see Figure 2. The undertaken software development was related to integration and customization of different visualization components based on the 3D Computer Graphics (Java3D) and Web (X3D, SOAP) technologies .

In the beginning of 90's, we mastered the object-oriented approach based on C++, (Vucinic 1991), which we have further oriented towards exploring Java3D™ solutions (Xj3D).

The presented visualization framework consists of extended graphical objects containing non-graphical (event information) used to related networks of such objects, which are aggregated to provide complex information in a more natural context dependent manner. Combining position and time parameters enables us to automate the creation of scenes and distribute them to the end-users; highlighting useful information, thus improving the situational awareness of the involved actors.

Another important aspect of the visualization framework is the user interaction possibilities to analyze the created 3D scenes and to browse through the history of events in an appropriate user friendly manner.

For managing crisis events, such as hurricanes, flooding, chemical, biological or radio-active incidents, maritime disasters and other large scale problems, we need the ability to generate simulations and to exchange these models by importing them into the 3D scene. Being able to freely tilt and rotate the stage, to choose the desired perspective, offers the user significantly improved insight into the crisis situation.

It could be argued that 2D maps have always been sufficient for locating objects on an area of interest. Traditionally, battlefield situations have been modelled with symbols on a large flat surface. It is obvious that 3D models make the understanding of the information easier (Blais, 2002). Such an approach is often found in museums to provide visitors with an enhanced experience. A problem related to their usage was that the 3D models needed for the real-time situations were costly to create, as their production required large amount of time and effort.

Today, the new visualization technology makes it possible to generate 3D content quickly and at a low cost, by simply inserting appropriate parameters into the existing pre-build templates. Examples are: overlaying 2D maps with satellite images (black and white, colour, or pseudo-colour, reveal more information than we could possibly see with the naked eye); extrusion models of 3D objects (e.g. buildings in a city). A further step is to filter and structure such models and to automatically create content dependent (virtual) "pictures" of the situation, which humans may intuitively understand and analyze through multiple "views", giving a different perspective on the same situation.

In this paper we present our software engineering approach, applied to the development of the visualization components through the requirements specification, the application design and the implementation phases. Finally, we give some indications on the usability testing of the presented distributed 3D information visualization framework.

2 Visualization Requirements

During the LASCOT project, we have performed an extensive analysis of the user needs and we have established the following requirements.

2.1 Dictionary of 3D Objects

A dictionary classifies 3D objects: e.g. plane, ship, submarine, etc... The behaviour of the objects is determined by the category to which an object belongs. For example: as ships do not fly, there is an automatic restriction imposed on their movement in the vertical direction. This restriction is reflected in the user interface. When positioning a ship by entering a numerical coordinate, the elevation position will be absent.

2.2 Library of 3D Objects

A library of 3D objects stores X3D (or VRML) formatted models. Each object is linked to one or more keywords. Categories are also linked to keywords. This allows flexible search and retrieval of the object (for example through a web oriented wizard): see Figure 13.

The library can only be updated or appended by an authorized user. It is necessary to assert that all X3D files are valid and that their profile matches the display capacities of the client application, in order to prevent possible corruption of the entire 3D scene (in case an invalid object could be loaded).

2.3 Actor Visualization

The position of the actors can be checked, monitored and displayed. It must be possible to select a particular actor and to scale each item as well as the entire LASCOT graphical space. An X3D object is chosen to represent the position of each actor and display the actor's data.

2.4 Information Visualization

Several information visualization components are required to enable the user to access:

- Weather data: the information is retrieved from weather forecast servers by the LASCOT server in XML format. The direct visibility of the weather information in one of the 3D Desktop panels is possible.

-GPS location: Localization of the objects, such as: ship, airplane etc. in the 3D world is available.

-Cartography maps offer possibility to visualize different maps: roads, cities, street map, countries, geopolitical maps, detailed maps of terrain, etc.

-Predefined locations: the location of important places (emergency centres, hospitals, police station, airports etc.) enables the direct communication with each of them to exchange information about particular needs.

2.5 Simulation Visualization

Performing 3D visualization of the crisis event simulation (e.g. oil spills). The 3D Graphical User Interface (GUI) allows the user to visualize and evaluate possible solutions related to the problem. The LASCOT application's desktop displays images, such as maps, photographs, data graphs, and animations of movies integrated in the 3D space. In addition, such 2D elements can be viewed through standard Java Swing components.

3   Application Design

3.1 3D Desktop (Client Application)

The visualization components are represented in the 3D desktop toolbar. They are subdivided into four elements:

1° 3D Viewer (geo-maps + actors);
2° Actor Tracking (ship, oil spill);
3° Data monitoring (e.g. temperature);
4° X3D objects modelling (editing, browsing).

3.2 Graphical Middleware (Application Server)

The graphical middleware contains the basic operational services for the database (MySQL database server), supporting retrieval, inserts, updates and removal of records.

The "Web Services" interfaces consist of SOAP server, as well as client, components.

In addition, the graphical middleware handles 3D scene management: generation, composition and history of 3D scenes ("event generation"), user session management and Web Services interaction (e.g. transmission of the user selected Focus Area via SOAP messaging).

3.3 X3D Modelling and Interaction

The X3D graphics package is responsible for the processing of graphical objects and consists of:

A) Interactive model for X3D objects:
1°) static objects: LASCOT coordinate system, elevation grid, sea surface, buildings, On/Off toggle for different layers);
2°) object positioning: general / flying / floating / underwater objects;
3°) grouping and association of the interactive behaviour of X3D objects.
B) Exposed End-user Interactivity:
1°) interactive viewing inside the X3D browser (zoom, pan, rotate the scene; view, fly, walk, examine modes);
2°) add and remove objects to/from the scene, rotate, position, scale, re-colour objects.

4 Implementation

4.1 Technology Platform

Our visualization software was designed with portability in mind. A Java-based implementation (see Figure 3) will run on Windows or any Linux platform, including Mac OS X.

The X3D ISO standard was used as the basis for the graphics content modelling. X3D remains compatible with VRML. It uses XML-based encoding, which enables hierarchical modelling (Kiss, 2003) and data-structures exchange across different platforms and between independent distributed applications. Because it is an ISO defined standard, X3D scenes, objects, environments will have predictable, reliable, reproducible behaviour towards the end-user, regardless of the system or specific software application being used. An open source conformant Java-based viewer

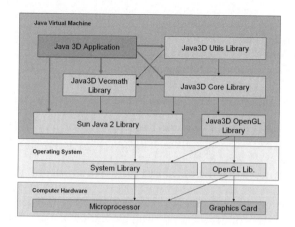

Fig. 3. Java and Java3D platform architecture

application was available (pre-release) and we used it as the underlying toolkit on which we based our 3D desktop development. For the 2D components, the Java Swing toolkit was used.

The selected application server was JOnAS, an open source implementation of the J2EE specification by ObjectWeb. JOnAS was used for the deployment of Java Servlets, Java Server Pages and Web Services.

The database is implemented in MySQL, but the developed components are compatible and portable to any SQL server product (such as, but not limited to, IBM DB2, Microsoft SQL Server, Oracle, mSQL, PostgreSQL, Sybase, etc.).

4.2 Client Application

The information visualization tools, each related to a specific data-source (existing or hypothetical), consist of:

1°) X3D EARTH GLOBE: a VisAD-based (Hibbard, 2000) component, showing a prototype of the 3D elevation model of the planet Earth, by augmented representation of elevation (false-colours + exaggeration of elevation).

2°) WEATHER SAT IMAGES: for retrieval of satellite images from web sources (see Figure 4), for example www.metoffice.gov.uk, on which coast-lines and lines of latitude and longitude have been added (they have been altered to polar stereographic projection).

3°) IDV DATA DISPLAY: for interactive display of various scientific data sources supported by Unidata's Integrated Data Viewer (IDV), an open-source, based on VisAD (Hibbard, 2000), for analyzing and visualizing data (see Figure 5) from heterogeneous sources, such as satellite imagery, surface observations, balloon soundings, NWS WSR-88D Level II and Level III RADAR data, and NOAA National Profiler Network data, within one unified interface.

4°) VIDEO CAPTURE AND DISPLAY: for retrieval and display of movies, as well as video capturing (if hardware is available), we have included Sun's JMStudio (an example application for the Java Media Framework 2.1).

Fig. 4. Weather imagery (web sources)

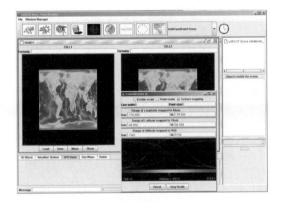

Fig. 5. Integrated Data Viewer

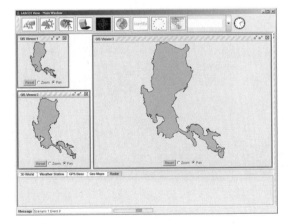

Fig. 6. GIS data viewer

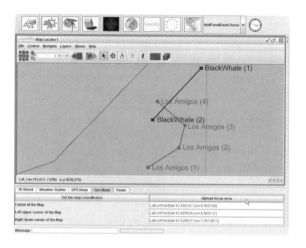

Fig. 7. 2D actor locator

5°) GIS Viewer: for display of 2D vector graphics (see Figure 6). Vector graphics are scalable image displays (as opposed to bitmaps, such as satellite photos).

6°) INTEGRATED WEB BROWSER: for systems which do not have a web browser installed, we provided a simple HTML capable client.

7°) GLOBAL POSITIONING TOOL: Vector graphics component (see Figure 7) based on BBN Technologies' OpenMap™, for displaying actor locations on a 2D map; also capable of event generation (transmits the area of interest to the middleware via SOAP messaging).

8°) 3D DESKTOP: This Xj3D based tool is a complex component, which can be used in scene authoring mode, or for event viewing (see Figure 8).

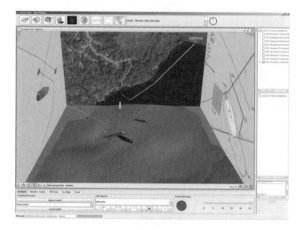

Fig. 8. 3D Desktop with 2 ships, helicopter and oil spill

The scene viewer represents a time-based scenario with time-slider for point-wise temporal object browsing (Daassi, 2000). Objects appearing in the scene are positioned according to event properties provided by the graphical middleware server. They can also be moved by the user, either by entering position coordinates numerically (using a slider), or intuitively by moving the mouse. Other operations available to the user include: rotation, re-colouring, removal of an object, adding of an object (selected from categories), re-scaling, playing of (pre-defined) animations and the adding or removing of instruments (visual tools) to or from the scene.

In our demonstrator we have implemented these functionalities from buttons inside the 3D scene, as well as from Java Swing buttons (2D components), outside the 3D world.

4.3 Graphical Middleware

The LASCOT graphical middleware (GM) consists of servlets and Java Server Pages available through the JOnAS application server. It acts as the bridge between the Common Information View (XML objects, provided by the Business Processor in the context of a LASCOT business process) and the 2D and 3D XML objects – provided by the 2D and 3D Visualization Services.

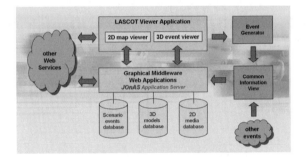

Fig. 9. Graphical middleware architecture

GM is an essential component, enabling the flow of externally generated data to the client application (see Figure 9). The uniqueness of the LASCOT concept is that, contrary to computer games, where content elements and their parameters are determined in advance (a closed system), GM provides the ability to visualize events, as they happen (open system).

The GM uses a classical relational database (RDB), because of proven reliability, for physical storage. The RDB stores attributes of events as pairs of: (identifier, value). The number of attributes per event is theoretically unlimited. While some parameters (see Figure 10) are stored in the "events" table (e.g. date and time), other "attributes" are modelled as a linked table (see Figure 11).

Each visualization component retrieves only the values of those identifiers that it is programmed (recognises) to deal with, while ignoring those that are used by other components. Such a setup makes the system very flexible, being loosely coupled, with

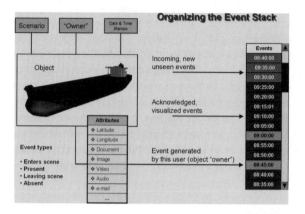

Fig. 10. Event properties

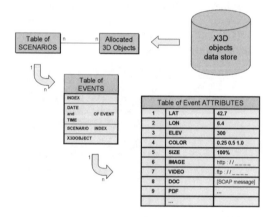

Fig. 11. Events and relationships

client components, which can be modified, added, removed or temporarily deactivated without any impact on the middleware code-base.

The identifiers are similar to the variables names in un-typed programming languages. The stored value can be an integer, string, URL, XML file, etc. Only the event generator and the display component need to understand the identifier, while the middleware handles it transparently. The identifier is not a simple variable name however, since it can itself be more complex, for example, it could also contain a set of commands (see Figure 11 and Figure 12).

In the relational database context, each event is seen as related to one object (see Figure 10). A collision of 2 ships would generate at least 2 two events. Each object has an "owner" (of it's "stream of events"). Any situation is represented as a series of events, within a given scenario context. The user can select different views on each situation.

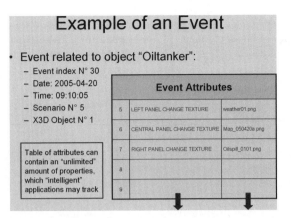

Fig. 12. One-to-many relation events and attributes

4.4 Web Components

A set of Web components (accessible through any web browser) provide additional functionalities of interaction (see Figure 13) with the graphical middleware.

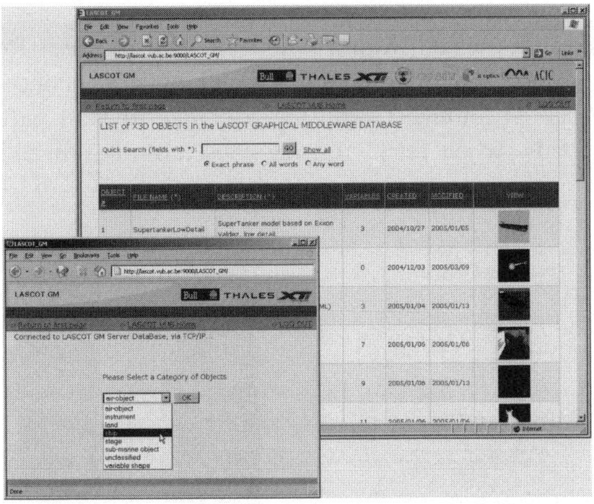

Fig. 13. X3D object access via wizard or table

The library of X3D/VRML objects can be accessed either via a listing in table format (sorting and selection functionalities are provided), or via a wizard. Objects can be visualized using an X3D/VRML viewer or browser plug-in.

5   Testing

The system resource monitoring (see Figure 14) showed that the memory allocation by the Java Virtual Machine remains below 100 MB, when using the most complex component (3D desktop). Of course, when using multiple components or several instances of the same component at the same time, requirements will increase. However, the application will not need more RAM than what is available in a desktop PC (500 MB to 1 GB).

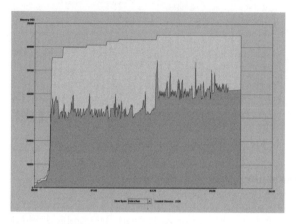

Fig. 14. Memory allocation and usage

Application speed was tested from a practical point of view. Responsiveness was deemed to be adequate, provided a high speed network connection is available (broadband or LAN). The longest time the user has to wait before the results are displayed is 6 seconds, when retrieving the most complex events in the 3D event viewer.

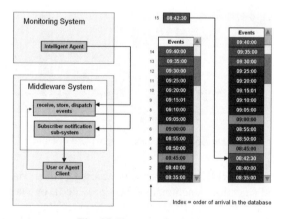

Fig. 15. Event stack sorting

The scenario of an oil spill crisis was chosen to represent a hypothetical crisis situation. Longitude and latitude coordinates for the trajectory of two ships were generated externally as input for the graphical middleware. Each event carries a timestamp. Events do not necessarily arrive in chronological order, but the middleware, as well as the client application, are capable of sorting the event stack (see Figure 10 and Figure 15).

6 Conclusion

We have demonstrated a level of integration of cutting edge 3D graphics technologies, which has not been reached before.

While the only Java-based X3D browser is still in the last development phase (version 1.0 to be expected soon), we not only managed to integrate it into the client application part of the LASCOT project, but we use Xj3D to visualize data which is coming, through our middleware from various external sources.

While presented software components provide highly flexible interactions and data-flows, the coupling between these components is very loose. Thus, the components can be upgraded (or even replaced) independently from each other, without loss of functionality. With SOAP messaging the communication between components is made completely independent of software platforms and communication transmission layers. In our approach Java components co-exist with Microsoft .NET front-end, as well as back-end implementations.

With our approach we aim to improve software development of 3D collaborative and visualization tools. Future development of an appropriate ontology could significantly improve the distributed visualization framework.

Acknowledgments

We would like to thank the European ITEA program for enabling the LASCOT project and the Belgium national authorities (IWT) for financing it, as without their direct support this work could not be accomplished. In addition, we thank the LASCOT Consortium: Bull, THALES, XT-i, Capvidia, MULTITEL, IT-OPTICS and ACIC, because without them this project would not have existed.

We would also like to thank Tomasz Luniewski for putting forward the 3D dashboard concept and Jef Vanbockryck for the WebService expertise.

References

Blais, C., Brutzman, D., Harney, J., Weekley, J.: Web-Based 3D Reconstruction of Scenarios for Limited Objective Experiments. In: Proceedings of the 2002 Summer Computer Simulation Conference, Society for Modeling and Simulation (SCS) (2002)

Daassi, C., Dumas, M., Fauvet, M., Nigay, L., Scholl, P.: Visual exploration of temporal object databases. In: Proceedings of 16ièmes Journées Bases de Données Avancées. BDA, French Conference on Databases (2000)

Hibbard, W.: An example of Unidata's future in new software: the VisAD component architecture for collaborative data analysis and visualization. In: Preprints, Conf. Interactive Information and Processing Systems for Meteorology, Oceanography, and Hydrology (2000)

Kiss, S., Nijholt, A., Zwiers, J.: Virtual Modelling. In: Proceedings Eurographics 2003: Modeling the real world, The Eurographics Association, Granada, Spain (2003)

Vucinic, D.: Object Oriented Programming for Computer Graphics and Flow Visualization, invited lecture, VKI Lecture Series on Computer Graphics and Flow Visualization in CFD, Brussels, Belgium (1991)

Vucinic, D., Pottiez, M., Sotiaux, V., Hirsch Ch.: CFView - An Advanced Interactive Visualization System based on Object-Oriented Approach. AIAA-92-0072. In: AIAA 30th Aerospace Sciences Meeting, Reno, Nevada, USA (1992)

Vucinic, D., Hazarika, B.K.: Integrated Approach to Computational and Experimental Flow Visualization of a Double Annular Confined Jet. Journal of Visualization 4(3) (2001)

Vuorenmaa, M.: Automatic Presentation of Model Data in MVC++ Applications. Master's thesis. Department of Computer and Information Sciences, University of Tampere, Finland (2000)

Interactive Editing of Live Visuals

Pascal Müller[1], Stefan Müller Arisona[2], Simon Schubiger-Banz[3],
and Matthias Specht[4]

[1] Computer Vision Lab, ETH Zürich
pmueller@vision.ee.ethz.ch
[2] Computer Systems Institute, ETH Zürich
sma@corebounce.org
[3] Swisscom Innovations
simon.schubiger@swisscom.com
[4] Anthropological Institute, University of Zürich
specht@ifi.unizh.ch

Abstract. This paper describes novel concepts for the interactive composition of artistic real-time graphics, so-called *live visuals*. By establishing two fundamental techniques dealing with the structured media integration and the intrinsic design process, we significantly increase the efficiency of interactive editing in live visuals applications. First, we present a media manager that supports the user in both retrieval and utilization of automatically annotated digital media. The computer-assisted application of individual media items permits the interactive control of non-linear editing (NLE) of video in real-time. Second, we optimize the design process by introducing the *design tree*, which collects and organizes the artist's work in an intuitive way. Design tree operations provide interactive high-level editing methods which allow for exploration, combination, reuse, and evolution of designs before and particularly during the performance. We examined the effectiveness of our techniques on numerous long-lasting live performances from which representative examples are demonstrated.

Keywords: Interactive Content Creation, Authoring Systems, Design Computation, Interaction Techniques, Live Visuals.

1 Introduction

From the very beginning, interactive graphics systems have been used for creating art (Sutherland, 1963). They have fascinated and deeply influenced visual performance artists who would eventually replace analog video mixing and effect consoles in favor of computer systems. Among other movements, "VJing", referring to the Video Jockey (VJ) who composes live visuals at music concerts, electronic dance music events, or media art performances in general, is nowadays becoming increasingly popular. An excerpt from a typical live visuals performance is illustrated in Figure 1. Performing such artistic real-time graphics live results in a tremendous need for state-of-the-art hardware and software systems. Today's systems virtually satisfy these needs in terms of performance and real-time processing. However, existing software tools mostly ignore the artistic design process before, and particularly during the performance. Furthermore,

J. Braz et al. (Eds.): VISAPP and GRAPP 2006, CCIS 4, pp. 169–184, 2007.
© Springer-Verlag Berlin Heidelberg 2007

Fig. 1. Real-time graphics composed live by a performing artist. The snapshot sequence represents a 5 minute excerpt from a typical live performance consisting of abstract imagery, video loops, font layouts and a live video stream.

they don't support the user in dealing with large media libraries or in applying individual media items in an "intelligent" manner. Hence, this work presents novel approaches to the issues of media utilization and interactive designing in live visuals applications.

First, we present a media manager, which supports the live visuals artist in retrieval and utilization of digital media based on annotated metadata. Using well-known computer vision methods, we automatically augment video clips with metadata by reverse-engineering their original shot list. Besides enabling efficient media retrieval, the metadata permits the media manager to assist *interactive* non-linear editing (NLE) of video *in real-time*. A video clip's individual shots are restructured in a "non-linear" style by the live visuals system. For example, shots are rearranged in order to fit musical features extracted in real-time. Hence, Eisenstein's *vertical montage* theory on the articulation of film and soundtrack (Eisenstein, 1994) can be approached in a live context using annotated media files and real-time audio analysis.

The second contribution addresses the problem of how artwork is dealt with during live performance. Rather than forcing the artist to fit into a fixed "preparation *vs.* performance" scheme, we provide mechanisms that give the artist freedom on which level individual design goals are placed. We introduce the high level concept of the *design tree*, which stores and organizes the artist's designs. The tree's nodes, representing individual designs, emerge by interactive composition or reuse during preparation, or as results of live composition during performance. Designs are "activated" (i.e., rendered) by selecting one or multiple design nodes. The series of activated designs results in a linear path, which implements Simon's theory of a *design path* (Simon, 1996). The path represents a temporal plot of the actual performance. In order to allow for smooth transition between different designs, we provide a number of design tree operations, such as merging or mixing design nodes.

The paper starts by briefly discussing relevant related work. Section 3 provides an overview of a typical live visuals system and how the media manager and the design tree have been integrated. In Section 4 and Section 5 the main contributions listed above are presented in detail. Section 6 will show how the actual implementations of the media manager and the design tree are used to create effective live visuals. The paper concludes with final remarks in Section 7.

2   Related Work

There is a wide range of existing software tools for creating live visuals. With the growing popularity of VJing, a large number of custom tools evolved (a comprehensive listing is found at (VJCentral, 2005)). Many of them resemble a digital counterpart of analog video mixers, where multiple video sources can be mixed and overlaid with visual effects. Others pick up the video mixing concept, but add features for digital compositing or rendering of arbitrary geometry, going far beyond the possibilities of analog video mixing (GarageCube, 2005). While most of these tools do a great job and are typically easy to use, their lack of generality imposes a major problem for visual artists that wish to go beyond predefined designs and without carrying a "footprint" of the software they were created with. Therefore, at the other end of the spectrum, applications with a general approach to creating live visuals (and often music as well) exist. They give a lot more freedom to the artist, but at the same time typically require at least some programming and signal processing knowledge. Two examples are Max, which has its origins in music and audio processing, and Touch, which roots in computer graphics modeling and animation.

Max (Pukette, 2002), and in particular Max/MSP and Jitter, represents a family of graphical programming environments. Max has become the *de facto* standard for many sound and visual artists. By applying the graphical programming paradigm objects of different types are interconnected to build *patches*. The patches represent a running program, and they as well serve as the user interface for interactive control. Therefore a programmer can create a "performing instrument", which can be used without programming skills. However, Max lacks means of organizing multiple patches beyond file system browsing or copy and paste. Thus, it is very hard creating several hours of visuals performance where a large number of differing designs is seamlessly arranged and mixed.

Derivative's *Touch* (its ancestor, *Houdini* was used to realize an interactive dance floor at the SIGGRAPH 98 Interactive Dance Club event (Ulyate and Bianciardi, 2002)) approaches the above problem by providing different environments for different levels of interaction: *Visual synthesizers* can be designed in Touch Designer, they can be mixed in Touch Mixer, or just played in Touch Player. At every level, the visual artist can interact (i.e., perform) in real-time.

In our work, the design tree navigation and manipulation methods act as the central means of design creation and modification. There is no distinction between preparation and performance, and our work emphasizes the actual "live design process" of a visual performance. This scheme not only addresses the mixing issues of long performances, it goes a step further and allows for true interpolation of different designs.

Another important task when compositing live visuals is the application of prepared media files. Interactive retrieval and annotation systems have been available for some time, for example (Tseng et al., 2002). However, to our knowledge, there exists no live visuals tool with an integrated media manager that incorporates metadata such as MPEG-7 annotations (Manjunath et al., 2002), making our solution a novelty in this area.

Audio analysis has been used for controlling and aligning visual parameters in a scene graph (Wagner and Carroll, 2001), as well as together with video segmentation methods (Lienhard, 1999; Rui et al., 1999) for automatic or semi-automatic alignment of music and video in interactive offline systems (Foote et al., 2002) and in non-interactive real-time systems (Jehan et al., 2003).

3   System Overview

From a system architecture viewpoint, the common denominator of existing tools for live visuals is real-time rendering engine, which is controlled by a user interface. More specifically, the user interface can manipulate a *processing graph*, which is processed by the rendering engine. The produced output images are typically directed to a preview monitor and one or multiple video projections. In our work, this set-up is enhanced by a media manager and the design tree. The system illustrated in Figure 2 has been implemented in a proprietary live visuals system called SOUNDIUM. Implementation details have been given in (Schubiger and Müller, 2003; Müller Arisona et al., 2006). For the remainder of this section we shall focus on concepts that are essential for understanding the functionality of the media manager and the design tree.

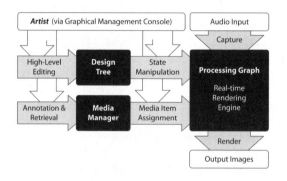

Fig. 2. Overview of the SOUNDIUM system. Our two contributions, the design tree and the media manager (left), increase the efficiency of existing live visuals systems (right).

The processing graph is a directed graph of interconnected *processing nodes*, where of each of them fulfills a certain purpose such as performing a 3D transformation, drawing a polygon, or calculating an audio signal level. Each processing node consists of a number of *input* and *output ports*, which are used for communication. The edges of the graph, interconnecting inputs and outputs, are called *connections*. With the processing graph, audio signal flow processing can be modeled as well as the hierarchical structures describing visual objects and their relations within a 3D world (similar to the well-known scene graph concept (Strauss and Carey, 1992)). Internally, the processing graph is stored as a sequence of SL2 statements. SL2 is an assembler-like scripting language designed for graph manipulation. Because of its simplicity, this textual representation is well suited for refactoring methods carried out by high-level design operations in Section 5.

A simple example is illustrated in Figure 3. The scene graph consists of a viewport, a camera, two transformations, and a node that draws a sphere. Simultaneously, the incoming audio is captured and processed, and the output of the level node is connected to the *Scale.X* input port of the first transformation node. The beat extrapolation node controls an animation curve node, effectively setting the duration of the curve to the beat duration, and restarting the curve with every beat trigger. Finally, the curve output

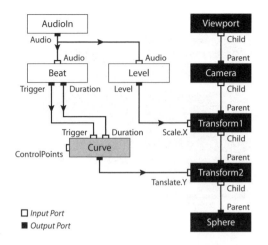

Fig. 3. Simple processing graph example which represents an animated sphere driven by audio. White colored nodes depict the audio signal flow and black nodes represent the 3D scene graph. Additionally, an animation curve node is illustrated in grey.

is connected to the *Translate.Y* input of the second transformation. Typically, only a few of all available input ports are connected. An example is the curve nodes' *ControlPoints* input (all others have been omitted for simplicity). These ports are available for external value assignment by the user interface.

To align visual content to music features, *real-time audio analysis* is needed to extract the latter. In SOUNDIUM, audio analysis methods are realized in terms of processing nodes. Currently, the system provides methods for spectral analysis, beat and onset detection (Scheirer, 1998; Goto, 2001; Brossier et al., 2004), and part detection (e.g., refrains) based on similarity analysis of the signal's spectral composition (Foote et al., 2002). Typically, the audio analysis nodes deliver continuous parameters, such as spectral levels or distributions, and discrete parameters, such as note onset triggers. How the parameters are connected to visual content is an artistic choice. However, SOUNDIUM supports the artist with a number of methods for the manipulation of audio analysis results in order to allow a better match to practical artistic goals, e.g., by providing dedicated processing nodes for modifying extracted rhythmical structures. Hence, manifold correlations between rhythm and visual content can be created.

SOUNDIUM includes a *graphical management console* where interaction between the performer and the system takes place (Figure 4). The main task of the management console is to maintain the current system state and consistent views of it. In addition, interactive state modification, high-level design manipulations, and media management takes also place through the console.

The SOUNDIUM system state is represented as a highlighted node in the design tree (Figure 4, top left). This design node has an expanded view as a processing graph (Figure 4, bottom left). Not shown in Figure 4 are the design's textual representation (SL2) and its visual rendering. Modifications can simultaneously take place through a node inspector (see Figure 4, right) or connected MIDI controllers. Changes are reflected in all views immediately. The management console is non-modal, enabling direct access

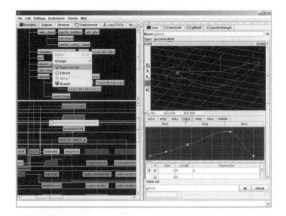

Fig. 4. Screenshot of the graphical management console. Top left: Design tree which permits high-level editing. Bottom left: Processing graph representing the current system state. Right: Node inspector for modification of a selected processing node.

to every object and follows standard interface conventions as well as a minimalist approach for easier learning. Several accelerators and shortcuts ensure a high degree of interactivity for the experienced user. Because error states are fatal during a live performance, modifications are statically checked against boundary conditions and type safety (e.g. input and output port types) before being applied to the system state. Such errors will lead to an invalid design which is signaled to the user without interrupting the performance.

4   The Media Manager

A typical media library of a live visuals artist contains several gigabytes of pictures, video footage, geometric models, and so on. Hence, an efficient media manager is needed to allow for quick interactive access, which is crucial during live performance. In SOUNDIUM, the media manager extracts metadata in a "pre-production" phase by automatically scanning media files according to their type. In addition, the media manager supports manual annotation of media files (e.g., for semantic content descriptions which cannot be acquired automatically). The resulting metadata is stored in XML format based on the MPEG-7 description standard (Manjunath et al., 2002). The digital library with its incorporated metadata can be accessed by using fast and intuitive high-level retrieval mechanisms. The media manager's GUI is embedded in the graphical management console.

4.1   Video Clip Integration

Since most live visual performances include video footage, the video clip is the most important media type a visual artist is working with. Traditionally, footage is prepared manually using video editing tools, which is a very time consuming task. Our approach employs automatic methods, which considerably facilitate dealing with footage and reduce time consuming manual tasks to a minimum: The media manager analyzes the unedited footage using video segmentation techniques for shot boundary detection (Lienhard, 1999) and video abstracting techniques for scene determination (Rui et al., 1999). The latter organizes the clip into *scenes*, *groups* and *shots*. Thus, a video clip is comprised of several scenes containing several groups, and a group itself consists of all visually similar shots within a scene (Figure 5). As a side effect of the scene determination algorithm, shots can be ordered within a group according to their group distance measure. This results in a measure for a group's "best" shot, which the visual artist will most likely use during performance. Furthermore, the media manager analyzes the motion of each shot, which results in a camera movement classification (pan/tilt/zoom/roll), and extracts the representative keyframes of each shot, which can be used for browsing. If desired, the user can modify the automatically generated video clip structure (e.g., by manually changing shot boundaries) and add content descriptions. For storage, the clip's source file is not modified, all editing information is stored exclusively in the metadata. Thus, the original clip is kept applicable to all kinds of scenarios.

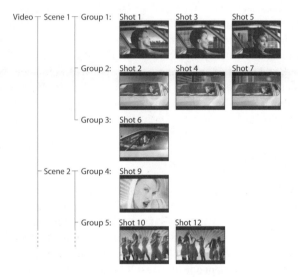

Fig. 5. The hierarchical structure of a video clip reverse-engineered by the media manager (schematic view)

For browsing video clips, the user has the choice of a temporal or a structural view. Particularly, the structural view gives an intuitive overview of the video clip. If the user selects a shot and its destination (i.e., a dedicated input port of a processing node), the media manager streams the corresponding frames to the rendering engine. In order to avoid long seek times within a video clip, each clip is encoded with keyframes at shot boundaries after the preparation phase. If requested, the engine caches the frames, so they remain available for random access later on.

4.2 Interactive NLE

Besides better retrieval capabilities, the extracted metadata of clips allows for a new form of video footage utilization: Interactive NLE of video, i.e., the (semi-)automatic rearrangement of a video clip's individual shots in real-time. In order to align live visuals to music, our approach applies film music theory in the reverse direction: The most popular film music procedure is to conduct the music according to given *visual action points* of a completely finished movie (Gorbmann, 1987). A visual action point is usually associated with a classical film cut, but it can also be within a continuous shot (e.g., the beginning of a pan) or refer to arbitrary types of dramatic events. In our case, visual action points have to be created in real-time for given "musical action points" resulting from audio analysis, for example extracted bar or beat borders may enforce cuts. Following these rules, the (short) clips of the dancers in Figure 1 have been synchronized to the incoming beat and extrapolated beat-durations by non-linearly stretching the clips between two beat boundaries.

In SOUNDIUM, the generation of visual action points is realized in terms of dedicated processing nodes for computer-assisted NLE. During performance, the user has interactive control over the selection of video footage and the node's configuration parameters. For instance, the user can assign a whole video scene or multiple groups to the NLE node, or tune editing parameters such as "cuts per second". The node then analyzes the associated metadata and – according to its configuration – decides which shots finally should be played, and how fast and for how long. SOUNDIUM includes NLE processing nodes implementing different editing techniques (Eisenstein, 1994) ranging from the functionality given above (simulating visual action points) to completely stochastic and audio-independent editing.

5 The Design Tree

In our case, a *design* is a complete description of the processing graph, including its nodes, value vectors, and edges. On a more abstract level, a design directly reflects the realization of an artistic idea. The artist's designs are stored in the *design tree*, a hierarchical data structure, where each node contains information about how the processing graph is to be modified in order to realize a design. Changes to the system state (by using the graphical management console) result in modification of the processing graph and, if desired, also in new nodes in the design tree.

5.1 Realization

In its simplest form, the design tree can be seen as a multilevel undo/redo facility: All user actions manipulating the system state are recorded and can be undone. These state manipulations are recorded as SL2 statements representing individual processing graph changes. The user can decide to commit a design to the design tree, where a new design node is created. When a design is committed, the minimal sequence of SL2 statements yielding the system state is computed and called the *normal form* of a design node.

During the design process, several design nodes are committed by the user in sequence with each node representing a revision of a previous design (Figure 6-b/c). This

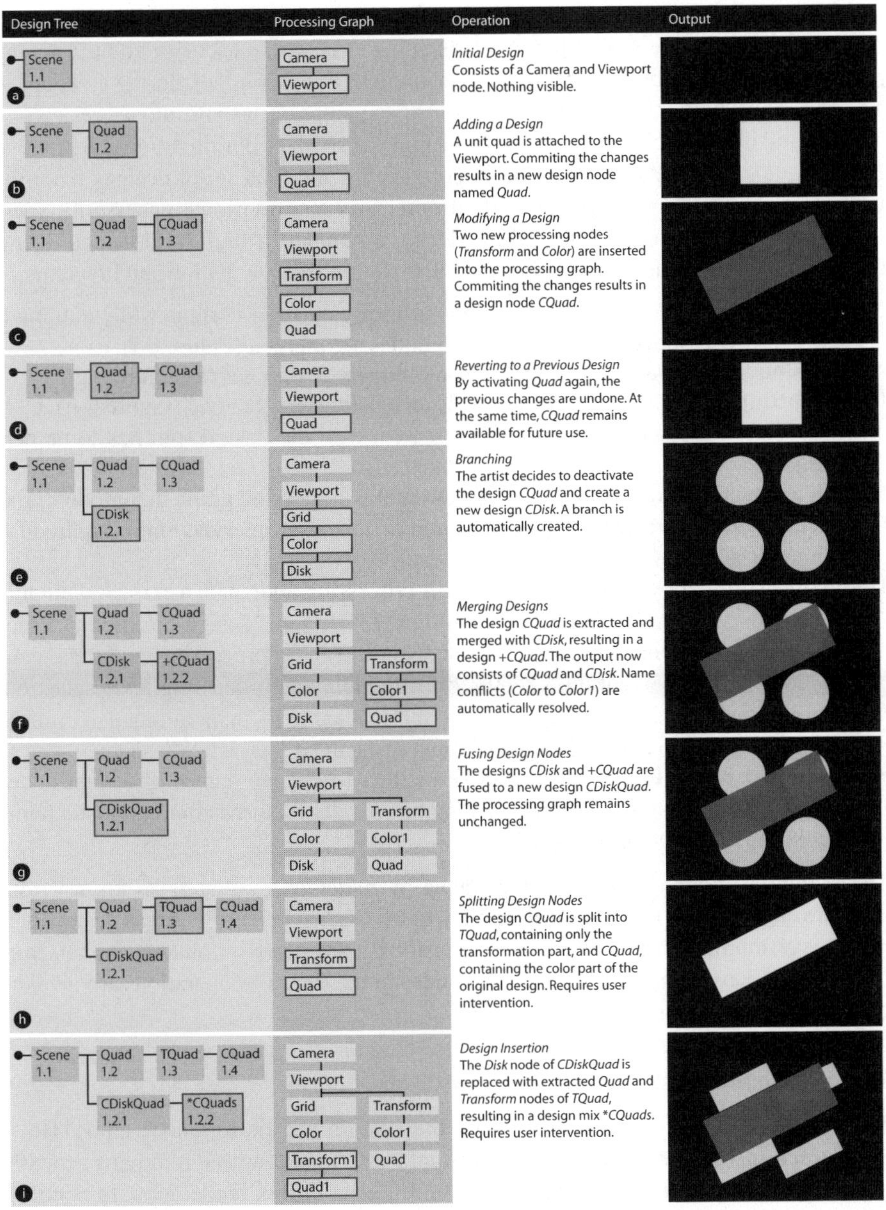

Fig. 6. Design tree operations (rows) and their effects on the processing graph. The framed boxes in the design tree column refer to the currently active design node. The framed boxes in the processing graph column indicate changes evoked by activating the corresponding design node.

is similar to a file versioning system (Cederqvist, 1993) that stores differences from one revision of a file to the next. Like in a versioning system, the user can go back to any previous design (Figure 6-d) and start a new branch (Figure 6-e), exploring a variant of a design. Thus, branching transforms the linear sequence of designs into a tree.

A natural ordering of nodes by time (revisions) takes place during the design process. However, this order has usually little importance for the final set of designs the artist wants to use during a performance. Furthermore, not every revision is necessarily a new design (Ramakrishnan and Ram, 1996). Hence, a number of high-level design operations acting on multiple design nodes complete design tree navigation and branching:

Node merging allows the user to combine arbitrary existing designs while automatically resolving identifier conflicts when nodes are merged (Figure 6-f).

Node fusion allows the user to unify two subsequent design nodes (Figure 6-g).

Node splitting allows the user to subdivide an existing design node (Figure 6-h). User intervention is required to inform the system how the design split has to be performed.

Module extraction encapsulates a subgraph of the processing graph in a module. Extracted modules are available for design insertion. User intervention is required for subgraph selection.

Design insertion allows the user to replace a processing node with a extracted module (Figure 6-i). Whereas node merging *unifies* two designs, design insertion *changes* a design by replacing a processing node by one or more processing nodes and connections. User intervention is required for module and processing node selection. The system proposes a default reconnecting scheme (e.g., maintaining parent-child relationships for scene graph connections) that can be interactively adapted.

SL2 identifier renaming is an interactive method to change names of design nodes and processing nodes. Explicit renaming is typically required after automatic name resolution of merge operations.

These high-level operations are implemented by *refactoring methods*, as known from software engineering (Fowler, 1999) applied to the SL2 code representing a design. Unlike file versioning systems, where every revision is considered immutable, the refactoring methods may change arbitrary design nodes in the tree. The operations are invoked by user interface actions.

5.2   System State Parameterization

The system does not distinguish between preparation and performance mode. However, *structural changes* to the processing graph, such as adding and removing processing nodes and connections are typically more frequent during preparation. In contrast, *parametrical changes*, i.e., assignment of values to input ports, are more common during performance. Changing multiple parameter of a design imposes a problem when switching designs during performance: Strictly following the undo/redo philosophy, all parameter changes will be reverted when deactivating a design node and visually important aspects of an artwork may abruptly change (e.g. motion or color).

In order to maintain visual consistency, the parameter spaces of SOUNDIUM may be treated orthogonal to the structural space consisting of processing nodes and connections. This is achieved by weighted parameter vectors called *valuesets*, whose scope can span multiple design nodes. Valuesets can be defined at every design node and comprise all or a subset of a design's parameters. Since valuesets only contain parameter changes, they can be applied weighted with respect to the current system state, and smooth transitions between the current parametrization and the valueset can be achieved. By changing a single weight, the user can interactively modify a potentially large number of design parameters at once.

Typical applications of valuesets are global and high-level properties of an artwork, such as "softness", "speed", or "entropy" that have general purpose application independent of the actual processing graph.

5.3   The Interactive Design Process

The interactive design process using the design tree can be split into two major stages: In a preparation phase, designs are created in terms of an upcoming performance. During performance, the predefined designs are selected and further modified during the performance. How detailed a performance is prepared is not technically constrained but rather the artist's choice, and often influenced by external factors such as the performance's duration.

Yet, a general procedure for preparation is inherent: The tree's root node generally contains a common setup, as indicated by the "Scene" node (1.1) in Figure 6. In practice, the setup includes a lot more than just a camera and a viewport. It typically comprises of a overall scene lighting, such as a traditional three-light setup (Alton, 1995; Kahrs, 1996), of global transformations (e.g., camera movement, or audio-sensitive dynamics), of real-time NLE nodes, and of full-scene post effects, such as motion blur, glow, or masking. The setup is normally placed in the design tree's root node, or in nodes close to the root. In addition, global valuesets (e.g., overall scene color modification) are placed at this point. Consequently, every design deeper in the tree's structure will inherit the particular global configuration.

The next step is the definition of the actual designs, which may be re-used and adapted from previous performances as needed. The design tree supports the artist in structuring the performance: Designs can be arranged as needed by creating design variations (e.g., *CQuad* is a variation of *Quad* in Figure 6-c) or branches containing a different design (*CDisk* in Figure 6-e). The arrangement may serve as a temporal plot or even as a script during performance, or assist multiple artists using the same common setup along with their individual designs.

Because several parameters (e.g., those resulting from real-time music analysis) are unknown during the preparation phase, these designs are typically anticipatory – their final visual rendering is partially unknown and only emerges in function of the environment during the live performance. This property is particularly effective for VJ performances that usually last several hours with musical content that is not predictable in advance. In addition, anticipatory designs provide enough space for improvisation during the performance.

Throughout the performance, the artist selects, fine-tunes, parameterizes, and applies designs, thereby countervailing the unknown and adding his perception of the moment. All changes to the system state (i.e., the processing graph) are tracked and can be committed to build new design nodes in order to be reused. Using the design operations presented earlier an interpolation from the current design to a target design is easily achieved. This powerful mechanisms implement the idea of a *design path* (Simon, 1996) and allow for a carefully adjusted and uninterrupted performance.

6   Results

SOUNDIUM has been used at numerous live performances ranging from large-scale VJ events to video art performances to interactive multimedia installations. The system has been evaluated by both novice visual artists as well as expert computer artists. For both groups we observed an immediate capability of using the media manager. On the other hand, getting accustomed to the design tree required a tutoring time of a day or two, but then resulting in a steep learning curve. While the novice artists mainly used the tree for recalling designs and as a undo/redo facility, the experts quickly explored the high-level design operations and used them to create their own designs. This section gives concrete examples that were realized interactively using SOUNDIUM.

The first example comprises a typical live performance scenario. It illustrates how the design tree and processing graph operations are applied to quickly evolve a sphere into an audio-driven "digital dance floor". The artist starts by modeling a simple 3D scene and gradually connecting it to extracted audio features: A sphere is scaled by the low frequency levels of the incoming audio signal and moves on an elliptical orbit, changing its direction on every bass drum onset (similar to Figure 3). Additionally, the bass drum onsets also change the faces' filled/wireframe state. The resulting output is shown in Figure 7 (top row). Now, the performer's design goal is to move the camera into the sphere and add a dance floor including dancers. Since this occurs during a live performance, the following steps must be executed reasonably fast and with the help

Fig. 7. Designing a digital dance floor. The top row shows the current design, visible to the audience on the main output while the artist prepares the transition into the sphere on the preview output (center row). Eventually the resulting scene is shown from different camera angles that are switched in context to the music (bottom row).

Fig. 8. Valueset example. The current design on the left is smoothly faded into a new appearance according to the settings of a user-defined valueset "bright". The valueset affects the color of the geometry, the three-light setup, the media selection in the corresponding NLE-node, and the glow node.

of a preview output (i.e., intermediate steps are not visible on the main outputs), which is illustrated in Figure 7 (center row). The dancing girls (Figure 1) are extracted from the artist's design tree and merged with the current design. A "multiple copy" processing node is inserted to generate a crowd of dancers. The dance floor consisting of a grid of quads is then modeled from scratch through direct manipulation of the processing graph. The quads' colors are defined by both the audio level and the grid position. Then, the dance floor and the dancers are transformed to fit into the sphere. Now, all components are in place and ready to be successively shown on the main output. Ultimately, the camera is moved into the sphere and a set of audio-driven different camera viewing-angles and transformation speeds is added (Figure 7, bottom row). Altogether, above steps take the (experienced) artist about 10 minutes.

Figure 8 demonstrates the application of valuesets. The user defined a valueset called "bright" as part of the root design and applied it to a design consisting of a geometry and the video clip of Figure 5. The valueset affects several processing graph nodes of the root design: The colors of geometry nodes, the luminance-based selection of video footage in corresponding NLE-nodes, the three-light setup and the glow node. Since these nodes and the valueset are part of the root design, the valueset is applicable to all other designs (as long as they make use of the nodes defined in the root design).

The third example illustrates how design operations (Section 5) are applied for efficient live design editing. The source design (Figure 9, left) is transformed into a target design, i.e. five cubes representing the audio spectrum (right). Two possible design transitions are shown. In both transitions, design insertion has been applied to transfer the target's background color to the source design while the source design's structural dominance has been gradually reduced. Application of the design operations including user intervention took about 5 minutes for each transition, provided that source and target design are given in advance.

In the last example, analyzed video footage has been rearranged in real-time by interactive NLE: Using the media manager, the video was automatically segmented into three scenes consisting of several shots. Scene 1 consists of five groups of shots showing a woman in blue color tones, scene 2 consists of two groups showing a close up of a man's face in dark color tones, and scene 3 consists of four groups of the woman and the man waiting for a train. During performance, the artist matches these three scenes to three different patterns detected by a dedicated "novelty measure" audio processing node (Foote et al., 2002). In addition to the computer-assisted alignment of scenes to

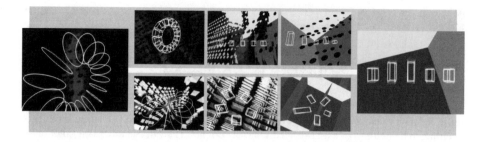

Fig. 9. Design transformation example. The design on the left is transformed into the one on the right by applying design operations. Two possible alternatives are illustrated.

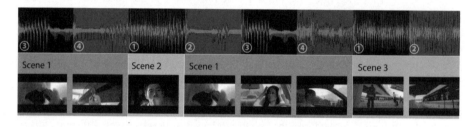

Fig. 10. Interactive real-time video editing example. Different shots of three scenes are aligned to different music parts using similarity analysis. The individual shots are non-linearly stretched to beat intervals. The beat numbers (4/4 measure) are denoted on the horizontal axis.

music parts, individual shots are non-linearly stretched in order to fit into beat intervals. Figure 10 illustrates two bars of music together with the representative keyframe of the emerging shots (the difference between musical pattern 2 and 3 is not visible in the waveform).

7   Conclusions

We presented two novel extensions for live visual performance systems. Together, the contributions raise live performance to a higher level, allowing the artist to focus on design and content instead of low level processing details.

First, the media manager substantially enhances the way the artist interacts with large media libraries. Most important, annotated and segmented video clips together with real-time audio analysis methods can be used for real-time non-linear video editing during performance. Although the computer vision methods applied for video segmentation impose certain limitations in terms of correctness, they have proven enormously valuable, and the method of automatic analysis and manual adjustment is much faster than manual segmentation. In addition, since we adhere to the MPEG-7 standard, annotated "ready-for-use" video footage databases will eventually become available. Nonetheless, a future work direction is the implementation of additional vision methods for visual semantic-based mining and retrieval (e.g., object recognition using local features). Interactive NLE could be facilated by introducing a control grammar (Wonka et al., 2003) to encode editing techniques. Furthermore, interactive video compositing tools could be integrated into SOUNDIUM (Wang et al., 2005).

Second, the novel concept of the design tree stores and organizes the visual artist's designs and acts as a link between preparation and performance. High level design operations and refactoring methods significantly reduce the time required to create and manipulate individual designs. They further provide means of design interpolation and allow for a seamless performance. For more intuitive usage and navigation of large design repositories (e.g., thousands of designs), future work may introduce a semantic-based annotation model for the design tree.

Both extensions have been implemented as part of the SOUNDIUM live visuals system. We however believe that both of them can be applied to other existing live visuals systems. In view of ever growing media libraries it is only a matter of time until other systems *must* provide a media manager. We further believe that the design tree, which is a unique and very general concept *per se*, is not only suited for live visuals systems but could be adapted for virtually any interactive software system, in the simplest case by just replacing the common one-dimensional undo/redo mechanism.

Finally, finding an optimal user interaction model for computer-based live performance certainly remains an attractive direction for future work. In particular, we focus on live composition and performance of music *and* visuals using the same software system.

Acknowledgements

We thank Jürg Gutknecht and Luc Van Gool of ETH Zürich, and Christoph P. E. Zollikofer of University of Zürich for supporting our work. Thanks are also due to Philippe Wüger, Mortiz Oetiker and David Stadelmann for implementing the vision algorithms. This research was supported in part by the NCCR IM2, by SNF grant 205321-102024/1, by Swisscom, and by the mighty Corebounce association.

References

Alton, J.: Painting With Light. University of California Press (1995)

Brossier, P., Bello, J.P., Plumbley, M.D.: Real-time temporal segmentation of note objects in music signals. In: Proceedings of the 2004 International Computer Music Conference, International Computer Music Association (2004)

Cederqvist, P.: Version Management with CVS. Signum Support AB (1993)

Eisenstein, S.: Selected Works 2: Towards a Theory of Montage. In: N. Glenny, R. Taylor, (eds.) British Film Institute (1994)

Foote, J., Cooper, M., Girgensohn, A.: Creating music videos using automatic media analysis. In: Proc. ACM Intl. Conf. on Multimedia, pp. 553–560. ACM, New York (2002)

Fowler, M.: Refactoring: Improving the Design of Existing Code. Addison-Wesley Object Technology Series. Addison-Wesley, Reading (1999)

Cube, G.: Modul8 real-time video mixing and compositing software. (2005),
    http://www.garagecube.com

Gorbmann, C.: Unheard Melodies: Narrative Film Music. Indiana University Press (1987)

Goto, M.: An audio-based real-time beat tracking system for music with or without drum sound. Journal of New Music Research 30(2), 158–171 (2001)

Jehan, T., Lew, M., Vaucelle, C.: Cati dance: Self-edited, self-synchronized music video. In: GRAPH '03: Proceedings of the SIGGRAPH 2003 Conference on Sketches & Applications, ACM Press, New York (2003)

Kahrs, J.: Pixel cinematography: Lighting for computer graphics. In: ACM SIGGRAPH 1996 Course Notes, ACM Press, New York (1996)

Lienhard, R.: Comparison of automatic shot boundary detection algorithms. In: Image and Video Processing VII. Proc. SPIE 3656-29 (1999)

Manjunath, B.S., Salembier, P., Sikora, T.: Introduction to MPEG-7: Multimedia Content Description Interface. John Wiley and Sons, Chichester (2002)

Müller Arisona, S., Schubiger-Banz, S., Specht, M.: A real-time multimedia composition layer. In: Proceedings of AMCMM, Workshop on Audio and Music Computing for Multimedia, ACM Press, New York (2006)

Pukette, M.: Max at seventeen. Computer Music Journal 26(4), 31–43 (2002)

Ramakrishnan, R., Ram, D.J.: Modeling design versions. The VLDB Journal, pp. 556–566 (1996)

Rui, Y., Huang, T.S., Mehrotra, S.: Constructing table-of-content for videos. ACM Multimedia Systems 7(5), 359–368 (1999)

Scheirer, E.: Tempo and beat analysis of acoustic musical signals. J. Acoust. Soc. Am. 103(1), 588–601 (1998)

Schubiger, S., Müller, S.: Soundium2: An interactive multimedia playground. In: Proceedings of the 2003 International Computer Music Conference, International Computer Music Association (2003)

Simon, H.A.: The Sciences of the Artificial. MIT Press, Cambridge (1996)

Strauss, P.S., Carey, R.: An object-oriented 3D graphics toolkit. In: Computer Graphics (Proceedings of SIGGRAPH 92), vol. 26(2), pp. 341–349. ACM, New York (1992)

Sutherland, I. E.: Sketchpad, a Man-Machine Graphical Communication System. PhD thesis, Massachusetts Institute of Technology (1963)

Tseng, B.L., Lin, C.-Y., Smith, J.R.: Video personalization and summarization system. In: Internet Multimedia Management Systems. SPIE Photonics East (2002)

Ulyate, R., Bianciardi, D.: The interactive dance club: Avoiding chaos in a multi-participant environment. Computer Music Journal 26(3), 40–49 (2002)

VJCentral (2005), http://www.vjcentral.com

Wagner, M.G., Carroll, S.: Deepwave: Visualizing music with VRML. In: VSMM '01: Proceedings of the Seventh International Conference on Virtual Systems and Multimedia (VSMM'01), p. 590. IEEE Computer Society Press, Los Alamitos (2001)

Wang, J., Bhat, P., Colburn, A., Agrawala, M., Cohen, M.: Interactive video cutout. In: Proceedings of ACM SIGGRAPH 2005 / ACM Transactions on Graphics, vol. 24(3), pp. 585–594. ACM, New York (2005)

Wonka, P., Wimmer, M., Sillion, F., Ribarsky, W.: Instant architecture. In: Proceedings of ACM SIGGRAPH 2003 / ACM Transactions on Graphics, vol. 22(3), pp. 669–677. ACM, New York (2003)

Part V

Image Formation
and Processing

Tolerance-Based Feature Transforms

Dennie Reniers and Alexandru Telea

Department of Mathematics and Computer Science, Eindhoven University of Technology
Den Dolech 2, 5600 MB, Eindhoven, The Netherlands
D.Reniers@tue.nl, alext@win.tue.nl

Abstract. Tolerance-based feature transforms (TFTs) assign to each pixel in an image not only the nearest feature pixels on the boundary (origins), but all origins from the minimum distance up to a user-defined tolerance. In this paper, we compare four simple-to-implement methods for computing TFTs on binary images. Of these methods, the Fast Marching TFT and Euclidean TFT are new. The other two extend existing distance transform algorithms. We quantitatively and qualitatively compare all algorithms on speed and accuracy of both distance and origin results. Our analysis is aimed at helping practitioners in the field to choose the right method for given accuracy and performance constraints.

Keywords: Feature transform, tolerance-based, distance transform, algorithms, image processing.

1 Introduction

A distance transform (DT) computes, for pixel p of an image, the distance $D(p) = \min_{q \in \delta\Omega} \|q - p\|$ to the nearest feature pixel, or *origin*, q on the boundary $\delta\Omega$ of some object Ω located in the image (Fig. 1). Non-object pixels will be denoted by $\bar{\Omega}$. There can be several equidistant origins q for a pixel p, i.e., the origin set $S(p) = \arg\min_{q \in \delta\Omega} \|q - p\|$ of p can have more than one element. The feature transform (FT) assigns to each pixel p the origin set $S(p)$. A *simple* FT computes only one origin per pixel, which is sufficient for some applications. We define a *tolerance-based* FT (TFT) as a map that assigns to each pixel the origin set $S_\epsilon(p) = \{q \in \delta\Omega \mid \|q - p\| \leq D(p) + \epsilon\}$, where ϵ is a user-defined tolerance. One use of the TFT is to compute exact Euclidean DTs, as first observed in (Mullikin, 1992) (see also Sec. 5). A second use of the TFT is to compute robust, connected skeletons or medial axes, as follows. Medial axis (MA) points can be detected as the FT points having at least two origins, one on each side of the axis (Foskey et al., 2003). However, this definition may yield disconnected skeletons in a discrete space. For example, for a rectangle of even height, no pixels lie exactly in the middle. Using a TFT with tolerance 1, origins from both axis sides are found, yielding a connected skeleton. Figure 2 shows the TFT for an object using four different tolerances ϵ. The pixel intensity denotes the origin set size $|S_\epsilon|$. The origin sets of four selected pixels are shown using white line segments. For $\epsilon = 0$, it can be seen that pixel p has only one origin because the horizontal rectangle is of even height. Using a tolerance $\epsilon \geq 1$, the origin set $S_\epsilon(p)$ contains origins from both sides of the rectangle.

J. Braz et al. (Eds.): VISAPP and GRAPP 2006, CCIS 4, pp. 187–200, 2007.

Fig. 1. The distance transform of an object. The pixel intensity denotes distance to the object boundary.

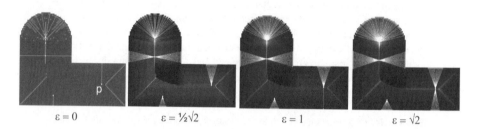

| $\varepsilon = 0$ | $\varepsilon = \frac{1}{2}\sqrt{2}$ | $\varepsilon = 1$ | $\varepsilon = \sqrt{2}$ |

Fig. 2. The TFT of an object using four different tolerances $\epsilon = 0, \frac{1}{2}\sqrt{2}, 1, \sqrt{2}$

Overall, both DTs and FTs have numerous applications in many domains (Cuisenaire, 1999; Ye, 1988) ranging from image processing, pattern recognition, and shape representation and modeling, to path planning, computer animation, skeletonization, and optimization algorithms.

DT and FT algorithms can be classified by the order in which they process the image pixels. Raster scanning algorithms (Danielsson, 1980) sequentially process pixels in scan-line order, needing multiple passes in which pixels are assigned new minimum distances. Ordered propagation methods (Ragnemalm, 1992) reduce the number of distance computations needed by updating only pixels in a contour set, which propagates from the object boundary $\delta\Omega$ inwards. Ordered propagation methods accommodate (distance-based) stopping criteria easier than raster scanning ones, thus being more efficient for some applications. A well-known class of ordered propagation methods are level-set and fast marching methods (FMM) (Sethian, 1999), which evolve the contour $\delta\Omega$ under normal speed (see Section 2). Although the FMM does not compute an exact Euclidean DT, the speed function it uses can be locally varied to compute more complex DTs, e.g., anisotropic, weighted, Manhattan, or position-dependent ones (Sethian, 1999; Strzodka and Telea, 2004). Recent FMM extensions compute an FT (Telea and van Wijk, 2002; Telea and Vilanova, 2003). However, this is only a simple FT, and can be quite inaccurate in many cases. Applications using this origin set, such as skeletonization, can deliver wrong results, as pointed out in (Strzodka and Telea, 2004).

As the above outlines, DT and FT methods have many, often subtle, trade-offs, which are not obvious to many practitioners in the field. In this paper, we discuss several competitive DT, FT, and TFT methods. Some of these methods extend existing ones, while others are new. We quantitatively and qualitatively compare the results of all methods with the exact TFT computed by brute force, and discuss the computational advantages and limitations of every method. The goal of our analysis is to provide a quantitative, practical guideline for choosing the "right" DT or (T)FT method to best match real-world application requirements, such as precision, performance, completeness, and implementation complexity.

This paper is structured as follows. In Section 2 we discuss the FMM and we detail on its inaccuracies. In Section 3, we modify the existing Augmented Fast Marching Method (AFMM) to yield exact simple FTs, and illustrate its use by skeletonization applications. In Section 4, we extend this idea to compute TFTs by adding a distance-to-origin tolerance. In Section 5, we analyze Mullikin's raster scanning DT, and get insight into how to set our TFT tolerance to compute exact DTs. In Section 6, we present a novel method, called ETFT, based on a different propagation order than the FMM. In Section 7, we compare our new ETFT with the related graph-search method of (Lotufo et al., 2000), and also extend the latter to compute TFTs. Finally, we quantitatively compare all of the above methods (Sec. 8) and come to a conclusion (Sec. 9).

2   Fast Marching Method (FMM)

Level set methods are an Eulerian approach for tracking contours evolving in time. The fast marching method (FMM) (Sethian, 1999) treats the special case of contours with constant sign speed functions F. The contour position p, given by its arrival time $T(p)$, is the solution of $\|\nabla T\|F = 1$ with $T = 0$ for the initial contour $\delta\Omega$. If $F = 1$, we obtain the Eikonal equation $\|\nabla T\| = 1$ whose solution is the Euclidean DT of $\delta\Omega$. The FMM efficiently computes T using the fact that $T(p)$ depends only on the T values of p's neighbors $N(p)$ for which $T(N(p)) < T(p)$. The FMM builds T from the smallest computed T values by maintaining the pixels in the evolving contour, or narrow band, sorted on T. Pixels are split into three types: *known* pixels p^{K} have an already computed T; *temporary* pixels (p^{T}) have a T subject to update; and *unknown* pixels (p^{U}) have not yet been assigned a T value. Invariant is $T(p^{\mathrm{K}}) \leq T(p^{\mathrm{T}}) \leq T(p^{\mathrm{U}})$. Initially, all pixels on $\delta\Omega$ are known to have $T = 0$ and their neighbors become temporary. Next, the temporary pixel p with smallest T becomes known (as its T cannot be influenced by other pixels), its unknown neighbors $N^{\mathrm{U}}(p)$ become temporary, and their T values are updated based on their own known neighbors, until all pixels become known. For a contour of length $B = |\delta\Omega|$ and area $N = |\Omega|$ pixels, the FMM needs $O(N \log B)$ steps, because it visits each object pixel once, and keeping the narrow band sorted on T in each iteration needs $O(\log B)$ steps.

The DT computed by the FMM is not exact. Errors occur due to the approximation of the gradient ∇T, usually of first or second order, the former being the most common. The errors are accumulated during the propagation. In (Sethian, 1999, Sec. 12.3), the FMM accuracy is briefly treated, but no comments are made on the implications for real-world applications. Figure 3 and Table 1 show the difference between the FMM and the exact DT for some typical shapes. High errors (bright areas in Fig. 3) seem to "diffuse" away from boundary concavities. Indeed, a temporary point at a narrow band

Fig. 3. Differences between the (approximate) FMM distance and the exact Euclidean distance for the 'bird', 'leaf', and 'dent' images. Black indicates no error, white indicates the maximum error. See Table 1 for the exact values.

Table 1. Differences between (approximate) FMM and exact Euclidean distances D (%e: ratio of erroneous pixels to object pixels; $\max e$: maximum error; $\bar{e}$: average error)

image	img.size	$\max D$	%e	$\max e$	$\bar{e}$
bird	238×370	49.82	89%	0.679	0.142
leaf	410×444	70.63	84%	1.013	0.290
dent	464×397	134.06	15%	1.210	0.082

concavity has just one known neighbor N^K, so its distance is updated from a single known $T(N^K)$ value. A point at a narrow band convexity has several known neighbors, so its distance T is updated using more information. The maximal DT error can easily exceed 1 pixel (cf. Table 1), and can grow arbitrarily with the image size.

3   AFMM Star

In (Telea and van Wijk, 2002), the Augmented FMM (AFMM) is presented, which computes one origin per pixel by propagating an arc-length parameterization U of the initial boundary $\delta\Omega$ together with FMM's T value. $U(p)$ basically identifies an origin $S(p)$. When a narrow band pixel p is made known and its unknown direct 4-neighbors $a \in N_4^U(p)$ are added to the narrow band, $U(a)$ is set to $U(p)$. After propagation has completed, for all points q where U varies with at least τ over $N_4(q)$, a segment of at least length τ from the original boundary collapses. Hence, the above point set $\{q\}$ represents a (pruned) skeleton, or medial axis, of $\delta\Omega$, with τ as the pruning parameter. AFMM's complexity remains the same as for the FMM, namely $O(N \log B)$, where N is the number of object pixels and B the boundary size, because it adds just the propagation of one extra value U. Similar methods are (Costa and Cesar, 2001) for digital images and (Ogniewicz and Kübler, 1995) for polygonal contours, respectively.

However efficient and effective for computing simple FTs and skeletons, the AFMM has several accuracy problems when computing U, as can be easily seen from the

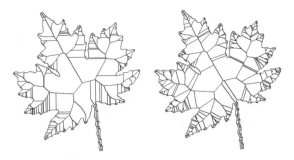

Fig. 4. AFMM skeletonization errors (left). AFMM Star skeletonization (right).

resulting skeletons. Errors show up as skeleton branches having the wrong angle, are too thick, or are disconnected (e.g., Fig. 4 left). The reason is that the value $U(a)$ is determined by only *one* pixel $p \in N_4(a)$, namely the p that is first made known. We propose to solve this problem as follows. For a point a that is made temporary, we set $S(a)$ (or equivalently $U(a)$) to the closest origin among the neighbor's origin sets, i.e.:

$$S(a) = \underset{q \in S(N_8^{\kappa,\tau}(a))}{\arg\min} \|q - a\|. \tag{1}$$

This method, which we call AFMM Star, solves AFMM's inaccuracy problems, i.e., yields a reliable simple FT method. AFMM Star robustly computes pixel-exact, pixel-thin, connected skeletons for arbitrarily complex noisy 2D boundaries (e.g., Fig. 4 right). One remaining problem is that we use the numerically inexact FMM DT (cf. Sec. 2). For practical applications, e.g. skeletonization, incorrect skeleton points will occur only where the FMM DT error exceeds 1 pixel. From Table 1, we see that this happens only at a very few pixels of relatively large objects. This gives a quantitative estimate of the AFMM Star limitations.

4   Fast Marching TFT

The AFMM Star is a simple FT, i.e., it computes just one origin per point. However, some applications, such as angle-based skeletonization (Foskey et al., 2003) require all origins to be found. Moreover, multiple-origin FTs are desired for the reasons outlined in Section 1.

We now propose the novel Fast Marching TFT (FMTFT) which computes for each pixel p an origin set S_ϵ whose size depends on a user-defined distance tolerance ϵ, i.e.:

$$S_\epsilon(p) = \left\{ q \in \delta\Omega \mid \|q - p\| \le D(p) + \epsilon \right\}. \tag{2}$$

The pseudo code is shown in Figure 5. The distances D^{f} are computed by the FMM (line 15), see e.g. (Sethian, 1999). We initialize the origin set $S(p) = \{q \in \delta\Omega \mid \|q - p\| \le \epsilon\}$ for $p \in \delta\Omega$. When the distance of a point a is updated during the FMM evolution, we simultaneously construct a candidate set C (line 16):

$$C(a) = \bigcup_{q \in N_s^{\kappa,\tau}(a) \cup \{a\}} S(q), \tag{3}$$

```
 1: for each p ∈ Ω ∪ Ω̄ do
 2:     if p ∈ Ω̄ then
 3:         f(p) ← K, Dᶠ(p) ← −1
 4:     else if p ∈ δΩ then
 5:         f(p) ← T, Dᶠ(p) ← 0, S(p) ← {q ∈ δΩ|‖q−p‖ ≤ ε}
 6:     else if p ∈ Ω ∧ p ∉ δΩ then
 7:         f(p) ← U, Dᶠ(p) ← ∞
 8:     end if
 9: end for
10: while ∃_q f(q) = T do
11:     p ← arg min Dᶠ(q)
             q:f(q)=T
12:     f(p) ← K
13:     for each a ∈ N₄^{U,T}(p) do
14:         f(a) ← T
15:         Dᶠ(a) ← min(Dᶠ(a),compdist(N₄^K(a)))
16:         C ← ⋃_{q∈N_s^{K,T}(a)∪{a}} (S(q))
17:         D(a) ← min_{q∈C} ‖q − a‖
18:         S(a) ← {q ∈ C | ‖q − a‖ ≤ D(a) + ε}
19:     end for
20: end while
```

Fig. 5. Fast Marching TFT (FMTFT)

where s is the neighborhood size. Next, let the distance $D(a) = \min_{q \in C(a)} \|q - a\|$. $D(a)$ is more accurate than the FMM distance $D^f(a)$, because it is computed directly as the distance from a to its nearest origin, while D^f is computed incrementally by a first-order approximation of the gradient. D^f is used only to determine the propagation order (line 11), as for the AFMM Star (Sec. 3). The tolerance-based origin set $S(a)$ is constructed by *pruning* C in line 18:

$$S_\epsilon(a) \leftarrow \left\{ q \in C \,\middle|\, \|q - p\| \leq D(p) + \epsilon \right\}. \tag{4}$$

Thus, this algorithm assumes that the origin set of a pixel a can be determined from the origin sets of a's neighbors. Statement (4) also occurs in all other to-be-discussed methods (line 30 in Fig. 7, line 17 in Fig. 8, and line 16 in Fig. 9).

The accuracy of D is influenced by the neighborhood size s and the tolerance ϵ. D can be made more accurate by increasing s. In general however, D cannot be made exact no matter the choice of s. This is because the Voronoi regions of origin pixels are not always connected sets on a discrete grid (Cuisenaire, 1999). In contrast, ϵ *can* be set so that all distance errors are eliminated. This was also observed by Mullikin, in a related context, as detailed in the next section.

5 ε-Vector Distance Transform

Mullikin presents in (Mullikin, 1992) a scan-based algorithm for computing exact Euclidean DTs. He first identifies pixel arrangements for which Danielsson's scan-based vector distance transform (VDT) with 4-neighborhoods (Danielsson, 1980) yields inexact distances. The problem of the VDT is that it stores only one origin. In Figure 6, the VDT computes that $S(q) = \{a\}$ and $S(r) = \{b\}$. For p, one of the nearest origins from

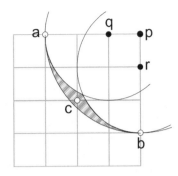

Fig. 6. Pixels a, b and c are object pixels. Pixel p is the pixel under consideration, q and r are its relevant 4-neighbors.

its 4-neighbors is taken. Thus $S(p) \in S(q) \cup S(r) = \{a, b\}$, while the actual nearest origin is $S(p) = \{c\}$. This situation occurs when there are three object pixels a, b, c so that $\|aq\| < \|cq\|$, $\|br\| < \|cr\|$, $\|cp\| < \|ap\|$, and $\|cp\| < \|bp\|$, i.e., when the hatched area contains a grid point. Mullikin proposes, in his ϵVDT, to store *all* nearest origins, and additionally all origins at a distance within a certain tolerance ϵ. Essentially, ϵVDT computes origin sets as defined in Equation (2). Mullikin shows that an exact distance transform is obtained when $\epsilon \geq \sqrt{D}/D$, where D is the number of spatial dimensions. This result can also be used for the other methods discussed in this paper.

The ϵVDT computes tolerance-based origin sets only as a means to compute exact DTs. Mullikin does not detail on the accuracy of the origin sets themselves in (Mullikin, 1992). Moreover, he uses only 4-neighborhoods as these are sufficient for exact Euclidean distances. We extended ϵVDT to also use 8-neighborhoods (see pseudo code in Fig. 7). These are useful for improving the origin set accuracy, as shown in Table 2. The pseudo code can be found in Figure 7. The ϵVDT is compared to the other methods in Section 8.

Besides the fact that the ϵVDT uses a scan-based approach, another conceptual difference with the FMTFT is that it uses a write formalism instead of a read formalism (Verwer et al., 1989). Whereas in the FMTFT the candidate origin set C of a pixel a is constructed by reading from all neighboring pixels (line 16 in Fig. 5), the ϵVDT writes information from a single neighbor to a (line 28 in Fig. 7).

6   Euclidean TFT

The FMTFT visits points in the order of the inaccurate FMM distances (Sec. 4). Although this keeps the original FMM advantage of using different speed functions, an erroneous propagation order potentially influences the distance and origin set accuracy (Sec. 1). The idea comes thus naturally to design an ordered propagation FT which visits the points in order of the accurately computed distances. We present the pseudo code of this new method, called Euclidean TFT, in Figure 8. The neighborhood size s (line 15) and tolerance ϵ (line 17) have the same meaning as for the FMTFT and ϵVDT discussed above. The initialization is the same as for the FMTFT, it also uses a read

```
 1: for each p ∈ δΩ do
 2:     S(p) ← {q ∈ δΩ| ‖q − p‖ ≤ ε}
 3: end for
 4: for y from 0 to N − 1 do
 5:     for x from 0 to M − 1 do
 6:         update( (x,y), (x-1,y-1) ) if s = 8
 7:         update( (x,y), (x,y-1) )
 8:         update( (x,y), (x+1, y-1) ) if s = 8
 9:         update( (x,y), (x-1, y) )
10:     end for
11:     for x from M − 1 downto 0 do
12:         update( (x,y), (x+1,y) )
13:     end for
14: end for
15: for y from N − 1 downto 0 do
16:     for x from 0 to M − 1 do
17:         update( (x,y), (x-1, y+1) ) if s = 8
18:         update( (x,y), (x, y-1) )
19:         update( (x,y), (x+1, y+1) ) if s = 8
20:         update( (x,y), (x-1, y) )
21:     end for
22:     for x from M − 1 downto 0 do
23:         update( (x,y), (x+1,y) )
24:     end for
25: end for
26: procedure update(a,b)
27: if a, b ∈ Ω then
28:     C ← S(a) ∪ S(b)
29:     D(a) ← min_{q∈C} ‖q − a‖
30:     S(a) ← {q ∈ C | ‖q − a‖ ≤ D(a) + ε}
31: end if
32: end procedure
```

Fig. 7. ϵ-Vector Distance Transform (ϵVDT). The image has dimensions $M \times N$.

formalism, and the propagation is still in the order of increasing distances. However, where the FMTFT propagates on D^f (Fig. 5, line 11), the ETFT propagates on the more accurate distances D (Fig. 8, line 11).

We found out that the above exact-distance propagation order yielded a comparable speed and accuracy, posing no advantage over the FMM order. Thus, we made the following change. Whereas the FMTFT updates all pixels $a \in N^{U,T}(p)$ (Fig. 5, line 13), the ETFT was made to update only pixels $a \in N^U(p)$ (Fig. 8, line 13). Now the ETFT updates pixels only once, trading accuracy for speed (see Table 2).

7   Graph-Search TFT

The FMTFT and ETFT resemble the graph-search approach of (Lotufo et al., 2000). However, the graph-search method uses a write formalism, and propagates only one

```
 1: for each p ∈ Ω ∪ Ω̄ do
 2:    if p ∈ Ω̄ then
 3:       f(p) ← K, D(p) ← −1
 4:    else if p ∈ δΩ then
 5:       f(p) ← T, D(p) ← 0, S(p) ← {q ∈ δΩ|‖q −
          p‖ ≤ ε}
 6:    else if p ∈ Ω ∧ p ∉ δΩ then
 7:       f(p) ← U, D(p) ← ∞
 8:    end if
 9: end for
10: while ∃_q f(q) = T do
11:    p ← arg min D(q)
              q:f(q)=T
12:    f(p) ← K
13:    for each a ∈ N_4^U(p) do
14:       f(a) ← T
15:       C ← ⋃_{q∈N_s^{K,T}(a)∪{a}} (S(q))
16:       D(a) ← min_{q∈C} ‖q − a‖
17:       S(a) ← {q ∈ C | ‖q − a‖ ≤ D(a) + ε}
18:    end for
19: end while
```

Fig. 8. The Euclidean TFT algorithm (ETFT)

origin per pixel, i.e., it is a simple FT. We extended Lotufo's algorithm to a TFT, so that it can be readily compared to the FMTFT, ϵVDT, and ETFT methods. Figure 9 gives the pseudo code for this extension, called the Graph-search TFT (GTFT). Now the differences between the ETFT and GTFT methods become visible. While GTFT uses only the flags T and K and updates all neighboring pixels a of p flagged as T (Fig. 9, line 13), ETFT also uses the flag U and only updates these pixels (Fig. 8, line 13). Since there are in general less pixels flagged U in ETFT than T in GTFT, ETFT updates less pixels per iteration. However, the update of a pixel in ETFT involves more work as all neighbors of a are used (Fig. 8, line 15), whereas in GTFT only p is used (Fig. 9, line 14). The running time differences are detailed in the next section.

8   Comparison

Unlike DT methods, the computational complexity of (T)FT methods depends on the origin set sizes and is therefore strongly input dependent. For example, the center of a circle is a worst case, as its origin set contains all boundary points. The origin set size, for points inside convex object-regions, increases with distance to boundary. When updating a pixel p, the whole candidate origin set for p must be inspected. For N image pixels, and B boundary pixels, this poses a worst case of $O(N(B+\log B))$ for the three propagation-based methods and $O(NB)$ for ϵVDT. Luckily, average real-world images are far from this worst case. However, it is difficult to mathematically characterize the average input image. Nevertheless, to give more insight into real-world running times, we empirically compare all discussed TFT methods on speed and accuracy of both

```
 1: for each p ∈ Ω ∪ Ω̄ do
 2:     if p ∈ Ω̄ then
 3:         f(p) ← K, D(p) ← −1
 4:     else if p ∈ δΩ then
 5:         f(p) ← T, D(p) ← 0, S(p) ← {q ∈ δΩ | ‖q −
           p‖ ≤ ϵ}
 6:     else if p ∈ Ω ∧ p ∉ δΩ then
 7:         f(p) ← T, D(p) ← ∞
 8:     end if
 9: end for
10: while ∃_q f(q) = T do
11:     p ← arg min D(q)
             q:f(q)=T
12:     f(p) ← K
13:     for each a ∈ N_s^T(p) do
14:         C ← S(a) ∪ S(p)
15:         D(a) ← min_{q∈C} ‖q − a‖
16:         S(a) ← {q ∈ C | ‖q − a‖ ≤ D(a) + ϵ}
17:     end for
18: end while
```

Fig. 9. The Graph-search TFT algorithm (GTFT)

distances and origin sets. We use images that are often used as typical input for image processing algorithms.

We implemented all methods and ran them on a Pentium IV 3GHz with 1 GB RAM. Some design decisions had to be made here. For the propagation-based methods (FMTFT, ETFT, GTFT) we used a priority queue to efficiently find the temporary pixel at minimum distance to the boundary. Origin sets are stored as STL multimaps (Musser and Saini, 1996) containing (distance,origin) pairs, so that merging two origin sets takes $O(n \log n)$ time (as we must avoid duplicates), while pruning the conservative set takes $O(\log n)$. To prevent floating point precision problems when performing Statement (4), it is needed to evaluate $\|q - p\| \leq D(p) + \epsilon + \tau$ instead, where τ is larger than the minimum representable difference between two floating point numbers. However, τ must be chosen smaller than $\left| \frac{1}{2} \min_{p,q,r \in \Omega} \|pq\| - \|pr\| \right|$: half of the minimum difference between two distances that can occur on the grid. Alternatively, integer arithmetic can be used when the equations were rewritten. In our experiments, the use of τ improved the accuracy by two orders of magnitude.

Table 2 compares the distances D^m and origin sets S^m produced by the methods m to the exact distances D^e and origins S^e, calculated using a brute-force approach. The table shows measurements on the 'leaf' image, and cumulative measurements on 10 different images. The considered methods are the FMM, FMTFT, GTFT, ϵVDT, and ETFT. We do not consider the AFMM Star, as it is a simple FT. For all methods, except the FMM, we ran the 4 and 8 neighborhood variants, and used 4 different tolerances: 0, $\frac{1}{2}\sqrt{2}$, 1, and $\sqrt{2}$. For the FMM, we used only the first-order distance gradient approximation (as mentioned in Sec. 2), which needs just the 4-neighborhood. The variants are

Table 2. In each row: distances D^m and origin sets S^m of method m are compared to the exact distances D^e and origins S^e. Left table: method comparison for the 'leaf' image. Right table: cumulative comparison of 10 different images. For distances (D), we show: the number of erroneous pixels ($\#e$), maximum distance error ($\max e = \max_p |D^m(p) - D^e(p)|$), and average distance error $\bar{e}$. For origins (S) we show: the number of pixels for which origin counts are different ($\#e$), and the average relative error $\bar{e}_r$ (see text). Timings are denoted in seconds in column t.

method m	D^m $\#e$	$\max e$	$\bar{e}$	S^m $\#e$	$\bar{e}_r$	t	D^m $\Sigma\#e$	S^m $\Sigma\#e$	$\overline{\Sigma\bar{e}_r}$	Σt
FMM	29381	1.01	0.25	170	0.182%	0.31	147938	1202	0.306%	1.47
FMTFT4 $\epsilon 0$	18	0.19	0.00	320	0.309%	0.31	674	2792	0.576%	1.58
ϵVDT4 $\epsilon 0$	22	0.19	0.00	218	0.147%	0.13	685	1889	0.304%	0.64
GTFT4 $\epsilon 0$	22	0.19	0.00	218	0.147%	0.28	685	1891	0.304%	1.28
ETFT4 $\epsilon 0$	18	0.19	0.00	317	0.304%	0.13	674	2779	0.573%	0.61
FMTFT8 $\epsilon 0$	1	0.04	0.00	1	0.001%	0.44	144	267	0.072%	2.09
ϵVDT8 $\epsilon 0$	1	0.04	0.00	1	0.001%	0.16	145	217	0.054%	0.89
GTFT8 $\epsilon 0$	1	0.04	0.00	1	0.001%	0.44	145	217	0.054%	2.11
ETFT8 $\epsilon 0$	1	0.04	0.00	1	0.001%	0.16	144	267	0.072%	0.83
FMTFT4 $\epsilon\frac{1}{2}\sqrt{2}$	0	0.00	0.00	12428	8.452%	0.50	0	35828	3.888%	3.31
ϵVDT4 $\epsilon\frac{1}{2}\sqrt{2}$	0	0.00	0.00	540	0.125%	0.31	0	2285	0.093%	2.60
GTFT4 $\epsilon\frac{1}{2}\sqrt{2}$	0	0.00	0.00	31835	23.120%	0.31	0	128672	21.655%	1.89
ETFT4 $\epsilon\frac{1}{2}\sqrt{2}$	0	0.00	0.00	26914	16.744%	0.19	0	146949	17.137%	1.19
FMTFT8 $\epsilon\frac{1}{2}\sqrt{2}$	0	0.00	0.00	34	0.006%	0.73	0	412	0.010%	5.16
ϵVDT8 $\epsilon\frac{1}{2}\sqrt{2}$	0	0.00	0.00	34	0.006%	0.45	0	392	0.009%	3.86
GTFT8 $\epsilon\frac{1}{2}\sqrt{2}$	0	0.00	0.00	34	0.006%	0.61	0	392	0.009%	3.59
ETFT8 $\epsilon\frac{1}{2}\sqrt{2}$	0	0.00	0.00	34	0.006%	0.31	0	410	0.010%	2.20
FMTFT4 $\epsilon 1$	0	0.00	0.00	7674	3.879%	0.66	0	23854	1.835%	4.39
ϵVDT4 $\epsilon 1$	0	0.00	0.00	162	0.025%	0.42	0	415	0.023%	3.42
GTFT4 $\epsilon 1$	0	0.00	0.00	22306	11.805%	0.41	0	107543	13.522%	2.53
ETFT4 $\epsilon 1$	0	0.00	0.00	15916	7.763%	0.25	0	89708	8.963%	1.76
FMTFT8 $\epsilon 1$	0	0.00	0.00	44	0.007%	0.94	0	151	0.004%	6.63
ϵVDT8 $\epsilon 1$	0	0.00	0.00	32	0.004%	0.63	0	89	0.002%	5.24
GTFT8 $\epsilon 1$	0	0.00	0.00	250	0.084%	0.69	0	1611	0.164%	4.36
ETFT8 $\epsilon 1$	0	0.00	0.00	284	0.089%	0.39	0	1404	0.129%	2.81
FMTFT4 $\epsilon\sqrt{2}$	0	0.00	0.00	17654	8.083%	0.75	0	59747	4.562%	5.27
ϵVDT4 $\epsilon\sqrt{2}$	0	0.00	0.00	142	0.018%	0.55	0	286	0.015%	4.77
GTFT4 $\epsilon\sqrt{2}$	0	0.00	0.00	36718	19.525%	0.42	0	169396	20.611%	2.64
ETFT4 $\epsilon\sqrt{2}$	0	0.00	0.00	29446	14.286%	0.30	0	152655	14.830%	1.98
FMTFT8 $\epsilon\sqrt{2}$	0	0.00	0.00	43	0.010%	1.13	0	165	0.005%	8.39
ϵVDT8 $\epsilon\sqrt{2}$	0	0.00	0.00	16	0.002%	0.81	0	27	0.000%	6.81
GTFT8 $\epsilon\sqrt{2}$	0	0.00	0.00	273	0.077%	0.78	0	1105	0.124%	5.25
ETFT8 $\epsilon\sqrt{2}$	0	0.00	0.00	279	0.080%	0.47	0	1130	0.157%	3.58

denoted as, e.g., FMTFT4 $\epsilon 0$ for the Fast Marching TFT using a 4-neighborhood and zero tolerance.

Table 2 shows that the distance errors decrease by increasing either the neighborhood size s or the tolerance ϵ. As previously noted, increasing the neighborhood size does not always eliminate all errors. Indeed, all methods produce one error for the leaf

Fig. 10. Locations of origin errors for the leaf image, $\epsilon = \sqrt{2}$. From left to right: FMTFT8, ϵVDT8, GTFT8, and ETFT8. The boundary and erroneous pixels are thickened for better display.

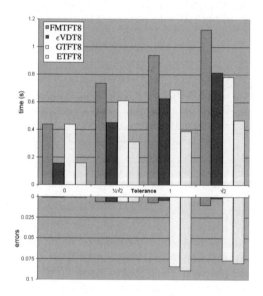

Fig. 11. Timings and relative error (e_r) of the 8-neighborhood variants for the 'leaf' image

image with $s = 8$ and $\epsilon = 0$. As predicted, using $\epsilon = \frac{1}{2}\sqrt{2}$ eliminates all errors for all methods; higher tolerances are not useful for computing exact distances. Finally, our novel method ETFT4 $\epsilon\frac{1}{2}\sqrt{2}$ is the fastest of all considered methods.

We next examine the accuracy of the computed origin sets. We compare origin sets by comparing the average relative differences between a method's origins and the exact (brute-force method) origins, denoted in column '$\bar{e}_r$'. Let the relative error e_r of a pixel p be $e_r(p) = \left| \frac{|S^m(p)| - |S^e(p)|}{|S^e(p)|} \right|$, then, $\bar{e}_r$ is the average of e_r over all pixels $p \in \Omega$. The tolerance ϵ is not only a means to compute exact distances, but is also a user parameter for computing origin sets. Unlike for distances, relaxing the tolerance ϵ increases the errors for origin sets. Indeed, it is more difficult to identify all origins that are within $D(p) + \epsilon$ for higher ϵ. For $\epsilon > 0$, none of the considered methods deliver the complete origin set, although some have only a few erroneous pixels. From Table 2, we see that the 8-neighborhood variants have the best accuracy ($< 0.1\%$). Of these, ETFT8 is the fastest (see also Fig. 11). For applications needing maximum accuracy, ϵVDT8 is the method of choice. Although ϵVDT8 has a better complexity, it is probably slower because of the hidden time constant: the image is scanned twice. Finally, we illustrate the locations of the pixels with erroneous origin sets for the leaf image in Figure 10.

9   Conclusion

In this paper, we both analyzed and extended several distance and feature transform methods for binary images. Our goal was to provide a guide for practitioners in the field for choosing the best method that meets application-specific accuracy, speed, and output completeness criteria. First, we perfected the existing simple FT method AFMM to deliver more accurate results (AFMM Star, Sec. 3). We next extended this method to a new tolerance-based feature transform, FMTFT, that allows e.g. overcoming undesired sampling effects when computing skeletons (Sec. 4). Next, we discussed three other easy-to-implement TFT methods: the existing ϵVDT (Sec. 5), the new ETFT (Sec. 6), and the GTFT extension of Lotufo's graph-searching method (Sec. 7).

For computing exact distances, ETFT4 $\epsilon\frac{1}{2}\sqrt{2}$ is the fastest of the considered methods. Although there are other, faster, exact DT methods, e.g. (Meijster et al., 2000), the ETFT4 $\epsilon\frac{1}{2}\sqrt{2}$ can accommodate early distance-based termination and has a simple implementation (cf. Fig. 8). For computing origin sets, all methods produce fairly accurate results ($< 0.1\%$ errors) for tolerances even up to $\sqrt{2}$. ϵVDT8 is the most accurate, while ETFT8 is the fastest. Finally, FMTFT8 is still useful, as it is the only considered method that can handle different speed functions.

We next intend to extend our TFT methods to 3D and investigate their relative performance and accuracy. This should be rather straightforward, as all considered methods either do not depend on dimension (FMTFT, GTFT, ETFT) or have equivalents in higher dimensions (FMM, ϵVDT). Next, we plan to apply the TFT methods to compute robust skeletons of 3D and higher dimensional objects.

Acknowledgements

This work was supported by the Netherlands Organisation for Scientific Research (NWO) under grant number 612.065.414.

References

Costa, L., Cesar Jr., R.: Shape analysis and classification. CRC Press, Boca Raton, USA (2001)

Cuisenaire, O.: Distance transformations: fast algorithms and applications to medical image processing. PhD thesis, Université catholique de Louvain, Belgium (1999)

Danielsson, P.-E.: Euclidean distance mapping. Computer Graphics and Image Processing 14(3), 227–248 (1980)

Foskey, M., Lin, M., Manocha, D.: Efficient computation of a simplified medial axis. In: Proc. of the 8th ACM symposium on Solid modeling and applications, pp. 96–107. ACM Press, New York (2003)

Lotufo, T., Falcao, A., Zampirolli, F.: Fast euclidean distance transform using a graph-search algorithm. In: Proc. of the 13th Brazilian Symp. on Comp, pp. 269–275 (2000)

Meijster, A., Roerdink, J., Hesselink, W.: A general algorithm for computing distance transforms in linear time. In: Goutsias, J., Vincent, L., Bloomberg, D. (eds.) Mathematical Morphology and its Applications to Image and Signal Processing, pp. 331–340. Kluwer Academic Publishers, Dordrecht (2000)

Mullikin, J.: The vector distance transform in two and three dimensions. CVGIP: Graphical Models and Image Processing 54(6), 526–535 (1992)

Musser, D., Saini, S.: STL tutorial and reference guide: C++ programming with the standard template library. Addison-Wesley Professional Computing Series. Addison-Wesley, Reading (1996)

Ogniewicz, R., Kübler, O.: Hierarchic voronoi skeletons. Pattern Recognition 28(3), 343–359 (1995)

Ragnemalm, I.: Neighborhoods for distance transformations using ordered propagation. CVGIP: Image Understanding 56(3), 399–409 (1992)

Sethian, J.: Level set methods and fast marching methods, 2nd edn. Cambridge University Press, Cambridge (1999)

Strzodka, R., Telea, A.: Generalized distance transforms and skeletons in graphics hardware. In: Proc. of EG/IEEE TCVG Symposium on Visualization (VisSym '04), pp. 221–230. IEEE Computer Society Press, Los Alamitos (2004)

Telea, A., van Wijk, J.: An augmented fast marching method for computing skeletons and centerlines. In: Proc. of the symposium on Data Visualisation, pp. 251–259 (2002)

Telea, A., Vilanova, A.: A robust level-set algorithm for centerline extraction. In: Proc. of the symposium on Data Visualisation, pp. 185–194 (2003)

Verwer, B., Verbeek, P., Dekker, S.: An efficient uniform cost algorithm applied to distance transforms. IEEE Transactions on Pattern Analysis and Machine Intelligence 11(4), 425–429 (1989)

Ye, Q.: The signed euclidean distance transform and its applications. In: Proc. of the 9th International Conference on Pattern Recognition, vol. 1, pp. 495–499 (1988)

A Unified Theory for Steerable and Quadrature Filters

Kai Krajsek and Rudolf Mester

J. W. Goethe University, Visual Sensorics and Information Processing Lab
Robert Mayer Str.2-4, D-60054 Frankfurt am Main, Germany
krajsek@vsi.cs.uni-frankfurt.de, mester@vsi.cs.uni-frankfurt.de

Abstract. In this paper, a complete theory of steerable filters is presented which shows that quadrature filters are only a special case of steerable filters. Although there has been a large number of approaches dealing with the theory of steerable filters, none of these gives a complete theory with respect to the transformation groups which deform the filter kernel. Michaelis and Sommer (Michaelis and Sommer, 1995) and Hel-Or and Teo (Teo and Hel-Or, 1996; Teo and Hel-Or, 1998) were the first ones who gave a theoretical justification for steerability based on Lie group theory. But the approach of Michaelis and Sommer considers only Abelian Lie groups. Although the approach of Hel-Or and Teo considers all Lie groups, their method for generating the basis functions may fail as shown in this paper. We extend these steerable approaches to arbitrary Lie groups, like the important case of the rotation group $SO(3)$ in three dimensions.

Quadrature filters serve for computing the local energy and local phase of a signal. Whereas for the one dimensional case quadrature filters are theoretically well founded, this is not the case for higher dimensional signal spaces. The monogenic signal (Felsberg and Sommer, 2001) based on the Riesz transformation has been shown to be a rotational invariant generalization of the analytic signal. A further generalization of the monogenic signal, the 2D rotational invariant quadrature filter (Köthe, 2003), has been shown to capture richer structures in images as the monogenic signal.

We present a generalization of the rotational invariant quadrature filter based on our steerable theory. Our approach includes the important case of 3D rotational invariant quadrature filters but it is not limited to any signal dimension and includes all transformation groups that own a unitary group representation.

Keywords: Steerable filter, quadrature filter, Lie group theory.

1 Introduction

Steerable filters and quadrature filters are well established methods in signal and image processing. Steerability is at least implicitly used when computing directional derivatives as this is the central operation in differential motion estimation. Quadrature filters are the choice for computing the local energy and local phase of a signal. In this paper we present a complete theory of steerable filters and derive a group invariant quadrature filter approach based on our steerable filter theory.

Although a large number of approaches dealing with the theory of steerable filters has been published (Danielsson, 1980; Freeman and Adelson, 1991; Perona, 1995;

J. Braz et al. (Eds.): VISAPP and GRAPP 2006, CCIS 4, pp. 201–214, 2007.

Simoncelli et al., 1992; Simoncelli and Farid, 1996; Michaelis and Sommer, 1995) (Teo and Hel-Or, 1996; Teo and Hel-Or, 1998; Yu et al., 2001) none of these provides a complete and closed theory. Such a theory should describe the general requirements which are necessary for a filter kernel to be a steerable filter. The benefit from this work is a deeper understanding of the concepts of steerable filters and enables the user to construct steerable filters for every Lie group transformation. None of the previously published approaches gives a general solution of the following problem: If one is confronted with a certain filter kernel and an arbitrary Lie group, what are the approbate basis functions to steer the filter kernel and how are the interpolation functions to be computed.

The steerable approach of Michaelis and Sommer (Michaelis and Sommer, 1995) gives a solution to this problem in the case of Abelian Lie groups, whereas the approach of Teo and Hel-Or (Teo and Hel-Or, 1996; Teo and Hel-Or, 1998) handles all Lie group transformations. But the latter approach may fail as we show in section 3.4. In contrast these approaches (Michaelis and Sommer, 1995; Teo and Hel-Or, 1996; Teo and Hel-Or, 1998) which either do not cover the case of non-Abelian groups (Michaelis and Sommer, 1995) or do not work for all filter kernels (Teo and Hel-Or, 1996; Teo and Hel-Or, 1998), our approach uses the full power of Lie group theory to generate the minimum number of basis functions also for non-Abelian compact Lie groups. It is a direct extension of the approach of (Michaelis and Sommer, 1995) in which the basis functions are generated by the eigenfunctions of the generators of the Lie group. In our approach a Casimir operator is used to generate the basis functions also for non-Abelian compact Lie groups. For non-Abelian, non-compact groups, we show that polynomials serve as appropriate basis functions.

The quadrature filter is a well established method in signal processing and low-level image processing for computing the local energy and local phase of a signal. Whereas the local energy is an estimate of the local intensity structure, the local phase provides information about the local shape of the signal. In the 1D case the quadrature filter is well defined by an even part, a bandpass filter, and an odd part, the Hilbert transformation of the bandpass filter. The filter output is the analytic signal, a representation of the signal from which the local energy and local phase can easily be computed. Large efforts have been made to generalize the analytic signal (Bülow and Sommer, 2001; Granlund and Knutsson, 1995) to the 2D case by projecting the scalar valued Hilbert transformation in the two dimensional space. The drawback of all of these methods is that they are not rotational invariant. The Riesz transformation has been shown to be a rotational invariant generalization of the Hilbert transformation generalizing the analytic signal to the monogenic signal (Felsberg and Sommer, 2001). A further generalization of the monogenic signal is the 2D rotational invariant quadrature filter (Köthe, 2003), based on rotated *steerable filters*, which is able to capture richer structures from an image than the monogenic signal.

Many interesting computer vision and image processing applications, like motion estimation, are not restricted to the two dimensional case. We present a generalization of the rotational invariant quadrature filter (Köthe, 2003) with respect to the signal dimension and the transformation group. This includes the important case of a 3D rotational invariant quadrature filter, but it is not limited to any signal dimension. Also other transformations than the rotation is considered, like shearing, which is the correct transformation group when describing motion in space time.

2 Steerable Filters

Let g denote an element of an arbitrary Lie group $\mathcal{G}$ and $\mathbf{x} \in \mathbb{R}^N$ the coordinate vector of a N dimensional signal space. We define a steerable filter $h_g(\mathbf{x})$ as the impulse response whose deformed version, with respect to the Lie group, equals the linear combination of a finite set of basis filters $\{b_j(\mathbf{x})\}$, $j = 1, 2, ..., M$. Furthermore, only the coefficients $\{a_j(g)\}$, denoted as the interpolation functions, depend on the Lie group element

$$h_g(\mathbf{x}) = \sum_{j=1}^{M} a_j(g)\, b_j(\mathbf{x}) \ . \tag{1}$$

Applying the deformed filter to a signal $s(\mathbf{x})$ is equivalent to the linear combination of the individual impulse responses of the basis filters

$$h_g(\mathbf{x}) * s(\mathbf{x}) = \sum_{j=1}^{M} a_j(g)(b_j(\mathbf{x}) * s(\mathbf{x})) \ . \tag{2}$$

Questions arising with steerable functions are:

- Under which conditions can a given function $h_g(\mathbf{x})$ be steered?
- How can the basis functions $b_j(\mathbf{x})$ be determined?
- How many basis functions are needed to steer the function $h_g(\mathbf{x})$?
- How can the interpolation functions $a_j(g)$ be determined?

In the last decade, several steerable filter approaches have been developed trying to answer these questions, but all of them, except for the approach of Teo and Hel-Or (Teo and Hel-Or, 1996; Teo and Hel-Or, 1998), tackle only a special case, either for the filter kernel or for the corresponding transformation group.

3 An Extended Steerable Approach Based on Lie Group Theory

In the following section, we present our steerable filter approach based on Lie group theory covering all recent approaches developed so far. It delivers for Abelian Lie groups and for compact non-Abelian Lie groups the minimum required number of basis functions and the corresponding interpolation functions. In order to complete the steerable approach the case of non-Abelian, non-compact Lie groups has to be considered separately. After presenting our concept, its relation to recent approaches is discussed and some examples are presented.

3.1 Conditions for Steerability

In the following section, we show the steerability of all filter kernels $h : \mathbb{R}^N \to \mathbb{C}$ which are expandable according to a finite number M of basis functions $\mathcal{B} = \{b_j(\mathbf{x})\}$. These basis functions should belong of a subspace $V :=\text{span}\{\mathcal{B}\} \subset L^2$ of all quadratic integrable functions. Since every element of L^2 can arbitrary exactly be approximated by a finite number of basis functions, we consider, at least approximately, all quadratic integrable filter kernels. The problem of approximating such a function by a smaller number of basis functions, allowing a certain error, has been examined in (Perona, 1995) and is not topic of this paper. With the notation of the inner product $\langle \cdot, \cdot \rangle$ in L^2 and the Fourier coefficients $c_j = \langle h(\mathbf{x}), b_j(\mathbf{x}) \rangle$ the expansion of $h(\mathbf{x})$ reads

$$h(\mathbf{x}) = \sum_{j=1}^{M} c_j b_j(\mathbf{x}) \ . \tag{3}$$

Furthermore, every basis function $b_j(\mathbf{x}) \in V$ should belong to an invariant subspace $U \subseteq V$ with respect to a certain Lie group $\mathcal{G}$ transformation.

Then, $h(\mathbf{x})$ is steerable with respect to $\mathcal{G}$.

Due to the assigned preconditions, this statement can be easily verified. Let $\mathcal{D}(g)$ denote the representation of $g \in \mathcal{G}$ in the function space V and $\mathbf{D}(g)$ the representation of $\mathcal{G}$ in the N-dimensional signal space. The transformed filter kernel $\mathcal{D}(g)h(\mathbf{x})$ equals the linear combination of the transformed basis functions

$$\mathcal{D}(g)h\,(\mathbf{x}) = \sum_{j=1}^{M} c_j \mathcal{D}(g) b_j(\mathbf{x}) \ . \tag{4}$$

Since every basis function $b_j(\mathbf{x})$ is, per definition, part of an invariant subspace, the transformed version $\mathcal{D}(g)b_j(\mathbf{x})$ can be expressed by a linear combination of the subspace basis. Let denote $m(j)$ the mapping of the index j of the basis function $b_j(\mathbf{x})$ onto the lowest index of the basis function belonging to the same subspace and $d(j)$ the mapping of the index of the basis function $b_j(\mathbf{x})$ onto the dimension d_j of its invariant subspace. The transformed basis function $\mathcal{D}(g)b_j(\mathbf{x})$ can be expressed, with the previous definition of $m(j)$ and $d(j)$, and the coefficients of the linear combination $w_{jk}(g)$ as

$$\mathcal{D}(g)b_j(\mathbf{x}) = \sum_{k=m(j)}^{m(j)+d(j)-1} w_{jk}(g)b_k(\mathbf{x}) \ . \tag{5}$$

Inserting equation (5) into equation (4) yields

$$\mathcal{D}(g)h(\mathbf{x}) = \sum_{j=1}^{M} c_j \sum_{k=m(j)}^{m(j)+d(j)-1} w_{jk}(g)b_k(\mathbf{x}) \ . \tag{6}$$

The double sum can be written such that all coefficients belonging to the same basis function are grouped together, where L denotes the number of invariant subspaces in V

$$\mathcal{D}(g)h(\mathbf{x}) = \sum_{b_k \in U_1} b_k(\mathbf{x}) \sum_{w_{jk} \in U_1} c_j w_{jk}(g) \tag{7}$$

$$+ \sum_{b_k \in U_2} b_k(\mathbf{x}) \sum_{w_{jk} \in U_2} c_j w_{jk}(g) + \dots$$

$$+ \sum_{b_k \in U_L} b_k(\mathbf{x}) \sum_{w_{jk} \in U_L} c_j w_{jk}(g) \ .$$

Thus, in order to steer the function h we have to consider all basis functions spanning the L subspaces.

3.2   The Basis Functions

The next question arising is how to obtain the appropriate basis functions spanning finite dimensional invariant subspaces. Furthermore, the invariant subspaces are desired to be as small as possible in order to lower computational costs. Group theory provides the solution of this problem and the functions fulfilling these requirements are, per definition, the basis of an irreducible representation of the Lie group. This has already pointed out by Michaelis and Sommer (Michaelis and Sommer, 1995) and a method for generating such a basis for Abelian Lie groups has been proposed. We extend this method for the case of non-Abelian, compact Lie groups. The case of non-Abelian, non-compact groups is discussed in subsection 3.2.2.

3.2.1   Basis Functions for Compact Lie Groups

The invariant space spanned by an irreducible basis cannot be decomposed further into invariant subspaces and thus, forming a minimum number of basis functions for the steerable function. Michaelis and Sommer showed that such a basis is given by the eigenfunctions of the generators in case of Abelian Lie groups. Since the generators of a non-Abelian groups do not commutate and thus have no simultaneous eigenfunctions, the method does not work in this case any more. But their framework can be extended with a slight change to compact non-Abelian groups. Instead of constructing the basis functions from the simultaneous eigenfunctions of the generators of the group, the basis function can also be constructed by the eigenfunctions of a *Casimir* operator $\mathcal{C}$ of the corresponding Lie group. In order to define the Casimir operator we first have to introduce the Lie bracket, or commutator, of two operators

$$[\mathcal{D}(a), \mathcal{D}(b)] := \mathcal{D}(a)\mathcal{D}(b) - \mathcal{D}(b)\mathcal{D}(a) \ . \tag{8}$$

Operators commuting with all representations of the group elements are denoted as Casimir operators

$$[\mathcal{C}, \mathcal{D}(g)] = 0 \quad \forall g \in \mathcal{G} \ . \tag{9}$$

Let $\{b_m(\mathbf{x})\}, m = 1, ..., d_\alpha$ denote the set of eigenfunctions of $\mathcal{C}$ corresponding to the same eigenvalue α. Then, every transformed basis function $\mathcal{D}(g)b_i(\mathbf{x})$ is an eigenfunction with the same eigenvalue α

$$\begin{aligned}
\mathcal{C}\mathcal{D}(g)b_i(\mathbf{x}) &= \mathcal{D}(g)\mathcal{C}b_i(\mathbf{x}) \\
&= \mathcal{D}(g)\alpha b_i(\mathbf{x}) \\
&= \alpha\mathcal{D}(g)b_i(\mathbf{x}) \ .
\end{aligned} \tag{10}$$

Thus, $\{b_m(\mathbf{x})\}$ forms a basis of a d_α dimensional invariant subspace U_α. Any transformed element of this subspace can be expressed by a linear combination of basis functions of this subspace

$$\mathcal{D}(\mathbf{u})b_i(\mathbf{x}) = \sum_{j=1}^{d_\alpha} w_{ij}b_j(\mathbf{x}) \ . \tag{11}$$

Thus, we have found a method for constructing invariant subspaces also for non-Abelian groups. A Casimir operator is constructed by a linear combination of products of generators of the corresponding Lie group where n denotes the number of generators

$$\mathcal{C} = \sum_{ij} f_{ij}\mathcal{L}_i\mathcal{L}_j, \quad i, j = 1, ..., n \ . \tag{12}$$

The coefficients f_{ij} are solved by the constraints

$$[\mathcal{C}, \mathcal{L}_k] = 0, \quad k = 1, ..., n \ . \tag{13}$$

If the Casimir operator of a compact group is self-adjoint with a discrete spectrum, the eigenfunctions constitute a complete orthogonal basis of the corresponding function space. It is a well known fact from functional analysis that in this case all eigenfunctions belonging to the same eigenvalue span a finite dimensional subspace. If furthermore the Casimir operator has the symmetry of the group $\mathcal{G}$, i.e. there exists no operation which does not belong to the group and under which the Casimir operator is invariant, then the eigenfunctions are basis functions of irreducible representation (Wigner, 1959). After computing one eigenfunction $b_1(\mathbf{x})$ corresponding to the eigenvalue α we can construct all other basis functions of this invariant subspace by applying all possible combinations of generators of the Lie group to $b_1(\mathbf{x})$. The sequence of generators is stopped when the resulting function is linear dependent from the ones which have already been constructed. This equals to the method for constructing the basis functions proposed by Teo and Hel-Or (Teo and Hel-Or, 1998) except for the fact that they propose to apply this procedure directly to the steerable function $h(\mathbf{x})$.

3.2.2   Basis Function for Non-compact Lie Groups

Since only Abelian Lie groups and compact non-Abelian Lie groups are proved to own complete irreducible representations, i.e. the representation space falls into invariant subspaces, we have to treat the case of non-Abelian, non-compact groups separately. Since we do only require an invariant subspace and not an entirely irreducible representation we can easily construct such a space from a polynomial basis of the space of square integrable functions. The order of a polynomial term does not change by an arbitrary Lie group transformation and thus the basis of a polynomial term constitute a basis for a steerable filter. In order to steer an arbitrary polynomial we have to determine the terms of different order. The sum of the basis functions of the corresponding invariant subspaces are a basis for the steerable polynomial.

We can now construct for every Lie group transformation the corresponding basis for a steerable filter. For Abelian groups and compact groups we chose the basis from the eigenfunction of the Casimir operator whereas for all other groups we choose a polynomial basis. The next section addresses the question how to combine these basis functions in order to steer the resulting filter kernel with respect to any Lie group transformation.

3.3   The Interpolation Functions

The computation of the interpolation functions $\{a_j(g)\}$ can already be deduced from equ.(7). In order to obtain the interpolation function corresponding to the basis function $b_m(\mathbf{x})$ the transformed version of the original filter kernel $h(\mathbf{x})$ has to be projected onto $b_m(\mathbf{x})$, $m = 1, ..., M$

$$a_m(g) = \langle \mathcal{D}(g)h(\mathbf{x}), b_m(\mathbf{x}) \rangle \tag{14}$$

$$= \left\langle \mathcal{D}(g) \sum_{n=1}^{M} c_n b_n(\mathbf{x}), b_m(\mathbf{x}) \right\rangle$$

$$= \sum_{n=1}^{M} c_n \langle \mathcal{D}(g)b_n(\mathbf{x}), b_m(\mathbf{x}) \rangle .$$

The relation between $\{c_k\}$ and $\{a_k\}$ is a linear map $\mathbf{P} \in \mathbb{R}^{M \times N}$ with the matrix elements

$$(\mathbf{P})_{ij} = \langle \mathcal{D}(g)b_i(\mathbf{x}), b_j(\mathbf{x}) \rangle \tag{15}$$

of the coefficient vector

$$\mathbf{c} := (c_1, c_2, ..., c_M) \tag{16}$$

onto the interpolation function vector

$$\mathbf{a}(g) := (a_1(g), a_2(g), ..., a_N(g)) . \tag{17}$$

As already pointed out by Michaelis and Sommer (Michaelis and Sommer, 1995), the basis functions have not to be the transformed versions of the filter kernel as assumed in other approaches (Freeman and Adelson, 1991; Simoncelli and Farid, 1996). It is sufficient that the synthesized function is steerable. If it is nonetheless desired to design basis functions which are transformed versions $h_g(\mathbf{x}) := \mathcal{D}(g)h(\mathbf{x})$ of the filter kernel $h(\mathbf{x})$ a basis change is sufficient

$$h(\mathbf{x}) = \sum_{j=1}^{M} a_j(g)b_j(\mathbf{x}) = \sum_{j=1}^{M} \tilde{a}_j h_{g_j}(\mathbf{x}) . \tag{18}$$

The relation between $\{a_j(g)\}$ and $\{\tilde{a}_j(g)\}$ can be found by a projection of both sides of equation (18) on $b_m(\mathbf{x})$, $m = 1, ..., M$

$$a_m(g) = \left\langle \sum_{j=1}^{M} a_j(g) h_{g_j}(\mathbf{x}), b_m(\mathbf{x}) \right\rangle \tag{19}$$

$$= \sum_{j=1}^{M} \tilde{a}_j(g) \underbrace{\left\langle h_{g_j}(\mathbf{x}), b_m(\mathbf{x}) \right\rangle}_{B_{jm}} .$$

This can be written as a matrix/vector operation with $\tilde{\mathbf{a}}^T := (\tilde{a}_1, \tilde{a}_2, \ldots, \tilde{a}_n)$ and $\mathbf{a}^T := (a_1, a_2, \ldots, a_n)$

$$\mathbf{a} = \mathbf{B}\tilde{\mathbf{a}} . \tag{20}$$

The matrix $\mathbf{B}$ describing the basis change is invertible

$$\tilde{\mathbf{a}} = \mathbf{B}^{-1}\mathbf{a} \tag{21}$$

and the steerable basis can be designed as steered versions of the original filter kernel.

3.4   Relation to Recent Approaches

We present a steerable filter approach for computing the basis functions and interpolation functions for arbitrary Lie groups. Since two steerable filter approaches based on Lie group theory (Michaelis and Sommer, 1995; Teo and Hel-Or, 1996; Teo and Hel-Or, 1998) have already been developed, the purpose of this section is to examine their relation to our approach.

Freeman and Adelson (Freeman and Adelson, 1991) consider steerable filters with respect to the rotation group in 2D and 3D, respectively. For the 2D case they propose a Fourier basis (of the function space) times a rotational invariant function as well as a polynomial basis (of the function space) times a rotational invariant function as basis functions of the steerable filter. They realized that the minimum required set of basis functions depend on the kind of basis itself but their approach failed to explain the reason for it. Michaelis and Sommer (Michaelis and Sommer, 1995) answer this question based on Lie group theory: the basis of an irreducible group representation span an invariant subspace of minimum size. Since the Fourier basis is the basis for an irreducible representation of the rotation group $SO(2)$, the required number of basis function is less as for the polynomial basis. Our approach can be considered as an extension of the approach of Michaelis and Sommer from Abelian Lie groups to arbitrary Lie group transformation. Whereas the approach of Michaelis and Sommer construct the basis function from the generators of the group, our approach uses a Casimir operator. Since the generators of an Abelian Lie group commutate with each other, their linear combination constitute a Casimir operator and thus both methods become equal in this case. But our method also works for the case of general compact groups, since in this case, a self-adjoint Casimir operator with a discrete spectrum delivers finite dimensional invariant subspaces. For non-compact, non-Abelian groups we showed that polynomials serve always as basis for an invariant subspace. The approach of Teo and Hel-Or significantly differs from our approach in the way how the invariant subspaces are generated. The basis functions of the invariant subspace are constructed by applying all combinations of Lie group generators to the function that is to be made steerable. A certain sequence of generators, denoted as generator chain in case of Abelian Lie groups and generator trees in the case of non-Abelian Lie groups, is stopped if the resulting function is linearly dependent to the basis functions which have already been constructed. In the following, we will show that this approach may fail.

Let us consider the function $h(x, y) = \exp(-x^2)$ and the rotation in 2D as the group transformation. Applying the generator chain which is simply the successive application of the group generator $\mathcal{L} = x\frac{\partial}{\partial y} - y\frac{\partial}{\partial x}$ does not converge since $h(x, y)$ is not expandable by a finite number of basis functions of a representation of the rotation group. In our approach, $h(x, y)$ is first approximated by a finite number of basis functions each belonging to a finite dimensional invariant subspace. Such a filter is always steerable by construction.

Table 1. Several examples of Lie groups, the corresponding operator(s), generator(s), Casimir operator(s) and basis functions. Terminology: $\mathbf{T}_N$: translation group in the N-dimensional Signal space; $SO(N)$: special orthogonal group; $\mathbf{U}_N$: uniform scaling group; $\mathbf{S}_N$: shear group.

Group	Operators	Generators	Casimir operator	basis functions
$\mathbf{T}_N$	$\mathcal{D}(\mathbf{a})h(\mathbf{x}) = h(\mathbf{x} - \mathbf{a})$	$\{\mathcal{L}_i = \frac{\partial}{\partial x_i}\}$	$\mathcal{C} = \sum_{i=1}^{N} \mathcal{L}_i^2$	$\{\exp(j\mathbf{n}^T\mathbf{x})\}$
$SO(2)$	$\mathcal{D}(\alpha)h(r, \varphi) = h(r, \varphi - \alpha)$	$\mathcal{L} = \frac{\partial}{\partial \varphi}$	$\mathcal{C} = \mathcal{L}^2$	$\{f_k(r)\exp(jk\varphi)\}$
$SO(3)$	$\mathcal{R}h(\mathbf{x}) = h(\mathbf{R}^{-1}\mathbf{x})$	$\{\mathcal{L}_k = x_j\frac{\partial}{\partial x_i} - x_i\frac{\partial}{\partial x_j}\}$	$\mathcal{C} = \sum_{i=1}^{3} \mathcal{L}_i^2$	$\{f_k(r)Y_{\ell m}(\theta, \varphi)\}$
$\mathbf{U}_N$	$\mathcal{D}(\alpha)h(\mathbf{x}) = h(e^{-\alpha}\mathbf{x})$	$\{\mathcal{L}_i = x_i\frac{\partial}{\partial x_i}\}$	$\mathcal{C} = \sum_{i=1}^{N} \mathcal{L}_i^2$	$\{r^k\}$
$\mathbf{S}_N$	$\mathcal{D}(\mathbf{u})h(\mathbf{x}, t) = h(\mathbf{x} - \mathbf{u}t, t)$	$\{\mathcal{L}_i = t\frac{\partial}{\partial x_i}\}$	$\mathcal{C} = \sum_{i=1}^{N} \mathcal{L}_i^2$	$\{f_k(t)\exp(jk\mathbf{x}/t)\}$

4 Group Invariant Quadrature Filters

Quadrature filters have become an appropriate tool for computing the local phase and local energy of one dimensional signals. They are obtained by a bandpass filter and its Hilbert transformation. The bandpass filter is applied to reduce the original signal to a signal with small bandwidth which is necessary to obtain a reasonable interpretation of the local phase. The Hilbert transformation is applied to shift the phase of the original signal by ninety degrees such that the squared sum of the output of the bandpass and its Hilbert transformation results in a phase invariant local energy. In order to apply this concept to image processing, large efforts have been made to generalize the Hilbert transform to 2D dimensional signals (Bülow and Sommer, 2001; Granlund and Knutsson, 1995). All of these approaches fail to be rotational invariant, but rotational invariance is an essential property of all feature detection methods. An appropriate 2D generalization of the analytic signal is the monogenic signal which is based on the vector-valued Riesz transformation (Felsberg and Sommer, 2001). The Riesz transformation is valid for all dimensions and reduces to the Hilbert transformation in the one dimensional case. A further generalization of 2D rotational invariant quadrature filters can be done by steerable filters which behave under certain conditions like quadrature filter pairs (Köthe, 2003). The monogenic signal is included in this approach. We will go a step further, using the theory of Lie groups and the steerable filter approach presented in the last section to develop a generalization of the rotational invariant quadrature filters to quadrature filters which are invariant to compact or Abelian Lie groups and is also valid for arbitrary signal dimensions. In particular, we are able to design rotational invariant quadrature filters in 3D. But also feature detection methods that are invariant with respect to other transformation groups are important as in the case of motion estimation. The signal in the space time volume is sheared and not steered by motion and thus filters for detecting this signal shall be designed invariant with respect to the shear transformation.

4.1 Properties of a General Quadrature Filter

We will first recall the main properties of a quadrature filter. The main idea of a quadrature filter is to apply two filters to a signal such that the sum of the square filter responses reflect the local energy of the signal. Also the local phase of the selected frequency band should be determined by the two filter outputs. Furthermore, the local energy should be group invariant, i.e. the filter outputs should be invariant with respect to the deformation of the signal by the corresponding group. In order to achieve group invariance, we construct our quadrature filter from the basis of a unitary group representation. Groups with a unitary representation are compact groups and Abelian groups (Wigner, 1959). The even $\mathbf{h}_e$ and odd $\mathbf{h}_o$ components of the quadrature filter are constructed by a vector valued impulse response consisting of the basis functions of a unitary representation of dimension m_e and m_o, respectively.

$$\mathbf{h}_e = \begin{pmatrix} h_{e1}(\mathbf{x}) \\ h_{e2}(\mathbf{x}) \\ \vdots \\ h_{em_e}(\mathbf{x}) \end{pmatrix}, \quad \mathbf{h}_o = \begin{pmatrix} h_{o1}(\mathbf{x}) \\ h_{o2}(\mathbf{x}) \\ \vdots \\ h_{om_o}(\mathbf{x}) \end{pmatrix} . \tag{22}$$

In the following we show that all basis functions of an invariant subspace generated by a Casimir operator which is point symmetric, i.e. commutates with the mirror group that acts on the coordinate vector like $\mathbf{Px} \rightarrow -\mathbf{x}$, own the same parity. Since the parity operator commutes with the Casimir operator, there exists simultaneous eigenfunctions. Applying $\mathcal{P}$ two times equals the identity operator and thus the eigenvalues of $\mathcal{P}$ are $\lambda = \pm 1$. Thus every basis function has a certain parity, i.e. is either point symmetric or point anti-symmetric

$$\mathcal{P}b_j(\mathbf{x}) = \pm b_j(\mathbf{x}) . \tag{23}$$

Let us consider an arbitrary basis function $b_d(\mathbf{x})$ with positive parity, i.e. $\mathcal{P}b_d(\mathbf{x}) = b_d(\mathbf{x})$. All other basis functions of the same subspace can be generated by linear combinations of generators of $\mathcal{G}$, where k_j^i denote the coefficients of the linear combination and n the number of generators of $\mathcal{G}$

$$\sum_{j=1}^{n} k_j^i \mathcal{L}_j b_d(\mathbf{x}) = b_i(\mathbf{x}), \quad i = 1, 2, ..., m_e . \tag{24}$$

Applying the parity operator on both sides of equ.(24) and considering that $\mathcal{P}$ commutates with all generators yields

$$\mathcal{P} \sum_{j=1}^{n} k_j^i \mathcal{L}_j b_d(\mathbf{x}) = \mathcal{P} b_i(\mathbf{x}) \tag{25}$$

$$\Leftrightarrow \sum_{j=1}^{n} k_j^i \mathcal{L}_j b_d(\mathbf{x}) = \mathcal{P} b_i(\mathbf{x})$$

$$\Rightarrow \mathcal{P} b_i(\mathbf{x}) = b_i(\mathbf{x}) \quad \forall i \ .$$

If we assume $\mathcal{P} b_d(\mathbf{x}) = -b_d(\mathbf{x})$ for an arbitrary basis function $b_d(\mathbf{x})$ we obtain with the same deduction $\mathcal{P} b_i(\mathbf{x}) = -b_i(\mathbf{x})$ for all basis functions of this subspace. Thus, all basis functions belonging to the same subspace attain the same parity. The filter responses of $\mathbf{h}_e$ and $\mathbf{h}_o$ are denoted as the filter channels $c_e = s(\mathbf{x}) * h_e(\mathbf{x})$ and $c_o = s(\mathbf{x}) * h_o(\mathbf{x})$, respectively. The square of the filter response of each channel are denoted as even and odd energies. Due to the unitary representation, both energies are invariant under the corresponding group action

$$E_s = (\mathbf{D}(g)\mathbf{c}_s)^T (\mathbf{D}(g)\mathbf{c}_s) = \mathbf{c}_s^T \mathbf{c}_s \ \ s \in \{e, o\} \ .$$

Note that the inner product is taken with respect to the invariant subspace, not with respect to the function space. The local energy of the signal is given by the sum of the even and odd energy. In the following we will examine the properties of the filter channels required to achieve a phase invariant local energy when applied to bandpass signals. In the ideal case, a simple[1] bandpass filtered signal consists of only one wave vector $\mathbf{k}_0$ and its Fourier transform[2] reads with the Dirac delta distribution $\delta(\mathbf{k})$

$$S(\mathbf{k}) = S_0 \delta(\mathbf{k} - \mathbf{k}_0) + S_0^* \delta(\mathbf{k} + \mathbf{k}_0) \ . \tag{26}$$

We start with examining the Fourier transform of the even and odd energies

$$E_s = \mathbf{c}_s^T \mathbf{c}_s = \sum_{j=1}^{m_s} (s(\mathbf{x}) * h_{sj}(\mathbf{x}))^2 \ . \tag{27}$$

Applying the convolution theorem to E_s reads

$$\mathcal{F}\{E_s\}(\mathbf{k}) = \sum_{j=1}^{m_s} (S(\mathbf{k}) H_{sj}(\mathbf{k})) * (S(\mathbf{k}) H_{sj}(\mathbf{k})) \ .$$

Inserting the signal (26) in the equation above, computing the convolution and performing the inverse Fourier transformation reads

---

[1] Simple signal: signal with intrinsic dimensionality one.
[2] Note that the Fourier transformed entities are labeled with capital letters.

$$E_s(\mathbf{x}) = S_0^2 \sum_{i=1}^{m_s} (H_{si}(\mathbf{k}_0))^2 \, e^{4\pi j \mathbf{k}_0^T \mathbf{x}} \tag{28}$$

$$+ S_0^{*2} \sum_{i=1}^{m_s} (H_{si}(-\mathbf{k}_0))^2 \, e^{-4\pi j \mathbf{k}_0^T \mathbf{x}}$$

$$+ |S_0|^2 \sum_{i=1}^{m_s} H_{si}(\mathbf{k}_0) H_{si}(-\mathbf{k}_0)$$

$$+ |S_0|^2 \sum_{i=1}^{m_s} H_{si}(-\mathbf{k}_0) H_{si}(\mathbf{k}_0) \ .$$

Note that the first two terms are phase variant whereas the last two ones are not. In order to achieve phase invariant local energy, the first two terms have to cancel when adding the even and odd energy. This is exactly the case when all basis functions of one invariant subspace are either even or odd and the sum of squared Fourier transformed filter components are equal

$$\sum_{i=1}^{m_e} |H_{ei}(\mathbf{k}_0)|^2 = \sum_{k=1}^{m_o} |H_{ok}(\mathbf{k}_0)|^2 \ . \tag{29}$$

All basis functions of one invariant subspace are either even (= their Fourier transforms are real and even), or odd (= their Fourier transforms are imaginary and odd). Thus, the Fourier transformed filter components become

$$\sum_{i=1}^{m_e} H_{ei}(\pm\mathbf{k}_0)^2 = \sum_{i=1}^{m_e} |H_{ei}(\mathbf{k}_0)|^2 \tag{30}$$

in the even case and

$$\sum_{i=1}^{m_o} H_{oi}(\pm\mathbf{k}_0)^2 = -\sum_{i=1}^{m_o} |H_{oi}(\mathbf{k}_0)|^2 \tag{31}$$

in the odd case. Since the inner product of the Fourier transform of both filter channels are equal, the first two terms cancel out resulting in a phase invariant local energy

$$E = 2|S_0|^2 \left(\sum_{j=1}^{m_e} |H_{ej}(\mathbf{k}_0)|^2 + \sum_{k=1}^{m_o} |H_{ok}(\mathbf{k}_0)|^2 \right) \ .$$

In the next section an example of a group invariant quadrature filter is presented.

4.2   An Example: 3D Rotational Invariant Quadrature Filters

We now apply the approach presented in the last section to the 3D rotational invariant quadrature filter. The even $\mathbf{h}_e$ and odd $\mathbf{h}_o$ vector valued impulse responses have to be the basis functions of a unitary representation of the rotation group $SO(3)$. A possible basis of a unitary invariant subspaces are the well known spherical harmonics times an arbitrary radial function $f_n(|\mathbf{x}|) \in L^2$

$$b_{n\ell m}(\mathbf{x}) = f_n(|\mathbf{x}|)Y_{\ell m}(\hat{\mathbf{x}}) \ . \tag{32}$$

The spherical harmonics are either even or odd, thus the even vector valued impulse responses can be constructed from all spherical harmonics of even order, the odd vector valued impulse response from all spherical harmonics of odd order. According to equ.(29), we have to show that the scalar product of the Fourier transformed vector valued impulse responses are equal. It is well known that a radial functions times a spherical harmonic is also spherical separable in the Fourier domain and vise versa. If we require, like in the 2D case (Köthe, 2003), the radial function $F_{n\ell m}(|\mathbf{k}_0|) = F(|\mathbf{k}_0|)$ in the Fourier domain to be the same for all transfer functions, the constraint equ.(29) becomes

$$\sum_{\ell}^{\text{odd}} \sum_{m=-\ell}^{\ell} |Y_{\ell m}(\hat{\mathbf{k}}_0)|^2 = \sum_{\ell}^{\text{even}} \sum_{m=-\ell}^{\ell} |Y_{\ell m}(\hat{\mathbf{k}}_0)|^2 \ . \tag{33}$$

Since the scalar product of the even as well as the odd spherical harmonics are rotational invariant the right and the left hand side of equ.(33) is constant. Therefore, the constraint equation can always be fulfilled by an appropriate scaling of the spherical harmonics.

5 Conclusion

We have presented a theory for steerable filters and quadrature filters based on Lie group theory. Both approaches are most general with respect to the signal dimension as well as with respect to the transformation Lie group. For the steerable filter case, we provide for every quadratic integrable function (at least approximately) the method for constructing the basis functions for every Lie group transformation. For compact and Abelian groups we even showed that this is the minimum required number of basis functions. Furthermore, we generalized the 2D rotational invariant quadrature filter approach with respect to arbitrary dimension of the signal space and to Lie group transformation which own a unitary representation. It turned out that the group invariant quadrature filter is a special steerable filter. The future work will be the integration of the general quadrature filter approach into a tensor representation and its application to motion and orientation estimation in 3D.

Acknowledgements

This work was funded by DFG ME 1796/5 - 3 and DAAD D/05/26027.

References

Bülow, T., Sommer, G.: Hypercomplex signals - a novel extension of the analytic signal to the multidimensional case. IEEE Transactions on Signal Processing 49(11), 2844–2852 (2001)
Danielsson, P.E.: Rotation-invariant linear operators with directional response. In: Miami, F.L. (ed.) Proc. Int. Conf. Pattern Recognition (1980)

Felsberg, M., Sommer, G.: The monogenic signal. IEEE Transactions on Signal Processing 49(12), 3136–3144 (2001)

Freeman, W., Adelson, E.: The design and use of steerable filters. IEEE Transactions on Pattern Analysis and Machine Intelligence 13(9), 891–906 (1991)

Granlund, G.H., Knutsson, H.: Signal processing for computer vision. Kluwer Academic Publishers, Dordrecht (1995)

Köthe, U.: Integrated edge and junction detection with the boundary tensor. In: Proc. of 9th International Conference on Computer Vision, Nice, France, vol. 1, pp. 424–431 (2003)

Michaelis, M., Sommer, G.: A Lie group approach to steerable filters. Pattern Recognition Letters 16, 1165–1174 (1995)

Perona, P.: Deformable kernels for early vision. IEEE Transactions on Pattern Analysis and Machine Intelligence 17(5), 488–499 (1995)

Simoncelli, E., Farid, H.: Steerable wedge filters for local orientation analysis. IEEE Transactions on Image Processing 5(9), 1377–1382 (1996)

Simoncelli, E.P., Freeman, W.T., Adelson, E.H., Heeger, D.J.: Shiftable multiscale transforms. IEEE Transactions on Information Theory 38(2), 587–607 (1992)

Teo, P., Hel-Or, Y.: A common framework for steerability, motion estimation and invariant feature detection. Technical Report STAN-CS-TN-96-28, Stanford University (1996)

Teo, P., Hel-Or, Y.: Lie generators for computing steerable functions. Pattern Recognition Letters 19(1), 7–17 (1998)

Wigner, E.: Group Theory and its Application to Quantum Mechanics of Atomic Spectra. Academic Press, London (1959)

Yu, W., Daniilidis, K., Sommer, G.: Approximate orientation steerability based on angular gaussians. IEEE Transactions on Image Processing 10(2), 193–205 (2001)

Part VI

Image
Analysis

Generalised Principal Component Analysis: Exploiting Inherent Parameter Constraints

Wojciech Chojnacki, Anton van den Hengel, and Michael J. Brooks

School of Computer Science, University of Adelaide
Adelaide, SA 5005, Australia
{wojciech.chojnacki,anton.vandenhengel,
michael.brooks}@adelaide.edu.au

Abstract. Generalised Principal Component Analysis (GPCA) is a recently devised technique for fitting a multi-component, piecewise-linear structure to data that has found strong utility in computer vision. Unlike other methods which intertwine the processes of estimating structure components and segmenting data points into clusters associated with putative components, GPCA estimates a multi-component structure with no recourse to data clustering. The standard GPCA algorithm searches for an estimate by minimising a simple algebraic misfit function. The underlying constraints on the model parameters are ignored. Here we promote a variant of GPCA that incorporates the parameter constraints and exploits constrained rather than unconstrained minimisation of a statistically motivated error function. The output of any GPCA algorithm hardly ever perfectly satisfies the parameter constraints. Our new version of GPCA greatly facilitates the final correction of the algorithm output to satisfy perfectly the constraints, making this step less prone to error in the presence of noise. The method is applied to the example problem of fitting a pair of lines to noisy image points, but has potential for use in more general multi-component structure fitting in computer vision.

Keywords: Generalised principal component analysis, constrained minimisation, multi-line fitting, degenerate conic.

1 Introduction

One of the challenges of image analysis and computer vision is to develop effective ways to fit a multi-component structure to data. A classical example problem is fitting multiple lines to data [Lou et al., 1997, Venkateswar and Chellappa, 1992]. Several methods have been proposed for solving this particular task, including those based on the Hough transform [Duda and Hart, 1972], K-subspaces [Ho et al., 2003], subspace growing and subspace selection [Leonardis et al., 2002], EM [Tipping and Bishop, 1999] and RANSAC [Forsyth and Ponce, 2003] algorithms. More recently, there has been interest in fitting multiple linear manifolds to data. This more general problem arose in the analysis of dynamical scenes in computer vision in connection with the recovery of multiple motion models from image data [Vidal et al., 2002, Vidal and Ma, 2004, Vidal et al., 2006]. To tackle it, a new approach has been put forth under the label of *generalised principle component analysis* (GPCA) [Vidal et al., 2003, Vidal et al., 2004,

J. Braz et al. (Eds.): VISAPP and GRAPP 2006, CCIS 4, pp. 217–228, 2007.

Vidal et al., 2005]. The GPCA method employs a parametric model in which parameters describe a multi-component, piecewise-linear structure to which various parts of a data set adhere. The number of linear components is assumed to be fixed and known beforehand. The relationship between data and components is encoded in a system of multivariate polynomial equations. When all components are hyperplanes, this system reduces to a single equation. In the special, but representative, case of fitting multiple lines to planar data, the order of the single polynomial describing the structure coincides with the number of the line components, and the recovery of the components is achieved by factoring the polynomial into a product of multivariate monomials, each corresponding to a separate line. The success of the whole procedure rests upon generation of a meaningful polynomial to factor.

This paper presents a variant of GPCA which advocates the use of *constrained* optimisation as a crucial step in component recovery. We concentrate on a particular problem of fitting two lines to data as in this case the underlying analysis is particularly simple and illuminating. Notwithstanding the specificity of our presentation, the multi-line and, more generally, multi-component fitting problems can be treated—upon suitable modification—within the same general framework.

At the technical level, the contribution of the paper is three-fold. First, it gives a statistically sound *cost function* measuring how well a given model instance describes the data. The cost function is evolved by applying the maximum likelihood principle to a Gaussian model of errors in the data. Second, a pair of lines is shown to be effectively estimated by minimising the cost function subject to a certain *parameter constraint*. A novel iterative method for computing an approximate constrained minimiser is given. Finally, a simple method is presented for converting nearly optimal estimates obtained by iterative constrained optimisation techniques (hyperbolae with high eccentricity) into estimates representing a *correct geometric structure* (pairs of lines).

The original GPCA algorithm [Vidal et al., 2003, Vidal et al., 2006] employs algebraic factorisation of a multivariate polynomial whose coefficients are obtained via *unconstrained* minimisation of a simple algebraic cost function, different from the one used in the present paper. The method does not require data segmentation and as such differs from iterative methods like K-subspaces and EM which alternate between estimating structure components and grouping the data around individual components. However, because of its reliance on computation of roots of polynomials—a numerically fragile operation—the GPCA algorithm is sensitive to noise. To curb adverse effects of noise, the subsequent version of GPCA [Vidal et al., 2004, Vidal and Ma, 2004, Vidal et al., 2005] uses polynomial differentiation instead of polynomial factorisation, but at the cost of employing some form of data segmentation—one data point per component is needed to effectuate the estimation step.

The present paper shows—and this is its main conceptual contribution—that the approach taken by the original version of GPCA can be sustained even in the presence of moderate noise if a statistically motivated cost function is minimised subject to appropriate constraints. We demonstrate empirically that constrained optimisation leads, in practice, to estimates that can be encoded into nearly factorisable polynomials. These estimates can be upgraded to estimates corresponding to perfectly factorisable polynomials by means of a simple correction procedure. Because a minor adjustment of the unconstrained minimiser is needed, the upgrading procedure operates reliably. Rather than use polynomial factorisation, the correction procedure in our version of the GPCA involves eigenvalue decomposition. Its simple form reflects the special nature of the estimation problem considered.

The estimate obtained by applying the method presented in the paper represents a pair of lines and as such is an instance of a conic—a degenerate conic. Thus, effectively, our variant of GPCA is a method for degenerate-conic fitting and can be viewed as an addition to the growing body of algorithms for fitting to data a conic of a type specified in advance [Fitzgibbon et al., 1999, Halíř and Flusser, 1998, Nievergelt, 2004, O'Leary and Zsombor-Murray, 2004].

2 Background

A *line* is a focus of points $x = [m_1, m_2]^T$ in the Euclidean plane $\mathbb{R}^2$ satisfying the equation

$$l_1 m_1 + l_2 m_2 + l_3 = 0.$$

Employing homogeneous coordinates $m = [m_1, m_2, 1]^T$ and $l = [l_1, l_2, l_3]^T$, the same line can be identified with the subset of the projective plane $\mathbb{P}^2$ given by $Z_l = \{m \in \mathbb{P}^2 \mid l^T m = 0\}$. A *conic* is a locus of points $x = [m_1, m_2]^T$ satisfying the equation

$$a m_1^2 + b m_1 m_2 + c m_2^2 + d m_1 + e m_2 + f = 0,$$

where a, b and c are not all zero. Introducing the symmetric matrix C

$$C = \begin{bmatrix} a & b/2 & d/2 \\ b/2 & c & e/2 \\ d/2 & e/2 & f \end{bmatrix},$$

the same conic can be described as $Z_C = \{m \in \mathbb{P}^2 \mid m^T C m = 0\}$. A *non-degenerate* conic satisfies $\det C \neq 0$ and is either an ellipse, or a parabola, or a hyperbola depending on whether the *discriminant* $\Delta = b^2 - 4ac$ is negative, zero or positive. If $\det C = 0$, then the conic is *degenerate*. A degenerate conic represents either two intersecting lines, a (double) line, or a point, as we now critically recall.

A union of two lines, $Z_{l_1} \cup Z_{l_2}$, obeys

$$l_1^T m \cdot l_2^T m = m^T l_1 l_2^T m = 0$$

or equivalently, given that $m^T l_1 l_2^T m = m^T l_2 l_1^T m$,

$$m^T (l_1 l_2^T + l_2 l_1^T) m = 0. \tag{1}$$

With $C = l_1 l_2^T + l_2 l_1^T$, a symmetric matrix, the above equation can be rewritten as $m^T C m = 0$, showing that $Z_{l_1} \cup Z_{l_2}$ is identical with the conic Z_C. The matrices $l_i l_j^T$ are rank-1, so the rank of C is no greater than 2 and the conic is degenerate. If $l_1 = l_2$, then Z_C represents a single, repeated line; in this case the conic equation $(l_1^T m)^2 = 0$

is equivalent to the line equation $l_1^T m = 0$. Finally, a point $[p_1, p_2]^T$ can be represented as the degenerate conic $(m_1 - p_1)^2 + (m_2 - p_2)^2 = 0$ corresponding to

$$C = \begin{bmatrix} 1 & 0 & -p_1 \\ 0 & 1 & -p_2 \\ -p_1 & -p_2 & p_1^2 + p_2^2 \end{bmatrix}.$$

To see that a pair of lines, a double line and a point are the only possible types of degenerate conic, suppose that C is a non-zero symmetric singular matrix. Then C admits an *eigenvalue decomposition* (EVD) of the form $C = VDV^T$, where V is an orthogonal 3×3 matrix and $D = \mathrm{diag}(\lambda_1, \lambda_2, \lambda_3)$, with λ_i ($i = 1, 2, 3$) a real number [Horn and Johnson, 1985]. The eigenvalue decomposition differs from the *singular value decomposition* (SVD) of C in that the latter uses two orthogonal, possibly different, matrices U and V, and that the former uses a diagonal matrix whose entries are not necessarily non-negative. However, the EVD and SVD of the symmetric C are closely related—any of the two orthogonal factors U, V in the SVD can serve as V in the EVD, and D in the EVD can be obtained from the diagonal factor in the SVD by placing a minus sign before each diagonal entry for which the corresponding columns in U and V differ by a sign, with all remaining entries left intact. For each $i = 1, 2, 3$, let v_i be the ith column vector of V. Then, clearly, v_i is an eigenvector of C corresponding to the eigenvalue λ_i, $Cv_i = \lambda_i v_i$, and, moreover, $C = \sum_{i=1}^{3} \lambda_i v_i v_i^T$. Now $\det C = \lambda_1 \lambda_2 \lambda_3 = 0$ so one eigenvalue, say λ_3, is zero, implying that $C = \sum_{i=1}^{2} \lambda_i v_i v_i^T$. If another eigenvalue, say λ_2, is zero too, then $C = \lambda_1 v_1 v_1^T$ and, since the remaining eigenvalue, λ_1, has to be non-zero, Z_C coincides with the line Z_{v_1}. If λ_3 is the only zero eigenvalue, then there are two possibilities— either λ_1 and λ_2 are of same sign, or λ_1 and λ_2 are of opposite sign. In the first case Z_C reduces to the linear span of $v_3 = [v_{13}, v_{23}, v_{33}]^T$ and represents a single point in $\mathbb{P}^2$; if $v_{33} \neq 0$, then this point is part of $\mathbb{R}^2$ and is given by $[v_{13}/v_{33}, v_{23}/v_{33}, 1]^T$. In the other case, Z_C represents a pair of lines in $\mathbb{P}^2$. Indeed, without loss of generality, we may suppose that $\lambda_1 > 0$ and $\lambda_2 < 0$. Then

$$\lambda_1 v_1 v_1^T + \lambda_2 v_2 v_2^T = l_1 l_2^T + l_2 l_1^T,$$

where $l_1 = \sqrt{\lambda_1} v_1 + \sqrt{-\lambda_2} v_2$ and $l_2 = \sqrt{\lambda_1} v_1 - \sqrt{-\lambda_2} v_2$. Consequently,

$$m^T C m = m^T l_1 l_2^T m + m^T l_2 l_1^T m = 2(l_1^T m)(l_2^T m),$$

so Z_C is the union of the lines Z_{l_1} and Z_{l_2}. The identification of Z_C with $Z_{l_1} \cup Z_{l_2}$ via the factorisation of the binomial $m^T C m$ as above exemplifies the general factorisation principle underlying GPCA.

3   Estimation Problem

The equation for a conic Z_C can alternatively be written as

$$\theta^T u(x) = 0, \tag{2}$$

where $\boldsymbol{\theta} = [\theta_1, \cdots, \theta_6]^T = [a, b, c, d, e, f]^T$ and $\boldsymbol{u}(\boldsymbol{x}) = [m_1^2, m_1 m_2, m_2^2, m_1, m_2, 1]^T$. The singularity constraint $\det \boldsymbol{C} = 0$ can be written as

$$\phi(\boldsymbol{\theta}) = 0, \tag{3}$$

where $\phi(\boldsymbol{\theta}) = \theta_1 \theta_3 \theta_6 - \theta_1 \theta_5^2/4 - \theta_2^2 \theta_6/4 + \theta_2 \theta_4 \theta_5/4 - \theta_4^2 \theta_3/4$. Note that ϕ is *homogeneous* of degree 3—that is such that

$$\phi(t\boldsymbol{\theta}) = t^\kappa \phi(\boldsymbol{\theta}) \tag{4}$$

for every non-zero scalar t, with $\kappa = 3$ the index of homogeneity.

Together, equations (2) and (3) form a parametric model that encapsulates the configuration comprising a pair of lines and a point at one of these lines. In this setting, $\boldsymbol{\theta}$ is the vector of parameters representing the lines and $\boldsymbol{x}$ is the *ideal* datum representing the point.

Associated with this model is the following estimation problem: Given a collection $\boldsymbol{x}_1, \ldots, \boldsymbol{x}_n$ of *observed* data points and a meaningful *cost function* that characterises the extent to which any particular $\boldsymbol{\theta}$ fails to satisfy the system of copies of equation (2) associated with $\boldsymbol{x} = \boldsymbol{x}_i$ ($i = 1, \ldots, n$), find $\boldsymbol{\theta} \neq \boldsymbol{0}$ satisfying (3) for which the cost function attains its minimum.

The use of the *Gaussian model of errors* in data in conjunction with the *principle of maximum likelihood* leads to the *approximated maximum likelihood* (AML) *cost function*

$$J_{\mathrm{AML}}(\boldsymbol{\theta}; \boldsymbol{x}_1, \ldots, \boldsymbol{x}_n) = \sum_{i=1}^n \frac{\boldsymbol{\theta}^T \boldsymbol{u}(\boldsymbol{x}_i) \boldsymbol{u}(\boldsymbol{x}_i)^T \boldsymbol{\theta}}{\boldsymbol{\theta}^T \partial_{\boldsymbol{x}} \boldsymbol{u}(\boldsymbol{x}_i) \boldsymbol{\Lambda}_{\boldsymbol{x}_i} \partial_{\boldsymbol{x}} \boldsymbol{u}(\boldsymbol{x}_i)^T \boldsymbol{\theta}},$$

where, for any length 2 vector $\boldsymbol{y}$, $\partial_{\boldsymbol{x}} \boldsymbol{u}(\boldsymbol{y})$ denotes the 6×2 matrix of the partial derivatives of the function $\boldsymbol{x} \mapsto \boldsymbol{u}(\boldsymbol{x})$ evaluated at $\boldsymbol{y}$, and, for each $i = 1, \ldots, n$, $\boldsymbol{\Lambda}_{\boldsymbol{x}_i}$ is a 2×2 symmetric *covariance matrix* describing the uncertainty of the data point $\boldsymbol{x}_i$ [Brooks et al., 2001, Chojnacki et al., 2000, Kanatani, 1996]. If J_{AML} is minimised over those non-zero parameter vectors for which (3) holds, then the vector at which the minimum of J_{AML} is attained, the constrained minimiser of J_{AML}, defines the *approximated maximum likelihood estimate* $\widehat{\boldsymbol{\theta}}_{\mathrm{AML}}$. The unconstrained minimiser of J_{AML} obtained by ignoring the constraint (3) and searching over all of the parameter space defines the *unconstrained approximated likelihood estimate*, $\widehat{\boldsymbol{\theta}}_{\mathrm{AML}}^u$. The function $\boldsymbol{\theta} \mapsto J_{\mathrm{AML}}(\boldsymbol{\theta}; \boldsymbol{x}_1, \ldots, \boldsymbol{x}_n)$ is homogeneous of degree zero and the zero set of ϕ is invariant to multiplication by non-zero scalars, so both $\widehat{\boldsymbol{\theta}}_{\mathrm{AML}}$ and $\widehat{\boldsymbol{\theta}}_{\mathrm{AML}}^u$ are determined only up to scale. Obviously, $\widehat{\boldsymbol{\theta}}_{\mathrm{AML}}$ is the preferred estimate of $\boldsymbol{\theta}$, with $\widehat{\boldsymbol{\theta}}_{\mathrm{AML}}^u$ being the second best choice.

4   Unconstrained Minimisation

The unconstrained minimiser $\widehat{\boldsymbol{\theta}}_{\mathrm{AML}}^u$ satisfies the *optimality condition* for unconstrained minimisation

$$[\partial_{\boldsymbol{\theta}} J_{\mathrm{AML}}(\boldsymbol{\theta}; \boldsymbol{x}_1, \ldots, \boldsymbol{x}_n)]_{\boldsymbol{\theta} = \widehat{\boldsymbol{\theta}}_{\mathrm{AML}}^u} = \boldsymbol{0}^T$$

with $\partial_{\theta} J_{\text{AML}}$ the row vector of the partial derivatives of J_{AML} with respect to θ. Direct computation shows that

$$[\partial_{\theta} J_{\text{AML}}(\theta; x_1, \ldots, x_n)]^T = 2 X_{\theta} \theta,$$

where

$$X_{\theta} = \sum_{i=1}^{n} \frac{A_i}{\theta^T B_i \theta} - \sum_{i=1}^{n} \frac{\theta^T A_i \theta}{(\theta^T B_i \theta)^2} B_i,$$

$$A_i = u(x_i) u(x_i)^T,$$

$$B_i = \partial_x u(x_i) \Lambda_{x_i} \partial_x u(x_i)^T.$$

The optimality condition rewritten as

$$[X_{\theta} \theta]_{\theta = \widehat{\theta}^u_{\text{AML}}} = 0 \tag{5}$$

serves as the basis for isolating $\widehat{\theta}^u_{\text{AML}}$. Two Newton-like iterative algorithms can be used for solving (5). The *fundamental numerical scheme* (FNS) [Chojnacki et al., 2000] exploits the fact that a vector θ satisfies (5) if and only if it is a solution of the *ordinary* eigenvalue problem

$$X_{\theta} \xi = \lambda \xi$$

corresponding to the eigenvalue $\lambda = 0$. Given a current approximate solution θ_c, the stable version of FNS [Chojnacki et al., 2005] takes for an updated solution θ_+ a normalised eigenvector of X_{θ_c} corresponding to the smallest eigenvalue. The iterative process can be started by computing the *algebraic least squares* (ALS) *estimate*, $\widehat{\theta}_{\text{ALS}}$, defined as the unconstrained minimiser of the cost function $J_{\text{ALS}}(\theta; x_1, \ldots, x_n) = \|\theta\|^{-2} \sum_{i=1}^{n} \theta^T A_i \theta$, with $\|\theta\| = (\sum_{j=1}^{6} \theta_j^2)^{1/2}$. The estimate $\widehat{\theta}_{\text{ALS}}$ coincides, up to scale, with an eigenvector of $\sum_{i=1}^{n} A_i$ for the smallest eigenvalue, and this can be found via singular value decomposition as the right singular vector of the matrix $[u(x_1), \ldots, u(x_n)]^T$ corresponding to the smallest singular value. Incidentally, we point out that the standard version of GCPA [Vidal et al., 2005] is based exclusively on ALS cost minimisation.

With $M_{\theta} = \sum_{i=1}^{n} (\theta^T B_i \theta)^{-1} A_i$ and $N_{\theta} = \sum_{i=1}^{n} (\theta^T A_i \theta)(\theta^T B_i \theta)^{-2} B_i$, equation (5) can equivalently be restated as

$$M_{\theta} \theta = N_{\theta} \theta, \tag{6}$$

where the evaluation at $\widehat{\theta}^u_{\text{AML}}$ is dropped for clarity. The *heteroscedastic errors-in-variables scheme* in its *basic* form, or *HEIV with intercept* [Leedan and Meer, 2000, Matei and Meer, 2000, Chojnacki et al., 2004a], is based upon the observation that a vector θ satisfies (6) if and only if it is a solution of the *generalised* eigenvalue problem

$$M_{\theta} \xi = \lambda N_{\theta} \xi$$

corresponding to the eigenvalue $\lambda = 1$. Given a current approximate solution θ_c, HEIV takes for an updated solution θ_+ a normalised eigenvector of the eigenvalue problem $M_{\theta_c} \xi = \lambda N_{\theta_c} \xi$ corresponding to the smallest eigenvalue. Again the iterative process can be seeded with $\widehat{\theta}_{\text{ALS}}$.

5   Approximate Constrained Minimisation

A natural means for isolating the constrained minimiser $\widehat{\boldsymbol{\theta}}_{\mathrm{AML}}$ is the *constrained fundamental numerical scheme* (CFNS) [Chojnacki et al., 2004b]. The scheme is a variant of FNS in which $\boldsymbol{X}_{\boldsymbol{\theta}}$ is replaced by a more complicated symmetric matrix. As it turns out, CFNS is sensitive to the choice of the underlying coordinate system and its practical success depends critically on good pre-conditioning. This is so because not only the initial estimate has to be sufficiently close to the sought-after solution (as is the case with all Newton-like methods), but also the smallest eigenvalue of the counterpart of $\boldsymbol{X}_{\boldsymbol{\theta}}$ used in iterations has to be well separated from the remaining eigenvalues. As a rule, to meet these conditions, a transformation of the data-related variables needs to be applied as a pre-process and a conformal transformation of the parameters-related variables has to follow in a post-process. Work on a suitable pre-conditioning for the case in question is in progress.

To find an estimate satisfying the singularity constraint and having the property that the value of J_{AML} at that estimate is only slightly increased compared to $J_{\mathrm{AML}}(\widehat{\boldsymbol{\theta}}_{\mathrm{AML}}^{u})$, we take a more conventional approach and adopt an *adjustment procedure*. It is a separate post-process operating on the result of unconstrained minimisation, $\widehat{\boldsymbol{\theta}}_{\mathrm{AML}}^{u}$. The estimate obtained via a post-hoc correction can be viewed as an approximate constrained minimiser.

A standard adjustment technique, due to Kanatani [Kanatani, 1996], generates iteratively a sequence of estimates, starting from $\widehat{\boldsymbol{\theta}}_{\mathrm{AML}}^{u}$, with the use of the update rule

$$\boldsymbol{\theta}_{+} = \boldsymbol{\theta}_{c} - [\partial_{\boldsymbol{\theta}}\phi(\boldsymbol{\theta}_{c})\boldsymbol{\Lambda}_{\boldsymbol{\theta}_{c}}\partial_{\boldsymbol{\theta}}\phi(\boldsymbol{\theta}_{c})^{T}]^{-1} \times \phi(\boldsymbol{\theta}_{c})\boldsymbol{\Lambda}_{\boldsymbol{\theta}_{c}}\partial_{\boldsymbol{\theta}}\phi(\boldsymbol{\theta}_{c})^{T}.$$

Here $\boldsymbol{\Lambda}_{\boldsymbol{\theta}} = \boldsymbol{Q}_{\boldsymbol{\theta}}(\boldsymbol{X}_{\widehat{\boldsymbol{\theta}}_{\mathrm{AML}}^{u}})^{-}\boldsymbol{Q}_{\boldsymbol{\theta}}$, with the notation $\boldsymbol{A}^{-}$ for the Moore-Penrose pseudo-inverse of $\boldsymbol{A}$, $\boldsymbol{Q}_{\boldsymbol{\theta}} = \boldsymbol{I}_{l} - \|\boldsymbol{\theta}\|^{-2}\boldsymbol{\theta}\boldsymbol{\theta}^{T}$, with $\boldsymbol{I}_{l}$ the $l \times l$ identity matrix and l the length of $\boldsymbol{\theta}$, here set to 6. The scheme is repeated until the value of the constraint residual $|\phi|$ is acceptably small. The final estimate delivers an approximation to $\widehat{\boldsymbol{\theta}}_{\mathrm{AML}}$.

In an effort to achieve a greater resemblance to CFNS, we have developed an alternative post-hoc correction (PHC) technique. It exploits the iterative process

$$\boldsymbol{\theta}_{+} = \boldsymbol{\theta}_{c} - [\partial_{\boldsymbol{\theta}}\phi(\boldsymbol{\theta}_{c})\boldsymbol{H}_{\boldsymbol{\theta}_{c}}^{-}\partial_{\boldsymbol{\theta}}\phi(\boldsymbol{\theta}_{c})^{T}]^{-1} \times \phi(\boldsymbol{\theta}_{c})\boldsymbol{H}_{\boldsymbol{\theta}_{c}}^{-}\partial_{\boldsymbol{\theta}}\phi(\boldsymbol{\theta}_{c})^{T}.$$

Here $\boldsymbol{H}_{\boldsymbol{\theta}}$ is the Hessian of J_{AML} at $\boldsymbol{\theta}$, given explicitly by $\boldsymbol{H}_{\boldsymbol{\theta}} = 2(\boldsymbol{X}_{\boldsymbol{\theta}} - \boldsymbol{T}_{\boldsymbol{\theta}})$, where

$$\boldsymbol{T}_{\boldsymbol{\theta}} = \sum_{i=1}^{n} \frac{2}{(\boldsymbol{\theta}^{T}\boldsymbol{B}_{i}\boldsymbol{\theta})^{2}} \left[\boldsymbol{A}_{i}\boldsymbol{\theta}\boldsymbol{\theta}^{T}\boldsymbol{B}_{i} + \boldsymbol{B}_{i}\boldsymbol{\theta}\boldsymbol{\theta}^{T}\boldsymbol{A}_{i} - 2\frac{\boldsymbol{\theta}^{T}\boldsymbol{A}_{i}\boldsymbol{\theta}}{\boldsymbol{\theta}^{T}\boldsymbol{B}_{i}\boldsymbol{\theta}}\boldsymbol{B}_{i}\boldsymbol{\theta}\boldsymbol{\theta}^{T}\boldsymbol{B}_{i} \right].$$

As in Kanatani's method, the process is initialised with $\widehat{\boldsymbol{\theta}}_{\mathrm{AML}}$ and is continued until the value of the constraint residual is sufficiently small.

It should be noted that while the value of the constraint residual at successive updates generated by any iterative (approximate) constrained minimisation technique like PHC systematically decreases as the computation progresses, the singularity constraint is hardly ever perfectly satisfied. The nearly perfect, but not ideal, satisfaction of the constraint means that, geometrically, the estimates are not pairs of lines, but are hyperbolae of high eccentricity—that is, hyperbolae that are elongated and have flat branches.

6   EVD Correction

To ensure that two-line fitting algorithms produce usable estimates, a method is required for enforcing the singularity constraint in a perfect manner. The method should be applicable to the final output of any two-line estimation procedure and, ideally, should deliver the result of the constraint enforcement in the form of a pair of lines. Here we describe one such correction technique based on EVD. It is tuned to fitting a pair of lines and does not directly generalise to fitting larger sets of lines. The method can be viewed as an alternative to the factorisation technique proposed in [Vidal et al., 2003].

A given estimate is first reshaped to take the form of a symmetric matrix C. Then EVD is performed on C yielding $C = V D V^T$ with $V = [v_1, v_2, v_3]$ orthogonal and $D = \mathrm{diag}(\lambda_1, \lambda_2, \lambda_3)$, $|\lambda_1| \geq |\lambda_2| \geq |\lambda_3|$. Finally, C is modified to $C_c = V D_c V^T$, where $D_c = \mathrm{diag}(\lambda_1, \lambda_2, 0)$. The corrected estimate C_c now perfectly satisfies the singularity constraint. This estimate can further be reinterpreted in accordance with the geometric nature of the associated set Z_{C_c}. If λ_1 and λ_2 are of opposite signs, then Z_{C_c} is the pair of lines

$$
\begin{aligned}
l_1 &= \sqrt{\mathrm{sgn}(\lambda_1)\lambda_1}\, v_1 + \sqrt{\mathrm{sgn}(\lambda_2)\lambda_2}\, v_2, \\
l_2 &= \sqrt{\mathrm{sgn}(\lambda_1)\lambda_1}\, v_1 - \sqrt{\mathrm{sgn}(\lambda_2)\lambda_2}\, v_2.
\end{aligned}
\tag{7}
$$

If $\lambda_2 = 0$, then Z_{C_c} is the double line v_1. If λ_1 and λ_2 are of same sign, then Z_{C_c} represents the point $v_3 = [v_{13}, v_{23}, v_{33}]^T$ in $\mathbb{P}^2$, which, when $v_{33} \neq 0$, belongs to $\mathbb{R}^2$ and is given by $[v_{13}/v_{33}, v_{23}/v_{33}, 1]^T$. The last case can be viewed as exceptional and is not expected to arise frequently. In a typical situation, the input estimate C is such that the associated values λ_1 and λ_2 have opposite signs and the corrected estimate C_c is geometrically represented by the lines l_1 and l_2 given in (7).

7   Experiments

To assess potential benefits stemming from the use of constrained optimisation in the realm of GPCA, we carried out a simulation study. Three algorithms, ALS, HEIV and PHC (described in Sections 4 and 5), were set to compute a pair of lines from synthetic data. We utilised a particular version of HEIV, namely the *reduced* HEIV scheme, or *HEIV without intercept*, that operates essentially over a subspace of the parameter space of one dimension less [Chojnacki et al., 2004a]. The covariances of the data employed by HEIV and PHC were assumed to be the default 2×2 identity matrix corresponding to isotropic homogeneous noise in image measurement.

To create data for our study, we randomly generated 100 pairs of lines. Along each line, in a section spanning 100 pixels in the x direction, 100 points were generated by sampling from a uniform distribution. To these points homogeneous zero-mean Gaussian noise was added at three different levels characterised by the standard deviation σ of 0.1, 0.55 and 1 pixel. This data was generated so as to represent the kinds of line segment that may be found by an edge detector. An example of the data is given in Figure 1.

Each estimator was applied to the points generated from each of the 100 pairs of lines and the resulting estimates were recorded and evaluated. As a measure of performance,

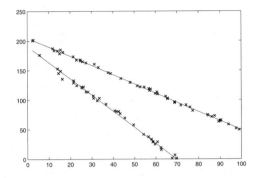

Fig. 1. An example data set and corresponding (true) pair of lines

Table 1. Averages of testing results

σ	Method	J_{AML}	Rank-2 J_{AML}
	ALS	1.286×10^{-1}	2.060×10^{1}
0.1	HEIV	1.084×10^{-2}	8.421×10^{-2}
	PHC	1.065×10^{-2}	1.065×10^{-2}
	ALS	1.444×10^{1}	5.977×10^{5}
0.55	HEIV	4.098	1.801×10^{2}
	PHC	9.190	9.195
	ALS	2.779×10^{2}	5.448×10^{2}
1.0	HEIV	4.448	3.652×10^{1}
	PHC	2.816	2.816

we used the AML cost function, with the standard value of J_{AML} averaged across the points in the image.

To ensure that the outputs of the algorithms can be interpreted as genuine pairs of lines, all estimates were post-hoc EVD corrected. The J_{AML} value of the corrected estimates, Rank-2 J_{AML}, is given in the rightmost columns in Tables 1 and 2. It is this Rank-2 J_{AML} number that is the most informative indicator of the performance of a particular method.

Tables 1 and 2 give the cost function values for 3 types of estimates. Table 1 shows that, on average, HEIV is an effective minimiser of J_{AML}, and that PHC coupled with EVD correction produces better results that the EVD-corrected HEIV scheme. Moreover—and this is a critical observation—when applied to the PHC estimate, EVD correction leaves the J_{AML} value virtually unaffected (unlike in the case of the HEIV estimate, where EVD correction markedly worsens the J_{AML} value). This confirms that the result of approximate constrained optimisation has an almost optimal form and that EVD correction in this case amounts to a tiny push, which can be stably executed in the presence of noise.

Table 2. Medians of testing results

σ	Method	J_{AML}	Rank-2 J_{AML}
	ALS	1.135×10^{-2}	1.113×10^{-2}
0.1	HEIV	9.517×10^{-3}	1.037×10^{-2}
	PHC	9.713×10^{-3}	9.713×10^{-3}
	ALS	3.738×10^{-1}	3.687×10^{-1}
0.55	HEIV	3.092×10^{-1}	3.277×10^{-1}
	PHC	3.121×10^{-1}	3.121×10^{-1}
	ALS	1.094	1.212
1.0	HEIV	9.498×10^{-1}	1.093
	PHC	9.509×10^{-1}	9.509×10^{-1}

Table 2 presents the results of the same tests but reports the median, rather than mean, of the J_{AML} values. As the median is usually more representative of the central tendency of a sample set than the mean, Table 2 provides a better indication of the performance of the algorithms on a typical trial.

8 Conclusions and Future Work

We have presented a novel version of GPCA for the case of fitting a pair of lines to data, with a message extending to the general case of multi-component estimation. At the core of our formulation lies the reduction of the underlying estimation problem to minimisation of an error function having solid statistical foundations, subject to a parameter constraint. We have proposed a technique for isolating an approximate constrained minimiser of that function. Preliminary experiments show that our algorithm provides better results than the standard GPCA based on unconstrained minimisation of a simple algebraic error function.

There are clearly a number of ways in which the work reported in this paper can be extended. The case of multiple lines can be approached starting from the observation that equation (1) characterising a pair of lines can equivalently be written as $(l_1 \otimes_s l_2)^T (m \otimes m) = 0$, where $l_1 \otimes_s l_2 = (l_1 \otimes l_2 + l_2 \otimes l_1)/2$ is the symmetric tensor product of l_1 and l_2, and $\otimes$ denotes the Kronecker (or tensor) product. More generally, the equation for an aggregate of k lines is $(l_1 \otimes_s \cdots \otimes_s l_k)^T (m \otimes \cdots \otimes m) = 0$, where $l_1 \otimes_s \cdots \otimes_s l_k = (k!)^{-1} \sum_{\sigma \in S_k} l_{\sigma(1)} \otimes \cdots \otimes l_{\sigma(k)}$ and S_k is the symmetric group on k elements. It is known that the totally decomposable symmetric tensors of the form $l_1 \otimes_s \cdots \otimes_s l_k$ constitute an algebraic variety within the space of all symmetric tensors [Lim, 1992]. However, no explicit formula for the underlying constraints is known (this is a fundamental difference with the case of totally decomposable antisymmetric tensors). Working out these constraints in concrete cases like those involving low values of k will immediately allow the new version of GPCA to cope with larger multi-line structures. More generally, progress in applying the constrained GPCA to estimating more complicated multi-component structures will strongly depend on successful identification of relevant constraints.

References

Brooks, M.J., Chojnacki, W., Gawley, D., van den Hengel, A.: What value covariance information in estimating vision parameters? In: Proc. Eighth Int. Conf. Computer Vision, vol. 1, pp. 302–308 (2001)

Chojnacki, W., Brooks, M.J., van den Hengel, A., Gawley, D.: On the fitting of surfaces to data with covariances. IEEE Trans. Pattern Anal. Mach. Intell. 22(11), 1294–1303 (2000)

Chojnacki, W., Brooks, M.J., van den Hengel, A., Gawley, D.: From FNS and HEIV: A link between two vision parameter estimation methods. IEEE Trans. Pattern Anal. Mach. Intell. 26(2), 264–268 (2004a)

Chojnacki, W., Brooks, M.J., van den Hengel, A., Gawley, D.: A new constrained parameter estimator for computer vision applications. Image and Vision Computing 22, 85–91 (2004b)

Chojnacki, W., Brooks, M.J., van den Hengel, A., Gawley, D.: FNS, CFNS and HEIV: A unifying approach. J. Math. Imaging and Vision 23(2), 175–183 (2005)

Duda, R.O., Hart, P.E.: Use of the Hough transform to detect lines and curves in pictures. Commun. ACM 15, 11–15 (1972)

Fitzgibbon, A., Pilu, M., Fisher, R.B.: Direct least square fitting of ellipses. IEEE Trans. Pattern Anal. Mach. Intell. 21(5), 476–480 (1999)

Forsyth, D.A., Ponce, J.: Computer Vision: A Modern Approach. Prentice-Hall, Englewood Cliffs (2003)

Halíř., Flusser, J.: Numerically stable direct least squares fitting of ellipses. In: Proc. Sixth Int. Conf. in Central Europe on Computer Graphics and Visualization, pp. 125–132 (1998)

Ho, J., Yang, M.-H., Lim, J., Lee, K.-C., Kriegman, D.J.: Clustering appearances of objects under varying illumination conditions. In: Proc. IEEE Conf. Computer Vision and Pattern Recognition, vol. 1, pp. 11–18. IEEE, Los Alamitos (2003)

Horn, R., Johnson, C.: Matrix Analysis. Cambridge University Press, Cambridge (1985)

Kanatani, K.: Statistical Optimization for Geometric Computation: Theory and Practice. Elsevier, Amsterdam (1996)

Leedan, Y., Meer, P.: Heteroscedastic regression in computer vision: Problems with bilinear constraint. Int. J. Computer Vision 37(2), 127–150 (2000)

Leonardis, A., Bischof, H., Maver, J.: Multiple eigenspaces. Pattern Recognition 35(11), 2613–2627 (2002)

Lim, M.H.: Conditions on decomposable symmetric tensors as an algebraic variety. Linear and Multilinear Algebra 32, 249–252 (1992)

Lou, X.-M., Hassebrook, L.G., Lhamon, M.E., Li, J.: Numerically efficient angle, width, offset, and discontinuity determination of straight lines by the discrete Fourier-bilinear transformation algorithm. IEEE Trans. Image Processing 6(10), 1464–1467 (1997)

Matei, B., Meer, P.: A general method for errors-in-variables problems in computer vision. In: Proc. IEEE Conf. Computer Vision and Pattern Recognition, vol. 2, pp. 18–25. IEEE, Los Alamitos (2000)

Nievergelt, Y.: Fitting conics of specific types to data. Linear Algebra and Appl. 378, 1–30 (2004)

O'Leary, P., Zsombor-Murray, P.: Direct and specific least-square fitting of hyperbolæ and ellipses. J. Electronic Imaging 13(3), 492–503 (2004)

Tipping, M.E., Bishop, C.M.: Mixtures of probabilistic principal component analysers. Neural Computation 11(2), 443–482 (1999)

Venkateswar, V., Chellappa, R.: Extraction of straight lines in aerial images. IEEE Trans. Pattern Anal. Mach. Intell. 14(11), 1111–1114 (1992)

Vidal, R., Ma, Y.: A unified algebraic approach to 2-D and 3-D motion segmentation. In: Pajdla, T., Matas, J. (eds.) ECCV 2004. LNCS, vol. 3021, pp. 1–15. Springer, Heidelberg (2004)

Vidal, R., Ma, Y., Piazzi, J.: A new GPCA algorithm for clustering subspaces by fitting, differentiating and dividing polynomials. In: Proc. IEEE Conf. Computer Vision and Pattern Recognition, vol. 1, pp. 510–517. IEEE, Los Alamitos (2004)

Vidal, R., Ma, Y., Sastry, S.: Generalized principal component analysis (GPCA). In: Proc. IEEE Conf. Computer Vision and Pattern Recognition, vol. 1, pp. 621–628. IEEE, Los Alamitos (2003)

Vidal, R., Ma, Y., Sastry, S.: Generalized principal component analysis (GPCA). IEEE Trans. Pattern Anal. Mach. Intell. 27(12), 1945–1959 (2005)

Vidal, R., Ma, Y., Soatto, S., Sastry, S.: Segmentation of dynamical scenes from the multibody fundamental matrix. In: ECCV Workshop Vision and Modelling of Dynamical Scenes (2002) Available at http://www.robots.ox.ac.uk/~awf/eccv02/vamods02-rvidal.pdf

Vidal, R., Ma, Y., Soatto, S., Sastry, S.: Two-view multibody structure from motion. Int. J. Computer Vision 68(1), 7–25 (2006)

Ellipse Detection in Digital Image Data Using Geometric Features

Lars Libuda, Ingo Grothues, and Karl-Friedrich Kraiss

Chair of Technical Computer Science
Aachen University, Germany
{libuda,grothues,kraiss}@techinfo.rwth-aachen.de

Abstract. Ellipse detection is an important task in vision based systems because many real world objects can be described by this primitive. This paper presents a fast data driven four stage filtering process which uses geometric features in each stage to synthesize ellipses from binary image data with the help of lines, arcs, and extended arcs. It can cope with partially occluded and overlapping ellipses, works fast and accurate and keeps memory consumption to a minimum.

Keywords: Ellipse Detection, Shape Analysis & Representation, Image Analysis.

1 Introduction

The detection of ellipses in digital image data is an important task in vision based systems as shapes of real world objects can often be described by geometric primitives like ellipses or be assembled by them (Sanz et al., 1988; Radford and Houghton, 1989). Applications include but are not limited to gaze tracking (Canzler and Kraiss, 2004), ball tracking in soccer games (d'Orazio et al., 2004), vehicle detection (Radford and Houghton, 1989), cell counting in breast cancer cell samples (Mclaughlin, 1998) or traffic sign detection (Piccioli et al., 1994).

Algorithms for ellipse detection have to cope with noisy image data and partially occluded ellipses and they also have to produce accurate results as fast as possible to be suitable for realtime applications. Furthermore, memory usage should be low, since ellipse detection is mostly just a preprocessing step for algorithms applied in later stages.

Ellipses are described by 5 parameters: center point (x_E, y_E), two semi-axes (a, b), and orientation α. The best known method to estimate these parameters is the standard Hough transform (Duda and Hart, 1972) and its derivatives, e. g. (Xu et al., 1990). Special versions of Hough transforms adapted to ellipse extraction also exists (Ho and Chen, 1996; Guil and Zapata, 1997). There is however a common disadvantage: Hough transforms demand a trade off between processing speed and accuracy and consume a lot of memory. This led to the development of methods independent of any Hough transform. McLaughlin (McLaughlin and Alder, 1998) proposed an algorithm called "UpWrite" for ellipse detection. It works faster and more accurate than the above mentioned methods, it fails however in case of partially occluded ellipses. The

J. Braz et al. (Eds.): VISAPP and GRAPP 2006, CCIS 4, pp. 229–239, 2007.

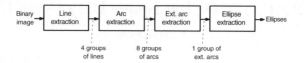

Fig. 1. Ellipse detection as four stage filtering process

latter problem is addressed by Kim et al. (Kim et al., 2002). They introduced a two-stage reconstruction algorithm which is able to detect partially occluded ellipses but do not treat memory consumption.

The algorithm presented in this paper can be added to the category of Hough transform independent algorithms and extends the work by Kim et al. Ellipse detection is regarded as a data driven four stage filtering process (Fig. 1). The first stage extracts short straight lines from a binary input image which is created with Canny's algorithm (Canny, 1986). In the second stage, these lines are combined to small arcs which are synthesized to extended arcs in the third stage. Extended arcs are finally used to create ellipses. Each stage uses geometric features of the extracted objects to synthesize them from objects extracted in the previous stage.

The remaining part of this paper is structured as follows: Section 2 gives an overview on the entire filtering process and basic definitions. Section 3 describes the process according to Fig.1 in detail. First results and performance of the algorithm are presented in section 4.

2   Overview and Definitions

The elements extracted in each processing stage are depicted in Fig. 2. A segment consists of at least two adjacent pixels and belongs to one of the line orientation groups denoted in Fig. 3. Within each separate group of segments lines are synthesized from adjacent segments which do not exceed a predefined quantization error with regard to the ideal analogue line represented by these segments. An arc is created from at least two adjacent lines of one line orientation group. The lines must not exceed a given error in the tangents to an estimated circle which these lines represent. During arc extraction each line orientation group is split in two arc orientation groups (Fig. 4) depending on the arc's orientation with respect to the ellipse's midpoint. Extended arcs consist of three adjacent arcs from consecutive arc orientation groups. Finally an ellipse is constructed from one ore more extended arcs which describe the same ellipse with a predefined tolerance and cover the circumference of the described ellipse to a predefined degree.

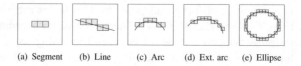

(a) Segment   (b) Line   (c) Arc   (d) Ext. arc   (e) Ellipse

Fig. 2. Extracted objects during ellipse detection

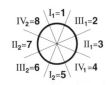

Fig. 3. Line groups

Fig. 4. Arc groups

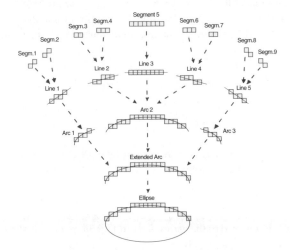

Fig. 5. Extracted elements and their relationships

During the filtering process it is necessary to access the base objects of a constructed element. Therefore, each synthesized object keeps a reference to all base objects it is composed of. Fig. 5 visualizes this concept which makes it possible to trace back each extracted object down to the single pixels belonging to this object.

3 Ellipse Detection

This section describes the used algorithms and the geometric features of the extracted objects in the single filter stages. All algorithms are described for orientation group I only. The same algorithms may be applied to all other groups after rotating the pixel coordinates by $\pm 45°$ and $90°$ respectively.

3.1 Line Extraction

In the first step lines are extracted from the binary input image using the algorithm proposed by Kim (Kim et al., 2003). The algorithm outputs for each line orientation group $g \in [I, II, III, IV]$ a set of n_g lines $\mathbf{LS}_g = \{\underline{\mathbf{L}}_i, i = 1..n_g\}$ with $\underline{\mathbf{L}}_i = (x_{si}, y_{si}, x_{ei}, y_{ei}, x_{Mi}, y_{Mi}, \Theta_i)$ describing the start position (x_{si}, y_{si}), end position (x_{ei}, y_{ei}), midpoint (x_{Mi}, y_{Mi}), and slope Θ_i of each line. The last three elements are calculated by the following equations:

$$x_{Mi} = \frac{x_{si} + x_{ei}}{2} \quad , \quad y_{Mi} = \frac{y_{si} + y_{ei}}{2}$$

$$\Theta_i = \tan^{-1}\left(\frac{y_{si} - y_{ei}}{x_{ei} - x_{si}}\right)$$

3.2 Arc Extraction

The second processing stage combines lines to small arcs for each line set $\mathbf{LS}_g$. The algorithm selects a target line $\underline{\mathbf{L}}_i$ from $\mathbf{LS}_g$ and stores it in an empty arc line set $\mathbf{LA}$. Subsequently it searches for a candidate line $\underline{\mathbf{L}}_j$ within an adaptive triangular search window (Fig. 6a). With the predefined maximum distance D_{line} the window parameters are calculated by:

$$GAP_{x1} = \frac{x_{ei} - x_{si} + 1}{2} - 1$$
$$GAP_{x2} = D_{line}$$
$$GAP_y = D_{line} - 1$$

If a candidate line $\underline{\mathbf{L}}_j$ is found $\underline{\mathbf{L}}_i$ and $\underline{\mathbf{L}}_j$ will be considered parts of the same arc if they satisfy the following two conditions:

1. The intersection angle $\Theta_{ij} = |\Theta_i - \Theta_j|$ has to be in the range $0° \leq \Theta_{ij} \leq 45°$ (Fig. 6b).
2. The error of Θ_j compared to the estimated circle tangent Θ_{est} in the midpoint (x_{Mj}, y_{Mj}) of $\underline{\mathbf{L}}_j$ must not exceed a given angle tolerance $\Theta_{err,line}$ (Fig. 6c). By using all lines in $\mathbf{LA}$ and the candidate line $\underline{\mathbf{L}}_j$ the circle midpoint $(\tilde{x}_C, \tilde{y}_C)$ and its radius $\tilde{R}$

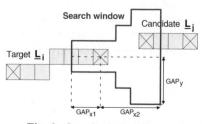

Fig. 6a. Search window for arcs

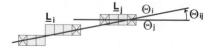

Fig. 6b. Intersection angle

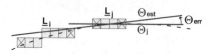

Fig. 6c. Tangent error

are estimated with the help of Thomas' algorithm (Thomas and Chan, 1989). Now, Θ_{est} can be calculated and the condition checked by:

$$\Theta_{est} = \tan^{-1}\left(\frac{x_{Mj}-\bar{x}_C}{\bar{y}_C-y_{Mj}}\right)$$

$$|\Theta_j - \Theta_{est}| \; < \; \Theta_{err,line}$$

If $\underline{\mathbf{L}}_j$ satisfies all conditions it is added to $\mathbf{LA}$ and a new iteration starts with $\underline{\mathbf{L}}_j$ as the new target. If $\underline{\mathbf{L}}_j$ is not found or fails either test and $\mathbf{LA}$ contains more than one element, a new arc is found. In this case the final circle parameters x_C, y_C and R are estimated from the lines contained in $\mathbf{LA}$ and stored in a vector $\underline{\mathbf{A}} = (\mathbf{LA}, x_C, y_C, R)$. Depending on the arc's position to the estimated circle midpoint, it is assigned to one of two possible arc groups (see Fig. 4). Afterwards the algorithm chooses a new target line from $\mathbf{LS}_g$ which is not already part of an arc and starts at the beginning. It terminates when all lines have been visited.

After application of this algorithm to all line sets the result is a set of n_g arcs $\mathbf{AS}_g = \{\underline{\mathbf{A}}_i, i = 1..n_g\}$ with $\underline{\mathbf{A}}_i = (\mathbf{LA}_i, x_{Ci}, y_{Ci}, R_i)$ for each group $g \in [1..8]$.

3.3 Extended Arc Extraction

In the third step arcs are combined to extended arcs. This is necessary because arcs are too small for an accurate ellipse estimation. For one extended arc three adjacent arcs $\underline{\mathbf{A}}_a$, $\underline{\mathbf{A}}_b$ and $\underline{\mathbf{A}}_c$ of consecutive arc groups have to be found. This can be achieved by selecting a target arc $\underline{\mathbf{A}}_b$ of the arc set $\mathbf{AS}_g$ and searching the sets $\mathbf{AS}_{g-1}$ and $\mathbf{AS}_{g+1}$ for the candidate arcs $\underline{\mathbf{A}}_a$ and $\underline{\mathbf{A}}_c$. To ensure that target and candidates describe the same ellipse, several conditions are checked. Conditions 1-3 apply to both arc pairs a/b and b/c, but are described for a/b only. Conditions 4-6 apply to all three arcs a/b/c. For arc pairs we define the gap vector $\overrightarrow{G}$ pointing from the endpoint of one arc to the start point of the other. We define $\angle(\underline{\mathbf{a}}, \underline{\mathbf{b}})$ to be the angle between the vectors $\underline{\mathbf{a}}$ and $\underline{\mathbf{b}}$.

1. The **absolute distance** of the arcs in horizontal and vertical direction given by $|G_x|$ and $|G_y|$ must not exceed the predefined maximum distance D_{arc}.

$$|G_x| \le D_{arc}$$
$$|G_y| \le D_{arc}$$

2. The **relative distance** d_{rel} of the arcs must be greater than the predefined minimum d_{min}. Vector $\overrightarrow{AB}$ connects the arc startpoints and $\overrightarrow{A}$, $\overrightarrow{B}$ are vectors pointing from start- to endpoint of each arc.

$$d_{rel} = \frac{|\overrightarrow{AB}|}{|\overrightarrow{A}|} > d_{min}$$

3. The **gap angles** of both arcs must be less than the predefined maximum $\Theta_{gap,max}$. With $\underline{\mathbf{L}}_a$ as last line of arc $\underline{\mathbf{A}}_a$ and $\underline{\mathbf{L}}_b$ as first line of $\underline{\mathbf{A}}_b$ the gap angles can be calculated as the angles between these lines and $\overrightarrow{G}$.

$$\Theta_{gap,a} = \angle(\underline{\mathbf{L}}_a, \overrightarrow{G})$$
$$\Theta_{gap,b} = \angle(\underline{\mathbf{L}}_b, \overrightarrow{G})$$

4. The **inner angles** of all arc line pairs must be less than $90°$. Let **LX** be the set of all lines of $\underline{\mathbf{A}}_a, \underline{\mathbf{A}}_b, \underline{\mathbf{A}}_c$ and $\underline{\mathbf{L}}_i, \underline{\mathbf{L}}_j$ be two lines of **LX**. The inner angles are the angles between their normal vectors $\vec{N_i}, \vec{N_j}$ and their startpoint connection $\vec{IJ}$ and $\vec{JI}$ respec-

tively.

$$\Theta_{in,i} = \angle(\vec{N_i}, \vec{IJ})$$
$$\Theta_{in,j} = \angle(\vec{N_j}, \vec{JI})$$

5. The **tangent error** of all arc lines compared to the estimated ellipse must be less than the predefined maximum $\Theta_{err,arc}$. Using $\underline{\mathbf{A}}_a, \underline{\mathbf{A}}_b, \underline{\mathbf{A}}_c$ the ellipse parameters $\tilde{x}_E, \tilde{y}_E, \tilde{a}, \tilde{b}, \tilde{\alpha}$ are estimated with the algorithm proposed in (Fitzgibbon and Fisher, 1999). For each arc line $\underline{\mathbf{L}}_i$ we compare the line tangent Θ_i and the ellipse tangent Θ_{est} in the midpoint

(x_{Mi}, y_{Mi}).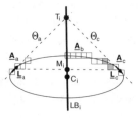

$$\Theta_{est} = \tan^{-1}\left(\frac{-\tilde{b}^2 \cdot x_{Mi}}{\tilde{a}^2 \cdot y_{Mi}}\right)$$
$$|\Theta_i - \Theta_{est}| < \Theta_{err,arc}$$

6. The **line beam** of the three extended arcs must run within the maximum distance D_{LB} from their estimated ellipse center point $C_i = (\tilde{x}_{Ei}, \tilde{y}_{Ei})$. With $\underline{\mathbf{L}}_a$ being the first line of $\underline{\mathbf{A}}_a$ and $\underline{\mathbf{L}}_c$ being the last line of $\underline{\mathbf{A}}_c$ the line beam LB_i can be calculated as the line passing through the points $\mathbf{T}_i$ and $\mathbf{M}_i$, whereas $\mathbf{T}_i$ is the intersection point of the line tangents Θ_a and Θ_c and $\mathbf{M}_i$ is the midpoint of the connection of the midpoints of $\underline{\mathbf{L}}_a$ and $\underline{\mathbf{L}}_c$.

If all three arcs satisfy all conditions, a new extended arc $\underline{\mathbf{X}}$ is created. After all arcs have been visited the result of this stage is a set of n extended arcs $\mathbf{XS} = \{\underline{\mathbf{X}}_i, i = 1..n\}$ with $\underline{\mathbf{X}}_i = (\underline{\mathbf{A}}_{ai}, \underline{\mathbf{A}}_{bi}, \underline{\mathbf{A}}_{ci}, \tilde{x}_{Ei}, \tilde{y}_{Ei}, \tilde{a}_i, \tilde{b}_i, \tilde{\alpha}_i, LB_i)$.

3.4   Ellipse Extraction

In the last step extended arcs are used to create ellipses. The algorithm merges extended arcs $\underline{\mathbf{X}}_i$ belonging to the same ellipse $\underline{\mathbf{E}}_j$ to a set $\mathbf{XE}_j = \{\underline{\mathbf{X}}_i, i = 1..n\}$ in three steps. Merged extended arcs $\underline{\mathbf{X}}_i$ are removed from the set $\mathbf{XS}$ because they can be part of one ellipse only.

Because each extended arc consists of three arcs, adjacent extended arcs can overlap in up to two arcs. In the first step, these overlapping arcs are identified by searching extended arcs composed of identical arcs. The identified objects are then checked by three conditions whether they describe the same ellipse:

1. The tangent error of all arc lines compared to the jointly estimated ellipse must be less than $\Theta_{err,arc}$. This is identical to condition 5 in section 3.3.
2. The line beams of all extended arcs have to intersect within the maximum distance D_{LB} from the ellipse center point.
3. The ellipse contour mismatch of the start- and endpoints (x_i, y_i) of all arc lines must not exceed the predefined maximum $\delta_{ell,max}$ and is checked by:

$$\left| \left(\frac{x_i}{\tilde{a}}\right)^2 + \left(\frac{y_i}{\tilde{b}}\right)^2 - 1 \right| \quad < \quad \delta_{ell,max}$$

In the second step non-overlapping extended arcs are taken from **XS** and it is tried to assign them to one of the merge sets $\mathbf{XE}_j$ created in the first step. An extended arc has to fulfill the same conditions 1-3 to become part of a set $\mathbf{XE}_j$.

The third step tries to merge the remaining extended arcs in **XS**. The algorithm compares the ellipse parameters of each extended arc and merges those that match with a predefined accuracy. The ellipse center must not differ more than D_{match} and the semi-axis have to match with a relative percentage r_{match}.

Finally the ellipse parameters x_{Ej}, y_{Ej}, a_j, b_j, and α_j are calculated for every merge set $\mathbf{XE}_j$. Subsequently, the ellipse circumference C_j is approximated by:

$$C_j \approx \pi \left(1.5 \left(a_j + b_j\right) - \sqrt{a_j b_j}\right)$$

If the set of all arc lines in $\mathbf{XE}_j$ covers C_j to a predefined percentage C_{min}, the ellipse is added to the final ellipse set $\mathbf{ES} = \{\underline{\mathbf{E}}_j, j = 1..n\}$ with $\underline{\mathbf{E}}_j = (\mathbf{XE}_j, x_{Ej}, y_{Ej}, a_j, b_j, \alpha_j)$.

4   Results

This section presents results which were obtained on a Pentium 4 system with 2.8 GHz. Fig. 7 visualizes all intermediate results during ellipse extraction on an outdoor real world image of size 800×600 pixels. Although there is lots of clutter in the binary edge image all relevant ellipses are found and no false positives are detected. However, false positives may be detected in case lines form a partial ellipse which actually do not belong to a real world ellipse as demonstrated in the top row of Fig. 8. This happens because lines and the derived structures are the only information used to search for ellipses. By incorporating more knowledge in the detection process, e.g. color or texture analysis within an ellipse candidate, false positives can be reduced. This is one task for future work.

Tab. 1 summarizes the amount of extracted objects in each filter stage, the memory consumption and processing time for the image in Fig.7. Each processing stage reduces the number of processed objects approximately by one order of magnitude, which means that the time consuming checks are only applied to very few objects. Memory is allocated only for the extracted objects. Of course memory consumption and processing time depend on the complexity of the original image. On an image of size 320×240 pixels the average processing time is 45 ms. However, with a more sophisticated preprocessing which narrows the search space, speed can be increased and

Fig. 7. Visualization of the different steps during ellipse detection in an outdoor real world image. *From top left to bottom right*: Input image, binary edge image, lines, arcs, extended arcs and ellipses. The extracted elements are superimposed on the input image (800 x 600 pixels).

Table 1. Memory consumption and processing time for image (800 x 600 pixels) in Fig. 7.

Object	Quantity	Memory usage	Time
Segments	89295	2092.9 KByte	62 ms
Lines	9094	931.8 KByte	172 ms
Arcs	540	63.7 KByte	47 ms
Ext. arcs	21	3.6 KByte	12 ms
Ellipses	5	0.3 KByte	3 ms
Total		3092.3 KByte	296 ms

memory consumption can be decreased even further. This optimization is the second task for future work.

The two bottom rows of Fig.8 show example images demonstrating the detection of overlapping and partially occluded ellipses. All ellipses are found in all images but their accuracy depends on the amount of their visible circumference. The more data is available for one ellipse the more precise are its estimated parameters.

Finally, the number of parameters introduced in section 3 has to be discussed. On the one hand many parameters allow to adapt the algorithm to nearly all situations but on the other hand it is sometimes hard to find the optimal configuration. For the latter case we ranked the parameters to identify the important ones. Tab. 2 shows which parameters should be changed first to adapt the algorithm in case it does not produce the desired results with its default settings. Parameters marked with "+" are most important for an adaption and have to be changed first. Parameters marked with "o" can be used for fine tuning the results and parameters marked with "-" do not influence the final results. They can be replaced by constant values in future versions of the algorithm. In this way

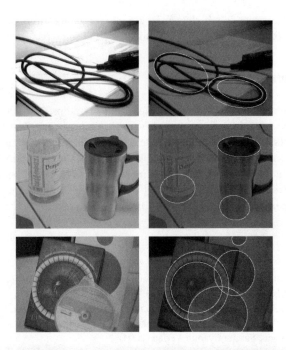

Fig. 8. Examples for the detection of false positives (top row) and overlapping and partially occluded (bottom rows) ellipses in real world images. All results were obtained with the same parameter settings (see Tab. 2).

Table 2. Importance of parameters. The 3rd column shows the values used to obtain the results in Fig. 8.

Symbol	Importance	Value	Ref.
D_{line}	-	3 pix.	3.2
$\Theta_{err,line}$	+	18.0°	3.2
D_{arc}	+	37 pix.	3.3
d_{min}	-	0.47	3.3
$\Theta_{gap,max}$	-	30.0°	3.3
$\Theta_{err,arc}$	+	14.0°	3.3, 3.4
D_{LB}	o	4 pix.	3.3, 3.4
$\delta_{ell,max}$	-	2.7	3.4
D_{match}	o	5.0	3.4
r_{match}	-	0.8	3.4
C_{min}	+	0.25	3.4

only four parameters remain which is a fair amount for an algorithm of this complexity. However, all ellipses in this paper were found using the same parameter settings.

5 Conclusion

This paper introduces a fast and robust algorithm for ellipse extraction from binary image data based on a four stage data driven filtering process. The obtained results support the conclusion that it is able to cope with partially occluded ellipses and noisy image data. It produces accurate results and keeps memory consumption to a minimum. Future work includes the incorporation of more knowledge, e.g. color information, to distinct between real ellipses and false positives and speed optimization. The algorithm is available as open source in the LTI-LIB project at http://ltilib.sourceforge.net.

References

Canny, J.: A computational approach to edge detection. IEEE Transactions on Pattern Analysis and Machine Intelligence 8(6), 679–698 (1986)

Canzler, U., Kraiss, K.-F: Person-adaptive facial feature analysis for an advanced wheelchair user-interface. In: Drews, P. (ed.) Conference on Mechatronics & Robotics, vol. Part III, pp. 871–876. Aachen, Sascha Eysoldt Verlag (2004)

d'Orazio, T., Guaragnella, C., Leo, M., Distante, A.: A new algorithm for ball recognition using circle hough transform and neural classifier. Pattern Recognition 37(3), 393–408 (2004)

Duda, R., Hart, P.: Use of the hough transformation to detect lines and curves in pictures. Communications of the ACM 15(1), 11–15 (1972)

Fitzgibbon, A.W., Pilu, M., Fisher, R.B.: Direct least-squares fitting of ellipses. IEEE Transactions on Pattern Analysis and Machine Intelligence 21(5), 476–480 (1999)

Guil, N., Zapata, E.: Lower order circle and ellipse hough transform. Pattern Recognition 30(10), 1729–1744 (1997)

Ho, C., Chen, L.: A high-speed algorithm for elliptical object detection. IEEE Transactions on Image Processing 5(3), 547–550 (1996)

Kim, E., Haseyama, M., Kitajima, H.: Fast and robust ellipse extraction from complicated images. In: Proceedings of the first International Conference on Information Technology & Applications, Bathurst, Australia (2002)

Kim, E., Haseyama, M., Kitajima, H.: Fast line extraction from digital images using line segments. Systems and Computers in Japan 34(10), 76–89 (2003)

Mclaughlin, R.: Randomized hough transform: Improved ellipse detection with comparison. Pattern Recognition Letters 19(3-4), 299–305 (1998)

McLaughlin, R., Alder, M.: The Hough transform versus the UpWrite. IEEE Transactions on Pattern Analysis and Machine Intelligence 20(4), 396–400 (1998)

Piccioli, G., Michelli, E., Parodi, P., Campani, M.: Robust road sign detection and recognition from image sequences. In: Proceedings of the IEEE Symposium on Intelligent Vehicles, Paris, FR, pp. 278–283. IEEE Computer Society Press, Los Alamitos (1994)

Radford, C., Houghton, D.: Vehicle detection in open-world scenes using a hough transform technique. In: Third International Conference on Image Processing and its Applications, Warwick, UK, pp. 78–82 (1989)

Sanz, J., Hinkle, E., Jain, A.: Radon and Projection Transform-Based Computer Vision. Springer, Heidelberg (1988)

Thomas, S., Chan, Y.: A simple approach for the estimation of circular arc center and its radius. Computer Vision, Graphics, and Image Processing 45(3), 362–370 (1989)

Xu, L., Oja, E., Kultanen, P.: A new curve detection method: Randomized hough transform (rht). Pattern Recognition Letters 11(5), 331–338 (1990)

A Comparison of Wavelet-Based and Ridgelet-Based Texture Classification of Tissues in Computed Tomography

Lindsay Semler and Lucia Dettori

Intelligent Multimedia Processing Laboratory
School of Computer Scienve, Telecommunications and Information Systems
DePaul University, Chicago IL, 60604, USA
lsemler@cs.depaul.edu, ldettori@cs.depaul.edu

Abstract. The research presented in this article is aimed at developing an automated imaging system for classification of tissues in medical images obtained from Computed Tomography (CT) scans. The article focuses on using multi-resolution texture analysis, specifically: the Haar wavelet, Daubechies wavelet, Coiflet wavelet, and the ridgelet. The algorithm consists of two steps: automatic extraction of the most discriminative texture features of regions of interest and creation of a classifier that automatically identifies the various tissues. The classification step is implemented using a cross-validation Classification and Regression Tree approach. A comparison of wavelet-based and ridgelet-based algorithms is presented. Tests on a large set of chest and abdomen CT images indicate that, among the three wavelet-based algorithms, the one using texture features derived from the Haar wavelet transform clearly outperforms the one based on Daubechies and Coiflet transform. The tests also show that the ridgelet-based algorithm is significantly more effective and that texture features based on the ridgelet transform are better suited for texture classification in CT medical images.

Keywords: Multi-Resolution Analysis, Texture Classification, Wavelet, Ridgelet, Computed Tomography.

1 Introduction

Over the past several years, 3D imaging equipment has been used on a more frequent basis, particularly in the medical field. On a daily basis, hospitals are witnessing a large inflow of digital medical images and related clinical data. This increase in workload has rapidly outpaced the increase in number of qualified radiologists to navigate, view, and interpret this data. Human analysis and visualization of 3D data received from such machines are often difficult to analyze due to the quantity of clinical data. Computerized analysis and automated information systems can offer help with dealing with the large amounts of data.

The research presented in this article is part of an ongoing project (Xu et al. 2005), (Channin et al. 2004), and (Semler, Dettori, & Furst 2005) aimed at developing an automated imaging system for classification of tissues in medical images obtained by

J. Braz et al. (Eds.): VISAPP and GRAPP 2006, CCIS 4, pp. 240–250, 2007.

Computed Tomography (CT) scans. Classification of human organs in CT scans using shape or grey level information is particularly challenging due to the changing shape of organs in a stack of slices in 3D medical images and the grey level intensity overlap in soft tissues. However, healthy organs are expected to have a consistent texture within tissues across multiple slices. This research focuses on using multi-resolution texture analysis for the classification of tissues from normal chest and abdomen CT scans. The approach consists of two steps: extraction of the most discriminative texture features of regions of interest and creation of a classifier that automatically identifies the various tissues. Four forms of multi-resolution analysis were carried on and texture features vectors were created from image transformations based on: the Haar wavelet, the Daubechies wavelet, the Coiflet wavelet, and the ridgelet. The classification step is implemented through a decision tree classifier based on the cross-validation Classification and Regression Tree (C&RT) approach. Multi-resolution analysis has been successfully used in image processing, and a number of applications to texture classification have been proposed over the past few years. Several studies have investigated the discriminating power of wavelet-based features applied to various domains, examples can be found in (Dara & Watsuji 2003) and (Mulcahy 1997). Recently, the finite ridgelet transform has emerged as a new multi-resolution analysis tool. Applications of ridgelet transforms to image contrast enhancement and image denoising have been developed in recent years as in (Do, & Vetterli 2003), however, to the authors' knowledge, applications to texture classification have only been investigated in the context of natural images (LeBorgne & O'Connor 2005).

Texture is a commonly used feature in the analysis and interpretation of images. It can be characterized by a set of local statistical properties of the pixel grey level intensity. Statistical, structural, or spectral techniques commonly used are: wavelets, run-length statistics, spectral measures, fractal dimensions, statistical moments, and co-occurrence matrices.

Multi-resolution analysis allows for the preservation of an image according to certain levels of resolution or blurring. Broadly speaking, multi-resolution analysis allows for the zooming in and out of the underlying texture structure. Therefore, the texture extraction is not effected by the size of the pixel neighborhood. This multi-resolution quality is one of the reasons why the wavelet transform have been useful in image compression, image de-noising, and image classification.

The discrete wavelet transform decomposes the image into several directional details obtaining low-pass bands that capture horizontal, vertical and diagonal activity. First and second order statistics of the wavelet detail coefficients provide texture descriptors that can discriminate contrasting intensity properties spatially distributed throughout the image, according to various levels of resolution. Wavelets have been an area of research in many texture classification applications and have been useful in capturing texture information and edge detection in natural images (Li, Jun 2003), such as detecting the vertical outline of a skyscraper. However, they are not able to capture enough directional information in noisy images, such as medical CT scans.

A better approach to texture classification for this type of image is to apply a ridgelet transform instead of a Wavelet transform. Ridgelets, like wavelets, capture directional information of an image, however, they are not limited to vertical, horizontal, and diagonal directions. Structural information derived from the ridgelet transform of an image is based on multiple radial directions in the frequency domain. For ridgelets, first order statistics can be calculated on the directional detail coefficients, providing texture descriptors that can be used in the classification of texture. Our tests confirm that the multi-directional capabilities of the ridgelet transform provide better texture information and prove to be more effective in the texture classification in medical images.

The article is organized as follows. Section 2 presents the continuous wavelet and ridgelet transforms. Section 3 describes the data set, the discrete wavelet and ridgelet transforms and the texture feature extraction process. The classification algorithm is detailed in Section 4. Tests and a comparison of wavelet-based and ridgelet-based features are presented in Section 5.

2 Texture Features

Three families of wavelets were investigated: Haar (H), Daubechies 4 (D4), and Coiflet (C6). The Haar wavelet was chosen since it is the oldest and simplest wavelet transform. Daubechies (D4) and Coiflet (C6) were chosen for their increasingly larger filters and smoother windows. It is interesting to note that, a posteriori, the simple Haar wavelet outperforms the other more complex wavelets. A wavelet can decompose a signal or an image with a series of averaging and differencing calculations. Wavelets compute average intensity properties as well as several detailed contrast levels distributed throughout the image. Wavelets can be calculated according to various levels of resolution (or blurring) depending on how many levels of averages are calculated. The general mother wavelet can be constructed from the following scaling $\phi(x)$ and wavelet functions $\psi(x)$:

$$\text{Equation 1: } \phi(x) = \sqrt{2}\sum h(k)\phi(2x - k),$$

$$\text{Equation 2: } \psi(x) = \sqrt{2}\sum g(k)\phi(2x - k)$$

where, $g(k) = -1^k h(N -1-k)$. Where N is the number of scaling and wavelet coefficients. The sets of scaling ($h(k)$) and wavelet ($g(k)$) function coefficients vary depending on their corresponding wavelet bases.

In the year 1998, Donoho introduced the ridgelet transform (Do & Vetterli 2003). The continous ridgelet transform can be defined from a 1-D wavelet function oriented at constant lines and radial directions. The continuous ridgelet transform (*CRT*) in R^2 is defined by:

$$\text{Equation 3: } CRT_f(a,b,\theta) = \int_{R^2} \psi_{a,b,\theta}(x)f(x)dx$$

where the ridgelets $\Psi_{a,b,\theta}(x)$ in 2-D are defined using a wavelet function:

$$\text{Equation 4: } \psi_{a,b,\theta}(x) = a^{-\frac{1}{2}}\psi((x_1\cos\theta + x_2\sin\theta - b)/a)$$

This is oriented at angles θ, and constant along the lines $x_1 \cos\theta + x_2 \sin\theta = const$. For details see, (Do & Vetterli 2003). Essentially, the ridgelet radial lines are defined by a slope θ, and an intercept b. The continuous ridgelet transform is similar to the continuous wavelet transform except that point parameters (x,y) are now replaced by line parameters (b, θ). Figure 1 illustrates the radial grid.

Generally speaking, wavelets represent objects with point singularities, while ridgelets are able to represent objects with line singularities.

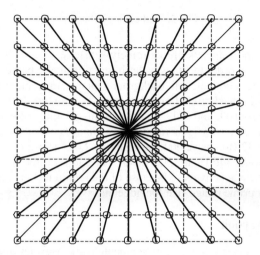

Fig. 1. Illustration of the radial grid of the ridgelet transform

3   Texture Features

The texture classification algorithm proposed in this article consists of four main steps: segmentation of regions of interest (organs), application of the discrete wavelet or ridgelet transform, extraction of texture features, and creation of a classifier. In this article, we analyze and compare texture classification techniques based on four different multi-resolution approaches: Haar (H) wavelet, Daubechies 4 (D4) wavelet, Coiflet (C6) wavelet, and the ridgelet. The general algorithm is summarized in the methodology diagram in Figure 2

3.1   The Data Set

The texture classification algorithms were tested on 3D data extracted from two normal chest and abdomen CT studies from Northwestern Memorial Hospital. The data consisted of 340 2D DICOM consecutives slices, each slice being 512 x 512 and having 12-bit grey level resolution. Using an Active Contour Models ("Snake") algorithm, five organs were segmented from the initial data: heart, liver, spleen, kidney, and backbone (Xu et al. 2005). The segmentation process generated 140 Backbone slices, 52 Heart, 58 Liver, 54 Kidney, and 40 Spleen.

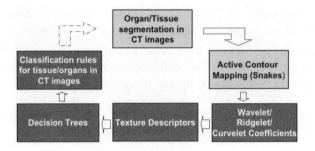

Fig. 2. Methodology Diagram

Both wavelets and ridgelets are extremely sensitive to contrast in the grey level intensity, therefore, in order to use wavelet-based or ridgelet-based texture description it was necessary to eliminate all background pixels to avoid mistaking the edge between the artificial background and the organ as a texture feature. Each slice was therefore further cropped, and only square sub-images fully contained in the interior of the segmented area were generated. These images were of sizes 31 x 31 (for ridgelets) or 32 x 32 (for wavelets), resulting in 2,091 slices of "pure" single-organ tissue (363 Backbone, 446 Heart, 506 Liver, 411 Kidney, 364 Spleen). These images were cropped to the respective size because of the requirements of an image of size 2^n for wavelets and a prime image size for ridgelets.

3.2 Feature Extraction

Once the medical images have been segmented, the wavelet and ridgelet discrete transforms are applied. Several texture features are then extracted from the wavelet and ridgelet coefficients generated by these transforms. First, the three different families of wavelets were investigated to determine which would yield a higher discriminating power.

3.2.1 Discrete Wavelet Transform
There are several ways of generating a 2D wavelet transform, this approach uses a filter structure for the Haar, Daubechies and Coiflet wavelets, each containing different scaling and wavelet function coefficients characteristic of their particular families. The constructions of these filters differ only in number of scaling and wavelet coefficients.

The Haar wavelet uses only two scaling and wavelet function coefficients, thus calculates pair wise averages and differences. The Haar transform uses non-overlapping windows, and reflects changes between adjacent pixel pairs. The Daubechies (D4) transform has four wavelet and scaling coefficients. A weighted averaging is computed over four pixels, thus resulting in a smoother transform. With the increase in wavelet and scaling coefficients, the filter constructions allows for overlapping windows, reflecting all changes between pixel intensities and resulting in over-complete information. The Coiflet wavelet uses six scaling and wavelet function coefficients.

For each of the wavelets, two levels of resolution were extracted. Three levels of resolution were originally tested, however in general two levels of resolution was found to be ideal. At each resolution level, the wavelet has three detail coefficient matrices representing the vertical, horizontal and diagonal structures of the image.

From each of the detail coefficient matrices, several first order and second order statistics were calculated: mean, standard deviation, energy, entropy, contrast, homogeneity, sum-mean, variance, maximum probability, inverse difference moment, and cluster tendency.

On average, using only two levels of resolution performed better than using all three resolution levels. Thus, a feature vector of: mean, standard deviation, energy, entropy, contrast, homogeneity, sum-mean, variance, cluster tendency, inverse difference moment, and maximum probability, calculated from wavelet details were used for two levels of resolution resulting in 22 descriptors.

3.2.2 Ridgelets

The Finite Ridgelet Transform as presented in (Do & Vetterli 2003), was also applied to each of the images. The Ridgelet Transform can be computed as illustrated in the flow chart, Figure 3.

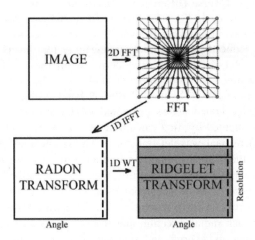

Fig. 3. Ridgelet transform flow graph

The ridgelet transform was computed by: first calculating a discrete radon transform, and then applying a one-dimensional wavelet transform. The radon transform was computed by: first calculating the 2-dimensional fast Fourier transform of the image, and then applying a 1-dimensional inverse Fourier transform on each of the 32 radial directions of the radon projection.

A one-dimensional Haar wavelet was applied to each of the radial directions, for three levels of resolution. The following texture descriptors were then calculated for each radial direction and resolution level of the wavelet details: mean, standard deviation, energy and entropy. For each level of resolution and each radial direction Energy, Entropy, Mean, and Standard Deviation were calculated. The discriminating power of the following four feature vectors were investigated: Energy and Entropy signatures averaged over radial directions (EE), Energy, Entropy, Mean, and Standard Deviation signatures averaged over radial directions (EEMS), Energy signatures (Eng), and Entropy signatures (Ent), neither averaged over radial directions. Each of these feature vectors was computed for three levels of resolution yielding: 6 descriptors, 12 descriptors, and 96 descriptors respectively.

Entropy texture descriptors were determined to yield the highest discriminating power; see Table 3 for more information. Several different combinations of resolution levels were also investigated, and two levels of resolution were determined to be best. Thus, the optimal ridgelet descriptor set yielded 64 descriptors, using two levels of resolution and entropy features from each radial direction.

Haar, Daubechies and Coiflet wavelet filters were applied to each of the images, using two levels of resolution. At each resolution level, three detail coefficient matrices were calculated capturing the vertical, horizontal and diagonal structures of the image.

The following first order statistics were calculated on each of the directional matrices: Mean and Standard Deviation. Also calculated from these matrices were 4-directional co-occurrence matrices on which the following second order statistics were calculated: Energy, Entropy, Contrast, Homogeneity Sum-mean, Variance, Maximum Probability, Inverse Difference Moment, and Cluster Tendency (Haralick, Shanmugame, & Dinstein 1973). This generated a 264-element texture descriptor vector per image. To avoid problems of overfitting for the decision trees the resulting feature vector was reduced to 22 features (using only two levels of resolution and averaging over wavelet details and co-occurrence directions). Further details on feature vector reduction and more in-depth analysis of the various wavelet-based texture features are provided in (Semler, Dettori, & Furst 2005).

The Finite Ridgelet Transform as presented in (Do & Vetterli 2003), was also applied. This was computed by: first calculating a discrete radon transform, and then applying a one-dimensional wavelet transform. The radon transform was computed by: first calculating the 2-dimensional fast Fourier transform of the image, and then applying a 1-dimensional inverse Fourier transform on each of the 32 radial directions of the radon projection. A one-dimensional Haar wavelet was applied to each of the radial directions, for two levels of resolution. The following texture descriptors were then calculated for each radial direction and resolution level of the wavelet details: mean, standard deviation, energy and entropy. Entropy texture descriptors were determined to yield the highest discriminating power; further details are presented in (Semler, Dettori & Kerr 2006). Several different combinations of resolution levels were also investigated, and two levels of resolution were determined best for both ridgelets and wavelets. The numbers of features extracted were limited since each descriptor is calculated over two resolution levels and for 32 directions, yielding 64 descriptors.

Although the ridgelet-based features contain more descriptors, it should not be assumed they would perform better than the wavelet-based features because of the increase in number of descriptors. In (Semler, Dettori, & Furst 2005), it was found that a wavelet-based feature vector of 33 descriptors outperformed another same-family wavelet-based feature vector of 99 descriptors.

4   Texture Classification

The classification step was carried out using a decision tree classifier based on the Classification and Regression Tree (C&RT) approach (Channin et al. 2004). A decision tree predicts the class of an object (organ) from values of predictor variables (texture descriptors). The most relevant texture descriptors are found for each specific organ, and based on those selected descriptors, a set of decision rules are generated. These set of rules are then used for the classification of the each region. Using the C&RT cross-validation approach, each tree's parameter was optimized, including depth of tree, number of parent nodes, and number of child nodes.

To evaluate the performance of each classifier, specificity, sensitivity, precision, and accuracy rates were calculated from each of the misclassification matrices.

A misclassification matrix is a table that lists each organ and its true positives, true negatives, false positives and false negatives. The number of true positives is the number of organs that are correctly classified as that organ. The number of true negatives is the number of other organs that are correctly classified as other organs. The number of false positives is the number of organs that are incorrectly classified as that organ. The number of false negatives is the number of organs that are incorrectly classified as other organ. From the misclassification matrix specificity, sensitivity, precision, and accuracy statistics were computed.

Table 1. Measures of classification performance

Measure	Definition
Sensitivity	True Positive / Total Positive
Specificity	True Negative / Total Negatives
Precision	True Positive / (True Positive + False Positives)
Accuracy	(True Positives + True Negatives) / Total Sample

Specificity measures the accuracy among positive instances, and is calculated by dividing the true negatives by the number of all other organ slices. Sensitivity measures the accuracy among negative instances, and is calculated by dividing the number of true positives by the total number of that specific organ slices. Precision measures show how consistent the results can be reproduced. Accuracy reflects the overall correctness of the classifier, and is calculated by adding the true positives and negatives together and dividing by the entire number of organ slices.

5   Wavelet - Ridgelet Comparison

Tables 2-5 in the Appendix show a comparison of accuracy, precision, specificity, and sensitivity results, for each tissue of interest for the three wavelet-based texture features and the ridgelet-based texture features respectively. Within all the wavelets, the Haar wavelet outperformed all others for most organs and performance measures. The only exception is the backbone, for which the Daubechies and Coiflet wavelets produce slightly better results. The performance for the Haar-based descriptors in all other organs was significantly higher, thus indicating that these descriptors yield the highest discriminating power among the wavelet-based features.

The results also show that the ridgelet-based texture features outperform all wavelet-based descriptors. Accuracy rates for Wavelet-based texture descriptors range between 85 - 93%, while ridgelet-based accuracy rates are in the 91 - 97% range. Precision rates for the wavelets are between 55 - 91%, compared to 73 - 93% for ridgelets. Specificity rates for the wavelets are in the 82-97% range, while specificity for the ridgelet descriptors is in the 92-98% range. Furthermore, sensitivity rates for the wavelets are in the 35-87% range, whereas ridgelets are between 72-94%. The lower bound of the sensitivity range for wavelets is due to the poor performance of those descriptors (especially Coiflets and Daubechies) for Heart and Spleen. The texture of the images for these two organs is quite similar and the classifier often mistakes the two organs for one another. Further investigation is needed to determine the underlying cause for the poor performance of the Heart and Spleen.

Overall, the ridgelet-based descriptors have significantly higher performance measures, with accuracy rates approximately four percent higher than any other feature set for all individual organs. This was expected due to the fact that the ridgelet transform is able to capture multi-directional features, as opposed to the wavelet transform which focuses mainly on horizontal, vertical, and diagonal features, which are not dominant in medical CT scan images. One of the limitations of using ridgelet-based descriptors is the fact that ridgelets are most effective in detecting linear radial structures, which are not the main component of medical images. A recent extension of ridgelets is the curvelet transform. Curvelets have been proven to be particularly effective at detecting image activity along curves instead of radial directions (Starck Donoho & Candes 1999). We are currently investigating the use of curvelet-based texture descriptors and we expect this to further improve the ability of our classifier to successfully classify each tissue sample.

References

Xu, D., Lee, J., Raicu, D.S., Furst, J.D., Channin, D.: Texture Classification of Normal Tissues in Computed Tomography. In: The 2005 Annual Meeting of the Society for Computer Applications in Radiology (2005)

Channin, D., Raicu, D.S., Furst, J.D., Xu, D.H., Lilly, L., Limpsangsri, C.: Classification of Tissues in Computed Tomography using Decision Trees. Poster and Demo. In: The 90th Scientific Assembly and Annual Meeting of Radiology Society of North America (2004)

Semler, L., Dettori, L., Furst, J.: Wavelet-Based Texture Classification of Tissues in Computed Tomography. In: Proceedings of the 18th IEEE International Symposium on Computer-Based Medical Systems, pp. 265–270. IEEE Computer Society Press, Los Alamitos (2005)

Do, M.N., Vetterli, M.: The Finite Ridgelet Transform for Image Representation. IEEE Transactions on Image Processing 12, 16–28 (2003)

LeBorgne, H.L., O'Connor, N, Natural Scene Classification and Retrieval Using Ridgelet-based Image Signatures. Advanced Concepts for Intelligent Vision Systems, pp. 20–23 (2005)

Starck, J.L., Donoho, D.L., Candes, E.J.: Astronomical Image Representation by the Curvelet Transform. Astronomy &Astrophysics 398, 785–800 (1999)

Semler, L., Dettori, L., Kerr, B.: Ridgelet-Based Texture Classification in Computed Tomography. In: IEEE Computer Society Conference on Computer Vision and Pattern Recognition (submitted 2006)

Dara, B., Watsuji, N.: Using Wavelets for Texture Classification. In: IJCI Proceedings of International Conference on Signal Processing, ISN 1304-2386 (2003)

Mulcahy, C.: Image Compression Using the Haar Wavelet Transform. Spelman Science & Math Journal 1, 22–31 (1997)

Li, J.: A Wavelet Approach to Edge Detection, Master of Science thesis, Sam Houston State University. Huntsville, Texas (2003)

Do, M., Vetterli, M.: Image Denoising Using Orthonormal Finite Ridgelet Transform. Proceedings of SPIE: Wavelet Applications in Signal and Image Processing 4119, 831–842 (2003)

Haralick, R.M., Shanmugam, D., Dinstein, I.: Texture Features for Image Classification. IEEE Transactions on Systems, Man, and Cybernetics 3(6), 610–621 (1973)

Appendix

Table 2. Wavelet-Ridgelet accuracy rates comparison

Accuracy						
Feature Set	Backbone	Heart	Liver	Kidney	Spleen	Average
Haar	93.7	85.0	88.6	92.8	89.5	89.9
Daubechies	93.6	84.0	88.0	83.6	88.2	87.5
Coiflets	93.1	85.3	88.3	85.8	88.6	88.2
Ridgelet	97.3	93.6	92.7	92.7	91.7	93.6

Table 3. Wavelet-Ridgelet precision rates comparison

Precision						
Feature Set	Backbone	Heart	Liver	Kidney	Spleen	Average
Haar	82.6	67.0	69.9	82.6	69.7	74.4
Daubechies	91.6	57.4	55.7	64.9	64.3	66.8
Coiflets	90.7	58.9	56.7	70.6	70.8	69.5
Ridgelet	93.5	90.8	79.4	88.5	72.9	85.0

Table 4. Wavelet-Ridgelet specificity rates comparison

Specificity						
Feature Set	Backbone	Heart	Liver	Kidney	Spleen	Average
Haar	96.1	92.1	91.4	94.4	94.3	93.7
Daubechies	97.3	91.8	92.0	82.9	96.2	92.0
Coiflets	96.8	89.4	92.2	87.4	97.6	92.7
Ridgelet	98.7	97.9	92.3	97.67	93.4	96.0

Table 5. Wavelet-Ridgelet sensitivity rates comparison

Sensitivity						
Feature Set	Backbone	Heart	Liver	Kidney	Spleen	Average
Haar	82.6	59.0	77.7	87.3	65.5	74.4
Daubechies	83.5	49.1	63.2	85.4	40.2	64.2
Coiflets	85.9	67.1	64.3	81.6	35.2	66.8
Ridgelet	90.9	77.8	94.2	72.5	83.8	83.8

Color Segmentation of Complex Document Images*

N. Nikolaou and N. Papamarkos

Image Processing and Multimedia Laboratory
Department of Electrical & Computer Engineering
Democritus University of Thrace
67100 Xanthi, Greece
papamark@ee.duth.gr

Abstract. In this paper we present a new method for color segmentation of complex document images which can be used as a preprocessing step of a text information extraction application. From the edge map of an image, we choose a representative set of samples of the input color image and built the 3D histogram of the RGB color space. These samples are used to locate a relatively large number of proper points in the 3D color space and use them in order to initially reduce the colors. From this step an oversegmented image is produced which usually has no more than 100 colors. To extract the final result, a mean shift procedure starts from the calculated points and locates the final color clusters of the RGB color distribution. Also, to overcome noise problems, a proposed edge preserving smoothing filter is used to enhance the quality of the image. Experimental results showed the method's capability of producing correctly segmented complex color documents while removing background noise or low contrast objects which is very desirable in text information extraction applications. Additionally, our method has the ability to cluster randomly shaped distributions.

Keywords: Color document segmentation, RGB color space, Mean shift, Edge preserving smoothing.

1 Introduction

Printed documents in color are very common nowadays. To be able to exploit their textual content, the identification of text regions is substantial. This can lead to built systems capable to index, classify and retrieve them automatically. The transformation of the text into its electronic form via OCR is also a very useful operation.

Objects on printed documents that appear uniform for human perception, become noisy with unwanted variations through the digitization process. So, digitized documents contain thousands of colors and a color reduction preprocessing step is necessary. The purpose is to create a simplified version of the initial image where

---

* This paper was partially supported by the project Archimedes 04-3-001/4 and Pythagoras 1249-6.

J. Braz et al. (Eds.): VISAPP and GRAPP 2006, CCIS 4, pp. 251–263, 2007.
© Springer-Verlag Berlin Heidelberg 2007

characters can be extracted as solid items, by utilizing a connected component analysis and labeling procedure.

Various types of methods for color reduction in text information applications have been proposed in the literature. Zhong (1995) used the smoothed RGB color histogram to detect local maxima and segment the color image. Chen's (1998) work is based on the YIQ color model and the resulted images contain 42 or less colors. Sobottka (2000) approaches the color segmentation of color documents with a graph-theoretical clustering technique. First the 3D histogram of the RGB color space is built and a pointer to its larger neighbor cell is stored. Chains of cells pointing to the same local maximum are identified and the color clusters are formed. Hase (2001) algorithm is based on the uniform color space CIE L*a*b*. Initially, the method partitions the three axes so that the color space is formed into many cubes. Those with frequency lower than 1/1000 or not larger than their neighbors are rejected. Remaining cubes define the representative colors and through a Voronoi tessellation procedure the final color centers are adopted. Strouthopoulos (2002) approach is based on an adaptive color reduction (ACR) method which first obtains the optimal numbers of colors and then segments the image. This is achieved by a self-organized feature map (SOFM) neural network. Wang (2005) uses the same approach as Sobottka (2000). Also, a similar work with the application of this paper (Hase, 2003) is presented from the viewpoint of the influence of resolution to color document analysis.

Dealing with complex color documents such as cover books or journal covers raises some challenging difficulties. Text is overlaid on images or graphics and often it is impossible to spatially define the background.

Generally, a color segmentation algorithm for text information extraction applications must be able to perform its task without oversegmenting characters and still preventing fusion with the background. Additionally, it is desirable to merge low contrast objects with their background and create large compact areas. This will result to a small number of connected components, so the outcome of a text information extraction algorithm will be extensively improved.

2   Description of the Method

In this paper, we propose an approach which efficiently approximates the RGB color distribution of the image by taking advantage an important property of the edge map. Specifically, we sub sample the image by selecting only those pixels which are local minima in the 8-neighborhood on the edge image. This ensures that the samples are taken from inner points of the objects so fuzzy areas are avoided. Also, all objects will be represented in the obtained sample set. The benefits of this approach are analyzed in section 4.1.

These samples are used in the next step to initially reduce the colors of the input image with a relatively large number of colors, usually no more than 100 (section 4.2). The extracted image at this stage is oversegmented.

The resulted color centers are then used by a mean shift operation (Fukunaga, 1975), (Cheng, 1995), (Comaniciu, 2002) to locate the final points of the RGB color space, on which the algorithm will be based to extract the final result (sections 4.3, 4.4).

In order to deal with noisy cases and to improve the performance of the system, a proposed edge preserving smoothing filter is used (section 3) as a preprocessing step.

The overall process consists of the following stages.

1. Edge preserving smoothing.
2. Color edge detection.
3. RGB color space approximation (Sub sampling).
4. Initial color reduction.
5. Mean shift
6. Finalization of the color reduction process.

The method is implemented in a visual environment and the computer system used for all tests is a PENTIUM 4 PC with 2.4GHz CPU speed and 512MB RAM.

In section 5 of this paper, experimental results are depicted where the efficiency of the method is demonstrated. Computation time is also mentioned.

3 Edge Preserving Smoothing

A common technique for removing noise from images is blurring them by replacing the center pixel of a window with the weighted average of the pixels in the window (Mean, Gaussian filters). Through this process valuable information is lost and the details of object boundaries are deformed. A solution to this problem is to use an anisotropic diffusion process (Perona, 1990). In this paper we present a filter which performs as well as anisotropic diffusion but requires less computation time.

First we calculate the Manhattan color distances d_i between the center pixel a_c and the pixels a_i in a 3x3 window. Values are normalized in [0,1]

$$d_i = \left| R_{a_c} - R_{a_i} \right| + \left| G_{a_c} - G_{a_i} \right| + \left| B_{a_c} - B_{a_i} \right| \tag{1}$$

To compute the coefficients for the convolution mask of the filter the following equation is used.

$$c_i = (1 - d_i)^p \tag{2}$$

In words, c_i receives larger values for smaller values of d_i. This concludes to the following convolution mask

$$\frac{1}{\sum\limits_{i=1}^{8} c_i} \begin{bmatrix} c_1 & c_2 & c_3 \\ c_4 & 0 & c_5 \\ c_6 & c_7 & c_8 \end{bmatrix} \tag{3}$$

Factor p in equation (2) scales exponentially the color differences. Thus it controls the amount of blurring performed on the image. As it gets larger, coefficients with small color distance from the center pixel increase their relative value difference

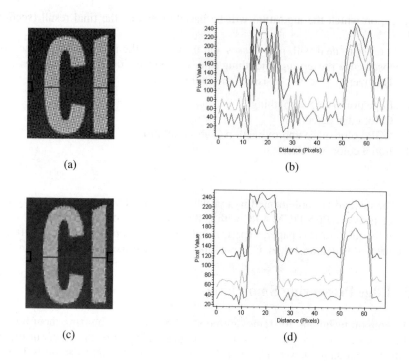

(a)

(b)

(c)

(d)

Fig. 1. The effect of the edge preserving smoothing filter on a color document. (a) Original noisy color document, (b) RGB pixel profile of line y=44 on the original document. (c)- (d) Filtered document ($p = 10$) and the pixel profile of the same line.

from coefficients with large color distance, so the blurring effect decreases. A fixed value 10 is used for all of our experiments since this resulted in very good performance.

The center pixel of the convolution mask is set to 0 in order to remove impulsive noise.

Figure 1 shows the effect of the filter on a color document. As it can be seen, noise is reduced without affecting edge points. The main benefit from this result is the extensive reduction of misclassifications on the segmented image.

4   Color Segmentation

4.1   Sub Sampling

In this section we propose a new technique for sub sampling a color image. The resulted set of samples will be used in the following steps of the algorithm in order to perform the task of color reduction.

With the use of the well known Sobel operator, we calculate the edge strength for each one of the three color channels.

(a) 87361 colors

(b) 602640 pixels (1620x372)

(c) 15959 colors

(d) 81123 pixel samples (13% sampling rate)

Fig. 2. (a) Original color document, (b) RGB color distribution of (a), (c) local minima pixels (d) RGB color distribution of local minima pixels

$$I G^r(x, y) \models \sqrt{(G^r_{row}(x, y))^2 + (G^r_{col}(x, y))^2} \tag{4}$$

$$I G^g(x, y) \models \sqrt{(G^g_{row}(x, y))^2 + (G^g_{col}(x, y))^2} \tag{5}$$

$$|G^b(x,y)| = \sqrt{(G^b_{row}(x,y))^2 + (G^b_{col}(x,y))^2} \tag{6}$$

where $|G^r(x,y)|$, $|G^g(x,y)|$, $|G^b(x,y)|$ the edge values for red, green and blue channel, respectively. To obtain the final edge value, we choose

$$G(x,y) = \max\left\{|G^r(x,y)|, |G^g(x,y)|, |G^b(x,y)|\right\} \tag{7}$$

The maximum value guarantees that edges will be detected even if variation occurs in only one of the three color channels. From the transformed image $G(x,y)$ the sample set is formed with those pixels (x_i, y_i) which satisfy the following criterion

$$G(x_i + n, y_i + m) \geq G(x_i, y_i)$$
$$where \ \ n = [-1,1], m = [-1,1] \tag{8}$$

These points will be referred as local minima. It is important to note that the watershed transformation algorithm (Roerdink, 2000) uses this methodology to initiate the segmentation process.

The resulted set of pixels has some interesting characteristics.

− Edge points are not represented in this set so fuzzy areas are avoided.
− Spatially, the samples are always inside the objects of the image.
− Every object's color is represented in the sample set.

As a conclusion, we can assume that every member of the local minima based extracted set of samples can be considered as a candidate cluster center. This assumption will be used in the next step of the algorithm to initially reduce the colors.

Figure 2 shows an example of approximating the original color distribution according to our sub sampling technique. It can be seen that the selected pixels are placed very close to the cluster centers of the initial image's RGB distribution.

The sampling rate depends on the structure of the input image but in most cases it is about 10%-15%. Also, the number of colors is extensively reduced.

4.2 Initial Color Reduction

Let S be the resulted set of samples obtained from the previous step and $p(r,g,b)$ ($r,g,b = [0,255]$) the 3D histogram of S. As already mentioned, every sample $s \in S$ is considered as a candidate cluster center. Based on this, the algorithm starts by choosing a random sample s_i and performs the following tasks.

Step 1. Define a cube with length of side $2h_1$. Considering $s_i = (r_i, g_i, b_i)$ as the center of the cube, calculate a new point $s_{m_i} = (r_{m_i}, g_{m_i}, b_{m_i})$ where $r_{m_i}, g_{m_i}, b_{m_i}$ the mean values of red, green, blue channels, respectively in the defined cube.

$$r_{m_i} = \frac{\sum_{r=-h_1}^{h_1} \sum_{g=-h_1}^{h_1} \sum_{b=-h_1}^{h_1} r \cdot p(r,g,b)}{\sum_{r=-h_1}^{h_1} \sum_{g=-h_1}^{h_1} \sum_{b=-h_1}^{h_1} p(r,g,b)} \tag{9}$$

$$g_{m_i} = \frac{\sum_{r=-h_1}^{h_1} \sum_{g=-h_1}^{h_1} \sum_{b=-h_1}^{h_1} g \cdot p(r,g,b)}{\sum_{r=-h_1}^{h_1} \sum_{g=-h_1}^{h_1} \sum_{b=-h_1}^{h_1} p(r,g,b)} \tag{10}$$

$$b_{m_i} = \frac{\sum_{r=-h_1}^{h_1} \sum_{g=-h_1}^{h_1} \sum_{b=-h_1}^{h_1} b \cdot p(r,g,b)}{\sum_{r=-h_1}^{h_1} \sum_{g=-h_1}^{h_1} \sum_{b=-h_1}^{h_1} p(r,g,b)} \tag{11}$$

Step 2. Label all points contained in the cube that has been examined.
Step 3. Choose a new unlabeled sample and go to step 1. If all samples are labeled then stop.

The new set of points S_m created by the algorithm just described is used to initially reduce the colors of the image (initial clustering). This is done by assigning to the pixels of the original image the color of their nearest neighbor (Euclidean distance) in S_m. The size of S_m (number of points) depends on the size of the cube, namely on h_1. After several experiments the value of h_1 was set to 32. With this value, the number of the obtained colors is relatively large and usually smaller than 100, thus the resulted image is oversegmented.

Figure 3(a) shows an example of initial clustering in the 2D space in a similar way of what is being discussed in the current section. The detected points (S_m) are referred as initial cluster centers. Adopting this approach, namely to first oversegment the clusters it is possible to solve a clustering problem where the clusters are randomly shaped by shifting the initial segments (as shown in Figure 3(a)) towards the mode point of the clusters. This is achieved by a mean shift operation which is described in the following section.

4.3 Mean Shift

Mean shift is a nonparametric and iterative technique, useful for estimating probability density functions. It was proposed by Fukunaga (1975) and extensively analyzed by Cheng (1995). Comaniciu (2002) used it to analyze complex multimodal feature distributions and also proposed a mean shift based color segmentation application.

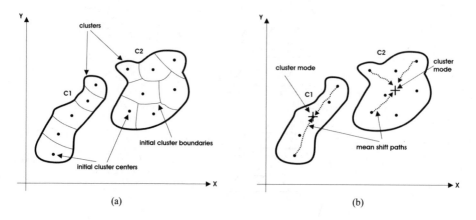

Fig. 3. Hypothetical case of clustering in the 2D space, (a) the two randomly shaped clusters C1 and C2 are initially oversegmented, (b) the final result is adopted by mean shifting the initial cluster centers (mode detection)

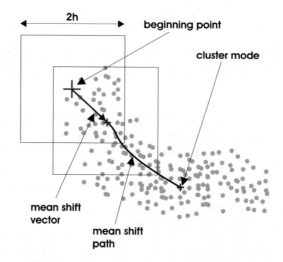

Fig. 4. Demonstration of the mean shift operation

It operates by iteratively shifting a data point to the average of points located in a specified neighborhood. As shown in Figure 4, starting from a beginning point x_i, the mean value of the points located in the square with side length $2h$ is calculated, considering point x_i as the center of the square. The resulted value, point x_j, is used in the next step with the same manner to locate a new point. The vector defined by two successive calculated points (x_i, x_j) is called mean shift vector. The algorithm continues until the norm of the mean shift vector ($\|x_i - x_j\|$) vanishes or becomes smaller than a specified lower bound (convergence condition).

In our case, beginning points of the mean shift procedure are the points of the set S_m calculated as described in section 4.2. For each point, we define a cube with length of side $2h_2$ in the 3D histogram and by utilizing equations (9), (10) and (11) for the calculation of the mean values, cluster modes are detected through the mean shift operation. A graphical example for the case of 2D space is given in Figure 3(b).

The convergence condition we adopt in our work is based on the calculation of the Manhattan color distance between two successive points in the 3D histogram $p(r,g,b)$.

$$d_m =| r_i - r_j |+| g_i - g_j |+| b_i - b_j |$$ (12)

In order to avoid a large number of repetitions and save computation time, we consider that the mean shift converges if

$$d_m \leq T_m$$ (13)

A small value $T_m = 3$ is used in our work. The final number of colors is affected by the side length of the cube ($2h_2$). A good choice for the value of h_2 is to set it equal to h_1 (section 4.2).

4.4 Final Color Reduction

To achieve the result of color segmentation, a final step which merges the shifted points is necessary because for each cluster, various values of modes have been extracted. These values are very close but do not have identical values.

Assuming that the final color cluster centers should not be closer than a specific distance, we employ a simple merging procedure where points with distance smaller than h_1 are considered to belong to the same color cluster, thus they are merged and their mean value represents the final color value which will be assigned to the cluster.

5 Experimental Results

To test the proposed method, a large database of color documents was created which consists of 1000 images. Some were scanned from color book covers and magazines (150 - 300 dpi) and others were obtained from the WWW. In all experiments we used the following parameters values

- Edge preserving smoothing factor $p = 10$
- Initial color reduction factor $h_1 = 32$
- Mean shift factor $h_2 = 32$

In Figures 5 and 6 we present experimental results of the proposed method on noisy color documents where we wish to demonstrate the effect of the edge preserving smoothing filter. The obtained results are summarized below in Tables 1 and 2.

(a) 378961 colors

(b) 82 colors

(c) 10 colors

(d) 339136 colors

(e) 134 colors

(f) 8 colors

Fig. 5. (a) Color document after edge preserving smoothing, (b) initial color reduction of (a), (c) final color reduction of (a), (d) color document without edge preserving smoothing, (e) initial color reduction of (d), (f) final color reduction of (d)

(a) 441567 colors

(b) 60 colors

(c) 8 colors

(d) 379088 colors

(e) 95 colors

(f) 10 colors

Fig. 6. (a) Color document after edge preserving smoothing, (b) initial color reduction of (a), (c) final color reduction of (a), (d) color document without edge preserving smoothing, (e) initial color reduction of (d), (f) final color reduction of (d)

Table 1. Experimental results for Fig. 5

	With edge preserving smoothing	Without edge preserving smoothing
computation time	2.68 sec	3.3 sec
initial color clusters	82	134
final color clusters	10	8
connected components	4913	20288

Table 2. Experimental results for Fig. 6

	With edge preserving smoothing	Without edge preserving smoothing
computation time	3 sec	3 sec
initial color clusters	60	95
final color clusters	8	10
connected components	8075	59195

It can be observed that when the edge preserving smoothing filter is not applied, the computation time increases or remains the same. This happens because the mean shift procedure requires more repetitions for converge. The explanation is that when the filter is applied, the density function of the RGB distribution becomes steeper and the mean shift vectors get larger values. In general, the structure of the RGB distribution affects significantly the computation cost. Another impact of the filter is that the initial classes are less in the case where preprocessing is applied. In all experiments that were made in order to test the method, this happened in all cases. The reason is that the filter shrinks the color variance and so less number of clusters is obtained from the initial color reduction procedure Also, the number of connected components is extensively reduced, a result that improves significantly the performance of text extraction applications.

In Figure 7 we demonstrate the application of the method on a complex color document. The image of Figure 7(b) represents the result of the algorithm after the initial color reduction procedure and Figure 7(c) shows the final image. The initial document (cover book) has 132106 colors and its size is 1096×1315 pixels. The quantitative results for this experiment are depicted in Table 3.

Table 3. Quantitative results for Fig. 7

computation time	3 sec
initial color clusters	28
final color clusters	7
connected components	5511

(a) Original color document with 132106 colors

(b) Document after initial color reduction
(28 colors)

(f) Document after final color reduction
(7 colors)

Fig. 7. Experimental result of color reduction

The resulted final image shows that text elements were segmented correctly without fusion with the background which has been identified as a single object.

6   Conclusions

A novel color segmentation method for text information extraction applications is presented in this paper. With an efficient sub sampling technique we first approximate the initial RGB distribution. The obtained samples are used to initially reduce the colors and by a mean shift procedure the final result is produced.

The method has been extensively tested on a large number of color documents and the results showed its capability of producing correct segmentation results where characters are not oversegmented or fused with the background. Also, unwanted low contrast objects are merged with their backgrounds and large compact areas are created. These results are very desirable in text information extraction applications.

References

Zhong, Y., Karu, K., Jain, A.K.: Locating text in complex color images. Pattern Recognition 28(10), 1523–1535 (1995)

Chen, W.Y., Chen, S.Y.: Adaptive page segmentation for color technical journals cover images. Image and Vision Computing 16, 855–877 (1998)

Sobottka, K., et al.: Text Extraction from Colored Book and Journal Covers. International Journal on Document Analysis and Recognition 2(4), 163–176 (2000)

Hase, H., Shinokawa, T., Yoneda, M., Suen, C.Y.: Character string extraction from color documents. Pattern Recognition 34(7), 1349–1365 (2001)

Strouthopoulos, C., Papamarkos, N., Atsalakis, A.: Text extraction in complex color documents. Pattern Recognition 35(8), 1743–1758 (2002)

Hase, H., Yoneda, M., Tokai, S., Kato, J., Suen, C.Y.: Color segmentation for text extraction. International Journal on Document Analysis and Recognition 6(4), 271–284 (2003)

Wang, B., Li, X.-F., Liu, F., Hu, F.-Q.: Color text image binarization based on binary texture analysis. Pattern Recognition Letters 26(11), 1650–1657 (2005)

Roerdink, J.B.T.M., Meijster, A.: The watershed transform: Definitions, algorithms and parallelization strategies. Fundamenta Informaticae 41, 187–228 (2000)

Perona, P., Malik, J.: Scale-Space and Edge Detection Using Anisotropic Diffusion. IEEE Trans. Pattern Analysis and Machine Intelligence 12, 629–639 (1990)

Fukunaga, P., Hostetler, L.D.: The Estimation of the Gradient of a Density Function, with Applications in Pattern Recognition. IEEE Trans. Information Theory 21, 32–40 (1975)

Cheng, Y.: Mean Shift, Mode Seeking, and Clustering. IEEE Trans. Pattern Analysis and Machine Intelligence 17(8), 790–799 (1995)

Comaniciu, D., Meer, P.: Mean Shift: A Robust Approach Toward Feature Space Analysis. IEEE Trans. Pattern Analysis and Machine Intelligence 24(5), 603–619 (2002)

Improved Reconstruction of Images Distorted by Water Waves

Arturo Donate and Eraldo Ribeiro

Department of Computer Sciences
Florida Institute of Technology
Melbourne, FL 32901
adonate@fit.edu, eribeiro@cs.fit.edu

Abstract. This paper describes a new method for removing geometric distortion in images of submerged objects observed from outside shallow water. We focus on the problem of analyzing video sequences when the water surface is disturbed by waves. The water waves will affect the appearance of the individual video frames such that no single frame is completely free of geometric distortion. This suggests that, in principle, it is possible to perform a selection of a set of low distortion sub-regions from each video frame and combine them to form a single undistorted image of the observed object. The novel contribution in this paper is to use a multi-stage clustering algorithm combined with frequency domain measurements that allow us to select the best set of undistorted sub-regions of each frame in the video sequence. We evaluate the new algorithm on video sequences created both in our laboratory, as well as in natural environments. Results show that our algorithm is effective in removing distortion caused by water motion.

Keywords: Image recovery, reconstruction, distortion, refraction, motion blur, water waves, frequency domain.

1 Introduction

In this paper, we focus on the problem of recovering a single undistorted image from a set of non-linearly distorted images. More specifically, we are interested in the case where an object submerged in water is observed by a video camera from a static viewpoint above the water. The water surface is assumed to be disturbed by waves. Figure 1 shows a sample of frames from a video of a submerged object viewed from above. This is an interesting and difficult problem mainly when the geometry of the scene is unknown. The overall level of distortion in each frame depends on three main parameters of the wave model: the amplitude, the speed of oscillation, and the slope of the local normal vector on the water surface. The amplitude and slope of the surface normal affect the refraction of the viewing rays causing geometric distortions while the speed of oscillation causes motion blur due to limited video frame rate.

Our goal in this paper is to recover an undistorted image of the underwater object given only a video of the object as input. Additionally, no previous knowledge of the waves or the underwater object is assumed. We propose to model the geometric distortions and the motion blur separately from each other. We analyse geometric distortions

J. Braz et al. (Eds.): VISAPP and GRAPP 2006, CCIS 4, pp. 264–277, 2007.

Fig. 1. An arbitrary selection of frames from our low energy wave data set

via clustering, while measuring the amount of motion blur by analysis in the frequency domain in an attempt to separate high and low distortion regions. Once these regions are acquired, we combine single samples of neighboring low distortion regions to form a single image that best represents the object.

We test our method on different data sets created both in the laboratory as well as outdoors. Each experiment has waves of different amplitudes and speeds, in order to better illustrate its robustness. Our current experiments show very promising results.

The remainder of the paper is organized as follows. We present a review of the literature in Section 2. In Section 3, we describe the geometry of refraction distortion due to surface waves. Section 4 describes the details of our method. In Section 5, we demonstrate our algorithm on video sequences acquired in the laboratory and outdoors. Finally, in Section 6, we present our conclusions and directions for future work.

2   Related Work

Several authors have attempted to approach the general problem of analyzing images distorted by water waves. The dynamic nature of the problem requires the use of video sequences of the target scene as a primary source of information. In the discussion and analysis that follow in this paper, we assume that frames from an acquired video are available.

The literature has contributions by researchers in various fields including computer graphics, computer vision, and ocean engineering. Computer graphics researchers have primarily focused on the problem of rendering and reconstructing the surface of the water (Gamito and Musgrave, 2002; Premoze and Ashikhmin, 2001). Ocean engineering researchers have studied sea surface statistics and light refraction (Walker, 1994) as well as numerical modeling of surface waves (Young, 1999). The vision community has attempted to study light refraction between water and materials (Mall and da Vitoria Lobo, 1995), recover water surface geometry (Murase, 1992), as well as reconstruct images of submerged objects (Efros et al., 2004; Shefer et al., 2001). In this paper, we focus on the problem of recovering images with minimum distortion.

A simple approach to the reconstruction of images of submerged objects is to perform a temporal average of a large number of continuous video frames acquired over an extended time duration (i.e., mean value of each pixel over time) (Shefer et al., 2001).

This technique is based on the assumption that the integral of the periodic function modeling the water waves is zero (or constant) when time tends to infinity. Average-based methods such as the one described in (Shefer et al., 2001) can produce reasonable results when the distortion is caused by low energy waves (i.e., waves of low amplitude and low frequency). However, this method does not work well when the waves are of higher energy, as averaging over all frames equally combines information from both high and low distortion data. As a result, the averaged image will appear blurry and the finer details will be lost.

Modeling the three-dimensional structure of the waves also provides a way to solve the image recovery problem. Murase (Murase, 1992) approaches the problem by first reconstructing the 3D geometry of the waves from videos using optical flow estimation. He then uses the estimated optical flow field to calculate the water surface normals over time. Once the surface normals are known, both the 3D wave geometry and the image of submerged objects are reconstructed. Murase's algorithm assumes that the water depth is known, and the amplitude of the waves is low enough that there is no separation or elimination of features in the image frames. If these conditions are not met, the resulting reconstruction will contain errors mainly due to incorrect optical flow extraction.

More recently, Efros et al. (Efros et al., 2004) proposed a graph-based method that attempts to recover images with minimum distortion from videos of submerged objects. The main assumption is that the underlying distribution of local image distortion due to refraction is Gaussian shaped (Cox and Munk, 1956). Efros et al., propose to form an embedding of subregions observed at a specific location over time and then estimate the subregion that corresponds to the center of the embedding. The Gaussian distortion assumption implies that the local patch that is closer to the mean is fronto-parallel to the camera and, as a result, the underwater object should be clearly observable through the water at that point in time. The solution is given by selecting the local patches that are the closest to the center of their embedding. Efros et al., propose the use of a shortest path algorithm that selects the solution as the frame having the shortest overall path to all the other frames. Distances were computed transitively using normalized cross-correlation (NCC). Their method addresses likely leakage problems caused by erroneous shortest-distances between similar but blurred patches by calculating paths using a convex flow approach. The sharpness of the image reconstruction achieved by their algorithm is very high compared to average-based methods even when applied to sequences distorted by high energy waves.

In this paper we follow Efros et al. (Efros et al., 2004), considering an ensemble of fixed local regions over the whole video sequence. However, our method differs from theirs in two main ways. First, we propose to reduce the leakage problem by addressing the motion blur effect and the refraction effect separately. Second, we take a frequency domain approach to the problem by quantifying the amount of motion blur present in the local image regions based on measurements of the total energy in high frequencies.

Our method aims at improving upon the basic average-based techniques by attempting to separate image subregions into high and low distortion groups. The K-Means algorithm (Duda et al., 2000) is used along with a frequency domain analysis for generating and distinguishing the two groups in terms of the quality of their member frames.

Normalized cross-correlation is then used as a distance measurement to find the single frame that best represents the undistorted view of the region being analyzed.

3 Distortion Analysis

In the problem considered in this paper, the local image distortions caused by random surface waves can be assumed to be modeled by a Gaussian distribution (Efros et al., 2004; Cox and Munk, 1956). The magnitude of the distortion at a given image point increases radially, forming a disk in which the center point contains the least amount of distortion. The center subregion can be determined by a clustering algorithm if the distribution of the local patches is not too broad (i.e., the diameter of the disk is small) (Efros et al., 2004). Our method effectively reduces the size of this distortion embedding by removing the subregions containing large amounts of translation and motion blur. In this section, we analyze how refraction and motion blur interferes with the appearance of submerged objects observed from outside the water. First, we analyze the geometry of refraction and its relationship to both the surface normals of the waves and the distance from the camera to the water. We then analyze the motion blur distortion caused by the speed of oscillation of the waves, and how it can be quantified in the frequency domain.

3.1 Refraction Caused by Waves

Consider a planar object submerged in shallow transparent water. The object is observed from a static viewpoint above the water by a video camera with optical axis perpendicular to the submerged planar object. In our modeling, we assume that only the water is moving in the scene (i.e., both the camera and the underwater object are stationary). Additionally, the depth of the object is assumed to be unknown and constant. Figure 2 illustrates the geometry of the scene. In the figure, d is the distance between the camera and a point where the ray of light intersects the water surface (i.e., point of refraction). The angle between the viewing ray and the surface normal is θ_n, and the angle between the refracted viewing ray and the surface normal is θ_r. These two angles are related by Snell's law (1). The camera $\mathbf{c}$ observes a submerged point $\mathbf{p}$. The angle α measures the relative translation of the point $\mathbf{p}$ when the viewing ray is refracted by the water waves.

According to the diagram in Figure 2, the image seen by the camera is distorted by refraction as a function of both the angle of the water surface normal at the point of refraction and the amplitude of the water waves. If the water is perfectly flat (i.e., there are no waves), there will be no distortion due to refraction. However, if the surface of the water is being disturbed by waves, the nature of the image distortion becomes considerably more complex. In this paper, we will focus on the case where the imaged object is planar and is parallel to the viewing plane (i.e., the planar object is perpendicular to the optical axis of the camera).

In the experiments described in this paper, the main parameters that model the spatial distortion in the image are the slant angle of the surface normal (θ_n) and the distance from surface to the camera (d). The two parameters affect the image appearance by translating image pixels within a small local neighborhood. More specifically, the varying slope of the waves and their amplitude will modify the angle of refraction that will

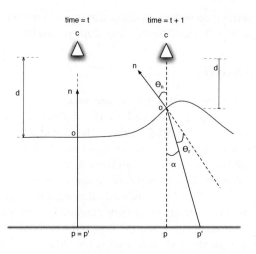

Fig. 2. Geometry of refraction on a surface disturbed by waves. The camera **c** observes a given point **p** on the submerged planar object. The slant angle of the surface normal (θ_n) and the distance from surface to the camera (d) are the main parameters of our distortion model. When θ_n is zero, the camera observes the point **p** at its original location on the object (i.e., there is no distortion in the image). If θ_n changes, the apparent position of **p** changes by a translation factor with magnitude $\|\mathbf{p}' - \mathbf{p}\|$. This magnitude also varies as a function of the distance from the water surface to the camera (e.g., due to the amplitude of the waves). The figure also illustrates the light refracting with the waves at two different points in time. The image at time t would appear clear while the image at time t+1 would be distorted by refraction.

result in the distortion of the final image. Additionally, considerable motion blur can occur in each video frame due to both the limited capture frequency of the video system, and the dynamic nature of the liquid surface. The blur will have different magnitudes across the image in each video frame. In our experiments, varying levels of motion blur will be present in each frame depending on the speed of change in the slant of the surface normals. Next, we show that the translation caused by refraction is linear with respect to the distance d and non-linear with respect to the slant angle of the water surface normal (θ_n).

We commence by modeling the refraction of the viewing ray. The refraction of light from air to water is given by Snell's law as:

$$\sin\theta_n = r_w \sin\theta_r \tag{1}$$

where θ_n is the angle of incidence of light. In our case, θ_n corresponds to the slant angle of the water surface normal. θ_r is the angle of refraction between the surface normal and the refracted viewing ray. The air refraction coefficient is assumed to be the unit and r_w is the water refraction coefficient (r_w = 1.33). From Figure 2, the angle that measures the amount of translation when θ_n varies is given by:

$$\alpha = \theta_n - \theta_r \tag{2}$$

Solving for θ_r in Equation 1 and substituting the result into Equation 2 we have:

$$\alpha = \theta_n - \arcsin(\frac{\sin\theta_n}{r_w}) \tag{3}$$

Considering the triangle $\triangle\mathbf{opp'}$, the magnitude of the underwater translation is given by:

$$\|\mathbf{p}_i - \mathbf{p}\| = d\tan\alpha \tag{4}$$

From (3), the overall translation is:

$$\|\mathbf{p}_i - \mathbf{p}\| = d\tan[\theta_n - \arcsin(\frac{\sin\theta_n}{r_w})] \tag{5}$$

Equation 5 describes the translational distortion of underwater points caused by two parameters: the slant angle of the surface normal and the distance between the camera and the point of refraction. The magnitude of translation in (5) is linear with respect to d and non-linear with respect to θ_n. These two variables will vary according to the movement of the water waves. For a single sinusoidal wave pattern model, the amplitude of the wave will affect d while the slope of the waves will affect the value of θ_n. The distortion modeled by Equation 5 vanishes when $d = 0$ (i.e., the camera is underwater), or the angle θ_n is zero (i.e., the surface normal is aligned with the viewing direction).

3.2   Motion Blur and Frequency Domain

Motion blur accounts for a large part of the distortion in videos of submerged objects when the waves are of high energy. The speed of oscillation of the surface waves causes motion blur in each frame due to limited video frame rate. Studies have shown that an increase in the amount of image blur decreases the total high frequency energy in the image (Field and Brady, 1997).

Figure 3 shows some examples of regions with motion blur distortion (top row) and their corresponding radial frequency histograms after a high-pass filter is applied to the

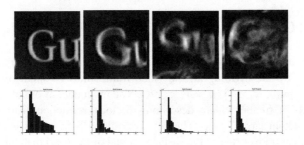

Fig. 3. Blur and its effect on the Fourier domain. Top row: images with increasing levels of blur. Bottom row: corresponding radial frequency histograms. Blur causes a fast drop in energy in the radial spectral descriptor (decrease in high frequency content).

power spectrum (bottom row). The decrease of energy in high frequencies suggests that, in principle, it is possible to determine the level of blur in images of the same object by measuring the total energy in high frequencies.

As pointed out in (Field and Brady, 1997), measuring the decay of high-frequency energy alone does not work well for quantifying motion blur of different types of images, as a simple reduction of the total number of edges in an image will produce power spectra with less energy in higher frequencies but no decrease in the actual image sharpness. Alternatively, blur in images from different scenes can be more effectively quantified using measures such as the phase coherence described in (Wang and Simoncelli, 2004).

In this paper, we follow (Field and Brady, 1997) by using a frequency domain approach to quantify the amount of motion blur in an image. We use the total energy of high-frequencies as a measure of image quality. This measurement is able to accurately quantify relative blur when images are taken from the same object or scene (e.g., images roughly containing the same number of edges).

In order to detect the amount of blur present in a set of images corresponding to the same region of the object, we first apply a high-pass filter to the power spectrum of each image. We express the filtered power spectrum in polar coordinates to produce a function $S(r, \theta)$, where S is the spectrum function, r and θ are the variables in this coordinate system. A global description of the spectral energy can be obtained by integrating the the polar power spectrum function into 1D histograms as follows (Gonzalez and Woods, 1992):

$$S(r) = \sum_{\theta=0}^{\pi} S(r, \theta) \tag{6}$$

Summing the high-frequency spectral energy in the 1D histograms provides us with a simple way to determine changes in the level of blur when comparing blurred versions of the same image. Figure 3 (bottom row) shows a sample of radial frequency histograms. The low frequency content in the histograms has been filtered out by the high-pass filter. The decrease in the high-frequency energy corresponds to an increase on the level of motion blur in the images.

4   Method Overview

Let us assume that we have a video sequence with N frames of a submerged object. We commence by sub-dividing all the video frames into K small overlapping sub-regions ($R_k = \{\mathbf{x}_1, \ldots, \mathbf{x}_N\}, k = 1, \ldots, K$). The input data of our algorithm consists of these K sets of smaller videos describing the local refraction distortion caused by waves on the actual large image. The key assumption here is that local regions will sometimes appear undistorted as the surface normal of the local plane that contains the region is aligned with the optical axis of the camera. Our goal is to determine the local region frame inside each region dataset that is closest to that fronto-parallel plane. We approach the problem by assuming that there will be two main types of distortion in the local dataset. The distortions are described in Section 3. The first type is the one caused by pure refraction driven by changes in both distance from the camera to the water and the angle of the water surface normal. The second type of distortion is the motion blur due to the speed of oscillation of the waves. Refraction and blur affect the local appearance of the frames in distinct ways. The first causes the local regions to translate across neighboring sub-regions while the second causes edges to become blurred. The exact interplay between these two distortions is complex. The idea in our algorithm is to quantify these distortions and select a reduced set of high-quality images from which we will choose the best representative region frames.

Algorithm 1. Multi-stage clustering.

Given N video frames:

1: Divide frames into K overlapping sub-regions.
2: Cluster each set of sub-regions to group the low distortion frames.
3: Remove the images with high level of blur from each group of low distortion frames.
4: Select the closest region to all other regions in that set using cross-correlation.
5: Create a final reconstructed single large image by mosaicking all subregions.
6: Apply a blending technique to reduce tiling artifacts between neighboring regions.

We start by clustering each local dataset into groups with the K-Means algorithm (Duda et al., 2000), using the Euclidean distance between the frames as a similarity measure. Since no previous knowledge of the scene is available, the K-Means centers were initialized with a random selection of sample subregions from the dataset. The clustering procedure mainly separates the frames distorted by translation. We expect the frames with less translation distortion to cluster together. However, some of the resulting clusters will contain frames with motion blur. In our experiments, the Euclidean distance measurement has shown good results in grouping most, if not all, of the lower distortion frames together, with some high distortion frames present. The initial number of clusters is very important. We found that the more clusters we could successfully split a data set into, the easier it was for the rest of the algorithm to obtain a good answer. To guarantee convergence, re-clustering was performed when one of the clusters had less than 10% of the total number of frames (e.g., in an 80-frame data set, each of the four clusters must have at least eight frames or we re-cluster the data). The algorithm initially attempts to divide the data into 10 clusters. If each cluster does not contain at least 10% of the total number of frames after a certain number of iterations, we reduce the number of clusters by one and repeat the process until the data is successfully clustered.

We assume that one of the resulting clusters produced by the K-Means algorithm contains mostly low distortion frames. To distinguish it from the other clusters, we take a statistical approach by assuming that the cluster containing most of the low distortion frames has the least amount of pixel change across frames. This is equivalent to saying that the frames should be similar in appearance to each other. We compute the variance of each pixel over all frames in the cluster using

$$\sigma^2 = \frac{1}{n} \Sigma_{i=1}^n (p_i - \bar{p})^2 \qquad (7)$$

where n is the number of frames in the cluster, p_i is the pixel value of the i-th image frame for that point, and $\bar{p}$ is the mean pixel value for that point over all frames in the cluster. We take the sum of the variances of all the pixels for each cluster, and the cluster with the minimum total variance is labeled as the low distortion group. Our experiments show that this technique is approximately 95% successful in distinguishing the best cluster. The algorithm discards all frames that are not in the cluster with the lowest total variance.

At this point, we have greatly reduced the number of frames for each region. The next step of the algorithm is to rank all frames in this reduced dataset with respect to their sharpness. As described in Section 3, the Fourier spectrum of frames containing motion blur tend to present low energy in high frequency. This allows us to remove the frames with high level of blur by measuring the decay of high frequency energy in the Fourier domain. We calculate the mean energy of all frame regions and discard the ones whose energy is less than the mean.

Finally, the algorithm produces a subset of frame regions which are similar in appearance to each other and have small amounts of motion blur. We then choose a single frame from this set to represent the fronto-parallel region. In (Efros et al., 2004), this was done using a graph theory approach by running a shortest path algorithm. We take a somewhat similar approach, computing the distances between all the frames via normalized cross-correlation then finding the frame whose distance is the closest to all the others. This is equivalent to finding the frame closest to the mean of this reduced set of frames. We then mosaic all sub-regions and use a blending algorithm (Szeliski and Shum, 1997) to produce the final reconstructed image.

Figure 4 illustrates the steps for finding the best frame of each set. The algorithm takes the frames in each subregion (Figure 4a) and use K-Means to produce four clusters (Figure 4b). After variance calculations, the algorithm determined the top-left cluster

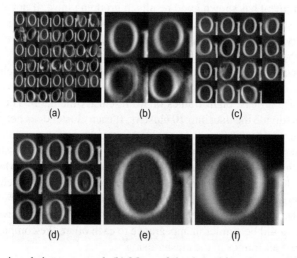

Fig. 4. (a) Subregions being compared. (b) Mean of the 4 resulting clusters, (c) frames belonging to the chosen sharpest cluster, (d) frames remaining after removing those with lower high frequency values, (e) final frame choice to represent subregion, (f) and average over all frames (shown for comparison).

of Figure 4b to be the one with the least overall distortion. The images in this cluster are then ranked in decreasing order of high-frequency energy and those frames whose energy is lower than the mean are removed in an attempt to further reduce the dataset. The remaining frames are shown in Figure 4d. From this reduced set, normalized cross correlation distances are computed in an attempt to find the best choice. Figure 4e shows the output, and Figure 4f shows the temporal average of the region for comparison.

5   Experiments

In this section we present experimental results for video sequences recorded in the laboratory and in natural environments. Current experiments show very promising results.

In the first experiment, we analyze an 80-frame video sequence (Figure 1). The waves in this data set were low energy waves, large enough to cause a considerable amount of distortion, yet small enough not to cause any significant separation or occlusion of the submerged object. The level of distortion in this dataset is similar to the one used in (Murase, 1992). Our method provides much sharper results when compared to simple temporal averaging. We extracted the subregions with 50% overlap. A simple blending process (Szeliski and Shum, 1997) is applied to reduce the appearance of "tiles" as observed in the final reconstructed image. The results can be seen in Figure 5. As expected, the blending process slightly reduced the sharpness of the image in some cases due to the fact that it is a weighted averaging function.

The next experiment shows the output of the algorithm when the input video sequence contains waves of high energy. These waves may occlude or separate the underwater object at times, temporarily making subregions completely blurry and unrecognizable. For a few regions of the image, the dataset does not contain a single frame in

Fig. 5. Low-energy wave dataset. (a) Average over all frames. (b) Output using our method.

Fig. 6. High-energy wave dataset. (a) Average over all frames. (b) Output using our method.

Fig. 7. Creek stream data set 1. (a) Average over all frames. (b) Output using our method.

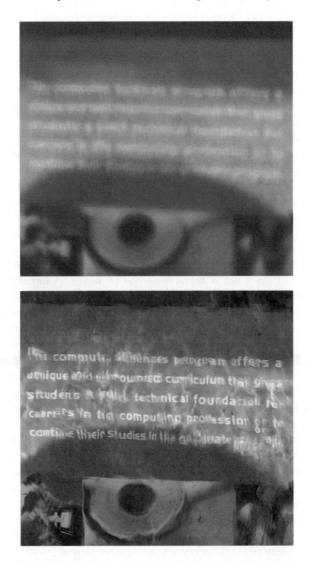

Fig. 8. Creek stream data set 2. (a) Average over all frames. (b) Output using our method.

which the object is clearly observed, making it difficult to choose a good frame from the set. The blur and occlusion complicate the reconstruction problem, but our algorithm handles it well by explicitly measuring blur and using it to select high-quality frames from each cluster. Figure 6 shows our results.

Our final experiments deal with datasets obtained in a natural outdoor environment. The videos were acquired from the moving stream of a small creek. The waves in this dataset are of high energy, but unlike the previous dataset, these are of low magnitude but very high frequency and speed, naturally generated by the creek's stream. Figures 7 and 8 show our results.

6 Conclusions

We propose a new method for recovering images of underwater objects distorted by surface waves. Our method provides promising improved results over computing a simple temporal average. It begins by dividing the video frames into subregions followed by a temporal comparison of each region, filtering out the low distortion frames via the K-Means algorithm and frequency domain analysis of motion blur.

In our method, we approach the problem in a way similar to (Efros et al., 2004) as we perform a temporal comparison of subregions to estimate the center of the Gaussian-like distribution of an ensemble of local subregions. Our approach differs from theirs in two main aspects. First, we considerably reduce the "leakage" problem (i.e., erroneous NCC correlations being classified as shortest distances) by clustering the sub-regions using a multi-stage approach that reduces the data to a small number of high-quality regions. Second, we use frequency-domain analysis that allows us to quantify the level of distortion caused by motion blur in the local sub-regions. Our results show that the proposed method is effective in removing distortion caused by refraction in situations when the surface of the water is being disturbed by waves. A direct comparison between our method and previously published methods (Efros et al., 2004; Murase, 1992; Shefer et al., 2001) is difficult due to the varying wave conditions between data sets, as well as the lack of a method for quantifying the accuracy of the reconstruction results.

Working with video sequences that contain high energy waves is a complex task due to occlusion and blurriness introduced into the image frames. Our algorithm handles these conditions well by explicitly measuring blur in each subregion. Additionally, large energy waves introduce the problem that a given embedding of subregions may not contain a single frame corresponding, or near, to a point in time when the water normal is parallel to the camera's optical axis. This affects the quality of our results.

Our plans for future research involve extending the current algorithm to improve results when dealing with high energy waves. We are currently researching the incorporation of constraints provided by neighboring patches. These constraints can, in principle, be added by means of global alignment algorithms. Further lines of research involve extending the current method to use explicit models of both waves and refraction in shallow water (Gamito and Musgrave, 2002), and the application of our ideas to the problem of recognizing submerged objects and textures. We are currently working on developing these ideas and they will be reported in due course.

Acknowledgements

The authors would like to thank Dr. Alexey Efros for kindly providing us with an underwater video sequence which we used to initially develop and test our algorithm.

References

Cox, C., Munk, W.: Slopes of the sea surface deduced from photographs of the sun glitter. Bull. Scripps Inst. Oceanogr. 6, 401–488 (1956)

Duda, R.O., Hart, P.E., Stork, D.G.: Pattern Classification, 2nd edn. Wiley-Interscience, Chichester (2000)

Efros, A., Isler, V., Shi, J., Visontai, M.: Seeing through water. In: Saul, L.K., Weiss, Y., Bottou, L. (eds.) Advances in Neural Information Processing Systems, vol. 17, pp. 393–400. MIT Press, Cambridge, MA (2004)

Field, D., Brady, N.: Visual sensitivity, blur and the sources of variability in the amplitude spectra of natural scenes. Vision Research 37(23), 3367–3383 (1997)

Gamito, M.N., Musgrave, F.K.: An accurate model of wave refraction over shallow water. Computers & Graphics 26(2), 291–307 (2002)

Gonzalez, R.C., Woods, R.E.: Digital Image Processing. Addison-Wesley, Reading, MA (1992)

Mall, H.B., da Vitoria Lobo, N.: Determining wet surfaces from dry. In: ICCV, pp. 963–968 (1995)

Murase, H.: Surface shape reconstruction of a nonrigid transparent object using refraction and motion. IEEE Transactions on Pattern Analysis and Machine Intelligence 10(10), 1045–1052 (1992)

Premoze, S., Ashikhmin, M.: Rendering natural waters. Computer Graphics Forum 20(4) (2001)

Shefer, R., Malhi, M., Shenhar, A.: Waves distortion correction using cross correlation (2001), http://visl.technion.ac.il/projects/2000maor/, http://visl.technion.ac.il/projects/2000maor/

Szeliski, R., Shum, H.-Y.: Creating full view panoramic image mosaics and environment maps. In: SIGGRAPH '97: Proceedings of the 24th annual conference on Computer graphics and interactive techniques, pp. 251–258. ACM Press/Addison-Wesley Publishing Co, New York, USA (1997)

Walker, R.E.: Marine Light Field Statistics. John Wiley & Sons, Chichester (1994)

Wang, Z., Simoncelli, E.P.: Local phase coherence and the perception of blur. In: Thrun, S., Saul, L., Schölkopf, B. (eds.) Advances in Neural Information Processing Systems, vol. 16, MIT Press, Cambridge, MA (2004)

Young, I.R.: Wind Generated Ocean Waves. Elsevier, Amsterdam (1999)

Part VII

Image
Understanding

Pose Estimation Using Structured Light and Harmonic Shape Contexts

Thomas B. Moeslund and Jakob Kirkegaard

Lab. of Computer Vision and Media Technology
Aalborg University, Denmark
tbm@cvmt.dk

Abstract. One of the remaining obstacles to a widespread introduction of industrial robots is their inability to deal with 3D objects in a bin that are not precisely positioned, i.e., the bin-picking problem. In this work we address the general bin-picking problem where a CAD model of the object to be picked is available beforehand. Structured light, in the form of Time Multiplexed Binary Stripes, is used together with a calibrated camera to obtain 3D data of the objects in the bin. The 3D data is then segmented into points of interest and for each a regional feature vector is extracted. The features are the Harmonic Shape Contexts. These are characterized by being rotational invariant and can in general model any free-form object. The Harmonic Shape Contexts are extracted from the 3D scene data and matched against similar features found in the CAD model. This allows for a pose estimation of the objects in the bin. Tests show the method to be capable of pose estimating partial-occluded objects, however, the method is also found to be sensitive to the resolution in the structured light system and to noise in the data.

Keywords: Bin-picking, rotational invariant features, surface mesh, time multiplexed binary stripes, CAD model.

1 Introduction

One of the remaining obstacles to a widespread introduction of industrial robots is their inability to deal with 3D objects that are not precisely positioned, e.g., objects supplied in bins, see figure 1. The general problem of robots handling objects located in bins or containers is known as the bin-picking problem (Torras, 1992).

Due to multiple objects in multiple layers, occlusion courses severe problems for any automatic bin-picking system. However, two issues make the problem tractable, i) the fact that only one type of object is usually present in a bin, and ii) the fact that a CAD model of the object type in the bin is normally known beforehand.

The automated bin-picking problem has been addressed using various technologies and different methods. One approach is to first find a plane region in an object, isolating it from the rest of the objects using a vacuum gripper and then do the final pose estimation using some computer vision techniques. In (Berger et al., 2000) the plane regions are identified using a grid projector combined with a binocular stereo setup placed above the bin. In (Saldner, 2003) a fringe placed in front of a video projector is used together with a high resolution camera.

J. Braz et al. (Eds.): VISAPP and GRAPP 2006, CCIS 4, pp. 281–292, 2007.

(a) A bin containing randomly organized stator housings.   (b) The stator housing object shown from four different viewpoints on a piece of A4 paper for reference.

Fig. 1. Depiction of the stator housings

A different approach is to match the CAD model directly with the objects in the bin. This can for example be carried out using the appearance (Balslev and Eriksen, 2002) or circular features (Moeslund and Kirkegaard, 2005). Alternatively, 3D data of the scene can be found[1] and matched directly with the CAD model, e.g., using a laser scanner (Schraft and Ledermann, 2003; Boughorbel et al., 2003), Active Depth From Defocus (Ghita and Whelan, 2003), or Structured Light (Salvi et al., 2004).

1.1   Content of the Paper

In this work we address the problem of automated bin-picking using structured light. The reason for using structured light is that it can support both the principle of finding plane regions in objects as well as finding the pose of an object directly in the bin. The problem is addressed generally, in the sense that nothing is assumed about the shape of the objects except that a CAD model is present. We use one particularly object type to validate our approach. This is a stator housing object, see figure 1, produced at Grundfos, one of the world's leading pump manufacturers (*www.grundfos.com*, 2005).

Since the detection of plane regions has been addressed thoroughly in the past we shall in this paper focus on finding invariant features for non-plane regions. The paper is structured as follows. In section 2 it is described how the 3D surface of the objects in the bin are reconstructed. In section 3 it is described how the invariant features are defined and extracted. In section 4 the matching between the CAD model and bin data is described. In section 5 the results are presented and finally section 6 concludes the work.

2   Reconstructing the 3D Surface

The structured light system is based on a standard LCD projector and a single JAI mono-chrome CCD camera. The encoding scheme used is *Time Multiplexed Binary Stripes* (Posdamer and Altschuler, 1982).

---

[1] See (Schwarte et al., 1999; Curless, 2000) for overviews of 3D imaging methods.

The basic principle is to project a series of patterns onto the scene encoding each scene point by a series of illumination values. The utilized patterns are binary Gray encoded multi stripe patterns, where the binary property refers to the use of two different illumination values (no and full) (Valkenburg and McIvor, 1998). More specifically the Gray codes ensure, that adjacent codewords only differ by a single bit, which in turn ensures that transitions between black and white stripes do not occur at the same position in all patterns concurrently. This principle is illustrated in figure 2.

Fig. 2. The principle behind the Gray coded binary representation. Each row indicates a given bit with the least significant bits placed in the top row. Each column indicates all the bits of one codeword.

We use 8 bits, i.e., encoding 256 stripes with the LSB pattern stripes being 4 pixels wide, see figure 3. Apart from the eight Gray encoded patterns ($I_0, \ldots, I_7$), two additional images are obtained of the scene, i.e., a full-illumination (I_H) and a zero-illumination image (I_L). These are used in equation 1 to compensate for ambient light and a possibly non-constant albedo of the objects in the scene. By subtracting I_L from the pattern images, they are compensated for ambient light effects. The denominator term is proportional to the object albedo, thereby creating an albedo normalized image, see figure 3.

$$J_k = \frac{I_k - I_L}{I_H - I_L} \tag{1}$$

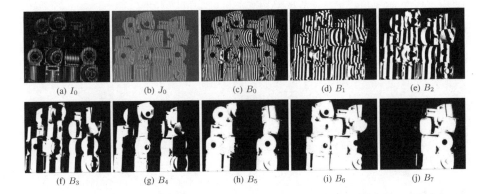

(a) I_0 (b) J_0 (c) B_0 (d) B_1 (e) B_2

(f) B_3 (g) B_4 (h) B_5 (i) B_6 (j) B_7

Fig. 3. The principle of Time Multiplexed Binary Stripes when using a resolution of 8 bits

2.1 Representing the Surface

After thresholding the albedo normalized images we have a series of binary images $B_0, \ldots, B_7$, which in turn provide the projector coordinate encoding of each pixel, see figure 3. Combining this with a calibration between the projector and the camera yields a number of 3D points representing the scene (Kirkegaard, 2005). These points are subjected to a Tessellation process, which yields a simple triangular mesh representing the surfaces in the scene. The basic assumption enabling the creation of the mesh is, that world points originating from neighboring pixels in the stripe image are also neighbors in the scene, i.e., these are connected.

Basically the reconstructed surface is a piecewise-linear surface consisting of triangles. These triangles will not be a perfect representation primarily due to the presence of noise in the reconstruction process, e.g., from the quantization due to the finite number of stripes and the crude approximation of object albedo. Therefore a smoothing of the rectangles is performed based on the weight of the three vertices in a triangle.

The weight of each vertex, i.e., the weight of each reconstructed 3D point, can be found from equation 1. The value of the pixels in the J_k images can give an indication of the quality or *fidelity* of the actual pixel. To give a quantitative measure of the pixel *fidelity* it is assumed that the normalized intensity images J_k are contaminated by zero-mean Gaussian noise $\xi(x, y)$ with variance σ^2. Given $J_k(x, y) > 0.5$ the pixel fidelity can be expressed as (Bronstein et al., 2003):

$$F_k(x, y) = P\{J_k(x, y) + \xi(x, y) > 0.5\} \quad \Leftrightarrow$$
$$F_k(x, y) = \Phi\left(\frac{0.5 - J_k(x, y)}{\sigma}\right) \quad (2)$$

where $\Phi(\cdot)$ denotes the cumulative distribution function for the normal distribution. Similar for $J_k(x, y) < 0.5$ we have:

$$F_k(x, y) = P\{J_k(x, y) + \xi(x, y) < 0.5\} \quad \Leftrightarrow$$
$$F_k(x, y) = \Phi\left(\frac{J_k(x, y) - 0.5}{\sigma}\right) \quad (3)$$

Errors in the most significant bit pattern effects the stripe image more severe than errors in the less significant patterns. Therefore it is necessary to weigh the fidelity by stripe significance. The pixel fidelity is defined by (Bronstein et al., 2003) as equation 4 where the term 2^{-k} is the stripe significance weighing. The variance σ^2 has been set to unity.

$$F(x, y) = \sum_{k=0}^{N-1} 2^{-k} F_k(x, y) \quad \Leftrightarrow$$
$$F(x, y) = \sum_{k=0}^{N-1} 2^{-k} \Phi\left(\left|\frac{0.5 - J_k(x, y)}{\sigma}\right|\right) \quad (4)$$

3   Extracting Features

The 3D mesh (and CAD model) provides a vast amount of different 3D positions from where features can be calculated. However, some locations are better than others. For example, features on a large smooth surface might not be the best choice since these by nature will result in ambiguities in the matching process. Therefore we do a segmentation of the mesh (and CAD model) in order to find positions where the ambiguity is low.

The general idea is to find positions where the curvature of the mesh changes (Trucco and Verri, 1998) and then calculate invariant features at these positions. The change of curvature is found by evaluating the change in the signs of the Principal Curvatures (Kirkegaard, 2005).

3.1 Shape Contexts

Before a matching between the segmented points and the CAD model can take place a number of features are to be extracted. We aim at a regional feature which characterizes the surface in a small finite region around each point of interest. A regional feature is a compromise between global and local surface features combining the noise robustness of the former with the occlusion robustness of the latter. Concretely we apply the *Harmonic Shape Contexts* as features. Since these are a generalization of the *Shape Context* features we start by explaining these.

Shape contexts are regional 3D shape features based on an oriented set of 3D points together with a multi-dimensional histogram. The support region for a shape context is a sphere centered at the point of interest with the sphere's north pole vector aligned with the normal vector of the mesh in this point (Frome et al., 2004), see figure 4.

The support region is divided linearly in the azimuthal (east-west) and in the co-latitudinal (north-south) directions of the sphere, while the support sphere is divided logarithmically in the radial dimension. The number of cells are S, T, and U for the azimuthal, colatitudinal, and radial dimensions, respectively. Altogether this division results in $S \times T \times U$ cells representing the support sphere around the point of interest. A single cell in the sphere corresponds to one element in a feature vector for the point of interest. The support region for the shape contexts is illustrated in figure 4.

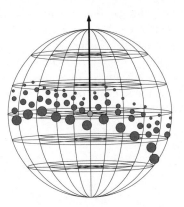

Fig. 4. The spherical support region of the shape contexts

A given cell accumulates a weighted count for each neighborhood point whose spherical coordinates fall within the ranges of the cell. The actual contribution (i.e., the weighting) to the cell count is given by the function $w\left(\cdot\right)$ (equation 5) for a given point $\mathbf{p_i}$.

$$w\left(\mathbf{p_i}\right) = \frac{1}{\rho_i \sqrt[3]{V}} \tag{5}$$

The element ρ_i in equation 5 is the local point density around the cell, while the function V denotes the volume of the cell. The normalization by the point density accounts for variations in sampling density, i.e., the same surface point may have varying numbers of neighborhood points given different image acquisition viewpoints. The normalization by the volume counteracts the effects of varying cell sizes. (Frome et al., 2004) found empirically, that normalizing by the cubic root of the cell volume retains discriminative power while leaving the feature robust to noise caused by points crossing cell boundaries.

Different shape contexts cannot be compared by simple correlation due to the shape contexts not being rotationally invariant, i.e., there exist a degree of freedom in the choice of orientation of the azimuthal direction. The shape contexts can however be made rotationally invariant by enhancing it by use of spherical harmonics - The Harmonic Shape Contexts (Kazhdan et al., 2003).

3.2 Harmonic Shape Contexts

Any given spherical function, i.e., a function $f(\theta, \phi)$ defined on the surface of a sphere parameterized by the colatitudinal and azimuthal variables θ and ϕ, can be decomposed into a weighted sum of spherical harmonics as given by equation 6.

$$f(\theta, \phi) = \sum_{l=0}^{\infty} \sum_{m=-l}^{l} A_l^m Y_l^m(\theta, \phi) \tag{6}$$

The terms A_l^m are the weighing coefficients of *degree* m and *order* l, while the complex functions $Y_l^m(\cdot)$ are the actual spherical harmonic functions of *degree* m and *order* l. Figure 5 depicts the principle of expressing a given spherical function by an infinite sum of weighted spherical harmonic basis functions.

The following states the key advantages of the mathematical transform based on the family of orthogonal basis functions in the form of spherical harmonics. A more thorough description can be found in (Kirkegaard, 2005).

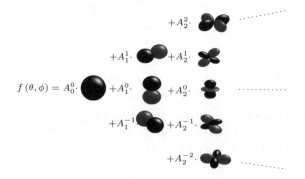

Fig. 5. A spherical function expressed as a linear combination of spherical harmonic basis functions. Black indicates positive values and gray negative values.

The complex function $Y_l^m(\cdot)$ is given by equation 7, where $j = \sqrt{-1}$.

$$Y_l^m(\theta, \phi) = K_l^m \, P_l^{|m|}(\cos\theta) \, e^{jm\phi} \qquad (7)$$

The term K_l^m is a normalization constant, while the function $P_l^{|m|}(\cdot)$ is the *associated Legendre Polynomial*. The key feature to note from equation 7 is the encoding of the azimuthal variable ϕ. The azimuthal variable solely inflects the *phase* of the spherical harmonic function and has no effect on the *magnitude*. This effectively means that $\|A_l^m\|$, i.e., the norm of the decomposition coefficients of equation 6 are invariant to parameterization in the variable ϕ.

The rotationally invariant property of the spherical harmonic transformation makes it suitable for use in encoding the shape context representation enabling a more efficient comparison. For a given spherical shell corresponding to all cells in a given radial division u, a function f_u is defined given by equation 8.

$$f_u(\theta, \phi) = SC(s, t, u) \qquad (8)$$

where $SC(s, t, u)$ means the shape context representation where s (azimuthal direction), t (colatitudinal direction), and u (radial division) are used to index a particular cell.

The primary idea in the encoding process, is then to determine the coefficients A_l^m for each of the functions f_u for $u \in [0; U-1]$. Based on the function in each spherical shell, a function $SH(\cdot)$ can be defined as given by equation 9.

$$SH(l, m, u) = \|(A_l^m)_{f_u}\| \qquad (9)$$

where $(A_l^m)_{f_u}$ denotes the spherical harmonic coefficient of order l and degree m determined from decomposition of the spherical function f_u. The function $SH(\cdot)$ is then an invariant regional surface feature based on the principle of the shape contexts.

The actual determination of the spherical harmonic coefficients is based on an inverse summation as given by equation 10, where N is the number of samples ($S \times T$). The normalization constant $4\pi/N$ originates from the fact, that equation 10 is a discretization of a continuous double integral in spherical coordinates, i.e., $4\pi/N$ is the surface area of each sample on the unit sphere.

$$(A_l^m)_{f_u} = \frac{4\pi}{N} \sum_{\phi=0}^{2\pi} \sum_{\theta=0}^{\pi} f_u(\theta, \phi) \, Y_l^m(\theta, \phi) \qquad (10)$$

In a practical application it is not necessary (or possible, as there are infinitely many) to keep all coefficient A_l^m. Contrary, it is assumed the functions f_u are band-limited why it is only necessary to keep coefficient up to some bandwidth $l = B$.

The band-limit assumption effectively means, that each spherical shell is decomposed into $(B+1)^2$ coefficients (i.e., the number of terms in the summation $\sum_{l=0}^{B}$ $\sum_{m=-l}^{l}$ in equation 6). By using the fact, that $\|A_l^m\| = \|A_l^{-m}\|$ and only saving coefficients for $m \geq 0$, the number of describing coefficients for each spherical shell is reduced to $(B+1)(B+2)/2$ coefficients (i.e., the number of terms in the summation

$\sum_{l=0}^{B} \sum_{m=0}^{l}$). Given the U different spherical shells, the final dimensionality of the feature vector becomes

$$D = U(B+1)(B+2)/2 \qquad (11)$$

The actual comparison between two harmonic shape contexts is done by the normalized correlation between two D dimensional feature vectors. A correlation factor close to unity resembles a good match, while a correlation factor close to zero represent a very poor match.

3.3 Tuning the Harmonic Shape Contexts

The number of azimuthal and colatitudinal divisions have no influence on the dimensionality of the harmonic shape context feature vector. However, the chosen divisions have influence on both the discriminative power as well as the matching efficiency. Furthermore, the number of angular divisions inflict the required computation when determining spherical harmonic coefficients based on the shape contexts (equation 10). As a trade-off between discriminative power and encoding time complexity **16** colatitudinal divisions and **32** azimuthal divisions are used. For the radial division we empirically found that **10** divisions spanned logarithmically between **5** and **25**mm is the best trade off. Finally the bandwidth parameter B is set to **15** and the final number of coefficients in each feature vector can be calculated from equation 11

$$10(15+1)(15+2)/2 = 1360. \qquad (12)$$

To get a better understanding of the harmonic shape contexts we illustrate some of the coefficients in the feature vectors for three points on a reconstructed mesh 7. The outer shell of the shape contexts for the three points are shown as the first row in figure 7. The three figures depict the count for each of 32×16 bins contained in the shell. The first colatitudinal bin corresponds to the bin around the north pole, while the last bin corresponds to the south pole bin. The three corresponding harmonic shape contexts for the three points are shown in the second row. The figures depict the spherical harmonic coefficients for each of the 10 shells together with the 36 first coefficients out of the total of 136 in each shell.

Fig. 6. Object mesh with three color-marked points

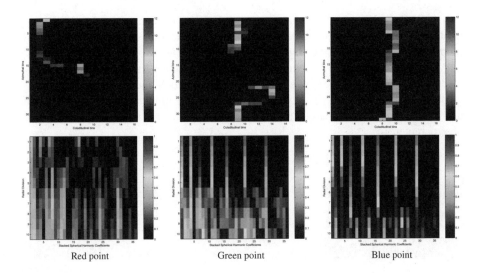

| Red point | Green point | Blue point |

Fig. 7. Illustrates shape contexts (first row) and harmonic shape contexts (second row) for the red, green, and blue points on the object mesh, respectively. Note that only the outer shell is visualized for the shape context and only the first 36 coefficients for the harmonic shape context.

4 Matching

The primary purpose of extracting harmonic shape contexts from the scene and CAD model is to perform a matching. Due to the rotational and translational invariance of the harmonic shape context, a feature vector extracted from the CAD model and the scene at positions originating from the same stator housing object point should correlate well. Since the objects in the scene are likely to be partial (self)occluded we divide the CAD model into 64 sub-models seen from different points of view and match each of these with the extracted data.

The quality of a match cannot be judge solely by one normalized correlation factor, i.e., it is necessary to consider more matches at a time. This is formulated as a graph search problem and solved using simulated annealing (Kirkegaard, 2005).

After having found a number of matches we are left with a number of corresponding 3D points from the scene and CAD model. We now minimize an error function in order to find the rigid transformation between the model and scene, i.e., the pose of the object in the scene (Kirkegaard, 2005).

5 Results

The primary evaluations performed on the method are based on synthetic data. This is done to be able to quantitatively judge the results of the method. We first evaluate the method's ability to handle occlusion, then noise and finally the resolution of the structured light system.

The CAD model is used to create the scene mesh by first using a simulated structured light system (using ray-tracing) and then doing a tessellation of the reconstructed 3D points (Kirkegaard, 2005). See figure 6 and 8 for examples.

A scene is constructed containing 12 randomly rotated, translated and partial occluded stator housings, see figure 8. The feature extraction and matching methods are applied and the results are visually inspected by transforming the models into the scene using the estimated pose parameters along with comparing the simulated and estimated pose parameters.

(a) The scene.

(b) The (rotated and translated) sub-model that matched best.

(c) The scene and transformed sub-model overlaid.

Fig. 8. Depiction of a correct 5 degree of freedom pose estimation

Six of the stator housings were pose estimated correctly down to five degrees of freedom, i.e., the "cylinder cup" where pose estimated correctly but without the remaining cylinder axis rotation, see figure 8. Two of the stator housings were pose estimated correctly with all six degrees of freedom. The primary reason for the many five degree of freedom results is due to the many symmetries contained in a stator housing object, i.e., it is only the particular terminal box of the stator housing object that enables the complete six degree of freedom pose estimation.

In table 1 we list the normalized frequency of correct pose estimations as a function of the level of random noise. The data is calculated by simulating a stator housing in 120 different configurations for each of the different noise levels. The random noise is added directly to the reconstructed 3D points and a correct pose estimation is defined

Table 1. Normalized frequency of correct pose estimations as a function of the level of simulated random noise [*mm*]

Noise	0.05	0.1	0.15	0.2	0.25	0.3
Pose	0.98	0.97	0.85	0.57	0.29	0.09

Table 2. Normalized frequency of correct pose estimations as a function of the resolution in the structured light system [*bit*]

Res.	10	12	14	16	18	20
Pose	0.24	0.97	0.98	0.98	0.99	1.0

to be when the $L2$ norm between the simulated and estimated rigid transformations is below 0.1 for both the rotation matrices and the translation vectors.

In table 2 we list the normalized frequency of correct pose estimations as a function of the resolution in the structured light system. The latter refers to the number of bits used to code the position of each pixel in the stripes. The same test setup as above is used.

6 Discussion

We have in this work addressed the general bin-picking problem where a CAD model of the object to be picked from the bin is available beforehand.

The performed tests showed that the proposed method is capable of pose estimating 8 objects in a scene containing 12 randomly organized and thereby occluding stator housings for the case of simulated noise free meshes. Even though this is only 2/3 of the objects it is still considered a success. Firstly because only one object is required to be pose estimated correct at a time (the scene will change after the robot has picked one object), and secondly because they are pose estimated very accurate even in the presence of occlusion.

In some cases only five out of the six degrees of freedom were correctly estimated. This is a common problem in many bin-picking applications due to self-symmetry but can be solve by using a two-step solution as mentioned in section 1, i.e., first isolating one object and picking it (based on the five estimated pose parameters) and *then* pose estimating it using standard vision techniques.

When adding noise to the data table 1 showed that the performance decreases. This is mainly due to the fact that the harmonic shape contexts are dependent on the direction of the normal vector. To some degree this problem can be handled by tuning the number of bins to the noise-level. Alternatively a better smoothing mechanism is required.

From table 2 we can see that the resolution has a high impact on the performance. Therefore a high number of bits should be used, which again means that the camera has to be placed closed to the objects (allowing only a few objects to be present within the field of view) or the resolution of the projector and the camera has to be very high. The concrete setup in this work only allowed a resolution of eight bits, which turned out to be too low for the system to operate reliably. This result is in total agreement with table 2 where resolutions below 12 bits produce poor results.

In conclusion it can be stated that using harmonic shape contexts is a solid approach due to the fact that they can model any rigid object without assuming anything about the shape of the object *and* can handle partially occluded objects. This is not the case with the traditional approaches where one assumes simple shapes, e.g., planes or ellipses, to be present. In fact, the harmonic shape contexts can model any free-form object, but works best when an object contains surfaces with different curvatures. Therefore it seems naturally that future *general* bin-picking approaches should combine the harmonic shape contexts with approaches using more global features since these two approaches compliment each other.

References

Balslev, I., Eriksen, R.D.: From belt picking to bin picking. In: Proceedings of SPIE - The International Society for Optical Engineering, vol. 4902, pp. 616–623 (2002)

Berger, M., Bachler, G., Scherer, S.: Vision Guided Bin Picking and Mounting in a Flexible Assembly Cell. In: Proceedings of the 13th International Conference on Industrial & Engineering Applications of Artificial Intelligence & Expert Systems, IEA/AIE2000, pp. 109–118, New Orleans, Louisiana, USA (2000)

Boughorbel, F., Zhang, Y., Kang, S., Chidambaram, U., Abidi, B., Koschan, A., Abidi, M.: Laser ranging and video imaging for bin picking. Assembly Automation 23(1), 53–59 (2003)

Bronstein, A.M., Bronstein, M.M., Gordon, E., Kimmel, R.: High-resolution structured light range scanner with automatic calibration. Technical report, Technion - Israel Institute of Technology (2003)

Curless, B.: Overview of active vision technologies. In: 3D Photography - Course Notes ACM Siggraph '00, ACM Press, New York (2000)

Frome, A., Huber, D., Kolluri, R., Bulow, T., Malik, J.: Recognizing objects in range data using regional point descriptors. In: Pajdla, T., Matas, J(G.) (eds.) ECCV 2004. LNCS, vol. 3024, pp. 224–237. Springer, Heidelberg (2004)

Ghita, O., Whelan, P.F.: A bin picking system based on depth from defocus. Machine Vision and Applications 13(4), 234–244 (2003)

Kazhdan, M., Funkhouser, T., Rusinkiewicz, S.: Rotation invariant spherical harmonic representation of 3d shape descriptors. In: SGP '03: Proceedings of the 2003 Eurographics/ACM SIGGRAPH symposium on Geometry processing, Sardinia, Italy, pp. 156–164. ACM, New York (2003)

Kirkegaard, J.: Pose Estimation of Randomly Organized Stator Housings using Structured Light and Harmonic Shape Contexts. Master's thesis, Lab. of Computer Vision and Media Technology, Aalborg University, Denmark (2005)

Moeslund, T.B., Kirkegaard, J.: Pose estimation of randomly organised stator housings with circular features. In: Scandinavian Conference on Image Analysis, Joensuu, Finland (2005)

Posdamer, J.L., Altschuler, M.D.: Surface measurement by space-encoded projected beam systems. Computer Graphics and Image Processing 18(1), 1–17 (1982)

Saldner, H.: Palletpicker-3d, the solution for picking of randomly placed parts. Assembly Automation 23(1), 29–31 (2003)

Salvi, J., Pags, J., Battle, J.: Pattern codification strategies in structured light systems. Pattern Recognition 37(4), 827–849 (2004)

Schraft, R.D., Ledermann, T.: Intelligent picking of chaotically stored objects. Assembly Automation 23(1), 38–42 (2003)

Schwarte, R., Heinol, H., Buxbaum, B., Ringbeck, T., Xu, Z., Hartmann, K.: Principles of Three-Dimensional Imaging Techniques in "Handbook of Computer Vision and Applications", 1st edn. vol. 1. The Academic Press, London (1999)

Torras, C.: Computer Vision - Theory and Industrial Applications, 1st edn. Springer, Heidelberg (1992)

Trucco, E., Verri, A.: Introductory Techniques for 3D Computer Vision, 1st edn. Prentice Hall, Englewood Cliffs (1998)

Valkenburg, R.J., McIvor, A.M.: Accurate 3d measurement using a structured light system. Image and Vision Computing 16(2), 99–110 (1998)

(2005), http://www.grundfos.com

Cognitive Vision and Perceptual Grouping by Production Systems with Blackboard Control – An Example for High-Resolution SAR-Images

Eckart Michaelsen[1], Wolfgang Middelmann[1], and Uwe Sörgel[2]

[1] FGAN-FOM, Gutleuthausstrasse 1, 76275 Ettlingen, Germany
mich@ fom.fgan.de
www.fom.fgan.de
[2] Institute of Photogrammetry and GeoInformation, University of Hanover,
Nienburger Satrasse 1, 30167 Hannover Germany
www.ipi.uni-hannover.de

Abstract. The laws of gestalt-perception play an important role in human vision. Psychological studies identified similarity, good continuation, proximity and symmetry as important inter-object relations that distinguish perceptive gestalts from arbitrary sets of clutter objects. Particularly, symmetry and continuation possess a high potential in detection, identification, and reconstruction of man-made objects. This contribution focuses on coding this principle in an automatic production system. Such systems capture declarative knowledge. Procedural details are defined as control strategy for an interpreter. Often an exact solution is not feasible while approximately correct interpretations of the data with the production system are sufficient. Given input data and a production system the control acts accumulatively instead of reducing. The approach is assessment driven features any-time capability and fits well into the recently discussed paradigms of cognitive vision. An example from automatic extraction of groupings and symmetry in man-made structure from high resolution SAR-image data is given. The contribution also discusses the relations of such approach to the "mid-level" of what is today proposed as "cognitive vision".

Keywords: Cognitive vision, Perceptual grouping, Production systems, Blackboard control, SAR images.

1 Introduction

A human subject can recognize and distinguish important gestalts even from pictorial data that he or she is not familiar with. Looking e.g. at the very high-resolution SAR-image displayed in Fig. 1 everyone will almost immediately perceive the important building features although only a minority of people is aware of the special properties of this kind of imagery. Yet SAR-experts have little success trying to code automatic building detection from such data. Partly, this results from the sheer size of these images – this one has decimetre resolution with an area of several hundred meters

J. Braz et al. (Eds.): VISAPP and GRAPP 2006, CCIS 4, pp. 293–304, 2007.
© Springer-Verlag Berlin Heidelberg 2007

covered – partly from the particular nature of noise in RADAR-data (Klausing & Holpp 2000). The important building features that humans perceive are of non-local nature; they disappear when only a small window of say 49x49 pixels is shown (such as is done in the lower part of Fig.1). Recall that most iconic operations are locally restricted on much smaller window sizes such as 7x7 pixels or even less. One may well argue that before processing these data should be scaled down. However, the antenna construction and the SAR-processing may well resolve fine structures of this

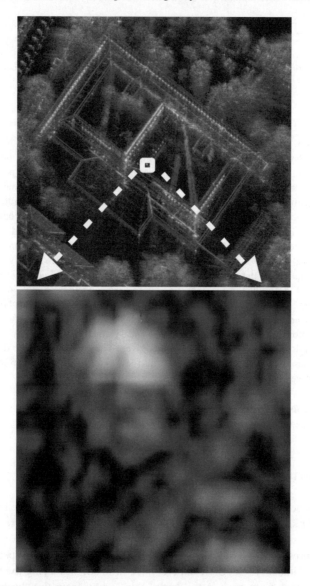

Fig. 1. X-band SAR image with a building and small section from it

size (Ender & Brenner 2003) and possibly important information that has been measured must not be neglected.

Numerous machine vision contributions rely on scale pyramid processing instead (e.g. Laptev et al. 2000). This repeats the methods on several scale levels of the image usually obtained by downscaling with factor 2 at each level. However, a line structure in these data may appear at a very fine scale – broken by gaps and yielding only small line segments at this scale, while it may disappear in noise in coarser scale completely. A considerable alternative is the large variety of Hough transform methods (Leavers 1993).

Being aware of the trouble that automatic systems have, we find that humans perform remarkably well. We emphasize that this holds for almost any kind of noisy high resolution pictorial data also including those from many kinds of e.g. medical sensors. In the literature these striking capabilities of human observers are known as the "gestalt perception" borrowing the word "Gestalt" from German language. It is now almost a hundred years that this topic is being studied. Psychological investigations identified the relations *similarity*, *good continuation*, *proximity* and *symmetry* as important inter-object relations that distinguish perceptive gestalts from arbitrary sets of clutter objects almost hundred years ago (Wertheimer 1927). Of these only proximity is of local nature. Research in incorporating perceptive capabilities based on these relations into machine vision also has a quite remarkable history (Marr 1982, Lowe 1985) There is joint work from psychologists, artificial-life researchers, neurophysiologists, Darwinists and computer vision experts to derive these principles from co-occurrence statistics of natural images and the principles of evolution of species (Guo et al. 2003). Yet much of the latest work on perceptive grouping concentrates on the implementation of local gap-filling techniques like tensor voting (Medioni et al. 2000).

This contribution focuses on automatically identifying symmetry and repetitive structure by a production system. To this end a multistage assessment driven process is set up. The first stage described in section 2 transforms the iconic image information into sets of structural objects like spots and short line segments. These primitive objects are combined to scatters, long lines, salient rows, and angles taking the laws of gestalt-perception into account, see section 3. The last stage of the production system consists of identifying and assessing the symmetry of angle pairs. Section 4 describes the methodology for efficient processing the production system. As result strong hypotheses of symmetry axes and scatterer rows are determined in section 5. Throughout the paper we discuss the relation to what is recently being discussed as "cognitive vision". This is particularly emphasized in the concluding section 6.

2 Transforming Iconic Information to Sets of Structural Objects

The image neighbourhood is closely connected to just one relation (proximity) among many others that interest us. Large image regions may contain nothing of interest just homogenous returns with some noise multiplied to it. Therefore the image matrix is not an appropriate representation. Instead we use *sets* of objects that are extracted from the image by feature extraction methods. Fig. 2 shows a set of spot pixel objects **P** with 4275 elements and Fig. 3 shows a set of short line objects **L** with 5527 elements. In comparison to the 2400x2300 grey value pixels of the original image this is a significant reduction, while the major building features remain in this representation.

Fig. 2. Set of primitive objects spot pixel – **P**

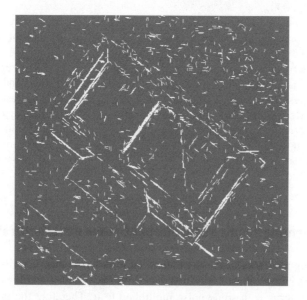

Fig. 3. Set of primitive objects line – **L**

Objects **P** are constructed using a spot-filter (Michaelsen et al. 2002) on a reduced version of the image by factor 4. The procedure has two parameters a window radius (set to 8 pixels) and a decision threshold (set to 10%) which is a factor of the maximal value found by the filter in the present image section. They are labelled with x- and y-coordinate and the strength above threshold. The latter gives their assessment. It is visualised as grey-value in Fig. 2. Bright colour means high assessment. Locations where no object **P** is present remain with the background grey value. Each object **P** states evidence for a bright spot in that position.

Objects **L** are constructed using the squared averaged gradient filter (Foerstner 1994). This filter gives a symmetric 2x2 matrix for each image position. Matrices with a big eigenvalue and a small one indicate evidence for an edge or for a line at the associated position. For the filter there is a radius parameter σ (set to 1 pixel here). For efficiency reasons this filter was run on 25 tiles of the image (in full resolution) separately. It makes sense to prolong these very short line segments in each tile of the image separately before joining the whole set for subsequent processing. This is done by running a trivial system containing only the production P_2 described in the next section for a fixed number of cycles. Thus the basis objects for structural analysis are computed.

The resulting set of primitive objects may be significantly improved (i.e. contain less noise but the same information) if a sophisticated iconic filter operation precedes the extraction process (Michaelsen et al. 2005). For simplicity we have replaced this step for the present contribution by simple morphological opening (for the **P** Objects) and closing (for the **L** Objects).

3 Coding Cognitive Vision and Gestalt Relations in Productions

Gestalt psychology teaches certain geometric relations as the key to perception. A set of parts fulfilling these constraints forms a whole that is described more briefly and distinctively. A straight forward way to code this for machines is to use production rules (or short productions). Such productions have occasionally been used for remote sensing and computer vision (Draper et al., 1989, Stilla et al. 1996). Main benefits from the use of production systems are modularity of knowledge and clear separation of the declarative knowledge – i.e. the productions - from the procedural decisions – i.e. the control. Each production P consists of an input side Σ, a constraint relation π, an output side Λ, and a function φ. The set of productions used for a given task is called production system. Compared to rule-based systems discussed in the AI and vision community long time ago (e.g. Matsuyama and Hwang, 1990) the system presented here contains only few productions. In Fig. 4 it is presented as production net and in Tab. 1 in tabular format. Circular nodes in Fig. 4 represent the productions while elongated nodes represent object concepts. Object names are short symbols, so there is one or two words with each object node to explain what kind of object it is.

The output side Λ most often only consists of a single symbol whereas the input side Σ may consist of a fixed tuple ($P_{3,...,6}$) or a set of objects ($P_{1,2,7}$) of the same type. Of most interest are productions P_4 and P_6. P_4 consecutively adds one scatterer object **Sc** after the other to row objects **R**. This recursive process is initialised using the direction of a neighbouring long line object **LL**. P_6 constructs symmetry axis from pairs of angle objects **A**. This alone is a non-local constraint and thus may cause excessive computational effort. For building detection we can further restrict one leg of one angle object **A** to be collinear with the other leg of the other angle object **A**. This makes the search more robust. Production P_7 codes clustering of detected symmetries so that a detected symmetry cue will not be based on one single pair of angles alone.

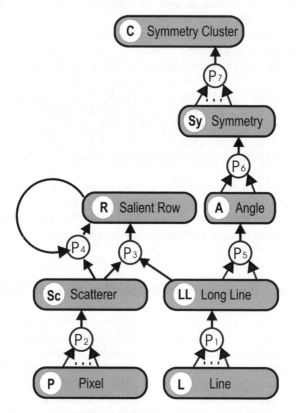

Fig. 4. Production-net visualisation

The cognitive vision paradigm – as it has been formulated in the research roadmap (ECVision, 2005) emphasizes automatic acquiring of such knowledge from large corpi of data. However, for many tasks – such as working towards automatic vision for SAR-sensors of the next generation – there are only some few sample images available. There also is no need to (machine-) learn the principles of perceptual grouping from large samples of data. They are known from nearly hundred years of psychological research. There is probably a potential for fostering robustness through adaptation of the thresholds and parameters inherent in the constraint relations π. We have proposed statistical calculus for this with models for background and target structure (Michaelsen & Stilla 2002). This needs a far bigger data corpus than is available now, and it requires tremendous human labour for the labelling of a learn set – and a test set for verification.

Table 1. Productions listed as table

	Σ	π	Λ	φ
P_1	{**P**,...,**P**}	proximity	**Sc**	mean
P_2	{**L**,...,**L**}	colinearity	**LL**	regression
P_3	(**SC,LL**)	proximity	**R**	copy
P_4	(**SC,R**)	good continuation $\wedge$ similarity	**R**	mean
P_5	(**LL,LL**)	proximity	**A**	intersect
P_6	(**A,A**)	symmetry $\wedge$ colinearity	**Sy**	mid axis
P_7	{**Sy**,...,**Sy**}	proximity	**C**	mean

4 The Accumulative Control a Paradigm for Cognitive Perception

The objective for the control of the production system is to handle robustly many thousand objects. Two possibilities for the control are discussed here.

Reduction: Standard interpretation of production systems following e.g. Matsuyama and Hwang (1990) works reductively: Given a set of productions and a set of data the productions are performed serially. For a system like the one presented above the interpreter would select a production and a subset that symbolically fits into the input side (e.g. a pair of objects (**LL, LL**) for P_5) test the constraint relation (in the example *proximity*) and carry out the production in case of success. Reduction means that the original object pair is removed and replaced by the new object **A**. Since selection of pairs is of quadratic computational complexity it is good advice to have one element of the input side triggering a search for partners that fulfil the constraint without listing all objects that are far away. We call such a pair of an object and a production to be tested with it a "working element". The main problem with this reduction technique is the administration of the control. It has to keep track of every step it took. Recall that there may be alternative possibilities for the selection step. The control may have to "undo" a sequence of steps and then try again with other selections. Thus the computational complexity of the search is bounded by no less than $\mathcal{O}(2^n)$ where n is the maximal serial depth of the search. If the production net contains cycles (like the one presented above) the serial depth will only be bounded by the number of objects (each reduction removes at least one object). Such control may be semantically correct but it will not be very robust concerning the computational effort dependency on the data. Particularly for recognition from image data it is necessary to trade the 100% semantic correctness for more robustness in the control. However, correct reducing approaches are still being pursued e.g. using PROLOG (Cohn et al. 2003).

Of particular interest today for the cognitive vision community is the logical structure best suited for vision tasks. The question is raised whether one should utilize deductive, inductive or even abductive logics. However, all of these attempts scale badly with rising number of data instances. In contrast to these works we believe that the key is in trading correctness for efficiency.

The Accumulating Interpretation Cycle: This follows the well known AI-paradigm of blackboard architecture. Given a production system $P = \{S, A, P\}$ where S is the set of symbols, A the attribute domain and P the set of productions, a working element is defined as quadruple $e=(s, i, as, pm)$ where s is a symbol from S, i is an object instance index, as is an assessment and pm is a production module index. Assessments are taken from the continuous ordered interval [0, 1]. A production module is always triggered by a particular object instance. It contains code that queries the database for partner instances which fulfil the constraint relation π of the production given the triggering object instance.

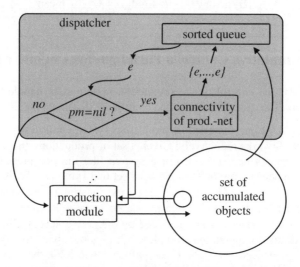

Fig. 5. The accumulative interpretation cycle

Usually search regions are constructed (e.g. a long stripe shaped region with the triggering Line instance in the centre for P_2). If the query results in a non-empty set the module will create new instances according to the functional part φ of the production. Some productions need more than one module (e.g. P_4 may be triggered by a row instance **R** or by a scatterer instance **Sc** requiring different queries). The set of module indices is expanded by *nil*. Always when a new object instance is created – either by an external feature-extraction process or by one of the production modules – also a corresponding new working element is added using this module index *nil* (meaning that there is no module assigned yet). The set of working elements is called the queue. It is sorted occasionally (e.g. after picking the best 100 elements) with respect to the assessments. The central control unit (AI-people call it dispatcher) always tackes working elements from the queue. If the module index of an element is *nil* it will be replaced by new working elements with appropriate module indices (recall that each connection from a symbol to a production in the production-net corresponds to a production module, i.e. a possibility to be tested). If there is a non-*nil* module index attached the dispatcher will trigger the indicated module by the corresponding object instances. The whole interpretation cycle is indicated in Fig. 5.

Modules may be run in parallel on different processors. The dispatcher can start picking elements from the queue the moment the first primitive instances are inserted. It terminates inevitably when the queue happens to run empty. But usually it will be terminated before, either by external processes or the user, or by limiting the number of cycles or time. Obviously the accumulative control features any-time capability. The advantages of the accumulating interpretation cycle have been originally described in the context of syntactic pattern recognition by Michaelsen (1998a, 1998b)

There is good evidence that a large portion of the remarkable visual capabilities of man is due to the visual motor system and its elaborated control. For the SAR-application we do not need to move physical sensors during recognition. The data provide high resolution everywhere and our control shifts the focus of attention around freely, because the data are organized as sets. The eye saccade control of a human observer is replaced by the assessment driven control of our blackboard. This stresses the importance of further research on the assessment functions.

5 Experimental Results for Strong Building Hypotheses

This is a methodological contribution meant to stimulate discussion on how to organize intermediate processes in computer vision. Human subjects are usually not aware of these intermediate processes – while performing them. The system presented does not extract buildings from high resolution SAR-images. These higher level decisions are preserved for later work based on the results presented here.

Table 2. Number of objects with increasing number of interpretation cycles, where each cycle picks 100 working elements from the queue

	P	L	Sc	LL	R	A	Sy	C
0	4275	5527	0	0	0	0	0	0
100	4275	5527	619	624	2052	219	4	1
200	4275	5527	820	881	4293	498	4	1
300	4275	5527	820	1031	7073	952	25	7

To demonstrate any-time capability the search run was terminated after 300 interpretation cycles with 100 working elements each. Tab. 2 gives intermediate statistics of the interpretation process. After 300 cycles the queue was still filled with

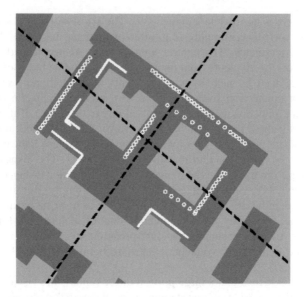

Fig. 6. Results overlayed to a GIS-building layer ground truth

many thousand working elements and growing. Fig. 6 shows the encouraging results. These results confirm the assessment driven ansatz as appropriate tool for perceptive building cue detection.

For better judgement the building layer of a GIS-base of the imaged area was chosen as background for the figures. Row objects **R** with more than 4 members are displayed. The two best symmetry objects **C** giving the axis dashed and in black. Objects **A** participating in the objects **C** are coloured white.

Assessments on the issue of appropriateness for remote sensing tasks need systematic testing and comparison with other methods on a representative dataset and definition of goals. There simply is not enough such high resolution SAR imagery around to start this yet.

6 Discussion and Conclusion

Citing form the research roadmap (ECVision, 2005) we affirm that: "... *The very essence of the cognitivist approach is that cognition comprises computational operations defined over symbolic representations and these computational operations are not tied to any given instantiation.* ..." (Section 6.1.2, page 29). This is what production-nets are about.

For next generation SAR-data an intermediate grouping process seems appropriate between feature extraction and final decision or description for automatic vision. Particularly the very high resolution devices generate imagery for which this is essential. Standard grouping techniques like clustering for local constraints like proximity and Hough transform or tensor voting for good continuation lack the flexibility and cooperative/competitive structure of the method presented here. On the other hand complex high-level AI reasoning schemes may not be capable of handling large amounts of data in a robust and quick way. The accumulative production-net search turns out a reasonable alternative for such tasks.

Repetitive structure and symmetry constitute strong relations that improve building detection significantly. The proposed production system with its accumulative control enables modular and robust utilization of these perceptive properties. Objectives of future work include symmetry of more complex objects e.g. generic descriptions of building parts. This leads also to theoretic investigations concerning decision theoretic inference of the constraint relations, computational complexity estimation and stop criteria.

Acknowledgements

We thank Dr. J. H. G. Ender and Dr. A. R Brenner from FGAN-FHR for providing us with the PAMIR SAR-data.

References

Cohn, A.G., Magee, D., Galata, A., Hogg, D., Hazarika, S.: Towards an architecture for cognitive vision using qualitative spatio-temporal representations and abduction. In: Freksa, C., Brauer, W., Habel, C., Wender, K.F. (eds.) Spatial Cognition III. LNCS (LNAI), vol. 2685, pp. 232–248. Springer, Heidelberg (2003)

Ender, J.H.G., Brenner, A.R.: PAMIR - a wideband phased array SAR/MTI system. IEE Proceedings - Radar, Sonar, Navigation 150(3), 165–172 (2003)

Foerstner, W.: A framework for low level feature extraction. In: Eklundh, J.-O. (ed.) ECCV 1994. LNCS, vol. 801, pp. 383–394. Springer, Heidelberg (1994)

Guo, C.-E., Zhu, S.C., Wu, Y.N.: Modelling visual patterns by integrating descriptive and generative methods. IJCV 53(1), 5–29 (2003)

Draper, B., Collins, R., Brolio, J., Hanson, A., Riseman, E.: The Schema System. IJCV 2, 209–250 (1989)

Klausing, H., Holpp, W.: Radar mit realer und synthetischer Apertur, Oldenburg Verlag, München (2000)

Laptev, I., Mayer, H., Lindeberg, T., Eckstein, W., Steger, C., Baumgartner, A.: Automatic Extraction of Roads from Aerial Images Based on Scale Space and Snakes. Machine Vision and Applications 12(1), 22–31 (2000)

Leavers, V.F.: Which Hough transform? CVGIP, Image Understanding, Vol. CVGIP, Image Understanding 58(2), 250–264 (1993)

Lowe, D.G.: Perceptual organization and visual recognition. Kluwer, Boston (1985)

Marr, D.: Vision, Freeman, San Francisco (1982)

Matsuyama, T., Hwang, V.S.-S.: Sigma a knowledge-based image understanding system. Plenum Press, New York (1990)

Medioni, G., Lee, M., Tang, C.: A computational framework for segmentation and grouping. Elsevier, Amsterdam (2000)

Michaelsen, E.: Über Koordinaten Grammatiken zur Bildverarbeitung und Szenenanalyse. Diss. Univ. of Erlangen (1998a), available online as http://www.exemichaelsen.de/Michaelsen_Diss.pdf

Michaelsen, E., Stilla, U.: Remark on the notation of coordinate grammers. In: Armin, A., Dori, D., Pudil, P., Freeman, H. (eds.) Advances in pattern recognition, JOINT IAPR Int. Workshop SPR-SSPR, pp. 421–428. Springer, Berlin (1998b)

Michaelsen, E., Stilla, U.: Probabilistic Decisions in Production Nets: An Example from Vehicle Recognition. In: Caelli, T.M., Amin, A., Duin, R.P.W., Kamel, M.S., de Ridder, D. (eds.) SPR 2002 and SSPR 2002. LNCS, vol. 2396, pp. 225–233. Springer, Heidelberg (2002)

Michaelsen, E., Soergel, U., Stilla, U.: Grouping salient scatterers in InSAR data for recognition of industrial buildings. In: Kasturi, R., Laurendeau, D., Sun, C. (eds.) 16th Int. Conf. on Pattern Recognition, ICPR 2002, vol. II, pp. 613–616 (2002)

Michaelsen, E., Middelmann, W., Sörgel, U., Thönnessen, U.: On the improvement of structural detection of building features in high-resolution SAR data by edge preserving image enhancement. Pattern Recognition and Image Analysis, MAIK, NAUKA, Moscow 15(4), 686–689 (2005)

Stilla, U., Michaelsen, E., Lütjen, K.: Automatic Extraction of Buildings from Aerial Images. In: F. Leberl, R. Kalliany, M. Gruber (eds.), Mapping Buildings, Roads and other Man-made Structures from Images, IAPR-TC7, Wien, Oldenburg, pp. 229-244 (1996)

Wertheimer, M.: Untersuchungen zur Lehre von der Gestalt II. Psychol. Forsch. In: Beardslee, D., Wertheimer, M. (eds.) Translated as 'Principles of Perceptual Organization, vol. 4, pp. 115–135. Princeton, N.J (1923)

ECVision: European research network for cognitive vision systems, A research roadmap of cognitive vision (2005), http://www.ecvision.org

Occlusion Invariant Face Recognition Using Two-Dimensional PCA

Tae Young Kim[1], Kyoung Mu Lee[2], Sang Uk Lee[2], and Chung-Hyuk Yim[3]

[1] Samsung Electronics Co. Ltd., Suwon, Korea
ty514.kim@samsung.com
[2] School of Electrical Eng., ASRI, Seoul National University, 151-600, Seoul Korea
kyoungmu@snu.ac.kr, sanguk@ipl.snu.ac.kr
[3] School of Mechanical Design and Automation Engineering,
Seoul National University of Technology
139-143, Seoul Korea
chyim@snut.ac.kr

Abstract. Subspace analysis such as the Principal Component Analysis (PCA) and Linear Discriminant Analysis (LDA) are widely used feature extraction methods for face recognition. However, since most of them employ holistic basis, local information can not be represented in the subspace. Therefore, in general, they cannot cope with the occlusion problem in face recognition. In this paper, we propose a new method that uses the two-dimensional principal component analysis (2D PCA) for occlusion invariant face recognition. In contrast to 1D PCA, 2D PCA projects a 2D image directly onto the 2D PCA subspace, and each row of the resulting feature matrix exhibits the distribution of corresponding row of the image. Therefore by classifying each row of the feature matrix independently, we can easily identify the locally occluded parts in a face image. The proposed occlusion invariant face recognition algorithm consists of two parts: occlusion detection and partial matching. To detect occluded regions, we apply a novel combined k-NN and 1-NN classifier to each row of the feature matrix of the test face. And for partial matching, similarity between feature matrices is evaluated after removing the rows identified as the occluded parts. Experimental results on AR face database demonstrate that the proposed algorithm outperforms other existing approaches.

Keywords: Face recognition, occlusion invariance, 2DPCA.

1 Introduction

Face recognition has been one of the most challenging and active research topics in computer vision for several decades (Zhao, 2000). The goal of face recognition is to identify one or more persons, given still or video scenes using stored faces in a database. A face recognition system should recognize a face robustly and independently as possible to the image variations such as pose, illumination, expression, and occlusion.

Face recognition approaches can be divided into two categories: feature based methods (Gao, 2002)-(Park, 2005) and appearance based methods (Turk, 1991)-(Georghiades, 2001). In the feature based methods, some features such as eyes, nose,

J. Braz et al. (Eds.): VISAPP and GRAPP 2006, CCIS 4, pp. 305–315, 2007.

and mouth are extracted, and the geometrical relationship between them are analyzed for recognition. This approach has some advantages such as low memory requirement and robustness to illumination changes. However, during the process of extracting low-level features, some distortions may arise. On the other hand, in the appearance based methods, the holistic intensity information of a face image is represented in terms of principal modes on a compact low dimensional subspace (Turk, 1991)-(Belhumeur, 1997). Appearance based approaches are known to be sensitive to illumination changes, and needs more memory than the feature based approaches. Although, many techniques have been proposed based on these two approaches, most of them produce relatively low recognition rate when occluded faces are presented. Occluded faces wearing sunglasses or scarfs are examples of partial information loss. These damaged regions usually degrade the performance of a face recognition system severely. Recently, some methods for reconstructing partially damaged face have been developed (Saito, 1999) (Hwang, 2003). They reconstructed damaged regions by interpolation or extrapolation using linear subspace analysis or a morphable face model. Note that occlusion problem can also be handled by partial matching after detecting and removing the lost features without direct reconstruction of the lost information. Leonardis et al. (Leonardis, 1996) rejected outliers and dealt with occlusions through a hypothesize-and-test paradigm using subsets of image points. On the other hand, Black et al.(Black, 1998) eliminated outliers by means of a conventional robust M-estimator. However, these methods usually need extensive training images or must satisfy some prior conditions, so they are not easily applicable to general situations.

In this paper, we propose a novel occlusion invariant face recognition method based on 2D PCA technique (Yang, 2004). In a subspace obtained by 2D PCA, we first detect the occluded parts by applying a combined k-NN (Earl, 1996) and 1-NN (Dick, 1998) classifier that considers the relative distance from a test data and its nearest neighbor, and then conduct partial matching only with the non-occluded parts after eliminating occlusion effect. So, the proposed algorithm recognizes a face by excluding unreliable and inconsistent features without reconstructing the lost information. In addition, unlike most conventional algorithms, since the proposed algorithm requires only a single training face image per person, it can be applied to more general situations where many training samples are not available.

2   Two-Dimensional PCA

In order to perform the conventional 1D PCA for face recognition, 2D face images must be transformed to 1D vectors in advance. The resulting image vectors of faces usually lead to a high-dimensional vector space (Turk, 1991). Contrast to the conventional 1D PCA, 2D PCA uses 2D matrices directly rather than 1D vectors. That is, an image does not need to be transformed into a vector. Also, the image covariance matrix can be constructed directly using the original image matrices, and the size of it is much smaller than that of 1D PCA. The details of 2D PCA can be found in (Yang, 2004).

Let $\mathbf{X}$ denote an n-dimensional unit column vector. The main idea of 2D PCA is to project image $\mathbf{A}$, an $m \times n$ random matrix, onto $\mathbf{X}$ by the following linear transformation.

$$\mathbf{Y} = \mathbf{AX}. \tag{1}$$

Thus, we obtain an m-dimensional projected vector $\mathbf{Y}$, which is called the projected feature vector of image $\mathbf{A}$. To make the performance of 2D PCA better, we have to determine a good projection vector $\mathbf{X}$. In fact, the total scatter of the projected samples can be introduced to measure the discriminative power of the projection vector $\mathbf{X}$. Moreover, the total scatter of the projected samples can be characterized by the trace of the covariance matrix of the projected feature vectors. Therefore, by maximizing the total scatter of the projected samples, we can determine a good projection vector $\mathbf{X}$. The physical significance of a good projection vector is to find a projection direction $\mathbf{X}$, onto which all samples are projected, so that the total scatter of the resulting projected samples is maximized. The covariance matrix of the projected feature vectors of the training samples can be denoted by

$$
\begin{aligned}
\mathbf{S}_x &= E[(\mathbf{Y} - E\mathbf{Y})(\mathbf{Y} - E\mathbf{Y})^T] \\
&= E[(\mathbf{AX} - E(\mathbf{AX}))(\mathbf{AX} - E(\mathbf{AX}))^T] \\
&= E[((\mathbf{A} - E\mathbf{A})\mathbf{X})((\mathbf{A} - E\mathbf{A})\mathbf{X})^T].
\end{aligned}
\tag{2}
$$

Therefore,

$$tr(\mathbf{S}_x) = \mathbf{X}^T E[(\mathbf{A} - E\mathbf{A})^T(\mathbf{A} - E\mathbf{A})]\mathbf{X}. \tag{3}$$

Let us define the following *image covariance matrix*.

$$\mathbf{G}_t = E[(\mathbf{A} - E\mathbf{A})^T(\mathbf{A} - E\mathbf{A})]. \tag{4}$$

We can calculate $\mathbf{G}_t$ directly using the training image samples. Suppose that the training set contains M samples in total, the j-th training image is denoted by an $m \times n$ matrix $\mathbf{A}_j (j = 1, 2, \cdots, M)$, and the average image of all training samples is denoted by $\bar{\mathbf{A}}$. Then, $\mathbf{G}_t$ can be evaluated by

$$\mathbf{G}_t = \frac{1}{M}\sum_{j=1}^{M}(\mathbf{A}_j - \bar{\mathbf{A}})^T(\mathbf{A}_j - \bar{\mathbf{A}}). \tag{5}$$

So, the Eq. (3) can be expressed by

$$tr(\mathbf{S}_x) = \mathbf{X}^T \mathbf{G}_t \mathbf{X}. \tag{6}$$

The unit column vector $\mathbf{X}$ that maximizes Eq. (6) is called the optimal projection axis. This means that the total scatter of the projected samples are maximized after the projection of an image matrix onto $\mathbf{X}$, so that the discriminative power of the projection vector $\mathbf{X}$ is also maximized.

The optimal projection axis $\mathbf{X}_{opt}$ is the unit column vector that maximizes Eq. (6), *i.e.*, the eigenvector of $\mathbf{G}_t$ corresponding to the largest eigenvalue (Yang, 2002). In general, since it is not enough to have only one optimal projection axis, we usually need to select a set of projection axes, $\mathbf{X}_1, \cdots, \mathbf{X}_d$, satisfying the following criterion,

$$\{\mathbf{X}_1, \cdots, \mathbf{X}_d\} = \arg\max tr(\mathbf{S}_x). \tag{7}$$

In fact, the optimal projection axes, $\mathbf{X}_1, \cdots, \mathbf{X}_d$, are the eigenvectors of $\mathbf{G}_t$ corresponding to the first d largest eigenvalues.

After finding the optimal projection axes of 2D PCA, they are used for feature extraction. For a given image sample **A**, we can obtain the following *principal component vectors*

$$\mathbf{Y}_k = \mathbf{A}\mathbf{X}_k, k = 1, 2, \cdots, d. \tag{8}$$

These principal component vectors are used to form an $m \times d$ matrix $\mathbf{B} = [\mathbf{Y}_1, \cdots, \mathbf{Y}_d]$ called the *feature matrix*, which characterizes the image sample **A** in the 2D PCA space.

3   Occlusion Detection and Partial Matching Using 2D PCA

3.1   Occlusion Detection

One interesting property of 2D PCA is that each row of an image **A** is projected onto the optimal projection axes and produces a corresponding row of the feature matrix (Fig. 1), *i.e.*, the i-th row of a feature matrix represents the projection of the i-th row of the image in 2D PCA subspace. Therefore, by analyzing each row of the feature matrix statistically and independently, we can identify the occluded rows or local regions in the image.

The process of occlusion detection is a type of one-class classification problem which discriminates face regions from non-face ones. In this case, a face regions belong to a target class and the occluded face regions belong to an outlier class. One-class classification techniques can be categorized into two types (Dick, 1998). One is the *unsupervised* method that uses only the samples of the target class for training. The other is the *supervised* method that employs the training samples of both target and outlier classes. Although it needs additional efforts for providing outlier samples during the training process, generally the supervised method gives better result than unsupervised one. Therefore, after obtaining the distributions of every row of both normal and occluded face images' feature matrices, we can apply a supervised one class classifier to each row for the detection of occluded face parts.

In this paper, we propose a new supervised one class classifier that combines the k-NN and a modified 1-NN classifier (Dick, 1998) sequentially. Note that usually the k-NN classifier shows good performance for one class classification. However, since no distance constraint is considered, misclassification may occur. One example is that when a test data is located far away from the training samples while most of the nearest neighbors belong to a target class, the test data is assigned to the target class even

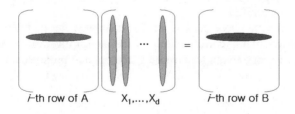

i-th row of A $X_1,...,X_d$ i-th row of B

Fig. 1. Matrix multiplication process of 2D PCA

though it is an outlier object. In order to resolve this problem, we employ the relative distance-based 1-NN classifier (Dick, 1998) for a post verification for the decision of target class.

The proposed classifier works as follows: For a test data x, k-NN classifier first seeks the k nearest samples among the training data. Among these k closest samples, if the number of outlier class samples is more than that of target class samples, the test data is classified as an outlier object. Otherwise, we apply 1-NN classifier to the target class samples only by using the relative distance from x to its first nearest neighbor in the training set defined by

$$\rho_{NN}(x) = \frac{||x - NN^{tr}(x)||}{||NN^{tr}(x) - NN^{tr}(NN^{tr}(x))||}, \tag{9}$$

where $NN^{tr}(x)$ denotes the nearest neighbor of object x in the training set. If it is smaller than a pre-specified threshold value, then the test data x is classified as a target object, otherwise, it is assigned to the outlier class. Let us denote $\mathbf{B}_i^T$ and $\mathbf{B}_i^O$ as the i-th feature matrices of training images in target class and outlier class, respectively. For a given k-th test image $\mathbf{A}_k$, we obtain its feature matrix denoted by

$$\mathbf{B}_k^{Test} = \begin{bmatrix} \mathbf{B}_{k,1}^{Test} \\ \mathbf{B}_{k,2}^{Test} \\ \vdots \\ \mathbf{B}_{k,m}^{Test} \end{bmatrix}. \tag{10}$$

The occlusion detection is done for each row vector, $\mathbf{B}_{k,j}^{Test}, j = 1, \ldots, m$ that corresponds to image row, independently by the method described above. Fig. 2 shows the examples of the proposed classification results for some row features. Note that although the row-based occlusion detection scheme shows a good result, it cannot cope with vertical occlusions efficiently. For example, If we apply the row-based occlusion detection scheme to the occluded face image in Fig. 3, the entire image is considered

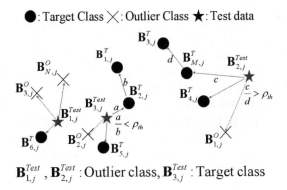

$\mathbf{B}_{1,j}^{Test}, \mathbf{B}_{2,j}^{Test}$: Outlier class, $\mathbf{B}_{3,j}^{Test}$: Target class

Fig. 2. Occlusion detection using a combined k-NN and 1-NN classifier

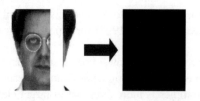

Fig. 3. The problem of occlusion detection by row

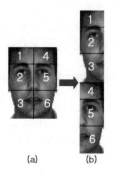

Fig. 4. Image partitioning and transformation

to be occluded since all the rows are identified as occluded. To overcome this horizontal localization problem, we divide a face image into two columns and concatenate them into a single one as shown in Fig. 4. After transforming all images in this way and performing the training with these transformed images, we apply a combined k-NN and 1-NN classifier to each row of the input feature matrix. Alternative method is to partition the column into several blocks as shown in Fig. 4 (b), and investigate the block-based occlusion by analyzing corresponding features of each block.

3.2 Partial Matching

We perform partial matching of faces using the corresponding feature matrices after removing the rows detected as occluded regions. Fig. 5 shows the idea. If feature matrices $\mathbf{B}_1$ and $\mathbf{B}_2$ are matched directly, the matching result may not be reliable due to the effect of the occluded part. While, by using $\mathbf{B}_3$ and $\mathbf{B}_4$ obtained after removing the occluded rows, we can achieve occlusion invariant matching results.

The dissimilarity measure between a target feature matrix $\mathbf{B}_i^T = [\mathbf{B}_{i,1}^T, \cdots, \mathbf{B}_{i,m}^T]^T$ and a test feature matrix $\mathbf{B}_k^{Test} = [\mathbf{B}_{k,1}^{Test}, \cdots, \mathbf{B}_{k,m}^{Test}]^T$, is defined by

$$d(\mathbf{B}_i^T, \mathbf{B}_k^{Test}) = \sum_{j=1}^{m} \omega_j \left\| \mathbf{B}_{i,j}^T - \mathbf{B}_{k,j}^{Test} \right\|_2, \tag{11}$$

where

$$\omega_j = \begin{cases} 0 \text{ if } \mathbf{B}_{k,j}^{Test} \text{ is an occluded row} \\ 1 \text{ otherwise} \end{cases} \tag{12}$$

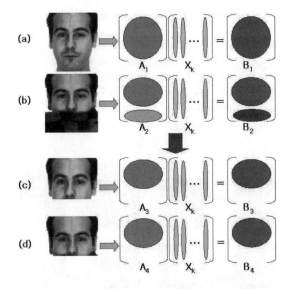

Fig. 5. Partial matching after removing occluded rows

and $||\mathbf{B}_{i,j} - \mathbf{B}_{k,j}||_2$ denotes the Euclidean distance between the two j-th rows of feature matrices $\mathbf{B}_i$ and $\mathbf{B}_k$.

4   Experimental Results

4.1   Experimental Environment

To evaluate the performance of the proposed algorithm, we tested it on the AR face database (AR, 1998). Specifically, we used neutral frontal images and occluded face images wearing sunglasses or scarfs. The performance of the proposed algorithm has been compared to those of the conventional approaches including 1-NN, Eigenface (Turk, 1991), NMF method (Lee, 1999), and modified local NMF (LNMF) (Li, 2001) method. In addition to these methods, it has been also compared to those of the LEM based method (LEM) (Gao, 2002) by Gao *et. al.*, the technique proposed by Martinez (AMM) (Martinez, 2002), and Park *et. al.*'s face-ARG technique (Park, 2005). Similar to our method, these three methods use a single frontal view image per person as a reference model, and the performances on the AR face database were reported in (Gao, 2002), (Martinez, 2002), and (Park, 2005), respectively. For comparison, we have referred their recognition rates. All 135 people (76 men and 59 women) in the AR face database were used. Among them, all 135 normal face images and 70 occluded face images (35 sunglass images and 35 scarf images of 20 men and 15 women) were used for the training of the target and the outlier classes, respectively. The remaining 100 sunglass images and 100 scarf images were used for the probe, and all the normal frontal faces were used for the gallery.

4.2   Occlusion Detection and Partial Matching Results

Fig. 6 and 7 show some results of occlusion detection by the proposed combined k-NN and 1-NN classifier to every row of feature matrix, in which the occluded rows are displayed by black lines. For most test images, occluded regions are detected accurately. However, there are some false alarms as shown in Fig. 7. Fig. 8 shows the results of the block-based occlusion detection with 6 regions, and Fig. 9 represents the results of applying occlusion detection to each individual row of the transformed images in

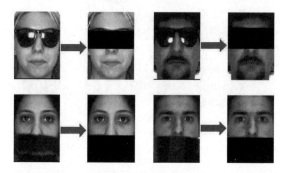

Fig. 6. Results of occlusion detection by row

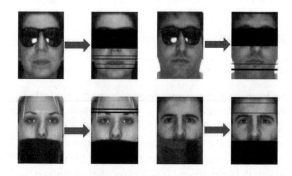

Fig. 7. Some false alarms

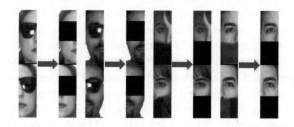

Fig. 8. Results of occlusion detection by block

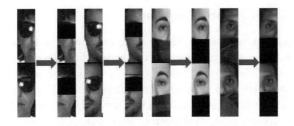

Fig. 9. Result of occlusion detection by row after image transformation

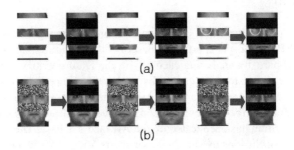

Fig. 10. Results of occlusion detection with virtual occlusions

Table 1. Comparison of the face recognition rates on the AR face database : Proposed method (a) occlusion detection by row, (b) occlusion detection by 6 block regions, and (c) occlusion detection by row after image transformation as shown in Fig. 4 (b)

Detection Method	Sunglasses	Scarfs
Proposed Method (a)	98.00%	99.00%
Proposed Method (b)	96.00%	98.00%
Proposed Method (c)	98.00%	98.00%
1-NN	43.18%	20.45%
PCA	43.18%	20.45%
NMF	25.00%	2.27%
LNMF	43.18%	13.64%
AMM	80.00%	82.00%
LEM	68.18%	63.64%
Face-ARG	73.48%	87.88%

Fig. 4 (b). We observed that the 'row after transformation' method gave the best detection results.

Face recognition test was conducted using the proposed algorithm explained in section 3, with the dissimilarity measure defined in Eq. (11). The recognition results of the proposed algorithm were compared to other algorithms and summarized in Table 1. Form these results, we can conclude that the proposed partial face recognition algorithm outperforms the conventional face recognition techniques.

4.3 Classifier Test to Synthetic Occlusions

Note that the occlusion patterns in AR database are limited to sunglasses and scarfs. Therefore, we have tested the proposed occlusion detection algorithm to other types of occlusions. Fig 10 (a) shows the results for the synthetic white occlusion masks, and Fig 10 (b) represents those for the occlusion masks generated by random noise. These experimental results demonstrate that the new combined k-NN and 1-NN classifier can work satisfactory to other types of occlusion patterns as well.

5 Conclusion

In this paper, we proposed a novel occlusion invariant face recognition algorithm using 2D PCA. In 2D PCA subspace, a face is described by a feature matrix. Therefore, by finding occluded parts by analyzing each row in the feature matrix accurately, we are able to remove severe distortions caused by occlusions. Since the proposed algorithm can detect and exclude unreliable and inconsistent parts by combining k-NN and 1-NN classifier sequentially, it recognizes occluded faces very accurately. The performance of the proposed algorithm has been tested on the AR face database. The results show that for the faces with occlusions by sunglasses or scarfs, the proposed algorithm produces more robust and reliable results over other existing methods.

Acknowledgements

This work has been supported in part by the ITRC (Information Technology Research Center) support program of Korean government and IIRC (Image Information Research Center) by Agency of Defense Development, Korea.

References

Zhao, W.Y., Chellappa, R., Rosenfeld, A., Phillips, P.J.: Face Recognition: A Literature Survey. In: UMD CfAR Technical Report CAR-TR-948 (2000)

Gao, Y., Leung, M.K.H.: Face Recognition Using Line Edge Map. IEEE Trans. Pattern Analysis and Machine Intelligence 24(6), 764–779 (2002)

Park, B.G., Lee, K.M., Lee, S.U.: A Novel Face Recognition Technique Using Face-ARG Matching. IEEE Trans. Pattern Analysis and Machine Intelligence 27(12), 1982–1988 (2005)

Turk, M., Pentland, A.: Eigenfaces for Recognition. Journal of Cognitive Neuroscience 3, 71–86 (1991)

Belhumeur, P.N., Hepanha, J.P., Kriegman, D.J.: Eigenfaces vs. Fisherfaces: Recognition Using Class Specific Linear Projection. IEEE Trans. Pattern Analysis and Machine Intelligence 19(7), 711–720 (1997)

Georghiades, A.S., Belhumeur, P.N., Kriegman, D.J.: From Few to Many: Illumination Cone Models for Face Recognition under Variable Lighting and Pose. IEEE Trans. Pattern Analysis and Machine Intelligence 23(6), 643–660 (2001)

Saito, Y., Kenmochi, Y., Kotani, K.: Estimation of eyeglassless facial images using principal component analysis. In: IEEE International Conference on Image Processing, vol. 4, pp. 192–201. IEEE, Los Alamitos (1999)

Hwang, B.W., Lee, S.W.: Reconstruction of partially damaged face images based on a morphable model. IEEE Trans. Pattern Analysis and Machine Intelligence 25(3), 365–372 (2003)

Leonardis, A., Bischof, H.: Dealing with Occlusions in the Eigenspace Approach. In: Proceedings of IEEE Conference on Computer Vision and Pattern Recognition, IEEE, Los Alamitos (1996)

Black, M., Jepson, A.: Eigentracking: Robust matching and tracking of articulated objects using a view-based representation. International Journal of Computer Vision 26(1), 63–84 (1998)

Yang, J., Zhang, D., Frangi, A.F., Yang, J.Y.: Two-Dimensional PCA: A New Approach to Appearance-Based Face Representation and Recognition. IEEE Trans. Pattern Analysis and Machine Intelligence 26(1) (2004)

Gose, E., Johnsonbaugh, R., Jost S.: The Book. Pattern Recognition and Image Analysis (1996)

Yang, J., Yang, J.Y.: From Image Vector to Matrix: A Straightforward Image Projection Technique-IMPCA vs. PCA. Pattern Recognition 35(9), 1997–1999 (2002)

Ridder, D., Tax, D.M.J., Duin, R.P.W.: An Experimental Comparison of One-Class Classification Methods. In: Proceedings of the Fourth Annual Conference of the Advanced School for Computing and Imaging, Delft (1998)

Martinez, A.M., Benavente, R.: The AR Face Database. In: CVC Technical Report, no.24 (1998)

Lee, D.D., Seung, H.S.: Learning the parts of objects by non-negative matrix factorization. Nature 401, 788–791 (1999)

Li, S.Z., Hou, X.W., Zhang, H.J., Cheng, Q.S.: Learning spatially localized, part-based representation. In: Proceedings of IEEE Conference on Computer Vision and Pattern Recognition, pp. 207–212. IEEE Computer Society Press, Los Alamitos (2001)

Martinez, A.M.: Recognizing Imprecisely Localized, Partially Occluded, and Expression Variant Faces from a Single Sample per Class. IEEE Trans. Pattern Analysis and Machine Intelligence 24(6), 748–763 (2002)

Multidirectional Face Tracking with 3D Face Model and Learning Half-Face Template

Jun'ya Matsuyama and Kuniaki Uehara

Graduate School of Science & Technology, Kobe University
1-1 Rokko-dai, Nada, Kobe 657-8501, Japan
junya@ai.cs.scitec.kobe-u.ac.jp, uehara@kobe-u.ac.jp

Abstract. In this paper, we present an algorithm to detect and track both frontal and side faces in video clips. By means of both learning Haar-like features of human faces and boosting the learning accuracy with InfoBoost algorithm, our algorithm can detect frontal faces in video clips. Furthermore, we map these Haar-like features to a 3D model to create the classifier that can detect both frontal and side faces. Since it is costly to detect and track faces using the 3D model, we project Haar-like features from the 3D model to a 2D space in order to generate various face orientations. By using them, we can detect even side faces in real time by only learning frontal faces.

Keywords: Face Tracking, Face Detection, AdaBoost, InfoBoost, 3D-Model, Half-Face, Cascading, Random Sampling.

1 Introduction

In recent years there has been a great deal of interest in detecting and tracking of human faces in video clips. To recognize people in a video clip, we must locate their faces. For example, to design a robot capable of interacting with humans, it is required that the robot can detect human faces within its sight and recognize the one it is interacting with. In this case, the speed of face detection is very important. However, when face detection is used in a surveillance system, it is very important that the system can detect all faces in the video clips.

Recently, Viola et al. proposed a very fast approach for multiple face detection (Viola and Jones, 2001), which uses AdaBoost algorithm (Freund and Schapire, 1996). This approach generates a fast strong classifier by applying AdaBoost to a weak learner. Then the classifier is applied to sub-images of the target image, and the sub-images classified into a face class are detected as faces in the target image. However, this approach has two problems:

First, AdaBoost has some problems when used for the human face detection. AdaBoost does not consider the reliability of the classification result of each weak learner. Furthermore, AdaBoost is based on a decision-theoretic approach, which does not take into consideration misclassified examples. Therefore, this algorithm cannot distinguish between misclassified faces and misclassified non-faces. We will discuss these problems in Section 3.

J. Braz et al. (Eds.): VISAPP and GRAPP 2006, CCIS 4, pp. 316–329, 2007.

Second, this algorithm can only detect frontal faces, although the number of frontal faces in video clips is less than the number of side faces. Additionally, some previous algorithms have problems in their initialization processes. Gross et al. (Gross et al., 2004) use a mesh structure to represent a human face, and detect and/or track the face with template matching. In the initialization process, all mesh vertices must be marked in every training example manually. Pradeep et al. (Pradeep and Whelan, 2002) represent a face as a triangle, whose vertices correspond to the eyes and the mouth, and track the face with template matching. In the initialization process, they need to manually initialize the parameters of the triangle in the first frame. Ross et al. (Ross et al., 2004) use eigenbasis to track faces and update the eigenbasis to account for the intrinsic (e.g. facial expression and pose) and extrinsic variation (e.g. lighting) of the target face. In the initialization process, they need to decide the initial location of the face in the first frame manually. On the other hand, Zhu et al. (Zhu and Ji, 2004) use a face detection algorithm in the first frame to initialize the face position. Thereby, they do not need a manual initialization process. However, the face detection algorithm can detect only a frontal face.

In this paper, we propose an algorithm, which classifies sub-images to a face class or a non-face class by using classifiers. This algorithm does not require a manual initialization process. We substitute InfoBoost algorithm (Aslam, 2000), which is based on an information-theoretic approach, for AdaBoost algorithm, which is based on a decision-theoretic approach. The reason of this is to solve the first problem and to improve the precision by using the additional information (hypothesis with reliability), which is ignored in AdaBoost. Additionally, our algorithm does not learn the whole human face but half of it and maps these half-face templates to a 3D model. Then the algorithm reproduces the whole-face template from the 3D model with some angle around the vertical axis. As a result, we can detect side faces, which are even rotated around the vertical axis, by using the reproduced whole-face templates.

2 Haar-Like Features

In this paper, Haar-like features are used to classify images into a face class or a non-face class. Some examples of Haar-like features are shown in Figure 1.

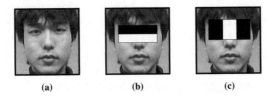

(a)   (b)   (c)

Fig. 1. Feature Example

Basically, the brightness pattern of the eyes distinguishes the face from the background. (a) is an original facial image. (b) measures the difference in brightness between the region of the eyes and the region under them. As shown in (b), the brightness of the eyes is usually darker than the skin under them. (c) measures the difference in brightness

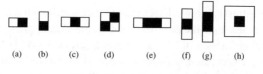

Fig. 2. Feature Prototypes

between the region of the eyes and the region between them. As shown in (c), the eyes are usually darker than the region between them. Thus, an image can be classified as a face class or a non-face class based on the brightness pattern described above. These features are generated from feature prototypes (Figure 2) by scaling these prototypes vertically and horizontally.

We calculate the average brightness B_b and B_w in the black region and the white region of the features respectively, and use their difference ($F = B_b - B_w$) as a feature value. The feature value provides a clue to classify an image into a face class or a non-face class. For example, consider the case where the feature shown in Figure 1 (b) is applied to a human face. Since the eyes are in the black region, B_b will be much lower than B_w. Thus, we can set a threshold for F to determine the class of the image. According to this feature, the image should be classified into a face class, if F is lower than the threshold. Otherwise, it should be classified into a non-face class. Finally, the image is classified taking the predictions of all the features into consideration.

Viola et al. used feature prototypes (a)-(d) shown in Figure 2. We use four additional prototypes (e)-(h). Prototype (e) will measure the difference in brightness between the region of the mouth and its both ends. The black region will match the region of the mouth, and the white regions will match both ends of the mouth. The black region of prototypes (f) and (g) will match the region of the mouth (the eyes), and the white regions will match the top and bottom of the region of the mouth (the eyes). The black region of prototype (h) will match the region of the eye (the nose or the mouth), and the white region will match the region around the eye (the nose or the mouth). Therefore, these feature prototypes will also be effective to classify images into face and non-face classes.

If we add these effective feature prototypes like (e)-(h), the learning time will somewhat increase, while the speed of classification will improve. If we add some compound feature prototypes, the computation time of the classification will decrease. For example, feature prototype (e) can be considered as the prototype which is made by combining the prototype (a) twice. In the regions where the feature prototype (e) can be used, we need to calculate twice the value of the feature generated from prototype (a). But now we need only one calculation for the value of the feature generated from the prototype (e). So the time complexity decreases for these regions, and the detection time can be reduced. In this case, if we need t seconds to detect a face with prototype (a), whereas only $\frac{1}{2}t$ seconds to detect a face with prototype (e).

3   Applying InfoBoost

Classification with Haar-like features is fast, but it is too simple and its precision is not very impressive. Hence, we apply a boosting algorithm to generate a fast strong classifier. AdaBoost is the most popular boosting algorithm.

3.1   AdaBoost

AdaBoost assigns the same weight to all training examples and repeats learning by weak learners while updating the weights of the training examples. If the weak classifier generated by the weak learner classifies a training example correctly, the weight of the example is reduced. If the weak classifier misclassifies a training example, the weight of the example is increased. By this repetition, the weak learner becomes more focused on the example which is difficult to classify. At the end, by combining these weak learners with the voting, AdaBoost generates one strong classifier and calculates the final hypothesis. The voting evaluates results of weak learners by majority decision and decides the final classification result. Nevertheless, we use InfoBoost to increase the precision of the classification because there are two problems in AdaBoost.

Weak learners do not consider the reliability of the classification result for each example. Hence, weak learners which classify the example with high reliability and those which classify the example with low reliability are combined without any consideration of their reliabilities.

For example, assume that the classifier consists of nine weak learners. If four of them classify an example into a face class with 95% accuracy, and five of them classify the same example into a non-face class with 55% accuracy, the example will be classified into a non-face class. If we introduce the reliabilities of these classifications, the example should have been classified into a face class.

Another problem is that AdaBoost is based on a decision-theoretic approach. AdaBoost algorithm only considers two cases, whether the classification is true or false, when the weights are updated. But actually there are the following four cases to be considered:

- A face image classified into a face class.
- A non-face image classified into a face class.
- A face image classified into a non-face class.
- A non-face image classified into a non-face class.

The incidences of these classifications are not always the same. For example, in a certain round of AdaBoost, if the number of misclassified face images and the number of misclassified non-face images are nearly equal, all we are required to do is to decrease the weights of correctly classified examples and to increase the weights of incorrectly classified examples. In contrast, if the number of misclassified non-face images is larger than the number of misclassified face images, the misclassified non-face images will be classified correctly in the next round or later, although the misclassified face images may not be correctly classified. The reason is that AdaBoost does not care about the difference of two misclassification cases. Therefore, we should not depend only on the classification result (true or false) for weight updating, but we must also consider the correct classes (positive or negative). When we update the weight of each example image we must consider these four cases individually.

3.2   InfoBoost

In this paper, we consider the two problems of AdaBoost and use InfoBoost algorithm, which is a modification of AdaBoost. We discuss three points where InfoBoost and AdaBoost differ:

First, InfoBoost repeats the round T times in the learning process. In round t ($t = 1, \cdots, T$), weak hypothesis h_t is shown by $h_t : X \rightarrow \mathbb{R}$. The hypothesis represents not only the classification result but also the reliability of the classification result. In order to make it easy to handle, we restrict the region of hypothesis h_t to $[-1, +1]$. The sign of h_t represents the class of prediction (-1 or $+1$), and the absolute value of h_t represents the magnitude of reliability. For example, if $h_1(x_1) = -0.8$, h_1 classifies the example x_1 into the class -1 with the reliability value 0.8.

Second, the accuracy of negative prediction $\alpha_t[-1]$ and the accuracy of positive prediction $\alpha_t[+1]$ are calculated. These values are calculated using equations (1) and (2).

$$\alpha[-1] = \frac{1}{2} \ln \left(\frac{1 + r[-1]}{1 - r[-1]} \right) \tag{1}$$

$$\alpha[+1] = \frac{1}{2} \ln \left(\frac{1 + r[+1]}{1 - r[+1]} \right) \tag{2}$$

$$r[-1] = \frac{\sum_{i:h(x_i)<0} D_t(i) y_i h_t(x_i)}{\sum_{i:h(x_i)<0} D(i)} \tag{3}$$

$$r[+1] = \frac{\sum_{i:h(x_i)\geq 0} D_t(i) y_i h_t(x_i)}{\sum_{i:h(x_i)\geq 0} D(i)} \tag{4}$$

y_i is the correct class of the example x_i, and $D_t(i)$ is the weight of the example x_i in round t. $\alpha_t[-1]$ and $\alpha_t[+1]$ reflect the magnitude of reliability and the precision of classification for each example. If hypothesis h_t classifies x_i into the class -1, $\alpha_t(h_t(x_i))$ is $\alpha_t[-1]$. If hypothesis h_t classifies x_i into the class $+1$, $\alpha_t(h_t(x_i))$ is $\alpha_t[+1]$.

Third, the weight D_t is updated according to equation (5)

$$D_{t+1}(i) = \frac{D_t(i) \exp(-\alpha_t(h_t(x)) y_i h_t(x_i))}{Z_t} \tag{5}$$

Z_t is a normalization factor. It is chosen in a way that $\sum_i D_{t+1}(i) = 1$. By executing this operation, the weight of the example classified correctly with hypothesis $h_t(x_i)$ is reduced, while the weight of the example classified incorrectly with hypothesis $h_t(x_i)$ is increased.

A total of T weak hypotheses are generated through the iteration process. Then the final hypothesis H is computed as the weighted sum of these weak hypotheses using $\alpha_t(h_t(x_i))$ as the weights. The output of H corresponds to the sign of the value of the weighted sum, i.e. $+1$ for a positive value and -1 for a negative value.

When we apply InfoBoost to weak learners, it is necessary to show how correct the classification results of training examples are. We calculate the feature value for each training example, the difference d of the feature value f, and the threshold t ($d = f - t$). The sign of the difference f represents the classification result. For example, if the absolute value of d is too small, the feature value f will be close to the threshold d. Therefore, the example classified as $+1$ might be classified into -1, so it is not trusty. Conversely, if the absolute value of d is too large, the classification result is trusty. Obtaining the difference between the feature value and the threshold, we can express the classification result and its reliability for each example. Therefore, we use the difference d between the feature value f and the threshold t as the classification result with evaluation of reliability.

Because InfoBoost is based on an information-theoretic approach, it does not only have the benefit of the improvement of the classification's precision, but also it can provide some flexibility to the classifier. For instance, in surveillance systems, we must detect all human faces while it is allowed to mis-detect few non-faces as faces. On the other hand, if a surveillance system of a building cannot detect some faces and those people commit a crime in the building, we cannot place their faces on the wanted list. Thus the surveillance system which cannot detect some human faces is not useful.

Hence, we can adapt the classifier for a surveillance system by adjusting of the weights of examples. InfoBoost divides misclassified examples into false negative predictions and false positive predictions, that is, face examples classified into the non-face class and non-face examples classified into the face class respectively. The weight given to a misclassified face example is different from the weight given to a misclassified non-face example. By increasing the weight of the misclassified face examples, the learning process focuses on the misclassified face examples and the final classifier will be able to detect almost all human faces accurately. As a result, the number of face examples classified into the non-face class can be decreased. Hence, we can adapt the classifier for a surveillance system by adjusting the weight to reduce false negative predictions.

4   3D Model and Learning Half-Face Template

In video clips, the probability of having complete frontal faces is not high. Most of them are side faces. Consequently, we map the classifier learned from facial features to a 3D model (Figure 3(a)(b)). The 3D model consists of three areas (r), (c), (l) (in Figure 3(b)). (r) is the right part of the 3D model, (c) is the center part of the 3D model, and (l) is the left part of the 3D model. These parts of the 3D model are plane faces, and their joint angles are $\frac{\pi}{4}$. By using this 3D template, the classifier will be able to detect not only frontal faces but also side shots of faces.

If we use the 3D model for face detection, time complexity increases and detection speed decreases, because the calculation of the 3D model is time consuming. Therefore, we create a new classifier by rotating the 3D model around the vertical axis and by projecting the 3D model classifier back to a 2D space again (Figure 3(c)(d)). By using these classifiers, we do not need to calculate of the 3D model during the detection process, so the time complexity does not increase much.

If the rotation angle is θ (positive for clockwise rotation), the width w_r of area (r) is modified to $\frac{cos(\theta - \frac{\pi}{4})}{cos\frac{\pi}{4}} w_r$, the width w_c of area (c) is modified to $cos(\theta)w_c$, and the width w_l of area (l) is modified to $\frac{cos(\theta + \frac{\pi}{4})}{cos\frac{\pi}{4}} w_l$. We execute these processes in every 30 degrees of the rotation angle and use these classifiers in parallel to prevent the increase of time complexity.

But, there is a self-occlusion problem. When the 3D model is rotated enough, (r) or (l) of the 3D model is occluded by (c), and some feature rectangles in the 3D model may be hidden and we cannot use these features. For example, if the 3D model in Figure 3 is rotated in clockwise direction, the part of the feature at the right eye in (r) will be hidden

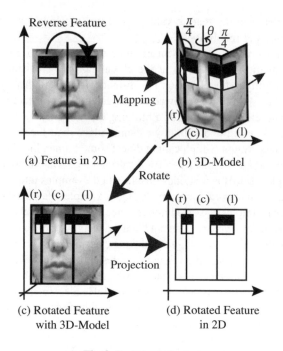

(a) Feature in 2D   (b) 3D-Model

(c) Rotated Feature
with 3D-Model

(d) Rotated Feature
in 2D

Fig. 3. Feature Projection

and we cannot use this feature. Hence, we do not use whole faces but use half-faces as learning examples.

Furthermore, because human faces are symmetric, we express the whole face by combining reversed facial features with the original ones (Figure 3(a)). Therefore, even if the 3D model is rotated, we can use all features of either the right half or the left half of the face.

Additionally, because we only learn half-faces, we do not have a problem with different illumination states between the left side and the right side of a face. We use the right side and the reversed left side of the whole face example as the half-face example, thus the half-face classifier is robust to the difference between the left side and the right side of the face.

The classifier generated from the boosting algorithm is a set of weak learners using Haar-like features. Each weak learner consists of the following elements: coordinates of the reference points, width and height of the white and black rectangles of Haar-like feature, and the threshold of Haar-like feature. In Figure 4, P_w is the reference point of the white rectangle of Haar-like feature, and P_b is the reference point of the black rectangle of Haar-like feature. The coordinates of these rectangles are shown as X_w, X_b, Y_w, Y_b, and widths and heights of these rectangles are shown as W_w, W_b, H_w, H_b respectively.

Therefore, the features are easily mapped to the 3D model shown in Figure 3(b). Then, we confine the 3D model to only rotate around the vertical axis, as a result feature rectangles are scaled only in horizontal axis (see Figure 3(a) and (d)). Therefore, the weak learner generated by projecting the features from the 3D model to a 2D space

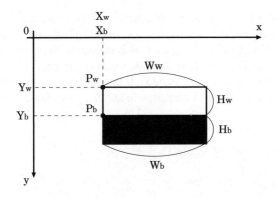

Fig. 4. Parameter of Haar-like Feature Rectangle

can be transformed by moving, expanding and/or shrinking the feature rectangles horizontally.

5   Extension of Cascading

Cascading is the algorithm to reduce the time complexity of classification. In the learning process, the following two conditions based on the true positive rate TP and the false positive rate FP should be satisfied:

$$TP > minTP \qquad (6)$$
$$FP < maxFP \qquad (7)$$

where

$$TP = \frac{\text{number of correctly classified faces}}{\text{total number of faces}} \qquad (8)$$

$$FP = \frac{\text{number of misclassified non-faces}}{\text{total number of non-faces}} \qquad (9)$$

The parameters $minTP$ and $maxFP$ are used to terminate the learning. In other words, the learning continues until the above conditions are satisfied. Thus, they should be appropriately determined considering the tradeoff between the number of false positive predictions and the efficiency of the learning process. We experimentally set the values of $minTP$ and $maxFP$ to 0.999 and 0.4 respectively.

We extend the boosting and the cascading process in the following three points to reduce the time complexity of face detection and learning time.

– The configuration of the cascading.
– The termination condition of the learning process.
– The number of examples used in the boosting process.

First, when we use half-face templates, we must evaluate them separately and aggregate the results of this evaluation. As shown in Figure 5, the classifier consists of two cascades. In this case, both of the calculations of these cascades are executed every time. However, when the target example is rejected in an early stage in one of these cascades, the calculation of another cascade makes no sense. Therefore we combine these cascades as shown in Figure 6 to reduce the unnecessary process. By using this new cascade, the unnecessary process is avoided. If the target example is rejected in an early stage in one of the cascades, the calculation in another cascade is stopped immediately.

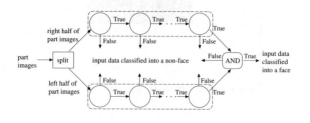

Fig. 5. Two Classifier Cascades

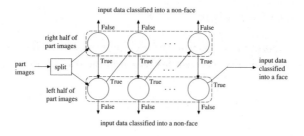

Fig. 6. Combining Two Classifier Cascades

Second, when we use half-faces as learning examples, characteristic features of a half-face are much fewer than those of a whole face. If we use whole faces as learning examples, we can use all features learned from the whole face images. However we cannot use some of these features (for example, the feature in Fig 1(b), (c)), because we use half-faces as learning examples. Thereby, we will use some new features that can be applied to half-faces to substitute for the features that we cannot use here. These new features are more delicate, hence their number is larger than that of the features that can only be applied to the whole faces. As a tradeoff, the speed of face detection will be decreased, because a simple feature based on the whole face is replaced by several small features based on the half-face. Accordingly, in the learning process, if the precision of the classification is enough to detect faces, we finish the learning process. As the learning process makes progress, the face detection rate will hit a peak. Simultaneously, the number of features which are necessary to classify both positive and negative examples will become larger. For this reason, we stop the process when both the precision and the recall are larger than 0.95.

Third, in the learning process, we must use many example images to detect almost all faces. However, when we use many example images, the time complexity of the learning process is very huge. Therefore, we use a subset of all examples to generate a classifier. These examples are selected by random sampling.

Random sampling is a sampling algorithm which picks out some examples from all examples randomly without overlapping. Random sampling is used where we cannot evaluate all examples (for example, marketing). The probability of each example to be picked out is the same. Therefore, the selected examples are miniature versions of all examples, and the learning result with selected examples will be similar to that with all examples.

We must decide the total number of selected examples. We decide the number based on "Chernoff bound" (Chernoff, 1952). The number of selected examples n are defined by inequality (10).

$$n > \frac{1}{2\epsilon^2} \ln \left(\frac{2}{\delta} \right) \tag{10}$$

According to "Chernoff bound", if the above inequality is satisfied for any ϵ $(0 < \epsilon < 1)$ and any δ $(0 < \delta < 1)$, the number of example n is enough for classification. We use this inequality as $\epsilon = 0.05$, $\delta = 0.01$, and get the minimum $n = 1,060$. Thus we select 530 positive examples and 530 negative examples in each stage to efficiently generate weak classifiers.

6 Experiments

We performed five experiments. We use a window to extract sub-images from the original image. The minimum size of the window is 38x38 pixels, the translation factor is $(0.5 \times window\ size)$ and the scale factor is 1.2.

First, we compare the precision of the classifier generated by InfoBoost with that of AdaBoost. We use Yale Face Database B (Georghiades et al., 2001) as positive examples. We use half of them as a training set, and the rest as a test set. We prepare negative example images in the learning process by ourselves. We generate additional negative examples by clipping and scaling these original ones. The total number of negative examples is 7,933,744, and we use half of these examples as training examples, and the rest as a test set.

The result of our experiment is shown in Figure 7. The horizontal axis shows the false positive rate and the vertical axis shows the true positive rate. The horizontal axis is a logarithmic axis to show the difference of the graph more clearly.

This graph shows that the precision of InfoBoost is higher than that of AdaBoost. The true positive rate of AdaBoost sharply degrades as the false positive rate decreases. InfoBoost can focus on both misclassified face and non-face examples. Thus, InfoBoost can reduce the false positive rate without the degradation of the true positive rate. In contrast, AdaBoost cannot focus on both of them because it does not divide misclassified examples into face examples and non-face examples. Therefore, AdaBoost cannot reduce the false positive rate without the degradation of the true positive rate.

Second, we perform the experiment of face tracking with the 3D model, and examine the accuracy of the classifier for each angle ($-60, -30, 0, 30, 60$ degrees). We use Yale Face Database B as a training set. We use Head Pose Image Database of Pointing

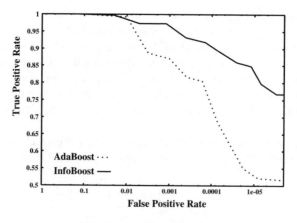

Fig. 7. Precision of Classifier

'04 (N. Gourier, 2004) as a test set. This data set contains multidirectional face images (vertical angle=$\{-90, -60, -30, -15, 0, +15, +30, +60, +90\}$, and horizontal angle=$\{-90, -75, -60, -45, -30, -15, 0, +15, +30, +45, +60, +75, +90\}$). We use a part of these examples, whose vertical angles are 0, and horizontal angles are $\{-75, -60, -45, -30, -15, 0, +15, +30, +45, +60, +75\}$. There are 30 example images for each degree, basically the maximum number of detected faces is 30. Besides, the number of evaluated sub-images is about 4,800,000. Thus the maximum number of detected negative examples is about 4,800,000.

We show two figures indicating the accuracy of the classification in Figure 8 and Figure 9. We represent the classifier aiming at detecting faces rotated with θ degrees as Classifier[θ], and examples rotated with θ degrees as Examples[θ]. Most classifiers can detect faces rotated with an angle close to that of the classifier, and there are not a lot of numbers of mis-detected non-faces. For example, Classifier[0] classifies Example[0] correctly with the high precision. However, there are two exceptions.

One of them is that Classifier[-30] and Classifier[$+30$] have the highest detection rate on Examples[-15] and Examples[$+15$]. The reason for the angle mismatch is as follows: The structure of the 3D face model is too simple to represent human faces correctly. Additionally, the test examples are taken by only one camera, and faces are turned toward a sign on the wall that indicates the direction. When the examples were being taken, some people only focused their eyes on the sign instead of rotating their heads, thus their face directions were not turned toward the sign correctly.

The other exception is that Classifier[-60] and Classifier[$+60$] have the highest detection rate on Examples[0]. In this case, we consider the reason is the self-occlusion of the 3D model. If the angle is -60 or 60 degrees, the self-occlusion of the 3D model emerges and we cannot use left or right half-face detectors respectively. Accordingly, the Classifier[-60] and the Classifier[$+60$] detect half of the whole face, thus the number of detected faces in Examples[0] is increased.

Third, we compare the detection speed between the classifier using the new cascading structure (Figure 5) and the classifier using the old one (Figure 6) by using all the examples of the second experiment. If we use the new cascading structure, we can

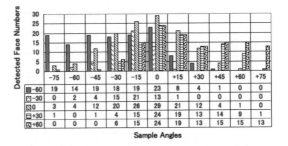

	-75	-60	-45	-30	-15	0	+15	+30	+45	+60	+75
-60	19	14	19	18	19	23	8	4	1	0	0
-30	0	2	4	15	21	13	1	0	0	0	0
0	3	4	12	20	26	29	21	12	4	1	0
+30	1	0	1	4	15	24	19	13	14	9	1
+60	0	0	0	6	15	24	19	13	15	15	13

Sample Angles

Fig. 8. Number of Detected Faces for Each Direction

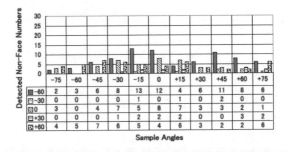

	-75	-60	-45	-30	-15	0	+15	+30	+45	+60	+75
-60	2	3	6	8	13	12	4	6	11	8	6
-30	0	0	0	0	1	0	1	0	2	0	0
0	3	0	4	7	5	8	7	3	3	2	1
+30	0	0	0	1	2	2	2	0	0	3	2
+60	4	5	7	6	5	4	6	3	2	2	6

Sample Angles

Fig. 9. Number of Detected Non-Faces for Each Direction

detect faces in an image whose size is 320x240 pixels, in about 0.036 seconds on 3.2GHz Pentium 4. If we do not use the new cascading structure, the calculation time is about 0.043 seconds. Hence, our new structure of cascading is effective for the reduction of time complexity.

Fourth, we execute the learning process with random sampling, and evaluate it. We extract training sets from the same data set, which is used as the training set in the second experiment. The learning time with random sampling is about 2.5 hours, and that without random sampling is about 2 days. Additionally, the result of face detection with random sampling is shown in Table 1. The numbers of detected faces and non-faces for each direction are decreased compared with the detection result without random sampling. Accordingly, precision is reduced and recall is improved. In conclusion, random sampling reduces the time complexity of learning without reducing the accuracy of the face detector.

Fifth, we reduce the weight of misclassified face examples in the learning process. The way we extract a training set is the same as that in the fourth experiment. After updating the weights of the examples, we double the weights of misclassified face examples. The result of face detection is shown in Table 2. From the results of Classifier[−30], Classifier[0] and Classifier[+30], we can see that the number of detected faces stays the same and the number of detected non-faces is decreased. The reason of this is that we use parameters $maxFP$ and $minTP$ to repeat and finish the learning process. These parameters are stronger than the modification of weights. Hence, the modification of weights cannot increase the precision of face detector. However, it can reduce its time

Table 1. Number of Detected Faces/Non-Faces for Each Direction With Random Sampling

	-60	-30	0	+30	+60
-75	23 / 10	0 / 0	1 / 0	0 / 0	0 / 14
-60	17 / 6	0 / 0	2 / 0	0 / 0	0 / 9
-45	11 / 9	1 / 0	2 / 0	0 / 0	0 / 6
-30	9 / 10	7 / 0	12 / 1	0 / 0	1 / 3
-15	8 / 11	14 / 0	20 / 0	3 / 0	5 / 1
0	6 / 5	13 / 0	25 / 0	17 / 0	11 / 3
+15	3 / 2	2 / 0	14 / 1	17 / 1	15 / 1
+30	1 / 2	1 / 0	5 / 0	7 / 0	5 / 3
+45	0 / 10	0 / 0	0 / 1	5 / 0	6 / 2
+60	0 / 10	0 / 0	0 / 1	2 / 0	12 / 4
+75	0 / 7	0 / 0	0 / 0	0 / 0	11 / 8

Table 2. Number of Detected Faces/Non-Faces for Each Direction With Random Sampling and biased InfoBoost

	-60	-30	0	+30	+60
-75	26 / 1	0 / 0	0 / 0	0 / 0	0 / 15
-60	22 / 2	0 / 0	0 / 0	0 / 0	0 / 10
-45	18 / 3	1 / 0	0 / 0	0 / 0	0 / 11
-30	13 / 8	1 / 0	4 / 0	0 / 0	9 / 2
-15	10 / 10	2 / 0	12 / 0	0 / 0	9 / 2
0	7 / 8	0 / 0	20 / 0	10 / 0	17 / 2
+15	3 / 6	1 / 0	9 / 0	8 / 0	14 / 9
+30	2 / 10	0 / 0	1 / 0	2 / 0	11 / 5
+45	0 / 10	0 / 0	0 / 0	0 / 0	12 / 8
+60	0 / 14	0 / 0	0 / 0	1 / 0	17 / 2
+75	0 / 11	0 / 0	0 / 0	0 / 0	18 / 5

complexity, because the learning process focuses more on the misclassified faces and converges faster. In this case, we can detect faces in an image whose size is 320 by 240 pixels, in about 0.023 seconds on 3.2GHz Pentium 4, which is faster than the detection without modifying the weights.

7   Conclusions and Future Work

In this paper, we tried to improve the precision of a classifier by using InfoBoost algorithm and tried to detect not only frontal faces but also side faces by using the 3D model and half-face templates. Additionally we extended the classifier cascade, and reduced the time complexity of learning and face detection.

However, we cannot detect faces rotated around the horizontal axis, or the axis vertical to the image. If we rotate the 3D model around these axes and project the features from the 3D model to a 2D space, these Haar-like feature rectangles are deformed. In our algorithm, we can only calculate upright rectangles. Thus, we must develop a fast algorithm to calculate these feature values.

Furthermore, with the extensions proposed in this paper, the time complexity of face detection is increased. We must reduce the time complexity by reducing the images evaluated with the face detector or by using some other method. In the process of extracting sub-images from the target image, if we use skin colors to detect face candidate regions, the number of evaluated sub-images can be reduced. Therefore, the precision of the classifier will be improved and time complexity will be reduced.

Likewise, we must perform additional experiments with different training and test examples. Since we performed the experiments depending on only two databases, we should verify that our method does not depend on data sets by using a wide variety of data sets.

References

Aslam, J.A.: Improving Algorithms for Boosting. In: Proc. of 13th Annual Conference on Computational Learning Theory (COLT 2000), pp. 200–207 (2000)

Chernoff, H.: A Measure of Asymptotic Efficiency for Tests of a Hypothesis Based on the Sum of Observation. Ann. Math. Stat. 23, 493–509 (1952)

Freund, Y., Schapire, R.E.: Experiments with a New Boosting Algorithm. In: Proc. of 13th International Conference on Machine Learning (ICML'96), pp. 148–156 (1996)

Georghiades, A., Belhumeur, P., Kriegman, D.: From Few to Many: Illumination Cone Models for Face Recognition under Variable Lighting and Pose. IEEE Trans. Pattern Anal. Mach. Intelligence 23(6), 643–660 (2001)

Gross, R., Matthews, I., Baker, S.: Constructing and fitting Active Appearance Models with occlusion. In: Proc. of the IEEE Workshop on Face Processing in Video (FPIV'04), IEEE Computer Society Press, Los Alamitos (2004)

Gourier, N., Hall, D.J.L.C.: Estimating Face Orientation from Robust Detection of Salient Facial Features. In: Proc. of Pointing 2004, International Workshop on Visual Observation of Deictic Gestures (2004)

Pradeep, P.P., Whelan, P.F.: Tracking of facial features using deformable triangles. In: Proc. of the SPIE - Opto-Ireland 2002: Optical Metrology, Imaging, and Machine Vision, vol. 4877, pp. 138–143 (2002)

Ross, D.A., Lim, J., Yang, M.-H.: Adaptive Probabilistic Visual Tracking with Incremental Subspace Update. In: Pajdla, T., Matas, J(G.) (eds.) ECCV 2004. LNCS, vol. 3021, pp. 470–482. Springer, Heidelberg (2004)

Viola, P., Jones, M.: Rapid Object Detection using a Boosted Cascade of Simple Features. In: Proc. of IEEE Conf. on Computer Vision and Pattern Recognition, pp. 511–518. IEEE Computer Society Press, Los Alamitos (2001)

Zhu, Z., Ji, Q.: Real Time 3D Face Pose Tracking From an Uncalibrated Camera. In: Proc. of the IEEE Workshop on Face Processing in Video (FPIV'04), IEEE Computer Society Press, Los Alamitos (2004)

Representing Directions for Hough Transforms

Fabian Wenzel and Rolf-Rainer Grigat

Hamburg University of Technology
Harburger Schloßstraße 20, Hamburg, Germany
wenzel@tu-harburg.de

Abstract. Many algorithms in computer vision operate with directions, i. e. with representations of 3D-points by ignoring their distance to the origin. Even though minimal parametrizations of directions may contain singularities, they can enhance convergence in optimization algorithms and are required e. g. for accumulator spaces in Hough transforms. There are numerous possibilities for parameterizing directions. However, many do not account for numerical stability when dealing with noisy data. This paper gives an overview of different parametrizations and shows their sensitivity with respect to noise. In addition to standard approaches in the field of computer vision, representations originating from the field of cartography are introduced. Experiments demonstrate their superior performance in computer vision applications in the presence of noise as they are suitable for Gaussian filtering.

Keywords: Parametrization, vanishing points, direction, unit sphere, Hough transform.

1 Introduction

Many algorithms in computer vision operate with minimal parameterizations of directions. Some of their applications can be found in the area of stereo or multiview geometry, treating directions literally when estimating rigid body or camera motions. However, the problem of representing directions is far more general. In a projective context, it is equivalent to representing the projective 2-plane with two components. A homogeneous coordinate $\mathbf{x} \in \mathbb{P}^2$ is equivalent to a globally scaled version $\lambda\mathbf{x}$. Hence, when fixing the scale such that $\|\mathbf{x}\| = 1$, the representation problem also becomes identical to parameterizing unit vectors or, in other terms, the surface of the unit sphere S^2.

Minimal parameterizations of homogeneous coordinates are used in optimization algorithms in order to avoid *gauge*, i. e. changes in the set of optimized parameters that have no effect on the value of the cost function. It has been mentioned that gauge freedoms introduce ambiguous optima and may lead to slower convergence (Morris, 2001).

Hough transforms are another example for methods that require minimal parameterizations, e. g. when locating vanishing points in an image. A vanishing point is the intersection of projected lines that are parallel in 3D space. In this context, the surface of the unit sphere S^2 acts as an accumulator space and is also called *Gaussian sphere* (Barnard, 1983). This way, finite or infinite vanishing points can be estimated.

Figure 1 shows an illustration of the vanishing point location problem. In this example, two projected lines appear parallel in an image. Thus, the vanishing point is

J. Braz et al. (Eds.): VISAPP and GRAPP 2006, CCIS 4, pp. 330–339, 2007.
© Springer-Verlag Berlin Heidelberg 2007

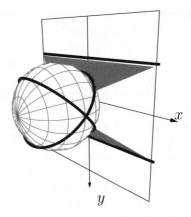

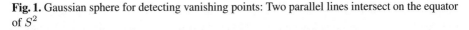

Fig. 1. Gaussian sphere for detecting vanishing points: Two parallel lines intersect on the equator of S^2

located at infinity so neither can it be found in the illustrated figure nor in any larger Euclidean image. However, the two lines may be mapped onto great circles on the Gaussian sphere. It can be seen that their intersection can also be found on S^2. In particular, vanishing points at infinity can be found on its equator if S^2 is oriented such that the polar and the optical axis coincide. The described orientation of S^2 will be assumed for the rest of this work.

Numerous parameterizations of points on S^2 exist with spherical coordinates (θ, φ) being the most obvious one. Here, θ represents the *co-latitude*, i.e. the angular deviance from the polar axis, whereas φ is called *longitude*. It is well-known, however, that parameterizations may either not be complete or contain singularities which makes them unsuitable for specific situations. As an example, spherical coordinates (θ, φ) are singular at the poles as φ is not unique for $\theta = \{0, 180°\}$.

This paper is organized as follows: After laying out some mathematical basics, an overview and comparison of existing parameterizations of S^2 is presented. Subsequent experiments show that parameterizations originating from the field of cartography are better suited for setting up accumulator spaces for Hough maps in case of noisy input data, not only because of their numeric properties but also as they may be used for Gaussian filtering.

2   Global and Local Parameterizations

This section shows that it is impossible to have a global one-to-one parametrization of S^2. The following details are closely based on (Stuelpnagel, 1964), in which a similar explanation for parameterizing the special orthogonal group $SO(3)$ can be found.

The unit sphere S^2 topologically is a 2-dimensional compact manifold. A global 1-1 parametrization hence necessarily requires a homomorphism h from S^2 to the Euclidean space E^2. A property of homomorphisms is that $h(U_i)$ for an open neighborhood U_i of a point i is open in E^2. Hence, $h(I)$, being the union of all $h(U_i)$ for $i \in S^2$, would still be open. On the other hand, $h(I)$ describes a continuous map of a compact space, thus is still compact. As no Euclidean space contains an open compact subset, such a homomorphism cannot be found.

Parameterizations also fail at *singular points* on S^2 that have infinitely many representations. However, a set of parameter patches, also called an *atlas*, circumvents this limitation. An atlas may contain infinitely many parameter patches. In this case, for a point of interest i, a unique parameter patch h_i can be chosen. This technique is also referred to as a *local parametrization* (Hartley and Zissermann, 2003). A particular h_i usually is constructed such that $h(U_i)$, the neighborhood of i, does not contain singular points and has advantageous numerical characteristics. It is interesting to note that local parameterizations still may suffer from singularity-like situations. As an example, (Hartley and Zissermann, 2003) suggests to use Householder transformations mapping a point of interest i to the origin o and choose a parametrization that "behaves well" in its vicinity. However, a Householder transformation does not exist if i is identical to the origin and is numerically unstable if i is close to it (Golub and Loan, 1996). Furthermore, some applications like the Hough transform explicitly require global parameterizations. Therefore, local parameterizations cannot be used in every situation.

A second possibility to circumvent singularities is to use an atlas with a few parameter patches only (Faugeras, 1993). Such an atlas is suitable for a projective setting as representing the complete unit sphere S^2 is not necessary. As two antipodal points $\mathbf{x}$ and its negative version $-\mathbf{x}$ on S^2 are equivalent, it is sufficient to focus on a *hemisphere*. Parameter patches that cover a complete hemisphere exist and are given in this paper.

3 Representations of Directions

Many global parameterizations of directions are mentioned in the literature (Snyder, 1987). Some of them can be found in the field of cartography and have not been used for Hough transforms before. This section gives an overview and shows characteristics (see also table 1). Besides spherical coordinates, we concentrate on different *azimuthal projections* on a hemisphere. Other types are not considered in this work as they have disadvantegous properties such as singular points, computational complexity or the lack of symmetry.

- Spherical coordinates (SPHERICAL):

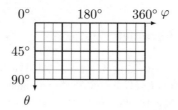

Even though spherical coordinates yield a singular point at each of the two poles of S^2, they are used in many computer vision algorithms (Medioni and Kang, 2004). Their advantage is the simple geometric interpretation.

Table 1. Overview of different global parameterizations

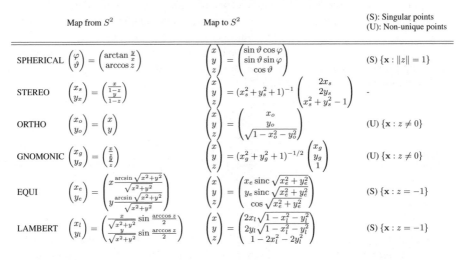

	Map from S^2	Map to S^2	(S): Singular points\n(U): Non-unique points
SPHERICAL	$\begin{pmatrix}\varphi\\\vartheta\end{pmatrix} = \begin{pmatrix}\arctan\frac{y}{x}\\\arccos z\end{pmatrix}$	$\begin{pmatrix}x\\y\\z\end{pmatrix} = \begin{pmatrix}\sin\vartheta\cos\varphi\\\sin\vartheta\sin\varphi\\\cos\vartheta\end{pmatrix}$	(S) $\{\mathbf{x} : \|z\| = 1\}$
STEREO	$\begin{pmatrix}x_s\\y_s\end{pmatrix} = \begin{pmatrix}\frac{x}{1-z}\\\frac{y}{1-z}\end{pmatrix}$	$\begin{pmatrix}x\\y\\z\end{pmatrix} = (x_s^2+y_s^2+1)^{-1}\begin{pmatrix}2x_s\\2y_s\\x_s^2+y_s^2-1\end{pmatrix}$	-
ORTHO	$\begin{pmatrix}x_o\\y_o\end{pmatrix} = \begin{pmatrix}x\\y\end{pmatrix}$	$\begin{pmatrix}x\\y\\z\end{pmatrix} = \begin{pmatrix}x_o\\y_o\\\sqrt{1-x_o^2-y_o^2}\end{pmatrix}$	(U) $\{\mathbf{x} : z \neq 0\}$
GNOMONIC	$\begin{pmatrix}x_g\\y_g\end{pmatrix} = \begin{pmatrix}\frac{x}{z}\\\frac{y}{z}\end{pmatrix}$	$\begin{pmatrix}x\\y\\z\end{pmatrix} = (x_g^2+y_g^2+1)^{-1/2}\begin{pmatrix}x_g\\y_g\\1\end{pmatrix}$	(U) $\{\mathbf{x} : z \neq 0\}$
EQUI	$\begin{pmatrix}x_e\\y_e\end{pmatrix} = \begin{pmatrix}x\frac{\arcsin\sqrt{x^2+y^2}}{\sqrt{x^2+y^2}}\\y\frac{\arcsin\sqrt{x^2+y^2}}{\sqrt{x^2+y^2}}\end{pmatrix}$	$\begin{pmatrix}x\\y\\z\end{pmatrix} = \begin{pmatrix}x_e\operatorname{sinc}\sqrt{x_e^2+y_e^2}\\y_e\operatorname{sinc}\sqrt{x_e^2+y_e^2}\\\cos\sqrt{x_e^2+y_e^2}\end{pmatrix}$	(S) $\{\mathbf{x} : z = -1\}$
LAMBERT	$\begin{pmatrix}x_l\\y_l\end{pmatrix} = \begin{pmatrix}\frac{x}{\sqrt{x^2+y^2}}\sin\frac{\arccos z}{2}\\\frac{y}{\sqrt{x^2+y^2}}\sin\frac{\arccos z}{2}\end{pmatrix}$	$\begin{pmatrix}x\\y\\z\end{pmatrix} = \begin{pmatrix}2x_l\sqrt{1-x_l^2-y_l^2}\\2y_l\sqrt{1-x_l^2-y_l^2}\\1-2x_l^2-2y_l^2\end{pmatrix}$	(S) $\{\mathbf{x} : z = -1\}$

- Stereographic projection (STEREO):

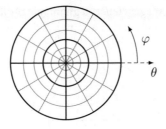

A standard approach in topology for finding a parametrization of S^2 is stereographic projection. Here, the center of projection is located at the north pole n, the Euclidean plane E^2 as the projection target is parallel to the equator. Corresponding points on E^2 and S^2 can be found on the same ray through n. It is obvious that n itself cannot be mapped onto E^2. For computational purposes, a stereographic projection has the advantage of being a *rational* parametrization of directions in $\mathbb{R}^3$. Hence, it does not involve trigonometric functions.

- Orthographic projection (ORTHO):

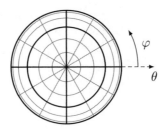

By omitting the z-coordinate of a vector in $\mathbb{R}^3$, the orthographic projection of a point can be achieved. This parametrization does not contain singularities, but an atlas is needed for representing the northern and southern hemisphere of S^2 uniquely. Its advantage is its computational simplicity given points in $\mathbb{R}^3$. It can be seen, however, that azimuthal resolution decreases near the equator. This drawback is important in section 4 when setting up Hough maps.

- Gnomonic projection (GNOMONIC):

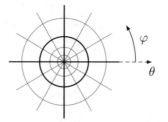

A gnomonic projection in cartography corresponds to the computation of a Euclidean representation given a homogeneous vector $\mathbf{x} \in \mathbb{P}^2$. Even though it is rational for points in $\mathbb{R}^3$, it is not unique for antipodal points and cannot find a Euclidean representation of the equator. Moreover, as the gnomonic projection inverts the process of homogenization of point coordinates, computations could directly be done on the original image. Hence, a gnomonic projection is suitable for Hough maps only if points of interest are in a camera's field of view.

- Azimuthal equidistant projection (EQUI):

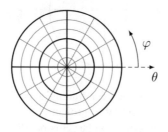

An azimuthal equidistant projection yields a 2D polar mapping of spherical coordinates. It preserves lengths of geodesics through the poles so that Euclidean distances on the map may be used as error terms.

- Azimuthal Lambertian projection (LAMBERT):

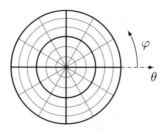

The last mapping considered in this paper is azimuthal Lambertian projection. It is area preserving, hence covariance ellipses on S^2 occupy the same area on the map. However, distances are not preserved.

4 Experimental Results

Vanishing point detection via intersecting lines on a Hough map served as an application for evaluating different parameterizations. We analyzed STEREO, ORTHO, EQUI and LAMBERT. In section 3 the two remaining mappings described in this paper have already been classified not to be suitable for Hough maps: SPHERICAL yields singular points at the poles whereas GNOMONIC cannot represent a hemisphere completely. As lines in an original image are mapped onto curves on the Hough map, a polar-recursive algorithm has been used for accessing corresponding accumulator cells.

In all following configurations, the position and orientation of intersecting lines has been linearly transformed prior to Hough transformation such that the width and height of an input image does not exceed a horizontal and vertical field of view of 90°. As a

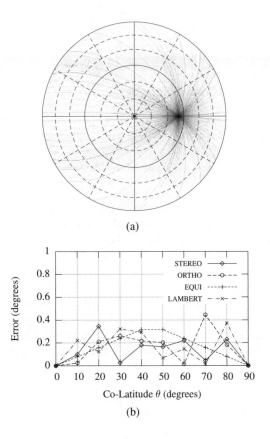

(a)

(b)

Fig. 2. (a) LAMBERT map for $\theta = 40°$, (b) Residual errors due to discretization

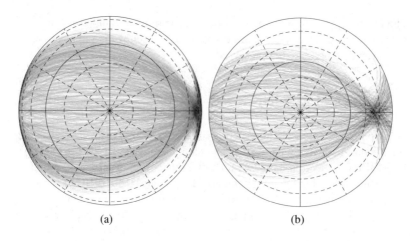

Fig. 3. (a) ORTHO map for $\sigma = 6°$, (b) LAMBERT map for $\sigma = 6°$

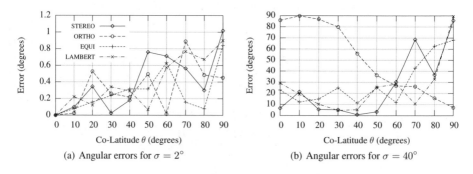

Fig. 4. Effects of different noise levels

result, the origin of the linearly transformed coordinate system coincides with the center of an image. Hence, Hough maps conform to the setup illustrated in figure 1.

A first experiment used synthetic data as input. An equirectangular point grid has been set up with line information at each position. Their individual orientations have been chosen such that all lines intersect at a single location on the x-axis. We examined 10 vanishing points with co-latitudes $\theta = 0°$ to $\theta = 90°$. Due to symmetry, analysis has been reduced to a single longitude $\varphi = 0°$. An example Hough map and the residual angular error between vanishing point estimates and their true positions can be seen in figure 2. In this case errors are only caused by spatial discretization of the parameter space, i.e. by the finite resolution of a Hough map. For the used size of 255×255 pixels, errors are below $0.5°$ and could be decreased further by increasing the map's resolution.

In order to evaluate robustness, we added gaussian noise with a preset standard deviation σ to all orientation angles. Figure 4 shows results for two noise levels which demonstrate the effects of the low resolution in θ for ORTHO: Starting from $\sigma = 4°$, vanishing point estimates incorrectly tend to be attracted by the equator. This problem

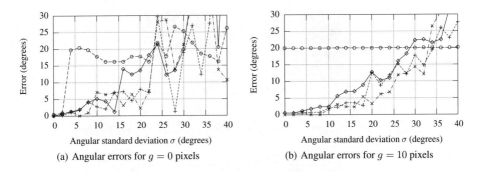

(a) Angular errors for $g = 0$ pixels

(b) Angular errors for $g = 10$ pixels

Fig. 5. Effects of different Gaussian filter sizes for $\theta = 70°$

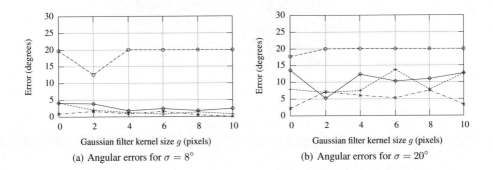

(a) Angular errors for $\sigma = 8°$

(b) Angular errors for $\sigma = 20°$

Fig. 6. Effects of different noise levels for $\theta = 70°$ if Gaussian smoothing is used

is caused by the spatial discretization of ORTHO and can be identified in figure 3(a). Other parametrizations, e. g. LAMBERT, see figure 3(b), do not suffer from this phenomenon.

The quality of vanishing point estimates is also affected by the finite number of intersecting lines. Therefore, in another experiment, we additionally applied a Gaussian filter with kernel size g to the Hough map. This approach is contrary to others in which special techniques like hierarchical (Quan and Mohr, 1989) or irregular Hough maps are used (Lutton, 1994). Results are shown in figures 5 and 6. It can be seen that the phenomenon of attractive equator cells in ORTHO could not be resolved by Gaussian smoothing. When using other parametrizations, maximum residual errors can approximately be halved at a moderate noise level (figure 6(a)). Best results could be achieved with EQUI and LAMBERT.

A final, qualitative experiment has been done using real input data without ground truth. We used a complex-valued filter for detecting edges (Perona, 1992), (D. Fleet and Jepson, 2000) and used the phase of the filter responses as orientation for lines on the Hough maps. Filter kernels are shown in figure 7.

Figure 8 shows a screenshot as well as a close-up of of the left vanishing point in the EQUI map. The marked locations denote point estimates before and after applying a Gaussian filter. Also in this case, estimates can be enhanced by Gaussian smoothing.

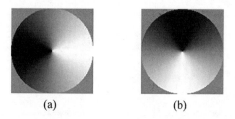

(a)   (b)

Fig. 7. (a) Real and (b) imaginary part of a complex filter kernel for edges

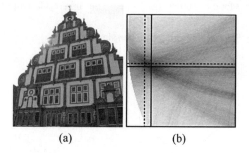

(a)   (b)

Fig. 8. (a) Input image, (b) Close-up of Hough map. Dashed mark: Estimate before Gaussian smoothing. Solid mark: Estimate after Gaussian smoothing.

5 Summary and Conclusion

We presented parameterizations of the Gaussian sphere S^2 for detecting directions using Hough transforms. We gave an overview of both known and novel projections for the field of computer vision. Spherical coordinates as well as gnomonic projection have been identified not to be suitable for generating Hough maps. Experiments show that azimuthal equidistant and Lambertian projection yield superior results compared to stereographic and orthographic projection. Finally, we applied a Gaussian filter to Hough maps that accounts for noise.

References

Barnard, S.T.: Interpreting perspective images. Artificial Intell. 21, 435–462 (1983)

Fleet, D., Black, M.Y., Jepson, A.: Design and use of linear models for image motion analysis. International Journal of Computer Vision 36(3), 171–193 (2000)

Faugeras, O.: Three-Dimensional Computer Vision - A Geometric ViewPoint. MIT Press, Cambridge (1993)

Golub, G.H., Loan, C.F.V.: MATRIX Computations. John Hopkins University Press (1996)

Hartley, R., Zissermann, A.: Multiple View Geometry, 2nd edn. Cambridge University Press, Cambridge (2003)

Lutton, M.L.-K.: Contribution to the determination of vanishing points using hough transforms. IEEE Transactions on Pattern Analysis and Machine Intelligence 16(4), 430–438 (1994)

Medioni, G., Kang, S.B. (eds.): Emerging Topics in Computer Vision. Robust techniques for computer vision. Prentice-Hall, Englewood Cliffs (2004)

Morris, D.D.: Gauge Freedoms and Uncertainty Modeling for 3D Computer Vision. PhD thesis, Robotics Institute, Carnegie Mellon University (2001)

Perona, P.: Steerable-scalable kernels for edge detection and junction analysis. In: Sandini, G. (ed.) ECCV 1992. LNCS, vol. 588, pp. 3–18. Springer, Heidelberg (1992)

Quan, L., Mohr, R.: Determining perspective structures using hierarchical hough transform. Pattern Recognition Letters 9, 279–286 (1989)

Snyder, J.P.: Map Projections; A Working Manual. U.S. Geological Survey, supersedes bulletin 1532 edn. (1987)

Stuelpnagel, J.: On the parametrization of the three-dimensional rotation group. SIAM Review, 6(4) (1964)

Part VIII

Motion, Tracking
and Stereo Vision

Dense Stereo Matching with Growing Aggregation and Neural Learning

Ignazio Gallo and Elisabetta Binaghi

Universita' degli Studi dell'Insubria, Varese, Italy
elisabetta.binaghi@uninsubria.it, gallo@uninsubria.it

Abstract. This work aims at defining a new method for matching correspondences in stereoscopic image analysis. The salient aspects of the method are -an explicit representation of occlusions driving the overall matching process and the use of neural adaptive technique in disparity computation. In particular, based on the taxonomy proposed by Scharstein and Szelinsky, the dense stereo matching process has been divided into three tasks: *matching cost computation, aggregation of local evidence* and *computation of disparity values.* Within the second phase a new strategy has been introduced in an attempt to improve reliability in computing disparity. An experiment was conducted to evaluate the solutions proposed. The experiment is based on an analysis of test images including data with a ground truth disparity map.

Keywords: Stereo, occlusion, disparity space, neural networks.

1 Introduction

The reconstruction of three-dimensional shape from two or more images is a well known and intensively investigated research problem within the Computer Vision community (Barnard and Fischler 1982; Barnard and Thompson W 1980; Dhond and Aggarwal 1989).

Major efforts have been devoted to the stereo matching sub-task aimed at computing correspondences in two (or more) images for obtaining dense depth maps. A substantial amount of work has been done on stereo matching giving rise to a variety of novel approaches (Scharstein and Szelinsky, 2002) attempting to improve upon existing early methods (Hannah, 1989) and satisfy the high accuracy demand in diversified application domains such as object recognition, robotics and virtual reality (McMillan and Bishop 1995).

Despite important achievements, the accuracy of most innovative stereo techniques may not be adequate especially in those situations where even isolated errors in the depth map create visible undesirable artefacts. The problem originates from the fact that most stereo algorithms ignore occlusions analysis or address it in a post processing stage within a more general smoothing task (Bobik and Intille 1999).

Occlusions are widespread in stereo imagery and even when images with small disparity jumps are processed, they drastically affect the accuracy of the overall reconstruction process being the major source of errors.

J. Braz et al. (Eds.): VISAPP and GRAPP 2006, CCIS 4, pp. 343–353, 2007.
© Springer-Verlag Berlin Heidelberg 2007

Recent works on stereo matching stem from the idea of mimicking the human visual system which uses occlusions to reason about the spatial relationships between objects during binocular stereopsis. Explicit representation of occlusions and direct processing within occlusion edges characterizes these approaches (Bobik and Intille 1999).

This paper proposes a novel algorithm for solving stereo correspondence based on an explicit representation of occlusions driving the overall matching process. In particular, based on the taxonomy proposed by Scharstein and Szelinsky, the dense stereo matching process has been divided into three tasks: *matching cost computation, aggregation of local evidence* and *computation of disparity values* (Scharstein and Szelisky, 2002) . Within the second phase a new strategy has been introduced in an attempt to improve reliability in computing disparity. An experiment was conducted to evaluate the solution proposed. The experiment is based on the analysis of test images including data with a ground truth disparity map and makes use of the quality metrics proposed by Scharstein and Szelinsky (Scharstein and Szelisky, 2002).

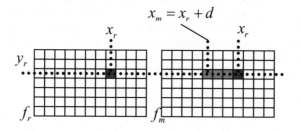

Fig. 1. Correspondence between a pixel (x_r, y_r) in reference image f_r and a pixel (x_m, y_r) in matching image f_m. The difference $d = (x_m - x_r)$ is the disparity value.

2 Representation

This section describes a data structure called *Disparity Space Image,* or *DSI,* already introduced in previous works (Okutomi and Kanade 1994; Bobik and Intille 1999). The DSI is an explicit representation of matching space and plays an essential role in the development of the overall matching algorithm which makes use of occlusion constraints.

The correspondence between pixel (x_r, y_r) in a Reference Image f_r and a pixel (x_m, y_m) in a Matching Image f_m is defined as

$$f_r(x_r, y_r) = f_m[x_r + s \cdot d(x_r, y_r), y_r] + \eta(x_r, y_r) \tag{1}$$

where $s = \pm 1$ is a sign chosen so that disparities are always positive; $d(x_r, y_r)$ is the disparity function and $\eta(x_r, y_r)$ is the Gaussian white noise.

From equation (1) we obtain

$$x_m = x_r + s \cdot d(x_r, y_r)$$ (2)

and from equation (2):

$$d(x_r, y_r) = s \cdot (x_m - x_r)$$ (3)

Introducing the *epipolar constraint,* we also have:

$$y_r = y_m$$ (4)

supposing the pixels move from right to left.

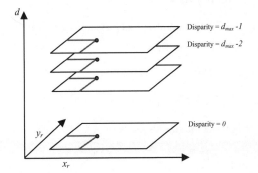

Fig. 2. Graphic Representation of Disparity Space Image (DSI)

Once the disparity space has been specified, the concept of DSI can be introduced and defined as any image or function over the disparity space (x_r, y_r, d). Values of DSI usually represent the *cost of a* particular match implied by the particular $d(x,y)$ considered.

Figure 2 shows a graphic representation of DSI: each slice indicates a level of disparity varying from 0 to a value d_{max} representing the maximum disparity for the pair of images considered.

3 Growing Template Algorithm

According to the taxonomy proposed by Scharstein and Szelinsky, the dense stereo matching process can be divided into four tasks (Scharstein and Szelisky, 2002):

1) *Matching Cost Computation*
2) *Aggregation Cost*
3) *Disparity Computation and Optimization*
4) *Disparity Refinement*

Many dense stereo matching methods have presented several different solutions to one or more of these tasks. The most common *matching costs* include *squared intensity differences (SD)* and *absolute intensity differences (AD)* (Cox et al., 1996; Scharstein and Szelisky, 2002).

The actual sequence of steps in the overall matching procedure depends on the matching algorithm and in particular, on its local or global nature.

Our approach, which follows a local strategy, extends the conventional Aggregation Cost phase including two novel sub-tasks:

   2.1) Growing Raw Cost
   2.2) Growing Aggregation Cost

3.1 Matching Cost Computation

Assuming the use of SD as matching function, by equation (3) the matching cost computed for a pixel (x_r, y_r) is defined as:

$$DSI(x_r, y_r, d) =$$
$$= [f_r(x_r, y_r) - f_m(x_m, y_r)]^2 \tag{5}$$

where d is the disparity associated with the pixel (x_r, y_r) and $0 \le d \le d_{max}$.

3.2 Aggregation Cost

Local and window-based methods aggregate the matching cost by summing or averaging over a support region in the DSI. The support region we use is a two-dimensional squared window of a fixed dimension.

In particular, this second step is performed by summing the calculated matching costs over a squared window with constant disparity $\overline{d}$. The aggregation cost $AC_{i,j}^d$ is defined as:

$$AC_{i,j}^{\overline{d}} = \sum_{m=a}^{a+W} \sum_{n=b}^{b+W} DSI(m, n, \overline{d}) \tag{6}$$

where $a = \left(i - \dfrac{W}{2}\right)$ and $b = \left(j - \dfrac{W}{2}\right)$.

Considering all the aggregation values obtained varying the disparity in the range $[0...d_{max}]$, we obtain:

$$\overrightarrow{AC}_{m,n} = \left[AC_{m,n}^0, AC_{m,n}^1, ... AC_{m,n}^{d_{max}}\right] \tag{7}$$

A classic Stereo Matching Algorithm, at this point, with a Winner Take All (WTA) technique for example, decides that the disparity is computed by selecting the minimal aggregated cost in $\overrightarrow{AC}_{m,n}$. The Growing Template Algorithm adds two new steps at the aggregation cost phase.

We now describe the two parts that characterize the Growing Template Aggregation Cost step.

3.3 Growing Raw Cost

Unlike conventional techniques that base further steps of matching algorithm on the minimal aggregated cost computed in $\overrightarrow{AC}_{m,n}$, our approach bases decisions on all the costs obtained. To this purpose, we introduce a new quantity $\overrightarrow{RC}_{m,n}$ defined as

$$\overrightarrow{RC}_{m,n} = \left[RC^0_{m,n}, RC^1_{m,n}, ..., RC^{d_{max}}_{m,n} \right] \tag{8}$$

where each element indicates the position in the sorted list of the element $AC^d_{i,j}$.

For example, if we have the vector $\overrightarrow{AC}_{m,n} = \left[12,1,16 \right]$ the corresponding vector of raw cost is $\overrightarrow{RC}_{m,n} = \left[2,1,3 \right]$.

At the end of this phase for every pixel of coordinates (m, n) in the reference image we have associated the $\overrightarrow{RC}_{m,n}$ calculated.

3.4 Growing Aggregation Cost

This sub-task calculates the number of confirmations in a given support window for a given cost l. Formally, from equation (8) we obtain the vector:

$$\overrightarrow{GA}_{m,n} = \left[GA^0_{m,n}, GA^1_{m,n}, ..., GA^{d_{max}}_{m,n} \right] \tag{9}$$

where

$$GA^d_{m,n} = \sum_{(m,n) \in W \times W} \left(RC^d_{m,n} \le l \right) \tag{10}$$

The salient aspect of our strategy is that of integrating contextual confirmation within the matching cost aggregation phase. The aggregation can be performed based on different cost values varying the l parameter in equation 10.

Figure 3 compares DSI's slices for fixed y obtained by means of a matching algorithm which uses SD matching cost within conventional AC computation performed with support window W=5 (a) and our algorithm which includes the GA task performed with the following parameters(c):

1. growing aggregation window GW=25
2. l=1

Both figures 3a and 3c highlight bands (dark lines and white lines respectively) indicating regions that match at a given disparity. They are more visible in figure 3c depicting disparity and occlusion situations without ambiguity.

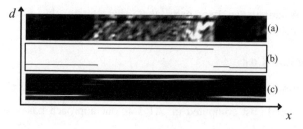

Fig. 3. DSI's slices obtained from the traditional AC values for each pixel of line 100 (a), and obtained from the GA on the same line (c). Slice (b) represents correct disparity information for line 100.

3.5 Disparity Computation

The next phase in the matching algorithm consists in the computation of the disparity map by selecting the $\overrightarrow{GA}_{m,n}$ components which satisfy a given criterion. Adopting a WTA strategy, the disparity associated with the minimum cost value is selected at each pixel.

The present work tested an adaptive strategy based on *neural networks* for disparity computation (Rumelhart et al. 1986; Pao, 1989). A Multilayer Perceptron neural model was adopted to compute the disparity based on specific local information extracted from the DSI slice.

The network is trained receiving input data from the DSI slices. In particular, at each position of a moving window over the DSI slice, an input pattern is extracted and presented to the network. A training example is constituted by a pair of elements

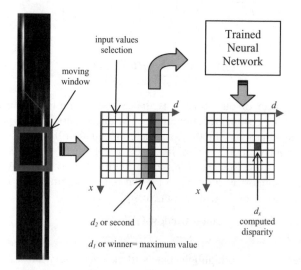

Fig. 4. Disparity computation procedure based on a trained neural network. The process extracts patterns from a window positioned over a DSI slice. For each x we select two values: d_1 and d_2. The trained neural network calculates the disparity associated with the center of the moving window.

(a,b) where a is the input pattern collecting a set $\{d_i\}$ and b corresponding disparity extracted from ground truth image for each x within the moving window. (Figure 4).

4 Experiments

The experiments illustrated in this section addressed the following questions:

- how did the performance depend upon their main parameters and upon the neural refinement stage?
- how did the Growing Template Algorithm compare with other matching approaches?

The overall experimental activity was supported by tools and test data available within the implementation framework proposed by Scharstein & Szelinski in their paper (Scharstein and Szelisky, 2002) and made available on the Web at www.middlebury.edu/stereo. We included our stereo correspondence algorithm in this framework, and applied it to the test data available.

Four stereo image pairs with different types of content are used to evaluate the performances of the proposed algorithm (see Figure 5).

Fig. 5. Left image and ground truth disparity maps of test set

Among the quality measures available within the framework, we adopted the RMS (root mean squared) error (measured in disparity units) between the computed disparity map $d_C(x, y)$ and the ground truth map $d_T(x, y)$

$$R = (\frac{1}{N}\sum(|d_C(x, y) - d_T(x, y)|^2)^{\frac{1}{2}}$$ (12)

These measures are intended computed over the whole image and five different kinds of regions in the whole image:

- textureless regions (TEXTRD): regions where the squared horizontal intensity gradient averaged over a square window of a given size (suggested value 3) is below a given threshold (suggested value 4.0)
- textured regions (TEXTRLS): regions complementary to the textureless regions
- occluded regions (OCCL): regions that are occluded in the matching image
- non occluded regions (NONOCCL): regions complementary to the occluded regions
- depth discontinuity regions (DISC): pixels whose neighboring disparity differs by more than a given threshold (suggested value 2.0), dilated by a window of a given width (suggested value 9)

These regions are computed by pre-processing reference images and ground truth disparity maps yielding binary segmentation.

4.1 Sensitivity Analysis

We attempted to evaluate the effects of systematically varying some of the key parameters of our stereo algorithm to find an optimal setting for all situations. Experiments were developed using SD and AD matching costs and windows of size 7, 15, 21, 35 for Growing Aggregation Cost.

Results obtained demonstrate that performances are not strongly influenced by the type of matching costs used. A large window can help for occlusion regions. Inversely, small windows perform better on discontinuity regions.

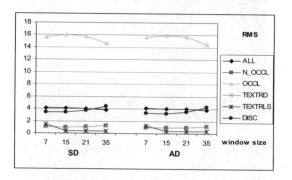

Fig. 6. Sensitivity Analysis of Growing Aggregation Algorithm

Dimensions of 35X35 were selected allotting the task of optimizing the balance between high accuracy in occlusion and discontinuity regions to the neural adaptive stage.

4.2 Performance Evaluation and Comparison Analysis

At first the evaluation procedure aimed to identify and evaluate the contribution of neural refinement within the global matching algorithm. To this purpose we compared the Growing Aggregation Algorithm including the neural stage with the same version including the WTA strategy for disparity computation. The evaluation was based on the monochromatic MAP pair of images. Training data for the neural stage has been selected from the Map image in a measure of 10% of global pixels.

As shown in Table 1, the algorithm GA presents   a competitive behaviour. However its principal merit consists in preparing ideal conditions for the subsequent neural stage as demonstrated by the fact that the algorithm   with neural refinement (GA+N) strongly prevails in all regions considered.

We compared performances obtained by means of the Growing Aggregation Algorithm including neural refinement with those obtained by running four algorithms implemented within the cited framework available, selected among those with better performances (Table 2).

Table 1. Results obtained with MAP image. GA=Growing Aggregation, GA+N=Growing Aggregation+ Neural Network for disparity computation.

	ALL	NON OCCL	OCCL	TEXT RD	TEXT RLS	DISC
GA	3.85	1.31	14.88	1.32	0.40	4.69
GA+N	1.66	1.42	3.82	1.42	0.72	4.86

Table 2. Results obtained with MAP image. DP= Dynamic Programming, SSD=Sum of Squared Difference, SO=Scanline Optimization, BD=Bayesian Diffusion.

	ALL	NON OCCL	OCCL	TEXT RD	TEXT RLS	DISC
DP	3.15	2.98	5.21	2.99	1.75	5.86
SSD	3.92	1.66	14.65	1.67	0.44	6.07
SO	4.39	2.02	16.09	2.02	2.57	5.25
BD	4.66	0.93	18.74	0.94	0.43	2.95

Figure 7 shows final disparity maps obtained by processing the four stereo image pairs considered.

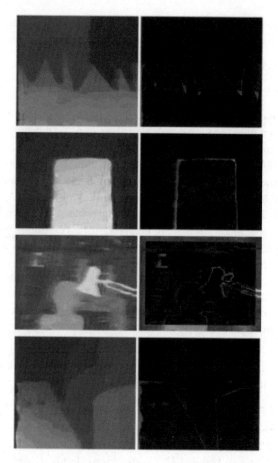

Fig. 7. Final disparity maps and difference images

5   Conclusions

Our objective in this study was to investigate the potentialities of a new method aimed at solving correspondence problem within a two-frame area matching approach and producing dense disparity maps.

The strategy was tested on standard data sets available on the Web. As seen in this experimental context the allied use of the growing aggregation strategy and neural adaptive techniques benefits the matching in general and in particular in occluded regions. The use of adapting techniques allow to process raw data directly extracted from DSI slices without formalizing explicitly the information useful for handling occlusions. The trained network encodes the knowledge about occlusions and efficiently uses it in generalization.

We consider this study preliminary to further investigation involving both methodological and experimental issues.In particular, the present solutions must be reinforced implementing an operative strategy for training neural network; strategies will be integrated in an attempt of improving generalization in such a way that trained networks could be reliably applied to different kind of images never seen during the training stage .

Further experiments dealing with Scanning Electron Microscopy imagery are planned.

References

Barnard, S.T., Fischler, M.A.: Computational Stereo. ACM Computing Surveys 14(4), 553–572 (1982)

Barnard, T., Thompson, W.B.: Disparity Analysis of Images. IEEE Trans. PAMI, 333–340 (1980)

Bishop, C.M.: Neural Networks for Pattern Recognition. Oxford University Press, Oxford (1995)

Bobik, A.F, Intille, S.S.: Large occlusion stereo. International Journal on Computer Vision 33, 181–200 (1999)

Cox, J.I., Higonani, S.L., Rao, S.P., Maggs, B.M.: A Maximum Likelihoods Stereo Algorithm. Computer Vision and Image Understanding 63, 542–567 (1996)

Dhond, U.R., Aggarwal, J.K.: Structure from Stereo – a review. IEEE Trans. On Systems, Man, and Cybernetics 19, 1489–1510 (1989)

Hannah, M.J.: A system for digital stereo image matching. Photogrammetric Engineering and Remote Sensing 55, 1765–1770 (1989)

McMillan, L., Bishop, G.: Plenoptic modelling:An image-based rendering system. In: Computer Graphics (SIG-GRAPH'95), pp. 39–46 (1995)

Kanade, T., Okutomi, M.: A Stereo Matching Algorithm with an Adaptive Window: Theory and Experiment. IEEE Trans. on PAMI 16(9), 920–932 (1994)

Pao, Y.H.: Adaptive Pattern Recognition and Neural Networks. Addison-Wesley, MA (1989)

Rumelhart, H., Hinton, G.E., Williams, R.J.: Learning Internal Representation by Error Propagation. In: Rumelhart, H., McClelland, J.L. (eds.) Parallel Distributed Processing, pp. 318–362. MIT Press, Cambridge, MA (1986)

Scharstein, D., Szeliski, R.: A Taxonomy and Evaluation of Dense Two-Frame Stereo Correspondence Algorithms. International Journal of Computer Vision 47, 7–42 (2002)

Improving Appearance-Based 3D Face Tracking Using Sparse Stereo Data*

Fadi Dornaika and Angel D. Sappa

Computer Vision Center
Edifici O Campus UAB
08193 Bellaterra, Barcelona, Spain
{dornaika,sappa}@cvc.uab.es

Abstract. Recently, researchers proposed deterministic and statistical appearance-based 3D head tracking methods which can successfully tackle the image variability and drift problems. However, appearance-based methods dedicated to 3D head tracking may suffer from inaccuracies since these methods are not very sensitive to out-of-plane motion variations. On the other hand, the use of dense 3D facial data provided by a stereo rig or a range sensor can provide very accurate 3D head motions/poses. However, this paradigm requires either an accurate facial feature extraction or a computationally expensive registration technique (e.g., the Iterative Closest Point algorithm). In this paper, we improve our appearance-based 3D face tracker by combining an adaptive appearance model with a robust 3D-to-3D registration technique that uses sparse stereo data. The resulting 3D face tracker combines the advantages of both appearance-based trackers and 3D data-based trackers while keeping the CPU time very close to that required by real-time trackers. We provide experiments and performance evaluation which show the feasibility and usefulness of the proposed approach.

Keywords: 3D face tracking, adaptive appearance models, evaluation, stereo, robust 3D registration.

1 Introduction

The ability to detect and track human heads and faces in video sequences is useful in a great number of applications, such as human-computer interaction and gesture recognition. There are several commercial products capable of accurate and reliable 3D head position and orientation estimation (e.g., the acoustic tracker system Mouse [www.vrdepot.com/vrteclg.htm]). These are either based on magnetic sensors or on special markers placed on the face; both practices are encumbering, causing discomfort and limiting natural motion. Vision-based 3D head tracking provides an attractive alternative since vision sensors are not invasive and hence natural motions can be achieved (Moreno et al., 2002). However, detecting and tracking faces in video sequences is a challenging task.

Recently, deterministic and statistical appearance-based 3D head tracking methods have been proposed and used by some researchers (Cascia et al., 2000; Ahlberg, 2002;

---

* This work was supported by the MEC project TIN2005-09026 and The Ramón y Cajal Program.

Matthews and Baker, 2004). These methods can successfully tackle the image variability and drift problems by using deterministic or statistical models for the global appearance of a special object class: the face. However, appearance-based methods dedicated to full 3D head tracking may suffer from some inaccuracies since these methods are not very sensitive to out-of-plane motion variations. On the other hand, the use of dense 3D facial data provided by a stereo rig or a range sensor can provide very accurate 3D face motions. However, computing the 3D face motions from the stream of dense 3D facial data is not straightforward. Indeed, inferring the 3D face motion from the dense 3D data needs an additional process. This process can be the detection of some particular facial features in the range data/images from which the 3D head pose can be inferred. For example, in (Malassiotis and Strintzis, 2005), the 3D nose ridge is detected and then used for computing the 3D head pose. Alternatively, one can perform a registration between 3D data obtained at different time instants in order to infer the relative 3D motions. The most common registration technique is the Iterative Closest Point (ICP) (Besl and McKay, 1992). The ICP algorithm and its variants can provide accurate 3D motions but their significant computational cost prohibits real-time performance.

The main contribution of this paper is a robust 3D face tracker that combines the advantages of both appearance-based trackers and 3D data-based trackers while keeping the CPU time very close to that required by real-time trackers. First, the 3D head pose is recovered using an appearance registration technique. Second, the obtained 3D head pose is utilized and refined by robustly registering two 3D point sets where one set is provided by stereo reconstruction.

The remainder of this paper proceeds as follows. Section 2 introduces our deformable 3D facial model. Section 3 states the problem we are focusing on, and describes the online adaptive appearance model. Section 4 summarizes the adaptive appearance-based tracker that tracks in real-time the 3D head pose and some facial actions. Section 5 gives some evaluation results associated with the appearance-based tracker. Section 6 describes the improvement step based on a robust 3D-to-3D registration and the appearance model. Section 7 gives some experimental results.

2 Modeling Faces

2.1 A Deformable 3D Model

In our study, we use the 3D face model *Candide*. This 3D deformable wireframe model was first developed for the purpose of model-based image coding and computer animation. The 3D shape of this wireframe model is directly recorded in coordinate form. It is given by the coordinates of the 3D vertices $\mathbf{P}_i, i = 1, \ldots, n$ where n is the number of vertices. Thus, the shape up to a global scale can be fully described by the $3n$-vector $\mathbf{g}$; the concatenation of the 3D coordinates of all vertices $\mathbf{P}_i$. The vector $\mathbf{g}$ is written as:

$$\mathbf{g} = \mathbf{g}_s + \mathbf{A}\,\tau_{\mathbf{a}} \tag{1}$$

where $\mathbf{g}_s$ is the static shape of the model, $\tau_{\mathbf{a}}$ the animation control vector, and the columns of $\mathbf{A}$ are the Animation Units. In this study, we use six modes for the facial Animation Units (AUs) matrix $\mathbf{A}$. Without loss of generality, we have chosen the six following AUs: lower lip depressor, lip stretcher, lip corner depressor, upper lip raiser, eyebrow lowerer and outer eyebrow raiser. These AUs are enough to cover most common facial animations (mouth and eyebrow movements). Moreover, they are essential for conveying emotions.

In equation (1), the 3D shape is expressed in a local coordinate system. However, one should relate the 3D coordinates to the image coordinate system. To this end, we adopt the weak perspective projection model. We neglect the perspective effects since the depth variation of the face can be considered as small compared to its absolute depth. Thus, the state of the 3D wireframe model is given by the 3D head pose parameters (three rotations and three translations) and the internal face animation control vector $\tau_{\mathbf{a}}$. This is given by the 12-dimensional vector $\mathbf{b}$:

$$\mathbf{b} = [\theta_x, \theta_y, \theta_z, t_x, t_y, t_z, \tau_{\mathbf{a}}^T]^T \tag{2}$$

2.2 Shape-Free Facial Patches

A face texture is represented as a shape-free texture (geometrically normalized image). The geometry of this image is obtained by projecting the static shape $\mathbf{g}_s$ using a centered frontal 3D pose onto an image with a given resolution. The texture of this geometrically normalized image is obtained by texture mapping from the triangular 2D mesh in the input image (see figure 1) using a piece-wise affine transform, $\mathcal{W}$. The warping process applied to an input image $\mathbf{y}$ is denoted by:

$$\mathbf{x}(\mathbf{b}) = \mathcal{W}(\mathbf{y}, \mathbf{b}) \tag{3}$$

where $\mathbf{x}$ denotes the shape-free texture patch and $\mathbf{b}$ denotes the geometrical parameters. Several resolution levels can be chosen for the shape-free textures. The reported results are obtained with a shape-free patch of 5392 pixels. Regarding photometric transformations, a zero-mean unit-variance normalization is used to partially compensate for contrast variations. The complete image transformation is implemented as follows: (i) transfer the texture $\mathbf{y}$ using the piece-wise affine transform associated with the vector $\mathbf{b}$, and (ii) perform the grey-level normalization of the obtained patch.

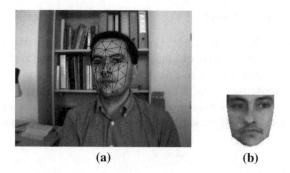

(a)   (b)

Fig. 1. (a) an input image with correct adaptation. (b) the corresponding shape-free facial image.

3   Problem Formulation

Given a video sequence depicting a moving head/face, we would like to recover, for each frame, the 3D head pose and the facial actions encoded by the control vector τ_a. In other words, we would like to estimate the vector $\mathbf{b}_t$ (equation 2) at time t given all the observed data until time t, denoted $\mathbf{y}_{1:t} \equiv \{\mathbf{y}_1, \dots, \mathbf{y}_t\}$. In a tracking context, the model parameters associated with the current frame will be handed over to the next frame.

For each input frame $\mathbf{y}_t$, the observation is simply the warped texture patch (the shape-free patch) associated with the geometric parameters $\mathbf{b}_t$. We use the HAT symbol for the tracked parameters and textures. For a given frame t, $\hat{\mathbf{b}}_t$ represents the computed geometric parameters and $\hat{\mathbf{x}}_t$ the corresponding shape-free patch, that is,

$$\hat{\mathbf{x}}_t = \mathbf{x}(\hat{\mathbf{b}}_t) = \mathcal{W}(\mathbf{y}_t, \hat{\mathbf{b}}_t) \tag{4}$$

The estimation of $\hat{\mathbf{b}}_t$ from the sequence of images will be presented in the next Section.

The appearance model associated with the shape-free facial patch at time t, A_t, is time-varying on that it models the appearances present in all observations $\hat{\mathbf{x}}$ up to time $(t-1)$. We assume that the appearance model A_t obeys a Gaussian with a center μ and a variance σ. Notice that μ and σ are vectors composed of d components/pixels (d is the size of $\mathbf{x}$) that are assumed to be independent of each other. In summary, the observation likelihood at time t is written as

$$p(\mathbf{y}_t|\mathbf{b}_t) = p(\mathbf{x}_t|\mathbf{b}_t) = \prod_{i=1}^{d} \mathbf{N}(x_i; \mu_i, \sigma_i) \tag{5}$$

where $\mathbf{N}(x; \mu_i, \sigma_i)$ is the normal density:

$$\mathbf{N}(x; \mu_i, \sigma_i) = (2\pi\sigma_i^2)^{-1/2} \exp\left[-\frac{1}{2}\left(\frac{x-\mu_i}{\sigma_i}\right)^2\right] \tag{6}$$

We assume that A_t summarizes the past observations under an exponential envelop, that is, the past observations are exponentially forgotten with respect to the current texture. When the appearance is tracked for the current input image, *i.e.* the texture $\hat{\mathbf{x}}_t$ is available, we can compute the updated appearance and use it to track in the next frame.

It can be shown that the appearance model parameters, *i.e.* μ and σ can be updated using the following equations (see (Jepson et al., 2003) for more details on Online Appearance Models):

$$\mu_{t+1} = (1-\alpha)\,\mu_t + \alpha\,\hat{\mathbf{x}}_t \tag{7}$$

$$\sigma_{t+1}^2 = (1-\alpha)\,\sigma_t^2 + \alpha\,(\hat{\mathbf{x}}_t - \mu_t)^2 \tag{8}$$

In the above equations, all μ's and σ^2's are vectorized and the operation is element-wise. This technique, also called recursive filtering, is simple, time-efficient and therefore, suitable for real-time applications. The appearance parameters reflect the most recent observations within a roughly $L = 1/\alpha$ window with exponential decay.

Note that μ is initialized with the first patch $\hat{\mathbf{x}}_0$. In order to get stable values for the variances, equation (8) is not used until the number of frames reaches a given value (*e.g.*, the first 40 frames). For these frames, the classical variance is used, that is, equation (8) is used with α being set to $\frac{1}{t}$.

Here we used a single Gaussian to model the appearance of each pixel in the shape-free patch. However, modeling the appearance with Gaussian mixtures can also be used on the expense of some additional computational load (e.g., see (Zhou et al., 2004; Lee, 2005)).

4   Tracking Using Adaptive Appearance Registration

We consider the state vector $\mathbf{b} = [\theta_x, \theta_y, \theta_z, t_x, t_y, t_z, \tau_{\mathbf{a}}{}^T]^T$ encapsulating the 3D head pose and the facial actions. In this section, we will show how this state can be recovered for time t from the previous known state $\hat{\mathbf{b}}_{t-1}$ and the current input image $\mathbf{y}_t$.

The sought geometrical parameters $\mathbf{b}_t$ at time t are related to the previous parameters by the following equation ($\hat{\mathbf{b}}_{t-1}$ is known):

$$\mathbf{b}_t = \hat{\mathbf{b}}_{t-1} + \Delta\mathbf{b}_t \tag{9}$$

where $\Delta\mathbf{b}_t$ is the unknown shift in the geometric parameters. This shift is estimated using a region-based registration technique that does not need any image feature extraction. In other words, $\Delta\mathbf{b}_t$ is estimated such that the warped texture will be as close as possible to the facial appearance A_t. For this purpose, we minimize the *Mahalanobis* distance between the warped texture and the current appearance mean,

$$\min_{\mathbf{b}_t} e(\mathbf{b}_t) = \min_{\mathbf{b}_t} D(\mathbf{x}(\mathbf{b}_t), \mu_t) = \sum_{i=1}^{d} \left(\frac{x_i - \mu_i}{\sigma_i} \right)^2 \tag{10}$$

The above criterion can be minimized using iterative first-order linear approximation which is equivalent to a Gauss-Newton method. It is worthwhile noting that the minimization is equivalent to maximizing the likelihood measure given by (5). Moreover, the above optimization is carried out using Huber function (Dornaika and Davoine, 2004). In the above optimization, the gradient matrix $\frac{\partial\mathcal{W}(\mathbf{y}_t, \mathbf{b}_t)}{\partial\mathbf{b}_t} = \frac{\partial\mathbf{x}_t}{\partial\mathbf{b}_t}$ is computed for each frame and is approximated by numerical differences similarly to the work of Cootes (Cootes et al., 2001).

On a 3.2 GHz PC, a non-optimized C code of the approach computes the 3D head pose and the six facial actions in 50 ms. About half that time is required if one is only interested in computing the 3D head pose parameters.

5   Accuracy Evaluation

The monocular tracker described above provides the time-varying 3D head pose (especially the out-of-plane parameters) with some inaccuracies whose magnitude depends on several factors such as the absolute depth of the head, the head orientation, and the

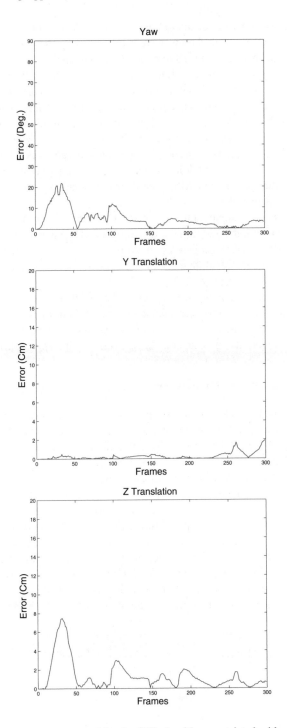

Fig. 2. 3D head pose errors computed by the ICP algorithm associated with a 300-frame long sequence

camera parameters. We have evaluated the accuracy of the above proposed monocular tracker using ground truth data that were recovered by the Iterative Closest Point algorithm (Besl and McKay, 1992) and dense 3D facial data.

Figure 2 depicts the monocular tracker errors associated with a 300-frame long sequence which contains rotational and translational out-of-plane head motions. The nominal absolute depth of the head was about 65 cm, and the focal length of the camera was 824 pixels. As can be seen, the out-of-plane motion errors can be large for some frames for which there is a room for improvement. Moreover, this evaluation has confirmed the general trend of appearance-based trackers, that is, the out-of-plane motion parameters (pitch angle, yaw angle, and depth) are more affected by errors than the other parameters. More details about accuracy evaluation can be found in (Dornaika and Sappa, 2005).

One expects that the monocular tracker accuracy can be improved if an additional cue is used. In our case, the additional cue will be the 3D data associated with the mesh vertices provided by stereo reconstruction. Although the use of stereo data may seem as an excess requirement, recall that cheap and compact stereo systems are now widely available (e.g., [www.ptgrey.com]).

We point out that there is no need to refine the facial feature motions obtained by the above appearance-based tracker since their independent motion can be accurately recovered. Indeed, these features (the lips and the eyebrows) have different textures, so their independent motion can be accurately recovered by the appearance-based tracker.

6   Improving the 3D Head Pose

The improved 3D face tracker is outlined in Figure 3. The remainder of this section describes the improvement steps based on sparse stereo-based 3D data. Since the monocular tracker provides the 3D head pose by matching the input texture with the adaptive facial texture model (both textures correspond to a 2D mesh), it follows that the out-of-plane motion parameters can be inaccurate even when most of the facial features project onto their true location in the image. We use this fact to argue that the appearance-based tracker will greatly help in the sense that it will provide the putative set of 3D-to-3D correspondences through the 2D projections. Our basic idea is to start from the 3D head pose provided by the monocular tracker and then improve it by using some sparse 3D data provided by stereo reconstruction. Here we use the estimated six degrees of freedom as well as the corresponding projection of all vertices. The estimated 3D head pose will be used for mapping the 3D mesh in 3D space while the 2D projections of the vertices will be processed by the stereo system in order to get their 3D coordinates.

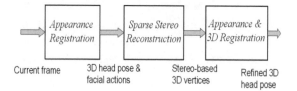

Fig. 3. The main steps of the developed robust 3D face tracker

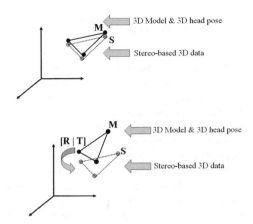

Fig. 4. (**M**) A 3D facial patch model positioned using the estimated 3D head pose. (**S**) the same 3D patch (three vertices) provided by stereo reconstruction. **Top:** An ideal case where the appearance-based 3D head pose corresponds to the true 3D head pose. **Bottom:** A real case where the appearance-based 3D head pose does not exactly correspond to the true 3D head pose. It follows that the improvement is simply the rigid 3D displacement [**R**|**T**] that aligns the two sets of vertices.

Improving the 3D head pose is then carried out by combining a robust 3D-to-3D registration and the appearance model. The robust 3D registration uses the 3D mesh vertices (the 3D model is mapped with the estimated 3D head pose) and the corresponding 3D coordinates provided by the stereo rig while the appearance model is always given by (10). Recall that the stereo reconstruction only concerns the image points resulting from projecting the 3D mesh vertices onto the image. Since our 3D mesh contains about one hundred vertices the whole refinement step will be fast.

Figure 4 illustrates the basic idea that is behind the improvement step, namely the robust 3D registration. Figure 4 (Top) illustrates an ideal case where the estimated appearance-based 3D head pose corresponds to the true 3D pose. In this case, the vertices of the 3D mesh after motion compensation coincide with their corresponding 3D points provided by the stereo rig. Figure 4 (Bottom) illustrates a real case where the estimated appearance-based 3D head pose does not correspond exactly to the true one. In this case, the improvement can be estimated by recovering the 3D rigid displacement [**R**|**T**] between the two sets of vertices.

We point out that the set of vertex pairs may contain some outliers caused for instance by occluded vertices. Thus, the 3D registration process must be robust. Robust 3D registration methods have been proposed in recent literature (e.g., see (Chetverikov et al., 2005; Fitzgibbon, 2003)). In our work, we use a RANSAC-like technique that computes an adaptive threshold for outlier detection. The whole improvement algorithm is outlined in Figure 5. As can be seen, the final solution (see the second paragraph in Figure 5) takes into account two criteria: i) the 3D-to-3D registration, and ii) the adaptive appearance model.

Inlier detection. The question now is: Given a subsample k and its associated solution $\mathbf{D}_k$, How do we decide whether or not an arbitrary vertex is an inlier? In techniques

Random sampling: Repeat the following three steps K times

1. Draw a random subsample of 3 different pairs of vertices. We have three pairs of 3D points $\{\mathbf{M}_i \leftrightarrow \mathbf{S}_i\}$, $i = 1, 2, 3$.
2. For this subsample, indexed by k ($k = 1, \ldots, K$), compute the 3D rigid displacement $\mathbf{D}_k = [\mathbf{R}_k | \mathbf{T}_k]$, where $\mathbf{R}_k$ is a 3D rotation and $\mathbf{T}_k$ a 3D translation, that brings these three pairs into alignment. $\mathbf{R}_k$ and $\mathbf{T}_k$ are computed by minimizing the residual error $\sum_{i=1}^{3} |\mathbf{S}_i - \mathbf{R}_k \mathbf{M}_i - \mathbf{T}_k|^2$. This is carried out using the quaternion method (Horn, 1987).
3. For this solution $\mathbf{D}_k$, compute the median M_k of the squared residual errors with respect to the whole set of N vertices. Note that we have N residuals corresponding to all vertices $\{\mathbf{M}_j \leftrightarrow \mathbf{S}_j\}$, $j = 1, \ldots, N$. The squared residual associated with an arbitrary vertex $\mathbf{M}_j$ is $|\mathbf{S}_j - \mathbf{R}_k \mathbf{M}_j - \mathbf{T}_k|^2$.

Solution:

1. For each solution $\mathbf{D}_k = [\mathbf{R}_k | \mathbf{T}_k], k = 1, \ldots, K$, compute the number of inliers among the entire set of vertices (see text). Let n_k be this number.
2. Select the 10 best solutions, i.e. the solutions that have the highest number of inliers.
3. Refine each such solution using all its inlier pairs.
4. For these 10 solutions, compute the corresponding observation likelihood (5).
5. Choose the solution that has the largest observation likelihood.

Fig. 5. Recovering the 3D rigid displacement using robust statistics and the appearance

dealing with 2D geometrical features (points and lines) (Fischler and Bolles, 1981), this is achieved using the distance in the image plane between the actual location of the feature and its mapped location. If this distance is below a given threshold then this feature is considered as an inlier; otherwise, it is considered as an outlier. Here we can do the same by manually defining a distance in 3D space. However, this fixed selected threshold cannot accommodate all cases and all noises. Therefore, we use an adaptive threshold distance that is computed from the residual errors associated with all subsamples. Our idea is to compute a robust estimation of standard deviation of the residual errors. In the exploration step, for each subsample k, the median of residuals was computed. If we denote by $\overline{M}$ the least median among all K medians, then a robust estimation of the standard deviation of the residuals is given by (Rousseeuw and Leroy, 1987):

$$\hat{\sigma} = 1.4826 \left[1 + \frac{5}{N-3} \right] \sqrt{\overline{M}} \qquad (11)$$

where N is the number of vertices. Once $\hat{\sigma}$ is known, any vertex j can be considered as an inlier if its residual error satisfies $|r_j| < 3\hat{\sigma}$.

Computational cost. On a 3.2 GHz PC, a non-optimized C code of the robust 3D-to-3D registration takes on average 15 ms assuming that the number of random samples K is set to 20 and the total number of the 3D mesh vertices, N, is 113. This computational time includes both the stereo reconstruction and the robust technique outlined in Figure 5. Thus, by appending the robust 3D-to-3D registration to the appearance-based tracker (described before) a video frame can be processed in about 70 ms.

7 Experimental Results

Figure 6 displays the head and facial action tracking results associated with a 300-frame-long sequence (only four frames are shown). The tracking results were obtained using the adaptive appearance described in Sections 4. The upper left corner of each image shows the current appearance (μ_t) and the current shape-free texture $(\hat{\mathbf{x}}_t)$. In this sequence, the nominal absolute depth of the head was about 80 cm.

As can be seen, the tracking results indicate good alignment between the mesh model and the images. However, it is very difficult to evaluate the accuracy of the out-of-plane motions by only inspecting the projection of the 3D wireframe onto these 2D images.

Therefore, we have used ground truth data for the 3D head pose parameters associated with a video sequence similar to the one shown Figure 6. The ground truth data are recovered by means of 3D registration between dense 3D facial clouds using the Iterative Closest Point algorithm. Figure 7 displays an accuracy comparison between the appearance-based tacker and the improved tracker using ground-truth data. The solid curves correspond to the errors obtained with the appearance-based tracker, and the dashed ones correspond to those obtained with the developed approach including the robust 3D-to-3D registration technique. The top plot corresponds to the pitch angle, the middle plot to the vertical translation, and the bottom plot to the in-depth translation. As can be seen, the most significant improvement affects the in-depth translation. The noisy value of the pitch angle error could be explained by the fact the 3D rotation (improvement) is estimated from a small set of 3D points. However, on average the value of the obtained error is equal to or less than the error obtained with the appearance-based tracker.

8 Conclusion

In this paper, we have proposed a robust 3D face tracker that combines the advantages of both appearance-based trackers and 3D data-based trackers while keeping the CPU time very close to that required by real-time trackers. Experiments on real video sequences indicate that the estimates of the out-of-plane motions of the head can be considerably improved by combining a robust 3D-to-3D registration with the appearance model.

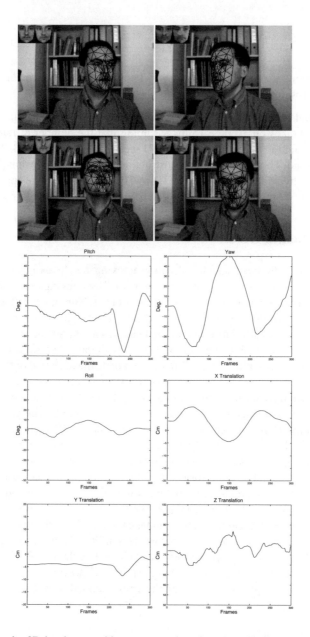

Fig. 6. Tracking the 3D head pose with appearance-based tracker. The sequence length is 300 frames. Only frames 38, 167, 247, and 283 are shown. The six plots display the six degrees of freedom of the 3D head pose as a function of time.

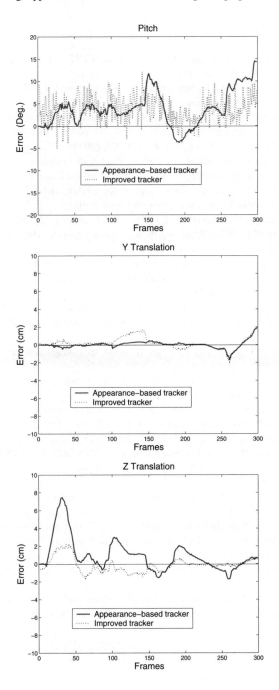

Fig. 7. 3D head pose errors associated with the sequence as a function of the frames. From top to bottom: pitch angle error, vertical translation error, and in-depth translation error. The solid curves display the errors obtained with the appearance-based tracker, and the dashed ones display those obtained with the improved tracker.

References

Ahlberg, J.: An active model for facial feature tracking. EURASIP Journal on Applied Signal Processing 2002(6), 566–571 (2002)

Besl, P., McKay, N.: A method for registration of 3-D shapes. IEEE Transactions on Pattern Analysis and Machine Intelligence 14(2), 239–256 (1992)

Cascia, M., Sclaroff, S., Athitsos, V.: Fast, reliable head tracking under varying illumination: An approach based on registration of texture-mapped 3D models. IEEE Transactions on Pattern Analysis and Machine Intelligence 22(4), 322–336 (2000)

Chetverikov, D., Stepanov, D., Kresk, P.: Robust Euclidean alignment of 3D point sets: the trimmed iterative closet point algorithm. Image and Vision Computing 23, 299–309 (2005)

Cootes, T., Edwards, G., Taylor, C.: Active appearance models. IEEE Transactions on Pattern Analysis and Machine Intelligence 23(6), 681–684 (2001)

Dornaika, F., Davoine, F.: Head and facial animation tracking using appearance-adaptive models and particle filters. In: IEEE Workshop on Real-Time Vision for Human-Computer Interaction, Washington DC, IEEE, Los Alamitos (2004)

Dornaika, F., Sappa, A.: Appearance-based tracker: An evaluation study. In: IEEE International Workshop on Visual Surveillance and Performance Evaluation of Tracking and Surveillance, IEEE, Los Alamitos (2005)

Fischler, M., Bolles, R.: Random sample consensus: A paradigm for model fitting with applications to image analysis and automated cartography. Communication ACM 24(6), 381–395 (1981)

Fitzgibbon, A.: Robust registration of 2D and 3D point sets. Image and Vision Computing 21, 1145–1153 (2003)

Horn, B.: Closed-form solution of absolute orientation using unit quaternions. J. Opt. Soc. Amer. A. 4(4), 629–642 (1987)

Jepson, A., Fleet, D., El-Maraghi, T.: Robust online appearance models for visual tracking. IEEE Transactions on Pattern Analysis and Machine Intelligence 25(10), 1296–1311 (2003)

Lee, D.: Effective Gaussian mixture learning for video background subtraction. IEEE Transactions on Pattern Analysis and Machine Intelligence 27(5), 827–832 (2005)

Malassiotis, S., Strintzis, M.G.: Robust real-time 3D head pose estimation from range data. Pattern Recognition 38(8), 1153–1165 (2005)

Matthews, I., Baker, S.: Active appearance models revisited. International Journal of Computer Vision 60(2), 135–164 (2004)

Moreno, F., Tarrida, A., Andrade-Cetto, J., Sanfeliu, A.: 3D real-time tracking fusing color histograms and stereovision. In: IEEE International Conference on Pattern Recognition, IEEE, Los Alamitos (2002)

Rousseeuw, P., Leroy, A.: Robust Regression and Outlier Detection. John Wiley & Sons, New York (1987)

Zhou, S., Chellappa, R., Mogghaddam, B.: Visual tracking and recognition using appearance-adaptive models in particle filters. IEEE Transactions on Image Processing 13(11), 1473–1490 (2004)

3D Tracking Using 2D-3D Line Segment Correspondence and 2D Point Motion

Woobum Kang[1,*] and Shigeru Eiho[2]

[1] Kyoto University
Gokasho, Uji, Kyoto 611-0011 Japan
kang@tigers-net.com
[2] The Kyoto College of Graduate Studies for Informatics
7 Monzen-cho, Tanaka, Sakyo-ku, Kyoto 606-8225 Japan
s_eiho@kcg.ac.jp

Abstract. In this paper, we propose a 3D tracking method which integrates two kinds of 2D feature tracking techniques. Our tracker searches 2D-3D correspondences used to estimate camera pose on the next frame from detected straight edges and projected 3D-CAD model on the current frame, and tracks corresponding edges on the consecutive frames. By tracking those edges, our tracker can keep correct correspondences even when large camera motion occurs. Furthermore, when the estimated pose seems incorrect, our tracker brings back to the correspondences of the previous frame and proceeds tracking of corresponding edges. Then, on the next frame, our tracker estimates the pose from those correspondences and can recover to the correct pose.

Our tracker also detects and tracks corners on the image as 2D feature points, and estimates the camera pose from 2D-3D line segment correspondences and the motions of feature points on the consecutive frames. As the result, our tracker can suppress the influence of incorrect 2D-3D correspondences and can estimate the pose even when the number of detected correspondences is not enough.

We also propose an approach which estimates both the camera pose and the correspondences. With this approach, our tracker can estimate the pose and the correspondence on the initial frame of the tracking.

From experimental results, we confirmed our tracker can work in real-time with enough accuracy for various applications even with a less accurate CAD model and noisy low resolution images.

Keywords: 3D tracking, CAD model, edge, feature point.

1 Introduction

Image-based markerless 3D tracking is one of the important issues. In one of the well-known approaches for the 3D tracking, called as model-based approach, the tracker estimates the camera pose from 2D-3D correspondences between 2D feature and 3D model. With the techniques (e.g. (Liu et al., 1990), (Christy and Horaud, 1999)) which estimates the pose from various kinds of 2D-3D feature correspondence (line, point,

---

* Most part of this research was done when the authors belonged to Kyoto University. The first author currently works for KEYENCE Corp.

J. Braz et al. (Eds.): VISAPP and GRAPP 2006, CCIS 4, pp. 367–380, 2007.
© Springer-Verlag Berlin Heidelberg 2007

etc.), we can estimate the pose correctly if sufficient number of correspondences are obtained on every frame of tracking. However, this is difficult in the real situation. Therefore, various correspondence estimation approaches for model-based 3D tracking have been proposed. Lowe (Lowe, 1992) proposed an edge-based iterative pose and correspondence estimation approach provided that approximate pose is obtained as the initial guess. Drummond et al. (Drummond and Cipolla, 2002) proposed real-time 3D tracking method using the 2D-3D edge point correspondence.

The weaknesses of 2D-3D model based approach are: (1)They cannot estimate or misestimate when the number of correspondences is not sufficient due to motion blur or measurement error of both 3D model and intrinsic parameters of the camera. (2)In the methods such as (Lowe, 1992) and (Drummond and Cipolla, 2002), which estimate 2D-3D correspondences by projecting the 3D model using the pose on the previous frame and nearest 2D feature search, once the tracker estimates an incorrect pose, it cannot obtain correct correspondences on the latter frames.

Vacchetti et al. (L. Vacchetti and Fua, 2004b) proposed a tracking method using 2D-3D feature point correspondences and feature point motions for the pose estimation. They also proposed a tracking method(L. Vacchetti and Fua, 2004a) which integrates their feature-point-based method(L. Vacchetti and Fua, 2004b) and the edge-based methods proposed in (Drummond and Cipolla, 2002), (Comport et al., 2003). By integrating 2D feature motions on the consecutive frames, they cover the first weakness of model-based approach. However, their tracker can only use the feature points on the surface of tracked object and does not use those on the back ground.

We here propose a markerless 3D tracking method which integrates image-based 2D feature tracking. We estimate the pose from (1) 2D-3D correspondences between straight edges and 3D line segments of the CAD model , and (2) feature point motions on the consecutive frames. We use the corners detected on images as the feature points.

Different from the method proposed on (L. Vacchetti and Fua, 2004b), our method does not restrict the position of feature points and can handle large camera motions by using a strong image-based straight edge tracking method. Moreover, our tracker can keep correct 2D-3D correspondences with a special 2D-3D correspondence update process even if quite a wrong pose is estimated for some numerical failures. And our tracker can recover to the correct pose on the latter frame by tracking corresponding edges and estimating the pose from preserved correspondences obtained just before the incorrect pose estimation.

On the initial frame of our 3D tracking, it is necessary to obtain both the 2D-3D correspondences and the pose. We also propose a method which estimates the pose and the correspondences by using the approximate initial guess of the pose. With this method, our tracker can estimate the pose and the correspondences on the initial frame automatically.

2   Overview of Our 3D Tracking Method

Our 3D tracker estimates the camera pose relative to the world coordinate system on every frame derived from a single camera. We assume that intrinsic parameters of the camera are known. We estimate the camera pose from (1) 2D-3D line segment correspondences between straight edges detected on the image and CAD model, and

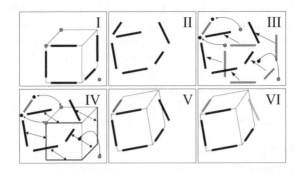

Fig. 1. Straight edge and feature point tracking, pose estimation, and 2D-3D correspondence update. [I:Projected CAD model (thin line), edges corresponding to the model (bold line), and detected feature points. II:Edges detected on the next frame of I. III:Our tracker tracks edges corresponding to the model (solid bold line) and motions of feature points. IV and V:Our tracker estimates the pose from 2D-3D line segment correspondences and feature point motions. VI:Our tracker eliminates incorrectly corresponding edges (dashed gray line) and searches newly found corresponding edges (solid gray line).].

(2) motions of the feature points on the consecutive frames. We use the corners on an image extracted with Tomasi-Kanade method(Shi and Tomasi, 1994) as feature points. Our tracker tracks these points on the consecutive frames by calculating their optical flow using Lucas-Kanade method(Lucas and Kanade, 1981), and uses their motions to estimate the pose. We assume that the pose and the 2D-3D line segment correspondences on the initial frame are provided.

We explain the outline of our method using fig.1. (I) shows projected 3D CAD model (thin line), straight edges corresponding to the model line segments (bold line), and detected feature points. When the new frame comes in, our tracker tracks the edges corresponding to the model line segments and the feature points detected on the previous frame shown as figures (II) and (III). By tracking those edges on the consecutive frames, our tracker can estimate the correct position of those edges even when the large camera motion occurs. After the 2D feature tracking, our tracker eliminates outliers of motions of feature points by fitting fundamental matrix with LMedS method. Then, as figure (IV), our tracker estimates the pose from both 2D-3D line segment correspondences and feature point motions on the consecutive frames. After the pose estimation, shown as the figures (V) and (VI), 2D-3D line segment correspondences are updated by checking the distances between straight edges detected on the current frame and projected 3D CAD model lines.

3 Straight Edge Tracking and Correspondence Update

3.1 Straight Edge Tracking and Detection

Straight edges corresponding to the 3D model line segments are tracked on the consecutive frames. This straight edge tracking is performed with two steps, estimation and matching.

On the estimation step, our edge tracker estimates the motion of the edges by calculating optical flow of all edge pixels for every tracked straight edge. And the tracker fits a line from calculated destinations of edge pixels and eliminates outliers. If those destinations are not on a line, our tracker regards the estimation was failed and stops tracking for that edge.

On the matching step, our tracker searches the edges near the estimated destination. If straight edges exist around there, the tracker regards the one on the nearest as corresponding edge. If there is no corresponding edge but most destinations of the edge pixels are on a line, the tracker constructs a straight edge from estimated destinations of edge pixels and regards it as the corresponding one. Different from the straight edge tracking method proposed by Chiba et al. (Chiba and Kanade, 1998), our edge tracker can track even when the corresponding edge is not detected properly due to motion blur and illumination changes.

On every frame, our tracker detects straight edges on the image by using Canny edge detector(Canny, 1986) for the edge detection. Like the method proposed by Lowe (Lowe, 1987), our tracker detects straight edges by splitting connected edges until all split edges become straight. Then, edges on the neighbor and on a line are merged in order to avoid the fragments.

3.2   Correspondence Update Process

After estimating the pose, our tracker updates 2D-3D correspondences by checking the distances between projected 3D model line segments and straight edges. In the model projection, hidden lines are removed in order to suppress incorrect 2D-3D correspondences. We define the distance and the overlapping ratio between a straight edge and its corresponding projected model line segment using the distances d_1, d_2 and the lengths l, l' as shown in fig.2. d_1 and d_2 are defined as the point-to-line distances between each end point of the projected 3D line segment and the line obtained by extending the straight edge. We define the distance d and the overlapping ratio γ as follows.

$$\begin{cases} d = \frac{1}{2} \left(d_1^2 + d_2^2 \right)^{\frac{1}{2}} \\ \gamma = \quad l/l' \end{cases} \tag{1}$$

Our tracker updates the correspondences with the following two steps; (1) elimination of incorrect correspondences from those currently used for the pose estimation, and (2) addition of new correspondences.

On the elimination step, our tracker calculates the distance for every 2D-3D line segment pair currently regarded as corresponding each other, and estimates the standard deviation of distances $\hat{\sigma}_d$ using MAD(Median Absolute Deviation)(G.A.F. Seber, 1981). Then, the correspondences whose distances d are larger than $\beta \hat{\sigma}_d$ are regarded as incorrect and eliminated. Where β is a constant and its value is around 2-3. As the threshold $\beta \hat{\sigma}_d$ becomes very large if the large displacements occur between the projected models and its corresponding edges, our tracker keeps 2D-3D correspondences of the previous frame if quite a different pose is estimated.

On the addition step, our tracker searches new correspondences by checking the distances between projected model line segments and straight edges, both of which has

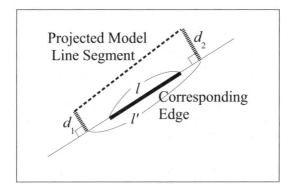

Fig. 2. Distance and overlapping ratio between a 3D model line segment and its corresponding straight edge

no corresponding edge or no corresponding model line segment. If their distance is $d < d_{corres}$ and the overlapping ratio is $\gamma > \gamma_{corres}$, our tracker adds this pair to the correspondences which are used in the pose estimation, where d_{corres} and γ_{corres} are constants, and we set d_{corres} around 2-3[pixel] and $\gamma_{corres} = 0.3$.

4 Pose Estimation for the Tracking

4.1 Pose from Known 2D-3D Line Segment Correspondence

In this method, we estimate the pose by minimizing the following objective function:

$$f(R_n, t_n) = \sum_{l=1}^{L} w_l \phi_l^2 + g(R_n) \tag{2}$$

where $\phi_l(R_n, t_n)$ is error term in 2D-3D correspondence, $g(R_n)$ is the constraint term for rotation matrix R_n, and w_l is weighting coefficients introduced to eliminate outliers.

We define the correspondence error between a 2D line segment (straight edge) and corresponding 3D line segment as follows: Considering fragments of straight edges, we define the error as the squared-sum of point-to-line distances between each end point of projected 3D line segment and extended straight edge as fig. 2.

When one of the end points of a 3D line segment is represented as $X = [X, Y, Z]^T$ in the world coordinate system and represented as $X' = [X', Y', Z']^T$ in the camera coordinate system, the relationship between X and X' is described as follows:

$$X' = RX + t \tag{3}$$

Therefore, squared point-to-line distance between projected an end point and a 2D line $l : ax + by + c = 0(a^2 + b^2 = 1)$ is described as follows.

$$d^2 = \left(a\frac{X'}{Z'} + b\frac{Y'}{Z'} + c\right)^2 \tag{4}$$

By substituting $1/Z'$ to a scale parameter μ in order to simplify the objective function, the distance is described as follows;

$$d'^2 = \mu^2 \left(aX' + bY' + cZ'\right)^2 = \mu^2 \left(\boldsymbol{n}^T \boldsymbol{X}'\right)^2$$
$$= \mu^2 \left[\boldsymbol{n}^T \left(R\boldsymbol{X} + \boldsymbol{t}\right)\right]^2 \tag{5}$$

where $\boldsymbol{n} = [a, b, c]^T$. 2D-3D line segment correspondence error is defined as the squared-sum of d'. When a 2D line segment l_i is corresponding to the 3D line segment L_j, its correspondence error ϕ becomes:

$$\phi(l_i, L_j, R, \boldsymbol{t}) = \sum_{k=1}^{2} \mu_{jk}^2 \left[\boldsymbol{n}_i^T \left(R\boldsymbol{X}_{jk} + \boldsymbol{t}\right)\right]^2 \tag{6}$$

where $\boldsymbol{X}_{jk}(k = 1, 2)$ is the end point of the 3D line segment L_j and μ_{jk} is its scale parameter.

Weighting coefficient w_l is determined from the correspondence error ϕ_l. We set w_l from Tukey's ρ function;

$$w = \begin{cases} \left[1 - \left(\frac{x}{C}\right)^2\right]^2 & |x| \leq C \\ 0 & |x| \geq C \end{cases} \qquad x = \frac{e}{\hat{\sigma}} \tag{7}$$

where e is the error (ϕ_l for w_l) and C is a constant. To determine w_l from eq.7, it is necessary to estimate the standard deviation of errors. According to MAD, standard deviation is estimated as;

$$\hat{\sigma}_{MAD} = 1.4826 \text{ median } \{|\phi_1|, ..., |\phi_L|\} \tag{8}$$

If we use MAD, however, 2D-3D correspondences necessary to estimate the pose uniquely are sometimes regarded as outliers. And the tracker cannot obtain the sufficient number of correspondences. We therefore set $\hat{\sigma}$ from maximum absolute correspondence error of those necessary to estimate the pose uniquely if only a few correspondences are obtained. By writing this maximum absolute error as $|\phi'|$, $\hat{\sigma}$ is determined as follows.

$$\hat{\sigma} = \max\{1.4826|\phi'|, \hat{\sigma}_{MAD}\} \tag{9}$$

To decrease the number of variables, we represent rotation component of the pose by a quaternion $\mathbf{r}_n$ instead of a rotation matrix R_n. The number of variables representing the camera pose is reduced from twelve (nine for R_n and three for $\boldsymbol{t}_n$) to seven (four for $\mathbf{r}_n$ and three for $\boldsymbol{t}_n$). The objective function is represented as follows;

$$f(\mathbf{r}, \boldsymbol{t}) = \sum_{l=1}^{L} w_l \phi_l^2 + g(\mathbf{r}) \tag{10}$$

On the above equation, $g(\mathbf{r})$ becomes the constraint term for the rotation quaternion. The minimization of the objective function is done by repeating weighting coefficients calculation and pose parameter estimation. Pose parameter estimation is done by using nonlinear minimization techniques such as Gauss-Newton approach. The pose estimation procedure is described as follows.

1. Set the weighting coefficients as $w_1 = w_2 = \ldots = w_L = 1$ and set R_{n-1}, t_{n-1} as initial guess of the pose parameters R_n, t_n.
2. Update the pose parameter by the following procedure.
   (a) Calculate the scale parameters $\mu_{lk} = 1/Z'_{lk}$, $(k = 1, 2)$ and ν_{m1}, ν_{m2} from currently estimated pose R_n, t_n.
   (b) Convert R_n to a quaternion $\mathbf{r}_n$, and update the pose to the one which decreases $f(\mathbf{r}_n, t_n)$. Then, convert updated $\mathbf{r}_n$ to a rotation matrix and substitute it to R_n.
   (c) Repeat above procedure until the objective function converges.
3. Calculate ϕ_l and ψ_m, and update the coefficients w_l.
4. Repeat 2 and 3 until the objective function $f(\mathbf{r}_n, t_n)$ becomes sufficiently small.

4.2   Pose from Known 2D-3D Correspondences and Motion Constraints

In this method, we add the motion constraint errors to the objective function of eq.2. The objective function becomes as follows:

$$f(R_n, t_n) = \sum_{l=1}^{L} w_l \phi_l^2 + \sum_{m=1}^{M} w'_m \psi_m^2 + g(R_n) \tag{11}$$

where $\psi_m(R_n, t_n)$ is the motion constraint error. ψ is defined from epipolar constraints for the motion of feature points on the consecutive frames.

When 2D coordinates of a feature point on $n - 1$ and n-th frame are x_{n-1} and x_n respectively, epipolar lines for x_{n-1}, x_n are represented by the following vectors.

$$\begin{cases} n_1 = \nu_1 E^T \tilde{x}_n = [a_1, b_1, c_1]^T \\ n_2 = \nu_2 E \tilde{x}_{n-1} = [a_2, b_2, c_2]^T \end{cases} \tag{12}$$

where E is the essential matrix composed of camera motion parameters on the consecutive frames (R', t'), ν_1, ν_2 are the scale parameters set to satisfy $a_k^2 + b_k^2 = 1 (k = 1, 2)$, and $\tilde{x}$ is the homogeneous representation of 2D point x, i.e., $\tilde{x} = [x, y, 1]^T$. The squared-error ψ^2 is defined as follows.

$$\begin{aligned} \psi^2 &= \left(n_1^T \tilde{x}_{n-1}\right)^2 + \left(n_2^T \tilde{x}_n\right)^2 \\ &= \left(\nu_1^2 + \nu_2^2\right) \left(\tilde{x}_n^T E \tilde{x}_{n-1}\right)^2 \\ &= \left(\nu_1^2 + \nu_2^2\right) \left[\tilde{x}_n^T \left\{t' \times (R' \tilde{x}_{n-1})\right\}\right]^2 \end{aligned} \tag{13}$$

Then, we express the right side of eq.13 by camera pose parameters R_{n-1}, t_{n-1}, R_n, t_n using the following equation which represents the relationship between the motion and the pose on each frame.

$$\begin{cases} R_n = R' R_{n-1} \\ t_n = R' t_{n-1} + t' \end{cases} \tag{14}$$

As we know the pose parameter on $(n - 1)$-th frame R_{n-1}, t_{n-1}, ψ^2 becomes the function of the pose parameter on n-th frame R_n, t_n.

Same as the method of 4.1, we represent the rotation component by a quaternion, and estimate the pose by repeating weight coefficients calculation and pose parameter estimation.

4.3 Pose from Decomposition of Essential Matrix and 2D-3D Line Correspondences

Essential matrix is composed of rotation and translation components of the camera motion R' and t', and we can obtain those parameters by decomposing essential matrix by using SVD(Hartley and Zisserman, 2000). However, motion parameters cannot be determined uniquely from SVD method. We need to choose rotation components from two rotation matrices R'_1, R'_2 obtained by the decomposition, and also need to determine the scale of translation vector t'. We therefore estimate the pose by the following procedure:

1. Decompose the essential matrix estimated from feature point motions and calculate $R'_1, R'_2, \bar{t}'$.
2. Choose R' from R'_1 and R'_2, and determine the scale of t' from 2D-3D line correspondences which are easily obtained from existing 2D-3D line segment correspondences.

In the following discussion, we represent 3D line L by point P on the line and direction D. Any point X on line L is represented using a coefficient κ as $X = P + \kappa D$. When a 3D line L is corresponding to the 2D line l, there exists the following equation:

$$\begin{cases} n^T R D & = 0 \\ n^T (R P + t) = 0 \end{cases} \tag{15}$$

From eqs.14 and 15, and representing the translation vector t' as the product of scale parameter α and normalized vector $\bar{t}'$ ($t' = \alpha \bar{t}'$), we obtain the following equations.

$$n^T (R' R_{n-1} D) = 0 \tag{16}$$

$$n^T \{ R_n P + (R' t_{n-1} + \alpha \bar{t}') \} = 0 \tag{17}$$

On the first, we choose rotation matrix R' from R'_1 and R'_2. We can regard the value of left side of eq.16 as 2D-3D line correspondence error, and we choose R' which gives less median of absolute error. If 2D-3D line correspondences (l_i, L_i), $(i = 1, 2, ..., M)$ are obtained on the n-th frame and two rotation matrices R'_1 and R'_2 appear, R' is chosen from the following equation.

$$R' = \arg \min_{R'_k} e_k \qquad (k = 1, 2) \tag{18}$$

$$e_k = \underset{i}{\text{median}} \left| n_i^T (R'_k R_{n-1} D_i) \right| (i = 1, 2, ..., M)$$

Next, we calculate the scale parameter α. We can calculate it from eq.17 :

$$\alpha = -\frac{n^T (R_n P + R' t_{n-1})}{n^T \bar{t}'} \tag{19}$$

This scale parameter is calculated from every line correspondences (l_i, L_i) and denoted as α_i, then, we determine the scale parameter α from the median of α_i:

$$\alpha = \underset{i}{\text{median}} \; \alpha_i \tag{20}$$

By using the median of parameters in the estimation process, we can eliminate the influence of some incorrect correspondences.

4.4 Switching the Two Pose Estimation Methods

On every frame, our tracker checks whether it has sufficient number of 2D-3D corre-spondences to estimate the pose from 2D-3D correspondences alone. If it has, it esti-mates the pose by the method of section 4.2. Otherwise, the method of section 4.3 is used for estimation.

If there are the sufficient number of 2D-3D correspondences, the tracker also es-timates the pose from 2D-3D correspondence alone using the method of section 4.1. Then, the tracker calculates the maximum absolute errors $|\phi'|$ of those two estimated poses, and chooses the pose whose $|\phi'|$ is smaller. By this choice of the pose from two, the tracker can estimate correct pose even when one of the estimated pose becomes quite wrong for various reasons. Especially, on the next frame after the incorrect pose is estimated, the feature motion constraint becomes incorrect because R_{n-1} and t_{n-1} are incorrect, and only 2D-3D correspondences are correct. On such frames, the tracker can obtain the correct pose estimated from 2D-3D correspondences alone.

5   Pose and Correspondences Estimation on the Initial Frame

On the initial frame of the tracking, it is necessary to know the camera pose and the 2D-3D line segment correspondence. However, it is difficult to estimate the pose and the correspondences automatically if the tracker doesn't have any prior knowledge about the pose. In this section, we propose a method which estimates camera pose and 2D-3D line segment correspondences simultaneously provided that we know approximate camera pose (initial guess).

5.1   Automatic Camera Pose and 2D-3D Line Correspondence Estimation

This method is based on ICP-algorithm(Besl and McKay, 1992) and integrates some robust statistics techniques. It can estimate camera pose and correspondences simulta-neously.

Our method is composed of two steps, namely correspondence step and pose step, just like EM algorithm. On the correspondence step, correspondences between 2D line segments $l = \{l_1, l_2, ..., l_i, ..., l_M\}$, and 3D line segments $L = \{L_1, L_2, ..., L_j, ..., L_N\}$ are fixed from the currently estimated camera pose. On the pose step, the pose is esti-mated from those correspondences. These two steps repeat until the pose parameter converges.

On the correspondence step, 3D line segments are projected using the currently es-timated pose. Then, the 2D line segment corresponding to a 3D line segment is de-termined as the one whose absolute line segment correspondence error $|\phi|$ defined on eq.6 is the smallest. 2D line segment l'_j corresponding to the 3D line segment L_j is determined as the following equation.

$$l'_j = \arg\min_{l_i} |\phi(l_i, L_j, R, t)| \tag{21}$$

On the pose step, camera pose is updated from the correspondences fixed above. We use the weighting coefficients again to decrease the bad effects of incorrect correspondences. The objective function used for updating the pose parameter is described as follows.

$$f(\mathbf{r}, \mathbf{t}) = \sum_{j=1}^{N} w_j \phi^2(l'_j, L_j, \mathbf{r}, \mathbf{t}) + g(\mathbf{r}) \qquad (22)$$

Coefficient w_j is determined from the correspondence error $\phi(l'_j, L_j, \mathbf{r}, \mathbf{t})$ and eq.7. Therefore, it is necessary to estimate standard deviation $\hat{\sigma}$ of line segment correspondence errors. If half or more correspondences are incorrect, we cannot correctly estimate $\hat{\sigma}$ using MAD. We therefore determine $\hat{\sigma}$ not from the distribution of ϕ but from the number of iteration. That is, we use large value of $\hat{\sigma}$ so that every coefficient w_j has almost the same value on the initial few iterations . Then, we gradually decrease $\hat{\sigma}$ as the number of iteration increases, and gradually regard the correspondences that have large errors as incorrect and give less effect to pose update process. Overall procedure of our method is described as follows.

1. Set $\hat{\sigma} = \hat{\sigma}_0$.
2. Repeat the following procedure until the pose parameter converges.
   (a) For every 3D line segment L_j, determine corresponding 2D line segment l'_j from eq.21.
   (b) Set coefficient w_j from eq.7.
   (c) Update the pose parameter to the one which decreases the value of objective function $f(\mathbf{r}, \mathbf{t})$.
   (d) For the next iteration, set $\hat{\sigma} := \gamma\hat{\sigma}$ $(\gamma < 1)$

5.2 Initial Pose and Correspondences Estimation

We applied this method to the initial pose and correspondence estimation problem. As we know the approximate initial guess of the camera pose, we can restrict candidates for the true correspondences in advance. To exclude the correspondences whose projected model line segment is not overlapping to the corresponding straight edge at all, we calculate the distances and the overlapping ratios defined on eq.1 for all possible 2D-3D correspondences and adopt only the correspondences as candidate whose distance is below d_{init} and overlapping ratio is above γ_{init}.

As we restrict the correspondences in advance, it is necessary to modify the criteria defined on eq.21. The modified criteria is described as follows:

$$l'_j = \arg\min_{l_i \in \boldsymbol{l}'_j} |\phi(l_i, L_j, R, \boldsymbol{t})| \qquad (23)$$

Where $\boldsymbol{l}'_j$ is the 2D line segments that are candidates for the one corresponding to the 3D line segment L_j.

After the estimation, it is necessary to choose the true correspondences from ones obtained on the correspondence step. As we have already obtained accurate camera pose, we determine the 2D-3D line segment correspondences same as the correspondence addition process described in section 2.

We applied this method to the pose and correspondences estimation on the initial frame of tracking. The top of fig.3 shows initial guess of the camera pose (bold line)

Fig. 3. Initial pose and correspondence estimation (Top : Initial guess of the pose and candidates for the corresponding edges, Bottom : Accurately estimated pose and edges corresponding to the line segments of CAD model

and the straight edges which are the candidate edges of those corresponding to 3D-Model line segments (thin line), and the bottom shows accurately estimated camera pose using our method.

6   Experimental Results

To evaluate our method, we took the image sequences of an object in a room (a CRT display) and a corridor scene. We used a conventional USB camera (Creative Webcam Pro eX, image size:320×240 pixels) which was calibrated with a conventional calibration software. We prepared CAD models of CRT display and corridor scene by measuring its 3D contours by hand. Because of the measurement error in the CAD model and intrinsic parameters of the camera, displacements sometimes appear between the target objects on the image and the projected model although we carefully estimated the correct pose by hand.

We have tested on two image sequences which are 1000 frames sequence for the CRT display and 300 frames sequence for the corridor scene, and our tracker could track in those sequences well. Snapshots from tracking result are shown in fig.4.

Fig. 4. Projected CAD model using tracking results (Top:CRT display[1000frames sequence], Bottom:corridor scene[300frames sequence])

Fig. 5. Projected model on the consecutive frames with large camera motion (Distance between the target on each frame are approximately 15-20pixels)

Fig. 6. Recovery from incorrect pose (Left : Incorrectly estimated pose, Right : Correctly estimated pose on three frames later from the left image)

Our tracker can track even when the camera moves rapidly. An example of such cases is shown in fig.5. Our tracker can also recover to the correct pose even if once it estimates an incorrect one. Fig.6 shows an example of such scene. The pose on the left side is apparently wrong and large displacements appear. However, we could get the pose with less displacement on the next frame as shown in right side.

One of the reasons for the incorrect pose estimation is the failure of numerical minimization in the pose estimation. As we use nonlinear minimization techniques for the estimation, the parameter sometimes falls into a local minimum and the tracker misestimates the pose. We have tried several nonlinear minimization methods such as proposed by Phong et al.(Phong et al., 1995) and Powell's Dog-leg method(Powell, 1970). However, the results were not good enough.

We implemented the tracker with C++ language. Our program is not optimized well. Even with this program, our tracker could track on 15-20 fps with a conventional PC (CPU : Intel Pentium4 Processor 2.2GHz, 1GB memory). We believe that our method can easily track over 30fps by using optimized program and a faster PC.

7   Conclusions

In this paper, we proposed a 3D tracking method which integrates the 2D feature tracking. By tracking edges and holding 2D-3D correspondences, our tracker can handle large camera motions and can recover to the correct pose even once the pose estimation fails. Moreover, our tracker estimates the pose from both 2D-3D line segment correspondences and motions of feature points. By fusing those two kinds of information, the tracker can suppress the influence of incorrect correspondences and can track even when the sufficient number of 2D-3D correspondences are not obtained. We also proposed an automatic camera pose and 2D-3D correspondences estimation method and succeeded to estimate the pose and correspondences on the initial frame automatically. From the experiments, we confirmed our tracker can track in real-time with noisy low resolution images taken by a cheap USB camera.

As the future work, we intend to measure the 3D position of feature points appeared during the tracking from their 2D positions and estimated poses on a few frame, and continue 2D tracking for them and use their 2D-3D correspondences on the latter frame of the 3D tracking.

References

Besl, P.J., McKay, N.D.: A Method for Registration of 3-D Shapes. IEEE Trans. Pattern Anal. Mach. Intell. 14(2), 239–256 (1992)

Canny, J.: A computational approach to edge detection. IEEE Trans. Pattern Anal. Mach. Intell. 8(6), 679–698 (1986)

Chiba, N., Kanade, T.: A Tracker for Broken and Closely Spaced Lines. In: ISPRS '98, vol. XXXII, pp. 676–683 (1998)

Christy, S., Horaud, R.: Iterative Pose Computation from Line Correspondences. CVIU 73(1), 137–144 (1999)

Comport, A., Marchand, E., Chaumette, F.: A real-time tracker for markerless augmented reality. In: ISMAR'03, pp. 36–45 (2003)

Drummond, T., Cipolla, R.: Real-Time Visual Tracking of Complex Structures. IEEE Trans. Pattern Anal. Mach. Intell. 24(7), 932–946 (2002)

Seber, G.A.F.C.: Nonlinear Regression. ch. 14, Wiley, Chichester (1981)

Hartley, R.I., Zisserman, A.: Multiple View Geometry in Computer Vision. Cambridge University Press, Cambridge (2000)

Vacchetti, L.V.L., Fua, P.: Combining Edge and Texture Information for Real-Time Accurate 3D Camera Tracking. In: ISMAR'04, pp. 48–57 (2004a)

Vacchetti, L., Fua, V.L.P.: Stable Real-Time 3D Tracking Using Online and Offline Information. IEEE Trans. Pattern Anal. Mach. Intell. 26(10), 1385–1391 (2004b)

Liu, Y., Huang, T.S., Faugeras, O.D.: Determination of Camera Location from 2-D to 3-D Line and Point Correspondences. IEEE Trans. Pattern Anal. Mach. Intell. 12(1), 28–37 (1990)

Lowe, D.G.: Three-Dimensional Object Recognition from Single Two-Dimensional Images. Artificial Intelligence 31(3), 355–395 (1987)

Lowe, D.G.: Robust model-based motion tracking through the integration of search and estimation. IJCV 8(2), 113–122 (1992)

Lucas, B., Kanade, T.: An Iterative Image Registration Technique with an Application to Stereo Vision. In: IJCAI'81, pp. 674–679 (1981)

Phong, T., Horaud, R., Yassine, A., Tao, P.: Object Pose from 2-D to 3-D Point and Line Correspondences. IJCV 15(3), 225–243 (1995)

Powell, M.J.D.: A Hybrid Method for Non-linear Equations. In: Rabinowitz, P. (ed.) Numerical Methods for Non-linear Equations, pp. 87–114. Gordon and Breach (1970)

Shi, J., Tomasi, C.: Good Features to Track. In: CVPR'94 (1994)

Vision-Based Tracking System for Head Motion Correction in FMRI Images

Tali Lerner[1], Ehud Rivlin[1], and Moshe Gur[2]

[1] Department of Computer Science, Technion-Israel Institute of Technology, Haifa 32000, Israel
{matali,ehudr}@cs.technion.ac.il
[2] Department of Biomedical Engineering, Technion-Israel Institute of Technology,
Haifa 32000, Israel
mogi@bm.technion.ac.il

Abstract. This paper presents a new vision-based system for motion correction in functional-MRI experiments. fMRI is a popular technique for studying brain functionality by utilizing MRI technology. In an fMRI experiment a subject is required to perform a task while his brain is scanned by an MRI scanner. In order to achieve a high quality analysis the fMRI slices should be aligned. Hence, the subject is requested to avoid head movements during the entire experiment. However, due to the long duration of such experiments head motion is practically unavoidable. Most of the previous work in this field addresses this problem by extracting the head motion parameters from the acquired MRI data. Therefore, these works are limited to relatively small movements and may confuse head motion with brain activities. In the present work the head movements are detected by a system comprised of two cameras that monitor a specially designed device worn on the subject's head. The system does not depend on the acquired MRI data and therefore can overcome large head movements. Additionally, the system can be extended to cope with inter-block motion and can be integrated into the MRI scanner for real-time updates of the scan-planes. The performance of the proposed system was tested in a laboratory environment and in fMRI experiments. It was found that high accuracy is obtained even when facing large head movements.

Keywords: fMRI, pose estimation, motion correction, tracking.

1 Introduction

Magnetic Resonance Imaging (MRI) technology plays a central part in human brain research in the last decade (Belliveau et al., 1991; Bandettini et al., 1992). The utilization of MRI for brain functionality studies is referred to as *functional MRI* (fMRI). In fMRI studies a subject is requested to perform a task while his brain is repeatedly scanned. These tasks may include viewing images, listening to different sounds, performing a mathematical calculation and others. Statistical techniques are applied on the acquired fMRI scans in order to analyze the functionality of the examined parts in the subject's brain. The duration of an fMRI experiment may be relatively long (tens of minutes). During this time the subject is requested to avoid head movements in order to acquire aligning MRI scans along the experiment. The subject's head is stabilized (with pads)

J. Braz et al. (Eds.): VISAPP and GRAPP 2006, CCIS 4, pp. 381–394, 2007.

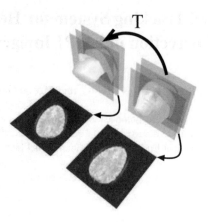

Fig. 1. Illustration of the slice misalignment caused by the head motion. The acquired slices after the motion do not align with the original slices.

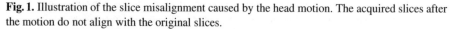

to prevent large head movements. However, small perturbations and slow drift of the head position are practically unavoidable. These motions deteriorate the alignment of scans that were acquired at different time instances, and therefore reduce the credibility and the accuracy of the statistical analysis (see Fig. 1). It is desirable to correct these displacement effects in the MRI slices before analyzing them.

The problem of motion correction in fMRI slices is discussed in several previous studies. Most studies derive the motion parameters from the acquired slices using different methods. These image-based techniques tend to fail in the presence of relatively large displacement. Additionally, due to brain activities, the gray levels of the image vary and may be confused with the head motion effects leading to a reduction in the accuracy of the motion estimates. Some of these studies handle 2D displacement in each slice separately and overlook the 3D nature of the head movement. Other studies extract the 3D motion parameters from the MRI slices under the assumption that no motion had occurred during the *block* (a set of subsequent MRI slices) acquisition but rather only between the different blocks.

The most traditional approach for finding the motion parameters is to compute the 2D transformation which best aligns a shifted image with a reference image. The alignment techniques can be classified into two groups: image intensity based and Fourier space based. The image intensity based group includes the works (Woods et al., 1992; Woods et al., 1993) which suggest defining images as being effectively the same when their voxel-by-voxel ratio is a constant. (Hajnal et al., 1995) suggests defining the difference between images using the mean square voxel-by-voxel error. Other intensity based works can be found in (Friston et al., 1996; Thesen et al., 2000; Ciulla and Deek, 2002). The Fourier space alignment techniques detect the motion parameters using Fourier methods that can be applied on the raw data of MRI images since it is collected in that domain. Examples of such techniques can be found in (Zoroofi et al., 1996; Kim et al., 2002; Caparelli et al., 2003). A different approach can be found in (Derbyshire et al., 1998). The described real-time system extracts the 3D position of the subject's head from an external source of information. Three coils are attached to the subject's head and their spacial location is monitored using magnetic resonance techniques. The computed motion is applied on the MRI scan-plane in order to chase the subject's head. The disadvantage of this system is the limited number of features (the coils) that lead to poor estimation of head position.

In the present work a new vision-based solution to the head motion correction problem is presented. The proposed system includes two calibrated and synchronized cameras for tracking the movements of a specially designed device which is worn on the subject's head. The monitored motion is utilized to produce motion-free MRI slices. Similarly to (Derbyshire et al., 1998) the system computes the 3D motion parameters using an external source of information (the optical tracking configuration), and therefore it can overcome extremely large head motion. Although the system presented here assumes no head motion during the block acquisition it can be easily extended to cope with inter-block motion when detecting the head position for each slice separately.

The rest of this paper is organized as follows: Section 2 gives a brief overview of the system. Section 3 describes the algorithms and devices used for the system calibration. The algorithms and devices used for the motion detection are described in Section 4. A method for correcting the MRI data is presented in Section 5. Section 6 elaborates on a series of lab experiments and Section 7 shows qualitative and quantitative results when applying the system in a real fMRI experiment. Finally, conclusions are noted in Section 8.

2   System Overview

The system presented in this work is composed of a specially designed tracking device which is strapped to the subject's head, and two cameras with zooming capability. The cameras are positioned on both sides of the MRI bed and monitor the movements of the tracking device (see Fig. 2). When using the system, three main stages are performed: system calibration, head motion detection, and MRI blocks correction.

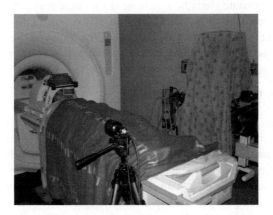

Fig. 2. The system configuration. The subject is wearing the device on his head and the two cameras monitor the movements of the tracking device.

Fig. 3. The calibration device designed for computing the relative position of the cameras

In the system calibration stage, the internal parameters of the two cameras and their relative position are computed. Once this information is evaluated the *pose* (position + orientation) of the subject's head w.r.t the cameras' coordinate systems can be accurately detected using stereopsis methods. Since the final objective is to correct the motion in the MRI slices, the head motion w.r.t the MRI system is required. For that aim the pose of the cameras w.r.t the MRI system is also extracted during the calibration phase.

Once the system is calibrated the fMRI experiment can begin. A head device is strapped to the subject's head during the experiment. Due to rigid body motion laws a single motion transformation applies to both the head and the head device. Therefore, by monitoring the pose of the head device the head movements can be deduced. Using the cameras relative position w.r.t the MRI, the head motion transformation can be expressed under the MRI coordinate system.

Finally, the MRI blocks can be corrected. Utilizing the head motion transformation, a compensating transformation can be applied on the MRI blocks. The generated motion-free blocks are the blocks that would have been obtained in the absence of head motion.

3   System Calibration

The calibration procedure starts by obtaining the internal parameters of each camera using a standard technique (Bouguet,). Next, the relative pose between the two cameras and their pose w.r.t the MRI system are estimated. The rest of this section elaborates on the methods and the custom made devices that participate in these procedures.

3.1   Finding the Cameras Relative Position

Extremely accurate pose estimates are required for a qualitative motion correction of the fMRI slices. For this purpose, a multi-camera pose estimation algorithm, referred to as *TwoCamPose*, is presented in Section 4.2. This algorithm requires the relative position and orientation between the two cameras. The accuracy of this connecting transformation significantly influences the obtained accuracies of the TwoCamPose algorithm. A calibration device composed of three planes is designed. Two planes create an angle of 120° and the third plane is orthogonal to both of them. On each plane a chessboard image was attached (see Fig. 3). The 3D locations of the corners on the three chessboards are known and serve as features for the device pose computation. The fact that

the features constellation is not coplanar drastically improves the accuracy of the obtained pose estimates. The device is placed in several positions and its poses w.r.t each
of the cameras are computed. The connecting transformation between the cameras is
computed as the composition of the device poses:

$$^{cam2}_{cam1}T = ^{cam2}_{device}T \cdot ^{device}_{cam1}T \tag{1}$$

where $^B_A T$ represents the Euclidean transformation from coordinate system A to B. The
parameters of these composed transformations are averaged to derive the final estimate
of the cameras relative position and orientation.

3.2 Cameras Pose w.r.t the MRI Coordinate System

Although the cameras' relative position enables the computation of the tracking device
pose w.r.t the cameras, the required information is its motion w.r.t the MRI coordinate
system. Therefore, the linking transformation from the cameras coordinate system to
the MRI coordinate system is necessary. For this purpose a device, referred to as *phantom*, is designed (see Fig. 4(b)). This device is composed of two main components. At
the front end a planar chessboard is installed. Using the TwoCamPose algorithm the
pose of the phantom device is obtained. At the back end, a $120 \times 120 \times 50$ mm water
container is attached see Fig. 4(a). This container is scanned by the MRI scanner using
high resolution parameters. Next, the slices produced by the MRI scanner are registered
to the geometrical model of the container. In order to acquire the 3D registration parameters with high accuracy, sixteen stakes were added to the geometrical structure of
the container. Once the poses of the phantom w.r.t the MRI system and the cameras are
known, the linking transformation between the cameras and the MRI system is derived.

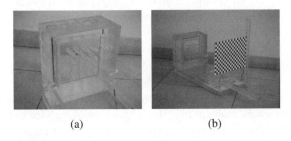

(a)   (b)

Fig. 4. The phantom device designed for linking the cameras to the MRI coordinate system

4 Motion Detection

This section details the heart of the system that is presented in this paper. The detection
of the subject's head motion is performed throughout the entire fMRI experiment. A
specially designed device is strapped to the subject's head and is monitored by the two
cameras. Later, the recorded information is analyzed in order to compute the compensating transformations for the MRI slices.

Fig. 5. The head device strapped to a subject's head

4.1   The Head Device

Monitoring the head movements is performed using a device that is worn by the subject. The device is composed of a strip which is placed on the subject's head, and two rods attached to it from both sides of the head near his temples. These rods are linked together in front of the chin to a *tracking device* that is monitored by the cameras (see Fig. 5). The tracking device is built of two 50×80 mm planes that create an angle of $90°$ between them. "L"-shaped features are arranged in four rows on the tracking device planes. The features in each row have a unique orientation which assist in the correspondence solution. The features orientation is detected by examining the direction of the vector from the center of the L-feature bounding-box to its gravity-center (see Fig. 6). The described configuration of the tracking device enables obtaining the head motion with high accuracy, as can be observed in Section 6.

4.2   The "TwoCamPose" Algorithm

During the system calibration procedure the relative position of the two cameras is computed. Utilizing this piece of information, the pose of the tracking device can be obtained in a straightforward manner: first, the 3D location of each feature is separately reconstructed w.r.t the cameras using a standard triangulation algorithm (Hartley and Zisserman, 2000). Next, the pose is computed from the 3D-to-3D feature registration (Umeyama, 1991). This approach is advantageous because both steps have closed-form solutions which make them computationally attractive. However, the triangulation step of the above approach overlooks the known 3D constellation of the features. Since the pose estimation computation is performed off-line, obtaining high accuracy is preferred over computational duration. Hence, an alternative method for the pose computation, referred to as *"TwoCamPose"*, is proposed. Let p_i be the 3D location of the i'th feature w.r.t the coordinate system of the model. Let t_{12} and R_{12} be the relative position and orientation, respectively, between the two cameras. Given the 2D

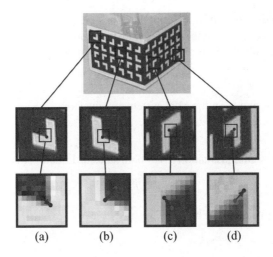

(a)   (b)   (c)   (d)

Fig. 6. Orientation classification method of the L-shaped features on the tracking device. The cyan dot represents the center of the feature's bounding box while the purple dot represents its center of gravity. The classification method utilizes the direction of the green arrows shown in (a)-(d).

measurements from each of the cameras - $\tilde{I}_{i,1}$ and $\tilde{I}_{i,2}$, this algorithm searches for the pose that minimizes the objective-function:

$$\sum_{i=1}^{n} \left(\frac{v_i}{(v_i)_z} - \tilde{I}_{i,1} \right)^2 + \left(\frac{R_{12}v_i + t_{12}}{(R_{12}v_i + t_{12})_z} - \tilde{I}_{i,2} \right)^2 , \qquad (2)$$

where $v_i = R \cdot p_i + t$, R and t are the pose hypothesis. The above function reflects the sum of the squared distances between the 2D extracted features from each camera and their reprojected 3D features given a pose hypothesis. This function was minimized using the Newton-Raphson optimization technique. Although the TwoCamPose algorithm is presented for only two cameras it can be easily extended to an arbitrary number of cameras. The TwoCamPose algorithm achieves more accurate pose estimates than the triangulation technique as will be shown in Section 6.

4.3 Construction of the Compensating Transformation

By composing two poses of the tracking device w.r.t the cameras, the device's motion, and thus the subject's head motion, is computed. Therefore, this motion transformation is also obtained w.r.t the cameras. Since the fMRI slices are acquired w.r.t the MRI system, the motion transformation must be expressed w.r.t the same system. Consider two time instances: t_0 and t_1, before and after a single movement of the head. Each time instance corresponds to a coordinate system D_0 and D_1 attached to the tracking device. Consider a point p_0 in the subject's brain. Due to the head movement this point is transferred to a new position p_1. Since it is assumed that the tracking device and the head move rigidly:

$$^{D_0}p_0 = {}^{D_1}p_1. \qquad (3)$$

In the above equation the left superscript describes the coordinate system in which the vector is represented. Let $\tilde{T}$ be the desired transformation between the points p_0 and p_1 under the MRI coordinate system. Using this transformation one can write:

$$^{MRI}p_1 = \tilde{T} \cdot {}^{MRI}p_0. \tag{4}$$

The positions of p_0 and p_1 in the MRI system are given by

$$^{MRI}p_i = {}^{MRI}_{D_i}T \cdot {}^{D_i}p_i \tag{5}$$

where $i = 1, 2$. Assigning Equation (5) to both sides of Equation (4) yields:

$$^{MRI}_{D_1}T \cdot {}^{D_1}p_1 = \tilde{T} \cdot {}^{MRI}_{D_0}T \cdot {}^{D_0}p_0. \tag{6}$$

Multiplying the left side of (6) by $^{D_1}_{MRI}T$ results:

$$^{D_1}p_1 = {}^{D_1}_{MRI}T \cdot \tilde{T} \cdot {}^{MRI}_{D_0}T \cdot {}^{D_0}p_0. \tag{7}$$

Recalling (3), the multiplication of the three transformations must be the identity transformation I:

$$^{D_1}_{MRI}T \cdot \tilde{T} \cdot {}^{MRI}_{D_0}T = I. \tag{8}$$

Multiplying by the inverse transformations yields the final result:

$$\tilde{T} = {}^{MRI}_{D_1}T \cdot {}^{D_0}_{MRI}T. \tag{9}$$

This transformation supplies a description of the subject's head motion between two time instances during the fMRI experiment.

In this work the first block is perceived as the reference block while the rest of the blocks are corrected according to its position. As a result, the movements between the reference block and the rest of the blocks w.r.t the MRI coordinate system are computed as described above. Similarly to (Derbyshire et al., 1998) the $\tilde{T}$ transformation could be supplied to the MRI scanner in order to update the scan-planes position. This way the slices chase the subject's head position during their acquisition and therefore no postprocessing motion compensation is necessary.

5   Motion Compensation in MRI Slices

The motion compensation is the final step of the system presented in this work. In this step, motion-free slices are synthesized from the existing MRI slices using the head movement transformation - $\tilde{T}$. As mentioned above, a single transformation is assigned to each block in the fMRI data. By applying this transformation on the block, its slices chase the subject's moving head. Each slice is represented by a 3D regular and planar grid. The grid points represent the center of voxels in the MRI scan. The location of the grid points w.r.t the MRI coordinate system is supplied by the MRI image format. In order to produce the motion-free slice, the $\tilde{T}$ transformation is applied on each of the grid points (see Fig. 7). The new gray level of the transformed grid point is determined by identifying its eight surrounding voxels in the origin block and applying trilinear interpolation on their gray level values.

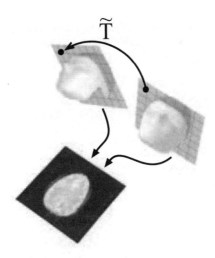

Fig. 7. Motion compensation in the fMRI slices. The head movement transformation $- \tilde{T}$ is applied to each of the MRI slices' grid points.

6 Lab Experiments

A series of lab experiments were conducted to evaluate the ability of the TwoCamPose algorithm described in section 4.2 to detect small motions and compare its accuracy to the triangulation based 3D reconstruction algorithm described in the same section. The tracking device was attached to a robotic arm and small motion was applied to it. The experiment involved moving the tracking device along a constant direction by ten steps of 0.1 mm in order to complete a trajectory of 1 mm. The motion was translational only, no rotation was involved. The eleven poses were estimated using the two evaluated algorithms. Although the structure of the true trajectory was known (pure translational motion along a constant direction), its relative position w.r.t the cameras was unknown. In order to overcome this obstacle, least squares alignment was performed between the true trajectory and the measured trajectory (the eleven poses), and the distances between the two fitted trajectories were measured. Three different trajectories were examined. Each one aligned with one of the main axes: X, Y, and Z. Tables 1 and 2 compare the mean and maximal errors of the two evaluated algorithms computed from the three trajectories. One can easily observe that the TwoCamPose algorithm achieves better results. The results of the experiment indicate that motions as small as 0.1 mm can be

Table 1. Comparison of the translation errors in each trajectory between the TwoCamPose and the Triangulation algorithms described in Section 4.2. The translation error is measured in mm.

Alg.	X		Y		Z	
	Mean	Max	Mean	Max	Mean	Max
TwoCamPose	0.0204	0.0335	0.0277	0.0721	0.0283	0.0559
Triangulation	0.0651	0.1308	0.0719	0.186	0.0602	0.1055

Table 2. Comparison of the rotation errors in each trajectory between the TwoCamPose and the Triangulation algorithms described in Section 4.2. The angular error is measured in degrees.

Alg.	ϕ		θ		ψ	
	Mean	Max	Mean	Max	Mean	Max
TwoCamPose	0.0131	0.0197	0.0117	0.017	0.0115	0.0162
Triangulation	0.0801	0.1734	0.0619	0.1418	0.0736	0.1195

detected with high accuracy using the TwoCamPose algorithm. These accuracies are very small compared to the fMRI image resolution which is at least 1.75 mm in X and Y axes and 2.8 mm in the Z axis.

7   Results

In this section the results that were obtained by the system described in this work are presented. fMRI experiments with a subject were conducted. The subject wore the head device and visual stimulations were presented to him while his brain was scanned (see Fig. 2 for the experiment's setup). Three experiments were recorded. In the first one the subject was asked to avoid motion as much as possible, in the second experiment the subject was asked to move slightly; and in the last experiment the subject was allowed to perform larger movements.

The algorithms described in this work were applied on the recorded MRI blocks producing new motion-free blocks. These corrected blocks were compared to the original (uncorrected) blocks both qualitatively and quantitatively. Figures 8 through 10 show an example of the displacement and the correction quality of a single slice. In each figure, the blue line represents the contour of the brain in the first block, the red dashed line represents the contour of the brain taken from another block, and the green dashed line represents the contour of the brain taken from the same block after compensation. As can be observed, the brain offset was correctly detected and compensated even in cases of large head motion. In Fig. 11 the average image of the corresponding slices taken from all the original blocks is compared to the same one taken from the corrected blocks. As can be observed, the average image of the original blocks is blurred and unclear while these artifacts are significantly reduced in its corrected counterpart.

In addition to the described qualitative results, a quantitative comparison between the original and the corrected blocks from the three experiments is presented in Table 3. Two measurements were used for this comparison: correlation coefficient and Forbenius norm. The correlation coefficient is computed by:

$$c = \frac{\sum_m \sum_n (R_{mn} - \bar{R})(A_{mn} - \bar{A})}{\sqrt{(\sum_m \sum_n (R_{mn} - \bar{R})^2)(\sum_m \sum_n (A_{mn} - \bar{A})^2)}} \tag{10}$$

where A is a slice and R is its corresponding reference slice. $\bar{R}$ and $\bar{A}$ are the mean values of the these slices. The Forbenius norm value is defined as:

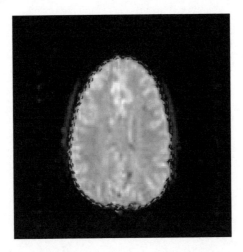

Fig. 8. Motion compensation in a slice from the first experiment (no intended motion)

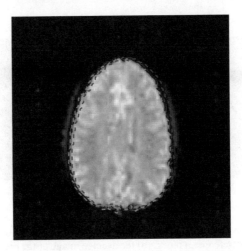

Fig. 9. Motion compensation in a slice from the second experiment (small intended motion)

$$f = \sqrt{\sum_m \sum_n (R_{mn} - A_{mn})^2}. \tag{11}$$

For both measurements the first block served as a reference block. The similarity between each slice and its corresponding slice in the reference block was evaluated by the two measurements. The similarity of the entire experiment was evaluated by averaging the similarity measurement of all its slices. As shown in Table 3 the alignment quality of the original blocks deteriorates when the motion's magnitude increases. The corrected

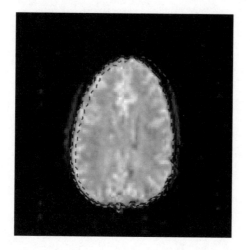

Fig. 10. Motion compensation in a slice from the third experiment (relatively large intended motion)

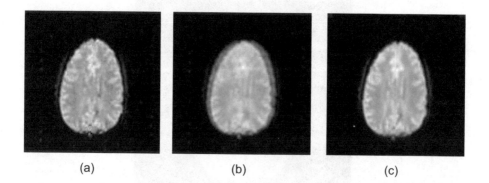

(a)   (b)   (c)

Fig. 11. Average images comparison of the third experiment (relatively large intended motion). (a) a slice from the first (reference) block. (b) the average image of the corresponding slices from all the original blocks. (c) the average image of the corresponding slices from all the corrected blocks.

Table 3. In this table the original and corrected blocks are compared by the average correlation coefficient (Equation 10) and average Forbenius norm (Equation 11) which were obtained from the three experiments

	Small Motion		Medium Motion		Large Motion	
	Correlation	Forbenius	Correlation	Forbenius	Correlation	Forbenius
Original	0.9865	6.1136	0.9816	7.3265	0.9411	13.569
Corrected	0.9963	3.8939	0.9957	3.8394	0.9946	4.3644

blocks, on the other hand, maintain high and almost constant alignment quality for all motion types. These results verify the advantage of utilizing the proposed system in fMRI experiments.

8   Conclusions

In this paper a new vision-based system for motion correction in fMRI experiments is proposed. The quality of the experiment's analysis significantly depends on the magnitude of the subject's head movements while the MRI scans were acquired. Due to the typical long duration of an fMRI experiment, head motion is practically unavoidable. Most of the previous work in this field addressed this problem by extracting the head motion parameters from the acquired MRI data. The system that was presented here detects the head movements using two calibrated cameras that monitor a head-device worn by the subject during the experiment. The system does not depend on the acquired MRI data and therefore can overcome large head movements. Additionally, the system can be extended to cope with inter-block motion and can be integrated into the MRI scanner for real-time updates of the scan-planes. As was shown in the lab experiments, the head motion is detected with sub-millimetric accuracy. The applicability of the system was tested with subjects and proved to achieve a high quality correction of corrupted MRI data even when dealing with large head motion.

References

Bandettini, P., Wong, E., Hinks, R., Tikofsky, R., Hyde, J.: Time course epi of human brain function during task activation. Journal of Magn. Reson. Med. 25, 390–397 (1992)

Belliveau, J., Kennedy, D., McKinstry, R., Buchbinder, B., Weisskoff, R., Cohen, M., Vevea, J., Brady, T., Rosen, B.: Functional mapping of the human visual cortex by magnetic resonance imaging. Science 254, 716–719 (1991)

Bouguet, J.: Camera calibration toolbox for matlab http://www.vision.caltech.edu/bouguetj/calib_doc

Caparelli, E., Tomasi, D., Arnold, S., Chang, L., Ernst, T.: K-spaced based summary motion detection for functional magnetic resonance imaging. NeuroImage 20, 1411–1418 (2003)

Ciulla, C., Deek, F.: Performance assessment of an algorithm for the alignment of fmri time series. Brain Tomography 14(4) (2002)

Derbyshire, J., Wright, G., Henkelman, R., Hinks, R.: Dynamic scan-plane tracking using mr position monitoring. Journal of Magn. Reson. Med. 5, 924–932 (1998)

Friston, K., William, S., Howard, R., Frackowiak, R., Tuner, R.: Movement-related effects in fmri time-series. Journal of Magn. Reson. Med. 35, 346–355 (1996)

Hajnal, J., Saeed, N., Soar, E., Oatridge, A., Young, I., Bydder, G.: A registration and interpolation procedure for subvoxel matching of serially acquired mr images. Journal of Computer Assisted Tomography 19, 289–296 (1995)

Hartley, R., Zisserman, A.: Multiple View Geometry in Computer Vision. Cambridge University Press, Cambridge (2000)

Kim, E., Park, N., Choi, M., Tamura, S.: Cancellation of mri motion artifact in image plane. In: IEEE Intrumentation and Measurements, IEEE Computer Society Press, Los Alamitos (2002)

Thesen, S., Hied, O., Mueller, E., Schad, L.: Prospective acquisition correction for head tracking for real-time fmri. Journal of Magn. Reson. Med. 44, 457–465 (2000)

Umeyama, S.: Least-squares estimation of transformation parameters between two point patterns. IEEE Trans. on Pattern Analysis and Machine Intelligence. Journal of Computer Assisted Tomography 13, 376–380 (1991)

Woods, R., Cherry, S., Mazziotta, J.: Rapid automated algorithm for aligning and reslicing pet images. Journal of Computer Assisted Tomography 16, 620–633 (1992)

Woods, R., Mazziotta, J., Cherry, S.: Mri-pet registration with automated algorithm. Journal of Computer Assisted Tomography 17, 536–546 (1993)

Zoroofi, R., Sato, Y., Tamura, S., Naito, H.: Mri artifacts cancellation due to rigid motion in the imaging plane. IEEE Tran. on Medical Imaging 15(6) (1996)

Learning Nonlinear Manifolds of Dynamic Textures

Ishan Awasthi[1] and Ahmed Elgammal[2]

[1] Department of Electrical and Computer Engineering, Rutgers University,
Piscataway, NJ, USA
awasthiishan@eden.rutgers.edu
[2] Department of Computer Science, Rutgers University, Piscataway, NJ, USA
elgammal@cs.rutgers.edu

Abstract. Dynamic textures are sequences of images of moving scenes that show stationarity properties in time. Eg: waves, flame, fountain, etc. Recent attempts at generating, potentially, infinitely long sequences model the dynamic texture as a Linear Dynamic System. This assumes a linear correlation in the input sequence. Most real world sequences however, exhibit nonlinear correlation between frames. In this paper, we propose a technique of generating dynamic textures using a low dimension model that preserves the non-linear correlation. We use nonlinear dimensionality reduction to create an embedding of the input sequence. Using this embedding, a nonlinear mapping is learnt from the embedded space into the image input space. Any input is represented by a linear combination of nonlinear bases functions centered along the manifold in the embedded space. A spline is used to move along the input manifold in this embedded space as a similar manifold is created for the output. The nonlinear mapping learnt on the input is used to map this new manifold into a sequence in the image space. Output sequences, thus created, contain images never present in the original sequence and are very realistic.

Keywords: Texture, Dynamic Texture, Image-based Rendering, Non Linear Manifold Learning.

1 Introduction

Our aim is to design an algorithmic framework that allows the creation of photorealistic, yet, arbitrarily long sequences of images for a dynamic scene, based on a short input sequence of a similar scene. Variously referred to as Dynamic Textures (Soatto et al, 2001), Video Textures (Schödl et al., 2000) or Temporal Textures (Szummer et al., 1996), these are image sequences that model motion patterns of indeterminate spatial and temporal extent. Waves in water, grass in wind, smoke, flame, fire, waterfall, etc. are a few examples of phenomena that fall in this category. There are two basic ways to approach this problem,

a) Physics based rendering
b) Image based rendering

Physics based rendering is primarily focused on creating a physical model derived from the standard principles, to recreate the dynamics of the system. To make the

J. Braz et al. (Eds.): VISAPP and GRAPP 2006, CCIS 4, pp. 395–405, 2007.
© Springer-Verlag Berlin Heidelberg 2007

output a little more realistic, approximations are then introduced and the model is simulated to synthesize an output sequence. The main advantage of this technique is that it provides extensive manipulation capability and an avenue to use the model for scientific calculations. But this technique suffers from the disadvantage of being computationally expensive and being less photorealistic. Perry and Picard (Perry et al., 1994) and Stam et al. (Stam et al., 1995) depicted the power and use of physics based models to synthesize sequences of gaseous phenomena like fire, flame, smoke, etc. Hodgins et al. (Hodgins et al, 1998) proposed a physical model for synthesizing and studying walking gaits. These provided sequences which could be easily manipulated but failed to produce visually appealing outputs.

Image based rendering techniques are focused on the creation of visually appealing and realistic output sequences. These could either follow a procedural technique generating synthetic images by clever concatenation or repetition of image frames. Or, these could be based on a model of the visual signal of the input sequence. Schödl et al. (Schödl et al., 2000) used a procedural technique to carefully choose sub-loops of an original video sequence and create new sequences. They found frames representing 'transition points', in the original sequence. By selecting the frames that did not end up at 'dead-ends', that is, places in the sequence from which there are no graceful exits, they created very realistic output sequences. But they only replayed already existing frames, and had to rely on morphing and blending to compensate for visual discontinuities. Sequences which did not have similar frames well spaced temporally, were very difficult to be synthesized. Many natural processes like fluids were thus, hard to synthesize. Kwatra et al. introduced a new seam finding and patch fitting technique for video sequences. They represented video sequences by 3D spatio-temporal textures. Two such 3D textures could be merged by calculating a 2D surface which could act as the optimal seam. However like in (Schödl et al., 2000), they first found transition points by comparing the frames of the input sequence. Then in a window of a few frames around this transition they found an optimal seam to join the two sequences, represented as 3D textures. Since they rely on transitions, they sometimes need very long input sequences to find similar frames and a good seam. Both (Schödl et al., 2000) and (13), offered little in terms of editability as the only parameter that could be controlled was the length of the output sequence. Simple control like slowing down or speeding up could not be achieved. It was only techniques based on a model of the visual signal in the input images, that provided this opportunity to control various aspects of the output. Szummer and Picard (Szummer et al., 1996) suggested a STAR model for generating temporal textures using an Auto Regressive Process (ARP). Fitzgibbon (Fitzgibbon et al., 2001) introduced a model based technique of creating video textures by projecting the images into a low-dimensional eigenspace, and modeling them using a moving average ARP. Here, some of the initial eigenvector responses (depicting non-periodic motions, like panning) had to be removed manually. Soatto et al. (Soatto et al, 2001) produced similar work. They modeled dynamic textures as a Linear Dynamic System (LDS) using either a set of principal components or a wavelet filter bank. They could model complex visual phenomena such as smoke and water waves with a relatively low dimensional representation. The use of a model not only allowed for greater editing power but the output sequences also included images that were never a part of the original sequence. However, the outputs were blurry compared to those from non-procedural techniques and for a few sequences the signal would decay rapidly and the intensity gets saturated. Yuan et al. (Yuan et al., 2004) extended this work by introducing feedback control and modeling the system as a closed loop LDS. The feedback loop corrected the problem of signal decay. But the output generated was still blurry. This is because these models assume a linear correlation between the various input frames.

In this paper, we propose a new modeling framework that captures the non-linear characteristics of the input. This provides clear output sequences comparable to those of the procedural techniques while providing better control on the output through model parameters. The organization of the paper is as follows: Section 2 describes the mathematical framework that forms the basis of our model. In section 3, we provide a brief overview of Non-Linear Dimensionality Reduction (NLDR). Section 4 describes the technique used to model the dynamics of the sequence in the embedded space. In section 5, we describe the methodology of transforming the model from the low dimension embedding space to the observed image space. Finally, section 6 presents the results of using our framework on a diverse set of input image sequences.

2 Model Framework

In this section we summarize the mathematical framework that we use for modeling the dynamic texture. The existing image based techniques model the input visual signal ((Soatto et al, 2001),(Fitzgibbon et al., 2001),(Szummer et al., 1996)) for creating dynamic textures, using a linear dynamic system of the following form:

$$x_t = Ax_{t-1} + v_t, \quad v_t \sim \mathbb{N}(0, \Sigma_v)$$
$$y_t = Cx_t + w_t, \quad w_t \sim \mathbb{N}(0, \Sigma_w)$$

Here, $y_t \in R^n$ is the observation vector; $x_t \in R^r, r \ll n$ is the hidden state vector, A is the system matrix; C is the output matrix and v_t, w_t are Gaussian white noises driving the system. In such a system, the observation is a linear function of the state. The limitation of this system is that this captures only the linear correlation between subsequent images. The lack of non-linear characteristics, lead to an output sequence that is not as crisp and detailed as the input.

We, propose a new model based on non-linear dimensionality reduction, which overcomes this shortcoming. The state representation is nonlinearly related to the observation and therefore, the parameters learnt, effectively model the non-linearities relating to substructures and small movements in the input sequence. The framework we propose is:

$$x_t = Ax_{t-1} + v_t, \quad v_t \sim \mathbb{N}(0, \Sigma_v)$$
$$y_t = B\psi(x_t) + w_t, \quad w_t \sim \mathbb{N}(0, \Sigma_w)$$

Where, $y_t \in R^n$ is the observation vector; $x_t \in R^r, r \ll n$ is the hidden state vector, A is the system matrix; B represents the coefficients of non-linear mappings; $\psi(x)$ is a function incorporating the basis functions to be used with B to define the non-linear mapping and v_t, w_t are Gaussian white noises driving the system.

We use NLDR using Locally Linear Embedding (LLE)(Roweis et al., 2000) and isometric feature mapping (Isomap) (Tenenbaum et al., 2000), to achieve a nonlinear embedding of the sequence. Given such an embedding, we explicitly model the transitions using a spline curve. This models the nonlinear manifold of the texture. Using the embedding, a RBF nonlinear mapping is fitted to the observation which leads to the nonlinear observation model in section 5-equation (2).

3   Non-linear Embedding

The model based approaches use dimensionality reduction to extract compact representations of relevant characteristics defining the data variability. Two popular forms of dimensionality reduction are principal component analysis (PCA) and multidimensional scaling (MDS). Both PCA and MDS are eigenvector methods that model variations in high dimensional data. PCA, finds a low-dimensional embedding of the data points that best preserves their variance as measured in the high-dimensional input space by computing the linear projections in the directions of greatest variance using the top eigenvectors of the data covariance matrix. Metric MDS, computes the low dimensional embedding that best preserves pair-wise distances between data points. If these distances correspond to Euclidean distances, the results of metric MDS are similar to those of PCA. Both methods are simple to implement, and their optimizations do not involve local minima, making these a popular choice despite their inherent limitations as linear methods. However, most scenes of simple natural phenomena depict non-linear dynamics and linear dimensionality reduction fails to capture the factors defining these non-linear characteristics. To overcome this shortcoming, we use non-linear dimensionality reduction to project the images into a low dimensionality embedding space. This is achieved using either the LLE or the Isomap algorithm. The following sub-sections discuss these methods in brief.

3.1   Locally Linear Embedding (LLE)

According to the LLE framework (Roweis et al., 2000), given the assumption that each data point and its neighbors lie on a locally linear patch of the manifold (Roweis et al., 2000), each point (image frame) y_i can be reconstructed based on a linear mapping $\sum_j w_{ij} y_i$ that weights its neighbors contributions using the weights w_{ij}. In our case, the neighborhood of each point is determined by its K nearest neighbors based on the distance in the input space. The objective is to find such weights that minimize the global reconstruction error,

$$E(w) = \sum_i \mid y_i - \sum_i w_{ij} y_i \mid^2, \quad \text{where } i, j = 1 \cdots N$$

The weights are constrained such that w_{ij} is set to 0 if point y_j is not within the K nearest neighbors of point y_i. This will guarantee that each point is reconstructed from its neighbors only. The weights obtained by minimizing the error in the above equation are invariant to rotations and re-scalings. To make them invariant to translation, the weights are also constrained to sum up to one across each row, i.e., the minimization is subject to $\sum_j w_{ij} = 1$. Such symmetric properties are essential to discover the intrinsic geometry of the manifold independent of any frame of reference. Optimal solution for such optimization problem can be found by solving a least-squares problem as was shown in (Roweis et al., 2000). Since the recovered weights W reflect the intrinsic geometric structure of the manifold, an embedded manifold in a low dimensional space can be constructed using the same weights. This can be achieved by solving, for a set of points $X = \{x_i \in R^e, i = 1..N\}$ in a low dimension space, wherein, $e \ll d$, and that minimize: $E(x) = \sum |x_i - \sum w_{ij}x_i|^2$ where i, j = 1 · · · N, and, the weights are fixed. Solving such problem can be achieved by solving an eigenvector problem as was shown in (Roweis et al., 2000).

3.2 Isomap Embedding

Isometric feature mapping (Tenenbaum et al., 2000), or Isomap, algorithm preserves the pair-wise distances between points in the image space. It adds the additional constraint of preserving the intrinsic geometry of the data as described by the geodesic manifold distances between all pairs of data points. For neighboring points, Euclidian distance provides a good approximation to geodesic distance. For faraway points, geodesic distance is approximated by adding up a sequence of "short hops" between neighboring points. These hops are computed by finding shortest paths in a graph with edges connecting neighboring data points. The algorithm as defined in (Tenenbaum et al., 2000) has three main steps:

The first step determines which points are neighbors on the manifold M, based on the distances $d_x(i, j)$ between pairs of points i, j in the high dimension, input space X. It either connects each point to all points within some fixed radius e, or to all of its K nearest neighbors. These neighborhood relations are represented as a weighted graph G over the data points, with edges of weight $d_x(i, j)$ between neighboring points. In its second step, Isomap estimates the geodesic distances $d_M(i, j)$ between all pairs of points on the manifold M by computing their shortest path distances $d_G(i, j)$ in the graph G. In the third and final step, MDS is applied to the matrix of graph distances $D_G = \{d_G(i, j)\}$, constructing an embedding of the data in a d-dimensional Euclidean space Y that best preserves this estimated intrinsic geometry. The coordinate vectors y_i for points in Y are chosen to minimize the cost function:

$$E = \| \tau(D_G) - \tau(D_Y) \|_{L^2}$$

Where, D_Y denotes the matrix of Euclidean distances $\{d_Y(i, j) = \| y_i - y_j \|\}$ and $\| A \|_{L^2}$ the L^2 matrix norm $= \sqrt{\sum_{i,j} A_{ij}^2}$. The τ operator converts distances to inner products, which uniquely characterize the geometry of the data in a form that supports efficient optimization. The global minimum of Eq. 1.2 is achieved by setting the coordinates y_i to the top d eigenvectors of the matrix $\tau(D_G)$.

4   Learning Dynamics

Non-Linear dimensionality reduction provides us a low dimensional embedding that closely captures the dynamics of the input sequence. Each input frame resides as a node on the embedded manifold. A new sequence, with similar dynamics, will also have a similar low dimensional embedding. The first step towards the creation of the output sequence is the creation of the output manifold in the same embedding space. To do so, first a model of the embedding is created and then this model is used to create a new manifold.

4.1   Modeling the Embedded Manifold

The non-linear dimensionality reduction techniques are used to create an embedding of the input sequence in 3D space. The embedded manifold is then modeled as a *3d-spline*. This is done by assuming consecutive frames to be equidistant in time and, using the 3D coordinates of each frame within the embedding space, to construct a piece-wise polynomial in each dimension. Thus, at any time t a point $A(x_t, y_t, z_t)$ on the embedding can be represented by

$$f(t) = (PPx(t), PPy(t), PPz(t))$$

Where, PPx, PPy and PPz are the piecewise polynomials fitting the *x, y and z* co-ordinates of the frames of the input sequence in the embedding space.

4.2   Creating the Output Manifold

The embedding manifold for the output is created by using the manifold for the input as a guide and walking through the embedding space. If T is the time used for an input sequence with m input frames, the average time-step between consecutive frames is

$$T_{av} = T / m$$

Starting at the first frame, and moving along the spline at steps equal to T_{av} would result in an exact trace of the input sequence. In order, to create a unique sequence, some noise is added to the time step between two consecutive frames. Also to allow for a rate of change of speed, an acceleration factor α is also introduced. Thus, the time step for the embedding for the output sequence can be represented as

$$T_{step} = \alpha T_{av} + \gamma$$

The use of T_{step} ensures the unique positioning of nodes representing frames of the output sequence, along the embedding manifold. However, the actual trajectory of the manifold for the output sequence still remains the same as that of the input sequence. In order to add variability to the trajectory for the output sequence, gaussian noise is also added to the 3d co-ordinates calculated by the piecewise polynomials PPx, PPy and PPz. The new spline function now becomes:

$$f_{new} = f(PPx(T_n) + \mu_x, PPy(T_n) + \mu_y, PPz(T_n) + \mu_z)$$

Where, μ_x, μ_y and μ_z represent Gaussian noise along x, y and z co-ordinates respectively. Thus, from a position at time T_{cur} on the output manifold, the next position is calculated as:

$$T_{cur} = T_{cur} + T_{step}$$
$$Pos_{new} = f_{new}(T_{cur})$$

(1)

Using, (1) we are able to create a new manifold within the 3d-embedding space that is restricted to within a cylindrical, twisted, shell with the manifold of the input sequence forming the axis of this shell.

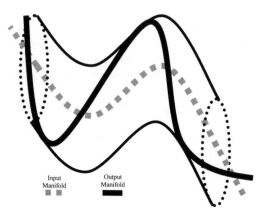

Fig. 1.

5 Observation Model

Once the manifold in the embedding space has been modeled, we need to map points from the low dimensional embedding space into the high dimensional visual input space. In order to learn such nonlinear mapping, a Radial basis function interpolation framework is used. In the Radial basis functions interpolation framework, the manifold is represented in the embedding space implicitly by selecting a set of representative points along the manifold.

Let the set of representative input instances be $Y = \{y_i \in R^d \quad i = 1, \cdots, N\}$ and let their corresponding points in the embedding space be $X = \{x_i \in R^e, \quad i = 1, \cdots, N\}$ where e is the dimensionality of the embedding space (e.g. $e = 3$ in our case). We can solve for multiple interpolants $f^k : R^e \to R$, where k is k-th dimension (pixel) in the input space and f^k is a radial basis function interpolant, i.e., we learn nonlinear mappings from the embedding space to each individual pixel in the input space. The functions used are generally of the form:

$$\mathbf{f}^k(x) = p^k(x) + \sum_i^N w_i^k \phi(|x - x_i|)$$

where $\phi(.)$ is a real valued basis function, w_i are real coefficients, $|.|$ is the norm on R^e (the embedding space) and p^k is a linear polynomial with coefficients c^k. The basis function we have used is the thin-plate spline $\phi(u) = u^2 \log(u)$. The whole mapping can be written in a matrix form as

$$f(x) = B.\psi(x) \tag{2}$$

Where B is a $d \times (N + e + 1)$ dimensional matrix with the k-th row $[w_1^k ... w_N^k \quad c^{k^T}]$ and the vector $\psi(x)$ is $[\phi(|x - x_1|) \cdots \phi(|x - x_N|) \quad 1 \quad x^T]^T$ The matrix B represents the coefficients for d different nonlinear mappings, each from a low-dimension embedding space into real numbers. To insure orthogonality and to make the problem well posed, the following additional constraints are imposed

$$\sum_{i=1}^N w_i p_j(x) = 0, j = 1, ..., m$$

where p_j are the linear basis of p. Therefore the solution for B can be obtained by directly solving the linear systems

$$\begin{pmatrix} A & P \\ P^T & 0 \end{pmatrix} B^T = \begin{pmatrix} Y \\ 0_{(e+1) \times d} \end{pmatrix}$$

Where, $A_{ij} = \phi(|x_j - x_i|)$, $i, j = 1...N$, P is a matrix with i-th row $[1 \quad x_i^T]$ and Y is $(N \times d)$ matrix containing the input images $[y_1...y_N]^T$.

6   Experimental Results

The algorithm was tested on various different input image sequences of varying length. The outputs were sequences with lengths, four times or greater than the input. Figure 2 shows the results for four sequences, each depicting different dynamics. The

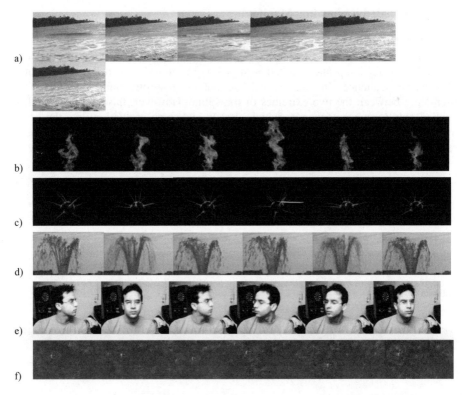

Fig. 2. a)Beach, b)Flame, c)Sparkling Ball, d)Fountain, e)Face, f)Boiling Water

output sequences can be viewed online at http://www.cs.rutgers.edu/~elgammal/ DynamicTexture. The input sequence for each was 70 frames in length. As can be seen, the synthesized images maintain both the dynamics and structure of the input. Depending on the shape of the input manifold, different approaches are used in generating the output manifold. The manifolds fell into one of three broad categories.

6.1 Closed Loop Embedding Manifold

When, the starting and the ending frames of the input sequence were either similar or at a small distance in the 3d-embedding space of the input manifold, the spline could be modified into a closed loop. This was achieved by introducing an edge between the first and the last points on the manifold (representing the first and the last frame) during the creation of the output manifold. The Flame, the Sparkling-ball and the Fountain sequences (Figure 2 (b),(c),(d)) show how the long output sequences, thus created. The output manifold for these sequences were created by looping around the closed loop of the input manifold as many times as was needed. Figure 3 (b), (c) & (d) show the manifold for the three sequences respectively.

6.2 Open Ended Embedding Manifold

When the starting and ending frames were far apart compared to the average distance between any 2 consecutive frames along the embedded manifold, closing the loop constituted a big jump and resulted in a jerk being introduced in the subsequently synthesized sequence. In such cases, the output manifold could be created by oscillating between the two extremes of the spline. However, this solution could be applied only to image sequences which already had some oscillation, like the beach and the turning face sequences. Figure 3 (a),(e) show the manifold for these, respectively.

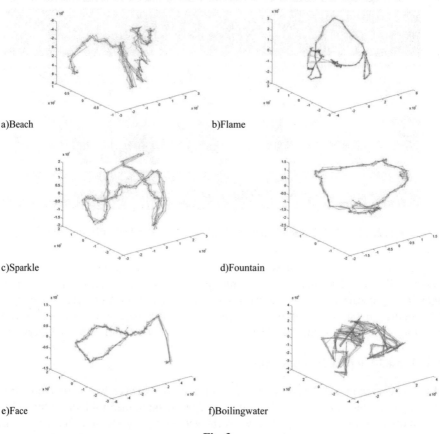

a)Beach

b)Flame

c)Sparkle

d)Fountain

e)Face

f)Boilingwater

Fig. 3.

6.3 Jerky Embedding Manifold

When, the input sequence comprises of relatively random and fast motion like in the boiling water sequence. The image frames are scattered within a small volume of the embedding space and the spline model constitutes a lot of sporadic jumps. In such a sequence, looping back to the first frame after the last has been reached, allows for a loop to be created with the associated jerk in the visual image space blending in with the rest of the jerks that the input sequence already depicts. Light and High-boiling water and the wavy river sequence have such a manifold. The manifold for the boiling water sequence is shown in Figure 3(f).

References

Stam, J., Fiume, E.: Depicting fire and other gaseous phenomena using diffusion processes. In: Proc. SIGGRAPH '95, 129–136 (August 1995)

Hodgins, J.K., Wooten, W.L.: Animating human athletes. In: Robotics Research: The Eighth International Symposium, pp. 356–367 (1998)

Popovićć, J., Seitz, S.M., Erdmann, M., Popović, Z., Witkin, A.: Interactive manipulation of rigid body simulations. In: Proc. of SIGGRAPH '00, pp. 209–218 (July 2000)

Perry, C.H., Picard, R.W.: Synthesizing Flames and Their Spreading. In: Proc. of the 5th Eurographics Workshop on Animation and Simulation, Oslo, Norway (September 1994)

Schödl, A., Szeliski, R., Salesin, D.H., Essa, I.: Video textures, In: Akeley, K. (ed.) Siggraph 2000 Computer Graphics Proceedings, ACMPress/ACM SIGGRAPH /Addison Wesley/ Longman, 2000, pp. 489–498 (2000)

Fitzgibbon, A.W.: Stochastic rigidity: image registration for nowherestatic scenes. In: Proceedings of the Eighth International Conference On Computer Vision, pp. 662–669 (2001)

Soatto, S., Doretto, G., Wu, Y.N.: Dynamic textures. In: International Conference on Computer Vision, pp. 439–446 (2001)

Kwatra, V., Schödl, A., Essa, I., Turk, G., Bobick, A.: Graphcut Textures: Image and Video Synthesis Using Graph Cuts. In: Proceedings of Siggraph'03, pp. 277–286 (2003)

Szummer, M., Picard, R.W.: Temporal Texture Modeling. IEEE International Conference on Image Processing 3, 823–826 (1996)

Yuan, L., Wen, F., Liu, C., shum, H.Y.: Synthesizing Dynamic Texture with Closed-Loop Linear Dynamical System. In: Pajdla, T., Matas, J(G.) (eds.) ECCV 2004. LNCS, vol. 3022, pp. 603–616. Springer, Heidelberg (2004)

Roweis, S., Saul, L.: Nonlinear dimensionality reduction by locally linear embedding. Science 290, 2323–2326 (2000)

Tenenbaum, J.B., de Silva, V., Langford, J.C.: A global geometric framework for nonlinear dimensionality reduction. Science 290, 2319–2323 (2000)

Author Index

Alexa, Marc   3
Ammon, Lorenz   78
Awasthi, Ishan   395

Batarilo, Zvonimir   155
Bieri, Hanspeter   78
Binaghi, Elisabetta   343
Brooks, Michael J.   217
Brosz, John   58

Chojnacki, Wojciech   217
Coombe, Greg   123

Deen, Danny   155
Dettori, Lucia   240
Donate, Arturo   264
Dornaika, Fadi   354

Eiho, Shigeru   367
Elgammal, Ahmed   395

Gallo, Ignazio   343
Gamito, Manuel N.   93
Grigat, Rolf-Rainer   330
Grothues, Ingo   229
Gur, Moshe   381

Holst, Mathias   31

Kang, Woobum   367
Kim, Tae Young   305
Kirkegaard, Jakob   281
Kraiss, Karl-Friedrich   229
Krajsek, Kai   201

Lacor, Chris   155
Lastra, Anselmo   123
Lee, Kyoung Mu   305
Lee, Sang Uk   305
Lerner, Tali   381
Libuda, Lars   229

Maddock, Steve C.   93
Matsuyama, Jun'ya   316
Mester, Rudolf   201
Michaelsen, Eckart   293

Middelmann, Wolfgang   293
Moeslund, Thomas B.   281
Müller Arisona, Stefan   169
Müller, Pascal   169

Nealen, Andrew   3
Nikolaou, N.   251

Oanta, Emil   155
Olsen, Ole Fogh   109

Papamarkos, N.   251
Park, Youngsup   139

Reniers, Dennie   187
Ribeiro, Eraldo   264
Rivlin, Ehud   381

Samavati, Faramarz F.   58
Sappa, Angel D.   354
Schjøth, Lars   109
Schubiger-Banz, Simon   169
Schumann, Heidrun   31
Semler, Lindsay   240
Sörgel, Uwe   293
Sousa, Mario Costa   58
Specht, Matthias   169
Sporring, Jon   109

Tal, Ayellet   44
Telea, Alexandru   187

Uehara, Kuniaki   316

van den Hengel, Anton   217
Vucinic, Dean   155

Wenzel, Fabian   330

Yim, Chung-Hyuk   305
Yoon, KyungHyun   139

Zuckerberger, Emanuel   44

Printing: Mercedes-Druck, Berlin
Binding: Stein + Lehmann, Berlin